To: Daddy..

Merry

MW00678653

' Courtney

To The scholar who
continues to teach so many
teachers... you are our
foundation, Daddy.
    Thank you -

INTERNATIONAL SOCIETY AND THE *DE FACTO* STATE

For my parents: my father, Gil M. Pegg (1935-1989), a consistent and vocal supporter of my pursuit of higher education, and my mother, Sharon Pegg, a constant source of love and support.

International Society and the *De Facto* State

SCOTT PEGG
Department of International Relations
Bilkent University
Ankara, Turkey

Ashgate
Aldershot • Brookfield USA • Singapore • Sydney

Published by
Ashgate Publishing Ltd
Gower House
Croft Road
Aldershot
Hants GU11 3HR
England

Ashgate Publishing Company
Old Post Road
Brookfield
Vermont 05036
USA

British Library Cataloguing in Publication Data
Pegg, Scott
   International society and the *de facto* state
   1. States, New 2. Postcolonialism 3. *De facto* doctrine
   4. Self-determination, National 5. Sovereignty
   6. International relations
   I. Title
   320.1

Library of Congress Cataloging-in-Publication Data
Pegg, Scott.
   International society and the *de facto* state / Scott Pegg.
      p. cm.
   Based on a doctoral dissertation at the University of British
Columbia.
   Includes bibliographical references and index.
   ISBN 1-84014-478-5 (hardbound)
   1. Sovereignty. 2. Recognition (International law) 3. *De facto*
doctrine. I. Title.
KZ4041.P44 · 1998
341.26--dc21
                            98-37112
                              CIP

ISBN 1 84014 478 5

Printed in Great Britain by The Book Company, Suffolk

Contents

List of Maps

List of Tables

Acknowledgments

This book could not have been written without the support and cooperation of a number of people both inside and outside of the academic community. For their various forms of assistance, I am eternally grateful.

In particular, I would like to thank the inter-library loan staff at the University of British Columbia in Vancouver, Canada. Ken Shivers and Siria Lopez at the US Department of State, Dr. Sazil Korküt at the Turkish Republic of Northern Cyprus representative office in New York, and Cathy Hsu at the Taipei Economic and Cultural Office in Seattle were all gracious in sharing their thoughts and information with me in interviews. Federico Chachagua, Jim Crawley, Mehmet Ali Doğan, Ali Karaosmanoğlu, Don Payzant, Jason Priestley, and Uli Rauch all assisted me in various ways during the preparation of this text. Andrew Nelson, Todd Roston, and the entire staff at Accurate Image graciously donated their time and energy free of charge to produce the four maps featured in this book. Thanks also to Lorenzo Patton for the flexibility in scheduling when I needed it.

This book is based on a doctoral dissertation at the University of British Columbia. For its financial assistance, I am grateful to the University of British Columbia for a graduate fellowship and a teaching assistantship. A number of my colleagues in the UBC political science department offered valuable support and advice along the way. My thanks go out to Amir Abedi, Janet Alford, Robert Crawford, Kevin Dwyer, Julie Fieldhouse, Jeremy Iveson, Matt James, Darryl Jarvis, Tom Lundberg, Haider Nizamani, Gideon Rahat, Carol Rice, Tony Sayers, Elizabeth Speed, Ian Wallace, Kim Williams, and Chao-Tzang Yawnghwe. For their encouragement and moral support, I thank my family and friends, Percy Amamasi, Bruce Chapman, Gerry Gelley, Wayne and Susan Michalowski, Ayesha Nizamani, Esperanza Rigo, Alan Tilchen, Larry Turner, and the late Reverend Dr. Odie Davis Brown.

The arguments put forth here have benefited from the comments, criticisms, suggestions, and feedback of a number of scholars. My deepest intellectual and academic debt is to my dissertation supervisor Kal Holsti. Professor Holsti's constructive criticism sharpened my arguments throughout the text and his calm and inspiring supervision enabled me to complete this project in a timely fashion. Special thanks also go to Brian Job and Alan James for their positive feedback and many helpful suggestions. I am sincerely indebted to these two gentlemen for the sundry ways in which this book has been improved by their insights. Maurice Copithorne, Robert Jackson, Peter Remnant, and Michael Wallace also offered useful comments. My scholarship has benefited previously from time spent at the University of Richmond, Virginia, and the London School of Economics. My thanks go out to David Evans, Fred Halliday, Richard Mateer, James Mayall, John Outland, and Michael Yahuda. The late Michael Hodges and John Vincent remain inspirational. My colleagues and students in the Department of International Relations at Bilkent University in Ankara, Turkey provided a warm and supportive environment in which to complete the final revisions to this book.

Most of what I needed to know about writing, I learned in the tenth grade: let me acknowledge my profound debt here to K. C. Raper.

My sincerest gratitude is also extended to Tom Lawton, who first put me in contact with Ashgate and who has consistently volunteered his assistance without ever having to be asked for it. Kirstin Howgate was an absolute pleasure to work with as an editor. I would also like to thank Tracey Daborn, Rachel Hedges, Sonia Hubbard, John Irwin, Ann Newell, and Val Saunders at Ashgate.

Lorraine Rigo suffered through the ups and downs of this project from the beginning. Her love and support is much appreciated.

This book could not have been written without the consistent and unflagging emotional and financial support of my mother, Sharon Pegg. The spirit of my late father, Gil M. Pegg, also remains with me to this day. He would have been proudest of all at this book's publication. I dedicate this book to my parents as a small token of my immense gratitude to them.

Any remaining errors of omission, content, or style are solely my own responsibility.

Scott Pegg
Ankara, October 1998

List of Abbreviations

ADB	-- Asian Development Bank
AIT	-- American Institute in Taiwan
APEC	-- Asia-Pacific Economic Cooperation
CCNAA	-- Coordination Council for North American Affairs
CSCE	-- Conference on Security and Cooperation in Europe (now OSCE)
DRET	-- Democratic Republic of East Timor
EC	-- European Community (now EU)
ECJ	-- European Court of Justice
ELF	-- Eritrean Liberation Front
EOKA	-- *Ethniki Orgánosis Kipriakoú Agónos*
EPLA	-- Eritrean People's Liberation Army (military wing of EPLF)
EPLF	-- Eritrean People's Liberation Front (now PFDJ)
EPRDF	-- Eelam People's Revolutionary Democratic Front
EPRLF	-- Eelam People's Revolutionary Liberation Front
EU	-- European Union (formerly EC)
FMLN	-- Faribundo Martí National Liberation Front
FRETELIN	-- *Frente Revolucianaria de Timor Leste Independente*
GATT	-- General Agreement on Tariffs and Trade (now WTO)
GNP	-- Gross national product
ICRC	-- International Committee of the Red Cross
IMF	-- International Monetary Fund
IPKF	-- Indian Peace-Keeping Force (in Sri Lanka)
JVP	-- *Janatha Vimukti Peramuna*
LTTE	-- Liberation Tigers of Tamil Eelam
NATO	-- North Atlantic Treaty Organization
OAS	-- Organization of American States
OAU	-- Organization of African Unity
OSCE	-- Organization on Security and Cooperation in Europe (formerly CSCE)
PA	-- Palestinian Authority
PAIGC	-- *Partido Africano da Independencia da Guine e Cabo Verde*
PFDJ	-- People's Front for Democracy and Justice (formerly EPLF)
PGE	-- Provisional Government of Eritrea (1991 - 1993)
PLO	-- Palestinian Liberation Organization

PLOTE	-- People's Liberation Organization of Tamil Eelam
PRC	-- People's Republic of China
ROC	-- Republic of China (Taiwan)
SADR	-- Saharan Arab Democratic Republic
SEF	-- Straits Exchange Foundation
SNL	-- Somali National League
SNM	-- Somali National Movement
SPM	-- Somali Patriotic Movement
SWAPO	-- South West Africa People's Organization
TELO	-- Tamil Eelam Liberation Organization
TFSC	-- Turkish Federated State of Cyprus (1975 - 1983)
TMT	-- *Türk Mukavemet Teskilati*
TPLF	-- Tigrean People's Liberation Front
TRA	-- Taiwan Relations Act
TRNC	-- Turkish Republic of Northern Cyprus
TULF	-- Tamil United Liberation Front
UDI	-- Unilateral declaration of independence
UK	-- United Kingdom
UN	-- United Nations
UNDP	-- United Nations Development Program
UNFICYP	-- United Nations Peace-keeping Force in Cyprus
UNITA	-- *União Nacional para a Independencia Total de Angola*
UNOSOM	-- United Nations Operation in Somalia
US	-- United States
USAID	-- United States Agency for International Development
USC	-- United Somali Congress
WTO	-- World Trade Organization (formerly GATT)

1 Introduction

1 Setting the Stage

If one takes 1960 as a convenient shorthand date for the ending of the vast majority of the decolonization process, then it can be argued that the three decades which followed that year were characterized by the greatest level of territorial stability ever seen in the history of international relations. With very few exceptions, the political map of the world's sovereign states remained unchanged during this period. James Mayall attributes this state of affairs to an ironic historical fate of the once-revolutionary principle of national self-determination which, in its post-World War II variant, has emphasized the sanctity of existing territorial boundaries and ended up 'attempting to freeze the political map in a way which has never previously been attempted' (1990, p. 56).

The delegitimization of territorial aggrandizement and the almost religious sanctity placed on existing borders marks a profound change in international relations. Whereas entities once had to demonstrate and maintain a certain level of military, economic, and governmental effectiveness in order to preserve their position in a competitive international system, the post-war era has witnessed the wholesale granting of statehood to large numbers of former colonies with few, if any, demonstrated empirical capabilities. Once acquired, sovereign statehood has become almost impossible to lose. Small and/or weak states which, in earlier eras, would have been carved up, colonized, or swallowed by larger powers, now have a guaranteed existence in international society. In the words of Robert Jackson, 'once sovereignty is acquired by virtue of independence from colonial rule, then extensive civil strife or breakdown of order or governmental immobility or any other failures are not considered to detract from it' (1987, p. 531). A lack of empirical viability no longer matters in a world where juridical statehood is underwritten by the new normative structures of international society.

One of the earliest and most influential attempts to analyze this novel situation of normatively-sanctified fixed territorial borders and internationally-guaranteed sovereignty appeared in a *World Politics* article by

1

Robert Jackson and Carl Rosberg (1982). In subsequent years, one might view the academic work which built upon Jackson and Rosberg's original article as branching out into three or four separate, yet interrelated, sub-fields of analysis. Perhaps the most fertile or vibrant area here has been the literature which has grown up around the subject of 'Third World' or 'weak state' security.[1] While this literature covers a wide range of topics, the security implications of fixed territorial borders and juridically-guaranteed statehood are central to its analysis.

A second main area of focus has been the impact of internationally-maintained sovereign boundaries on economic development. Jeffrey Herbst (1990), for example, notes that

> the absence of a truly competitive states system that penalizes military weakness means that even those states that have no other prospects than long-term dependence on international aid will survive in their crippled form for the foreseeable future.... The presence of permanently weak states that will not be eliminated... poses novel development challenges.[2]

In this regard, Jackson and Rosberg (1986) maintain that juridically-guaranteed statehood has had a profound impact on the development process. Specifically referring to sub-Saharan Africa, these authors do not claim that juridical statehood provides an adequate explanation for economic underdevelopment. They do, however, argue that it 'is a significant partial explanation that has hitherto gone largely unnoticed' and that 'its impact has frequently been more adverse than favourable' (1986, p. 28).

In some ways, this examination of the impact of fixed territorial borders on the economic prospects of poorer states is merely a unique sub-set of a larger critique of the impact of sovereignty on the global political economy. Charles Beitz (1991), for example, sees the states system's respect for each state's exclusive domestic jurisdiction as a kind of collective property right which 'effectively sanctions the existing international distribution of wealth as well as that of power'.[3] Similarly, Michael Barnett and Alexander Wendt view the collective acceptance of sovereignty without any commitment to material equality as constituting 'a structurally coercive mechanism of decentralized social control that institutionalizes territorial and therefore resource inequalities' (1992, p. 104).

A third major focus of recent research has been on the international implications of the growing number of 'collapsed' or 'failed' states. Much of the work in this regard has proceeded from the conventional assumption that these states must and should be reconstituted as viable entities within their existing territorial boundaries; debate in this area has mainly centered around the question of how best to go about this difficult task of state reconstruction.[4]

Finally, the fourth line of inquiry that can be identified is Robert Jackson's own attempt (1990) to broaden and develop his ideas into a general study of international relations. As Jackson sees it, what is novel about the way international relations is practiced today is not the existence of inequality between the states of the world. Inequality has always been a feature of the states system and there is nothing particularly recent or unique about it. What is distinctive about international relations in the post-1945 era is: 1) how statehood is acquired; and 2) how international society deals with weak and underdeveloped states. In traditional international law, recognition was acquired only after successfully demonstrating the capacity to govern. To acquire sovereignty, one had first to be sovereign: 'states historically were empirical realities before they were legal personalities'. In the new era, however, 'rulers can acquire independence solely in virtue of being successors of colonial governments' (1990, p. 34). Independence need not positively be earned; rather it now comes as a moral entitlement. Factors like a lack of qualified personnel, small territories or populations, questions of economic viability or inadequate military defenses no longer militate against sovereign recognition.

The second novel feature of this new system concerns the ways in which international society deals with its weakest members. States may no longer be deprived of their sovereignty through colonialism, conquest, or partition. The sanctity of existing borders and the international aid regime (albeit as limited as it is) combine to operate as a kind of safety net propping up states which earlier would have fallen prey to the imperial ambitions of other, more successful states.

This 'new sovereignty game' thus produces a world characterized by large numbers of 'quasi-states': states which are internationally recognized as full juridical equals, possessing the same rights and privileges as any other state, yet which manifestly lack all but the most rudimentary empirical capabilities. In Jackson's (1990, pp. 27-30) terms, these states possess 'negative sovereignty'—a formal-legal condition that can be equated with non-intervention and the freedom from outside interference. What they lack is 'positive sovereignty'—a substantive condition that allows governments actively to function and to deliver political goods and services to their citizens. International society confers and maintains these states' juridical equality and their negative sovereignty. It does little, however, to assist them in developing their empirical capabilities so they can acquire positive sovereignty. In Naeem Inayatullah and David Blaney's (1995) terminology, these quasi-states are unable to 'realize' their sovereignty substantively.

The existence of large numbers of recognized sovereign states that fundamentally lack many of the capabilities traditionally associated with independent statehood brings forward a number of questions. If sovereignty is now granted as a moral right and not earned on the battlefield or through a demonstrated capacity to govern, and if existing state boundaries have acquired such a sanctity so as to 'freeze' the political map, then what happens to the various groups who are fundamentally dissatisfied at the way they have been 'frozen' off the political map and denied admission to the exclusive club of sovereign states? If scores of existing sovereign states are, as it seems, so manifestly lacking in terms of legitimacy, effectiveness, power, popular support, and the ability to provide governmental services, then what happens when a breakaway state group is able to establish some sort of effective territorial control and demonstrate governance capabilities of the sort that once led to full recognition as an independent sovereign state?

This is not a study of secession or self-determination *per se* and it is not a general assessment of governmental breakdowns in weak or failed states. My aim is to investigate another facet of the 'new sovereignty game' which has not received sufficient attention in the existing literature. This is the '*de facto* state'. In essence, these are entities which feature long-term, effective, and popularly-supported organized political leaderships that provide governmental services to a given population in a defined territorial area. They seek international recognition and view themselves as capable of meeting the obligations of sovereign statehood. They are, however, unable to secure widespread juridical recognition and therefore function outside the boundaries of international legitimacy.

The *de facto* state can be seen as the flip side of the quasi-state coin. This is not to suggest that for every quasi-state there must be a *de facto* state; indeed, even the most cursory research would reveal that there are far more quasi-states than there are *de facto* states—at least in the way that I define them. Rather, it is to suggest that some of the same normative logic in international society that produces quasi-states may also facilitate the creation of something that is more or less their inverse: the *de facto* state.

The quasi-state's juridical equality was internationally enfranchised by the existing society of states. Previously, colonialism was predicated on the fact that independence was a question of empirical conditions—levels of development, qualified personnel, military capabilities, national unity, and the like. It was only when the anti-colonial movement succeeded in normatively defeating this intellectual framework and turning independence into a natural right of all dependencies that quasi-states were able to come into being (Jackson, 1993b, pp. 117-125). Once they succeeded in changing the criterion for independence from empirical viability to a categorical moral right of all former dependencies regardless of their assorted lack of qualifications, the international consensus against the dismemberment of existing states or the redrawing of territorial borders served as the foundation which supported the quasi-state regardless of its failings. Even if the government's writ did not run throughout most of its territory, the juridical existence of the state was guaranteed.

International norms which support existing quasi-states also deny the legitimacy of any would-be challengers. The same logic that supports the quasi-state also prevents the acceptance of other groups regardless of how legitimate their grievances, how broad their popular support, or how effective their governance. Quasi-states and *de facto* states are thus both children of the new sovereignty regime.

Whereas the quasi-state has recognized territorial borders, a seat at the UN, and the ability to participate in intergovernmental organizations, in many cases it does not effectively control large swathes of its own countryside. Though it seeks recognition, the *de facto* state, on the other hand, has been denied its seat at the UN and its place at the international table. No matter how long or how effective its territorial control of a given area has been, that control is neither recognized nor is it considered legitimate. The quasi-state is legitimate no matter how ineffective it is. Conversely, the *de facto* state is illegitimate no matter how effective it is. The quasi-state's juridical equality is not contingent on any performance criteria. Even if the entire state apparatus has collapsed, the quasi-state (à la Cambodia and Lebanon) will be supported and maintained through international efforts. At times, it may be more of an abstract idea than it is a hard reality. The *de facto* state, on the other hand, is a functioning reality that is denied legitimacy by the rest of international society.

One way to distinguish between these two very different entities is to conceptualize them in terms of power versus recognition. According to Janice Thomson, 'if recognition without power capabilities characterizes most contemporary states, cases of power capabilities without recognition exist as well' (1995, p. 220). Following this terminology, the quasi-state would have recognition and lack power capabilities while the *de facto* state would have power capabilities but lack recognition.

This distinction can also be conceptualized in terms of authority versus control. Thomson makes the distinction here

> Between the claim to exclusive right to make rules (authority) and the capability of enforcing that claim (control).... Authority... is contingent on recognition; control depends on concrete capabilities to monitor and enforce compliance with the rules that are made under that authority (1995, p. 223).

This is similar to Michael Oakeshott's (1975) objections to the misuse of the word sovereign: 'Invoked to specify "authority", it has been used to specify the "power" which *may* partner authority in an office of rule....'[5] In these terms, it is the authority of quasi-states that is so actively supported by the other members of international society. Having that authority, however, does not mean that they will be able to exercise any meaningful degree of control over their jurisdictions. *De facto* states, on the other hand, despite lacking (recognized) authority are still able to exercise some degree of control through their empirical capabilities.

Finally, another distinction might be made using Jackson's terminology of negative sovereignty vs. positive sovereignty. Negative sovereignty, in the sense of non-intervention and the recognition of a state's exclusive domestic jurisdiction, is an absolute formal-legal condition that one either has or does not have. Quasi-states have it; *de facto* states do not. Positive sovereignty, in the sense of actual capabilities which allow governments to act and to 'realize' their sovereignty, is a relative and substantive condition that one can have or not have in varying degrees. The argument here is not that quasi-states have no positive sovereignty and that *de facto* states are in full possession of it. Rather, quasi-states generally lack positive sovereignty. Conversely, it would not make sense to speak of a *de facto* state which did not have some degree of positive capacity for governmental action.

In essence then, we have a distinction between a large number of sovereign states that have full juridical recognition but lack substantive empirical capabilities and a much smaller number of non-sovereign entities that lack any form of widespread recognition yet are able, more or less effectively, to function as governing authorities over specific territorial domains. It is this latter group that we refer to as *de facto* states.

This study examines four *de facto* states: Eritrea before it won its independence from Ethiopia; the Republic of Somaliland; the areas of Sri

Lanka controlled by the Liberation Tigers of Tamil Eelam (LTTE, popularly known as the 'Tamil Tigers'); and the Turkish Republic of Northern Cyprus (TRNC). At various points in time, and depending on the criteria one were to use, other potential *de facto* states might include Biafra; Rhodesia after its unilateral declaration of independence (UDI); Charles Taylor's Liberia; the Southern Sudan; Chechnya; Krajina; the Bosnian Serb Republic; Kosovo; the Trans-Dniester region of Moldova; the Abkhazia region of Georgia; Kurdistan; the Karen and Shan states of Myanmar; the Muslim-controlled areas of Mindanao in the Philippines; the Khmer Rouge-controlled areas of Cambodia; and the Republic of China (Taiwan).

It should be noted that the term '*de facto* state' has been used prior to this study. Hussein Adam has referred to Somaliland as a *de facto* state (1994b, p. 21). R. Sean Randolph has also used the term in reference to Taiwan (1981, p. 257). His choice of this terminology was subsequently criticized by Ya Qin (1992, pp. 1081-1082). In the popular media, *The Guardian*[6] and *Agence France Presse*[7] have both used this term in reference to the LTTE-controlled areas of Sri Lanka. *The Economist* has also used it in reference to Somaliland.[8] Secessionists have, on occasion, even used this term in reference to themselves.[9] I first used this term in a 1994 article (Pegg, 1994, p. 5).

2 The *De Facto* State in the Wider Academic Context

Despite the vast extent of the academic literature on such topics as international society, secession, self-determination, sovereignty, the state, ethnic conflict, and weak state security, the *de facto* state has received scant academic attention to date. While some work has been done, for example, on Northern Cyprus or on the Tamil conflict in Sri Lanka, there is no general analysis of *de facto* states as a category of actor in international politics. It is this gap in the literature that this study aims to fill.

Before doing this, however, one must first examine the reasons for this near-complete academic neglect to date. One leading reason has to do with the inherently imprecise nature of the concept '*de facto* state'. In an academic discipline that rewards precise clarity and quantifiable empirical work, the *de facto* state may be too fuzzy a concept for many scholars. In reference to juridical states, James Mayall contends that

> The important point to note is that all these formal states, whose governments take part in the ritual quadrille of international diplomacy and enjoy the dignity of mutual recognition and membership of the United Nations, actually exist: they can be located on the map; they have more or less defined boundaries; they have settled populations and identifiable social and political institutions (1990, p. 7).

While one might contest Mayall's point on settled populations and identifiable institutions, his larger message remains valid: juridical states actually exist and they can be analyzed by social scientists in a variety of ways. The *de facto* state, however, often has a more tenuous existence. The date of Chad's independence, for example, is much easier to deal with than trying to decide at what point did Chechnya graduate from being a dissatisfied Russian republic to becoming a *de facto* state. *De facto* states are often much harder to analyze precisely and quantify than are juridical states. Even if one were to argue that the entire category of 'states' was an intellectual construct, the juridical state would still be a more readily grasped construct than the *de facto* state. The inherent ambiguity that adheres to this concept must, in some ways, discourage rigorous academic analysis.

Another reason for the *de facto* state's academic neglect relates to international society's prior success at freezing the territorial map. This attempt to preserve the territorial status quo was so successful and the degree of consensus supporting it so strong that very little discussion of other options even occurred. Former UN Secretary-General U Thant's famous quote from a 1970 press conference in Dakar, Senegal perhaps best sums up the international community's thinking in this regard:

> As far as the question of secession of a particular section of a Member State is concerned, the United Nations' attitude is unequivocable. As an international organization, the United Nations has never accepted and does not accept and I do not believe that it will ever accept the principle of secession of a part of its Member States.[10]

Rather than being worthy of careful study, places like Biafra and Northern Cyprus merely became problems to be solved and situations to be ritually denounced in UN resolutions. If the territorial map is seen as unalterable, there is little incentive to devote much attention to *de facto* states because their ultimate defeat and reincorporation into existing states is both assumed and sought. While there were some academics who questioned whether or not the post-war interpretation of self-determination, with its emphasis on fixed territorial borders, really promoted stability (Kamanu, 1974, p. 359) or who argued that the international community should develop consistent criteria by which to assess secessionist claims rationally,[11] most were content to view any challenges to existing sovereign states as problems in need of solutions.

Since 1989 this situation has, of course, altered considerably. In addition to the reunifications of the Germanys and the Yemens, the post-Cold War period has also seen the peaceful dissolutions of Czechoslovakia and the Soviet Union and the violent break-ups of Ethiopia and Yugoslavia. In all, more than twenty new states have assumed UN membership during this period. The exact significance of the ending of the Cold War on irrevocably fixed territorial borders remains open to question. As Barry Buzan (1991a) puts it,

> It is not yet clear whether it is the norm of fixed boundaries that is under assault or only the practice in specific locations. But it is clear that this norm is vulnerable to the counter-norm of national self-determination, and that some of the restraints on boundary change have been weakened by the ending of the Cold War.[12]

This new situation has naturally stimulated or renewed academic interest in a number of areas pertinent to the subject of this study. Ethnic conflict and ethnic identity formation has once again become a salient topic in the study of international relations (Gurr, 1993; Gurr, 1994; Posen, 1993). The principle of national self-determination has been revisited (Halperin and Scheffer with Small, 1992), with strong arguments made both for (Binder, 1993) and against (Etzioni, 1992-93) the concept. The adequacy or inadequacy of academic international relations' treatment of the state is again a lively topic of debate (Halliday, 1994, chapter four; Navari, 1991; Shaw, 1991). The changing nature of sovereignty has been examined (Barkin and Cronin, 1994; Lapidoth, 1992), with particular emphasis placed on the question of what are the limits to non-intervention (Deibel, 1993; Duke, 1994; Vincent and Wilson, 1993; C. Weber, 1992). Similarly, the role of territoriality in international relations has again come under renewed scrutiny (Elkins, 1995; Ruggie, 1993). One can even find authors who now argue that territorial boundaries in Africa may need to be changed (Chege, 1991-92, pp. 152-153; Herbst, 1996, pp. 168-169). This is a significant departure from the earlier consensus against even considering such an option. Perhaps the area which has been most affected by the changing international environment has been the academic study of secession. The earlier reflex opposition to anything relating to secession has now given way to a series of efforts designed to illuminate specific criteria under which 'just' or 'legitimate' secession attempts may be distinguished from 'unjust' or 'illegitimate' attempts.[13]

Clearly, the end of the Cold War has sparked or reignited vigorous intellectual debate in a number of areas pertinent to the subject matter of this study. And yet, little or no work has been done on the *de facto* state *per se*. One suspects that this might point to a third reason for the *de facto* state's academic neglect: it is simply not the sexiest or most important topic in the field of international relations. The four *de facto* states examined in this study are all fairly small places with minor populations. This is not to say that *de facto* states are unimportant. Yet, all the *de facto* states in the world put together and their impact on the international system would not rank in importance alongside the US-Soviet strategic rivalry during the Cold War or issues such as migration flows, global governance, foreign direct investment, or nuclear proliferation today. Their relatively peripheral importance to international politics thus counts as a third reason for the general neglect of this topic.

Why then study the *de facto* state? Although small in numbers and generally small in size, the evidence indicates that many *de facto* states can survive for quite extended durations of time. One reason to study this phenomenon therefore is to evaluate the ways in which international society copes with the presence of such non-juridical entities in its midst. Spelling out the advantages and disadvantages of particular methods of dealing with these entities should be of some policy relevance to international decision-makers. A second reason to study *de facto* states is that these entities do have measurable impacts on world politics. Their impact can be felt in the area of global political economy but is most readily apparent in regard to conflict and war. The sheer numbers of refugees and fatalities produced in the assorted struggles that result in the creation of these entities is, in and of itself, a compelling reason to study them. In this sense, a greater focus on *de facto* states would be one part of what K. J. Holsti identifies as a shift in the study of international politics 'from exclusive focus on the activities of the great powers to a concern with what have traditionally been considered peripheral actors' (1996, p. 207). A third reason to examine *de facto* statehood is to assess its potential significance for academic international relations theory. *De facto* states may be useful vehicles from which to generate insights on such larger questions as are we witnessing a return to a more diverse international system?; and what are the extent of challenges facing the states system today? The existence of these entities may also suggest interesting avenues of future inquiry within specific theoretical traditions such as realism, rationalism, and post-modernism.

3 Methodology

While there was not necessarily any hard and fast separation between them, my research was essentially composed of two main components: 1) general academic and theoretical work; and 2) more detailed empirical research on the four specific case studies themselves. In regards to the general theoretical section, as there is no academic literature on the *de facto* state *per se*, my research draws upon a wide range of other existing literatures. A number of the literatures consulted, such as secession, self-determination, sovereignty, territoriality, and weak state security have already been mentioned. Another literature revolves around the state: theories of the state; the criteria and requirements for statehood; the recognition process; state-making and nation-building; challenges to the state; and federalism and other forms of autonomy designed to accommodate demands for greater representation within the state. Ethnic conflict, ethnic identity formation, and the problems of national minorities within sovereign states constituted another major focus. Obviously, many of these assorted works are interrelated and intertwined.

I selected the four specific case studies for three main reasons. The first concerns geography. The selection of two African, one Asian, and one European case study is intended to show that the *de facto* state is a generic phenomenon not limited to one region of the globe. The second, and more important, line of reasoning behind the selection has to do with some of the unique characteristics of each case. As the only *de facto* state ever to graduate successfully to sovereign statehood, Eritrea stands out for this reason alone. Northern Cyprus merits attention both for its extended longevity and for its unique degree of dependence on external support—in this case from Turkey. The more than 30-year UN peacekeeping presence on Cyprus also distinguishes this case. Somaliland offers a particularly sharp lens from which to view the workings of international society. Despite its comparatively strong democratic credentials, its former separate colonial status, and its functional effectiveness, the international community still insists that this *de facto* state remain harnessed to the collapsed functional bankruptcy that is Somalia today. This case certainly indicates some of the limits to the supposedly changed attitudes toward secession and fixed territorial boundaries. The LTTE-controlled areas of Sri Lanka were selected for two main reasons: 1) the LTTE's impressive ability to survive under adverse conditions, and 2) its uniquely brutal, violent, and intolerant leadership. A third reason for the selection of these four case studies is that all four are contemporary. The four cases selected have also all been in existence long enough that adequate literature has grown up around them.[14] I excluded other potential case studies such as Chechnya and the Bosnian Serb Republic on the grounds that they were already receiving substantial attention from other scholars and media commentators.

The selection of only contemporary case studies leads to the question: Is the *de facto* state only a contemporary phenomenon of the post-war era or do its roots go back further in the international system? The answer is probably yes to both parts of this question. Following Robert Jackson (1990), I argue that the post-1945 international consensus on the preservation of existing states within their fixed territorial borders marks a dramatic break in the history of international relations. The *de facto* state is one of the unintended by-products of this new normative environment. The various macro-level factors discussed in chapter five that help create a setting conducive to the emergence of these entities are all unique to the postwar era. Historically, though, the *de facto* state does have antecedents. Disputed, yet effective *de facto* political control of a given territorial area has been a recurrent feature of international relations for centuries. Yet, the *de facto* state itself—at least in the way it is conceptualized in this study—is limited in time to the contemporary postwar decolonization era.

One problem doing research on contemporary cases is the frequency of highly-biased or polemical narratives. The static-to-noise ratio of emotional passion versus detached analysis is often quite high. Wherever possible, to minimize the ill-effects of this, I consulted a variety of sources that included local sources from both sides of the issue (i.e., Greek *and* Turkish Cypriot scholars; Sinhalese *and* Tamil scholars); 'outside' scholars (usually westerners); and media sources. The strongly pro-whichever group articles have more or less been balanced out by the strongly anti-whichever group articles.[15]

A few caveats are, however, in order here. First, as one might expect, the mere fact that someone is a Sinhalese scholar does not make them pro-government and the fact that someone is a Tamil scholar does not make them pro-LTTE. Second, in some cases it is difficult to find opposing views. For example, the Egal administration in Somaliland has not been subjected to much more than mild criticism. On the other hand, one struggles to find anyone who is even moderately positive about the LTTE. Third, my aim is only to ensure that all views are represented and considered. No attempt has been made to balance out the respective number of scholars consulted.

As has already been noted, the *de facto* state is an inherently more imprecise concept than the juridical state. Therefore, while I will use empirical data on such things as human rights violations, population, refugee flows, per capita gross national product (GNP), and the extent of territory controlled to buttress the arguments in this study, much of the analysis will inevitably remain arguable. This should not come as a surprise, for many of the key concepts remain what W. B. Gallie (1962) has termed 'essentially contested'. For example, in reference to sovereignty, Alan James (1986b) argues that 'there is in existence on this subject a substantial intellectual quagmire...'.[16] Similarly, when considering the state, James Rosenau (1988) remains 'disconcerted by the wavering, multiple uses and elusive formulations of this concept...'.[17] This need not, however, be a cause for despair. As Barry Buzan elaborates on essentially contested concepts, 'Paradoxically, the utility of these concepts stems in part from whatever it is that makes them inherently ambiguous, not least because ambiguity stimulates theoretical discussion about them' (1991b, p. 7). The intent of this study is to stimulate that theoretical discussion. It is also to advance knowledge on *de facto* states, thereby hopefully leading to small advances in knowledge in other, larger subject areas.

Finally, this study examines a particular subject matter in a particular way. No claim to exclusivity is made: my way is not the only way and it is not necessarily the 'best' way. For example, one of the criteria to be elaborated in chapter two distinguishes the *de facto* state from peaceful secession movements. This, therefore, rules out any substantial consideration of Québec in this study. Someone else, however, might decide that they wish to compare Northern Cyprus not with the three other case studies here, but with Québec. Considering the similarities readily discerned between these two situations,[18] this would be perfectly valid research to undertake. My claim is not that my research program is 'better' than the Northern Cyprus-Québec research program or any other; merely that it is different.

4 Value Biases and Assumptions of the Author

This study incorporates several significant assumptions, shown in the table on the following page. The theoretical framework that informs the analysis is the Grotian, rationalist, or 'English' school of international relations. The extensive literature on this topic[19] is too well-known to go into much detail here. Suffice it to say that the specific conception from which I am working views the international society of sovereign states as a practical association with the mutual recognition of sovereignty as its foundation.

Table 1.1 Ten Value Assumptions Underlying This Study

One	The theoretical framework views the international society of states as a practical association with the mutual recognition of sovereignty as its foundation.
Two	State sovereignty is neither permanent nor inevitable.
Three	Current state borders are neither natural nor inevitable. There are no territorial givens.
Four	Both territory and statehood still matter.
Five	The traditional bias against secession is rejected.
Six	The 'domino theory' of unlimited and never-ending 'Balkanization' is rejected.
Seven	The post-1945 interpretation of self-determination has either a) not promoted international stability, or b) has promoted a particular kind of international stability that is not necessarily the only or the best kind of stability available.
Eight	Self-determination claims need to be evaluated on a case-by-case basis, and not on the basis of abstract principle alone.
Nine	*De facto* states are a diverse group. Some may be deemed more worthy of support (or less worthy of active opposition) than others.
Ten	The states system is seen as viable and able to accommodate territorial change and change in the status of its units without being thrown into crisis.

The distinction between international society as either a purposive or a practical association comes from Terry Nardin (1983). According to Nardin, a purposive association consists of those 'who are associated in a cooperative enterprise to promote shared values, beliefs, or interests...' (1983, p. 9). A practical association, on the other hand, is not defined or governed by the pursuit of shared goals. Rather, it is based upon 'a framework of common practices and rules capable of providing some unifying bond where shared purposes are lacking' (1983, p. 5). Thus, in the practical conception of international society,

> what unites the separate states in a larger society is not any similarity of language, religion or government. Nor is there unity to be found in geographical proximity, in their transactions with one another, or in any interests they may happen to share. It is, rather, the formal unity of an association of independent political communities each pursuing its own way of life within certain acknowledged limits: that is, according to generally recognized rules through which cultural individuality and communal liberty are guaranteed, subject only to the constraints of mutual toleration and mutual accommodation (1983, p. 50).

This view of international society sees sovereign states as the primary actors in world politics. They form a society that is based not on shared goals or purposes, but on a set of minimal rules that allows each state to pursue its own particular aims, subject only to mutually reciprocal constraints on how those aims may legitimately be pursued.

Does such a society of states actually exist? Evidence that it does comes from both Hedley Bull and Thomas Franck. Bull (1977) contends that

> Most states at most times pay some respect to the basic rules of coexistence in international society, such as mutual respect for sovereignty, the rule that agreements should be kept, and rules limiting resort to violence. In the same way, most states at most times take part in the working of common institutions... (1977, p. 42).

Franck (1988) focuses his argument specifically on individual states' compliance with international law. As he puts it,

> The surprising thing about international law is that nations ever obey its strictures or carry out its mandates.... That they should do so is much more interesting than, say, the fact that most citizens usually obey their nation's laws, because the international system is organized in a voluntarist fashion, supported by so little coercive authority. This unenforced rule system can obligate states to profess, if not always to manifest, a significant level of day-to-day compliance, even, at times, when that is not in their short-term self-interest (1988, p. 705).

The final thing that must be said in regards to my conception of international society is that it is based upon the mutual recognition of sovereignty. In other words, each individual state claims exclusive domestic jurisdiction subject to no higher governing body (authority in Oakeshott or Thomson's terms) over a specific territory and it correspondingly recognizes other states' claims to their own exclusive domestic jurisdictions. The entire states-system is premised upon this mutual recognition of sovereignty. Diplomacy, international law, treaties, and all the other institutions that enable states to communicate and interact with each other rest upon 'the mutual recognition among government leaders that they represent a specific society within an exclusive jurisdictional domain'(Barkin and Cronin, 1994, p. 110). A corollary of this mutual recognition of sovereignty is some sort of general non-intervention principle. In this regard, John Vincent describes non-intervention as a 'first principle' of international society because the observance of such a principle demonstrates 'the recognition by states of the existence of others and the legitimacy of their separateness in a society bound together only by the mutual acknowledgment of the autonomy of its parts...' (1974, pp. 330-331).

A second assumption of this study is that state sovereignty is neither permanent nor inevitable. Sovereignty is not divinely ordained; it is an artificially-created political arrangement that can be reformed or radically uprooted. While there are strong institutional and practical reasons not to expect its imminent demise, sovereignty may be viewed as a socially constructed concept which can, perhaps within certain limits, be deconstructed and/or reconstructed. Sovereignty is thus a distinct historical phenomenon, not an inevitable feature of human life. F. H. Hinsley captures the essence of this sentiment when he argues that,

> Although we speak of it as something concrete that may be lost or acquired, eroded or increased, sovereignty is not a fact. It is an assumption about authority—a concept men have applied in certain circumstances to the political power that they or other men were exercising (1967, p. 242).

A third assumption relates to boundaries: current state borders are neither natural nor inevitable. In short, there are no territorial givens. As Ravi Kapil notes,

> Boundaries demarcate sharp discontinuities in political jurisdictions; except where land reaches the sea, such sharp breaks do not occur either in topography and vegetation or in the natural distribution of social, economic, linguistic, or cultural traits of human populations (1966, p. 657).

Even when it comes to islands, there is nothing particularly natural or definitive about existing political boundaries. The islands of Hispaniola (divided between the Dominican Republic and Haiti) and Borneo (divided between Brunei, Indonesia and Malaysia) could each be governed as single entities; as entities with even more subdivisions (i.e., more than two governments on Hispaniola, more than three on Borneo); or as entities with the same number of sub-divisions but with different territorial jurisdictions (i.e., Hispaniola divided between the Dominican Republic and Haiti, but with different borders than at present). There are no compelling natural reasons for the planet to be divided into its present 185+ sovereign states. International society could exist in a more or less similar fashion with either fewer than 100 sovereign jurisdictions or with more than 300. All political borders are mutable human constructs that can be altered or abolished; none is sacrosanct. This is not to deny that there may be compelling arguments for maintaining existing territorial jurisdictions; it is merely to state that such arguments must be based on something other than the 'naturalness' or the 'inevitability' of existing boundaries.

A fourth assumption is that both territory and statehood still matter. This may seem so obvious as not to bear mentioning, but in an era when it is increasingly fashionable to talk about the myriad challenges facing the state and the states system, it is worth asserting explicitly: the possession of territory and recognition as a sovereign state both remain fundamentally important. This is not to deny that the sovereign state may increasingly have to share the world stage with multinational corporations, non-governmental organizations, intergovernmental organizations, social movements, ethnic groups, and even individuals. Rather, it is to argue that statehood still counts as the ultimate prize in international relations. The presence of so many secessionist movements in the world today bears witness to this fact. Similarly, in regard to territory, my point is not to deny that non-territorial forms of organization may be increasing in importance or that modern technology has opened up new ways to organize governmental services on non-territorial bases (Elkins, 1995). It is not even to deny that territory may at times be a limiting factor that hinders adaptation and highlights state vulnerabilities.[20] Instead, it is to argue that territory remains a valuable commodity in international relations. In contrast to Richard Rosecrance (1996), territory is not seen as becoming 'passé' (1996, p. 45). Rather, even in an era of quasi-states and negative sovereignty, the possession of territory remains 'the pre-condition for the exercise of legitimate political authority on the international level' (Kratochwil, Rohrlich and Mahajan, 1985, p. 3).

Fifth, this study explicitly rejects the traditional bias against secession. Integration is not necessarily a 'good' and disintegration is not necessarily a 'bad'. Depending on one's perspective, particular forms of integration may be disastrous while other forms of disintegration might lead to lasting benefits. The point is that secession should not automatically be prejudged in all cases. Conversely, as secession is quite a complicated process which often descends into violence and necessarily entails substantial restructuring, it is not something to be flippantly supported in all cases either.

One of the main arguments against secession is the so-called 'domino theory'—essentially a fear of unlimited and never-ending 'Balkanization' due to an unqualified right to secede that is exercised by increasing numbers of ethnic or national groups. My sixth assumption is to reject the domino theory for both intellectual and empirical reasons. From the intellectual or philosophical viewpoint, Allen Buchanan (1991) points out that

> This argument proceeds by sleight of hand. It assumes, quite without warrant, that a right to secede must be an *unlimited* right—a right of virtually anyone to secede for virtually any reason. But one doesn't have to allow everything just because one allows something.... the right to secede cannot be an unlimited right.[21]

Perhaps even more compelling is the empirical evidence to date. One could cite Norway's secession from Sweden; Iceland's secession from Denmark; Singapore's secession from Malaysia; and Bangladesh's secession from Pakistan as examples of cases where one successful secession did not lead to further secessions either from the newly independent state, the former parent state, or from any other states in the regions concerned. Conversely, the failure of the Katangans and the Southern Sudanese did not seem to have any substantial deterrent effect on Biafra.[22] The demonstration effects of both successful and unsuccessful secession attempts are limited. While the Eritrean example may offer modest encouragement to Somaliland, it has definitely not led to any wholesale redrawing of the political map in Africa. Rejecting the domino theory does not mean that one has to support independence for either Québec or Northern Cyprus. It merely requires that the opposition to their independence be based on something more substantial than the fear of unlimited secession in North America or the Mediterranean.

A seventh assumption of this study is that the post-1945 interpretation of self-determination has either: a) not promoted international stability, or b) has promoted a particular kind of international stability that is not necessarily the only or the best kind of stability available. I believe that the empirical evidence available supports proposition (a) above. Even if one does not accept that, proposition (b), which is the weaker form of the argument, is a sufficiently compelling reason to temper any religious-like reverence attributed to the contemporary interpretation of self-determination.

To simplify the history of self-determination, one can view the principle as having widespread international acceptance or popularity in two main periods: the Wilsonian era after World War I and the anti-colonial period after World War II. The essential underpinning of self-determination, the question of who is the 'self', has shifted dramatically between these two periods. In essence, the earlier Wilsonian concept which was based on ethnic, cultural, or national groups has given way to a new territorial conception of self-determination where the eligible units are primarily former colonies and non-self-governing territories as defined under Chapter XI of the UN Charter. As Rupert Emerson (1971) has argued, the point of contradiction between these two periods lies

> in the fact that the peoples involved in the Wilsonian period were ethnic communities, nations or nationalities primarily defined by language and culture, whereas in the present era of decolonization, ethnic identity is essentially irrelevant, the decisive, indeed, ordinarily the sole, consideration being the existence of a political entity in the guise of a colonial territory (1971, p. 463).

Along with this shift in emphasis from national peoples to colonial territories has come the belief that self-determination is now not a process, but rather a one-off event. Once an acceptable form of self-determination[23] takes places at the time of decolonization, the issue is permanently settled. No further exercises of self-determination need take place. The readily-apparent irony in this situation is that

> precisely the condition which was held to justify self-determination in the earlier period, *i.e.*, that ethnically different peoples were subjected to alien rule, is now wholly unacceptable as a justification once the colonial territory has achieved its independence.... once the newly created or newly independent state is in existence, no resort to further self-determination is tolerable (Emerson, 1971, pp. 463-464).

The driving force behind the new interpretation of self-determination was an attempt to restrict the scope of who was entitled to be a 'self'. Considering the potentially revolutionary nature of an unlimited right to self-determination and the ethnic heterogeneity so prevalent in many of the former colonies, it is not surprising that this attempt to limit self-determination received such widespread international support. In the post-war era, the 'selves' eligible for self-determination essentially came to comprise three main groups: former colonies or other similar non-self-governing territories; territories under military occupation; and territories where majority colored populations were subjected to institutionalized racism or *apartheid* by Europeans.[24] This latter category was defined quite narrowly so as to exclude all forms of institutionalized racism or discrimination by one non-European group against another non-European group. Thus, while black South Africans and Rhodesians were entitled to self-determination, other groups such as Tibetans, Tamils, and black southern Sudanese who also suffered from institutionalized discrimination were not entitled to this same right.

Most UN members hoped that this novel and quite limited interpretation of self-determination would promote international stability. After all, an international society of sovereign states does seem more stable than an international society of (much more nebulously defined) sovereign nations. One must, however, question the success of the post-war interpretation of self-determination in this regard from both empirical and intuitive perspectives. Empirically, the post-1945 world has seen more than 21 million civilian and military casualties resulting from interstate wars and internationalized civil wars. More than 99 percent of these casualties have been in the so-called Third World (Holsti, 1992, p. 37). Certainly not all of these casualties can be blamed on the post-war interpretation of self-determination. Yet, in a study of 58 conflicts from 1945 - 1989, K. J. Holsti finds that state creation issues were major sources of war in 52 percent of the fifty-eight conflicts. He goes on to conclude that 'in terms of the relative frequency of issues it [state-creation] ranks highest by a considerable margin' (1991, pp. 282 and 311). Clearly this doctrine's intended message of severely restricting the number of eligible 'selves' has not quite gotten through to many of those supposedly non-eligible 'selves'.

From an intuitive perspective, Onyeonoro Kamanu (1974) questions whether the attempt to ban the right of self-determination from all but majorities in accepted political units has really enhanced stability. He believes that

> It has probably had the reverse effect since it leaves no choice to minorities seeking separate nationhood except resort to force. An anarchic situation now prevails whereby the only solution to a demand for secession in other

than a colonial context is armed conflict, a condition that, far from discouraging impermissible use of force across state boundaries, multiplies the opportunities and temptations for such action (1974, p. 359).

Denied the possibility of pursuing their (often legitimate) grievances in any other manner, disaffected groups are forced to turn to armed struggle. The consensus around freezing the map that the new interpretation of self-determination helped promote thus fails to ensure international stability.

One can certainly argue against this point. Counterfactually, it is difficult to refute the possibility that the levels of both conflicts and casualties would have been much higher in a world where self-determination applied to entities other than just former colonies, areas under military occupation, or majority colored populations suffering from institutionalized *apartheid* at the hands of Europeans. Maybe a looser interpretation of self-determination would have led to more instability. But, just as easily, maybe it would not have. It is impossible to resolve this question adequately. Whatever one's position here, I believe that the weaker form of the argument (proposition (b) above) is irrefutable. Even if one firmly believes that this new interpretation of self-determination has promoted international stability, the fact remains that it has produced only one particular kind of stability. Judging from the myriad conflicts that have arisen and the vast array of political, social, and economic problems that still plague so many Third World and former socialist countries, it is doubtful that this form of international stability was the best one available. It was certainly not the only possibility.

The eighth assumption or premise that this study works from is that self-determination claims need to be evaluated on a case-by-case basis, and not on the basis of abstract principle alone. Self-determination remains an essentially contested concept. Consensus or agreement has never been reached on such key points as who is the self?; is self-determination a political principle or a legal right?; and if self-determination is a legal right, does it include secession? All of these intellectual questions are compounded by the traditional inconsistency with which the principle of self-determination has been applied.[25] As such, it is extremely difficult to translate from the abstract principle of national self-determination into the cold, hard reality of whether or not Biafra or Bangladesh has a legitimate right to secede. As Stanley French and Andres Gutman (1974) put it,

> there may be instances where it is quite justifiable for a population to try to secede from the state of which it is part.... Such arguments should be

considered on their own merits.... national self-determination cannot be sanctioned by appeal to the *principle* of national self-determination (1974, p. 153).

One can argue over what criteria should be applied in assessing the legitimacy of a particular secession attempt. My point is merely that the answer to the question 'Who has the right to self-determination?' will not be found solely in abstract formulations of the principle of national self-determination. Self-determination may be generally supported or generally opposed for a variety of reasons. Specific attempts at self-determination must, however, be evaluated on an individual case-by-case basis.

My ninth premise is that just as particular self-determination claims may be deemed more worthy of support than others, so may particular *de facto* states be deemed more worthy of support (or less worthy of active opposition) than others. These entities form a diverse group. Particular readers may find some *de facto* states more 'just' or morally appealing than others. This author, for example, would object far less strenuously to being described as a 'friend' of the Eritrean People's Liberation Front (EPLF) or of the Egal administration in Somaliland than he would to being considered a 'friend' of the Tamil Tigers. All *de facto* states are not created equal. One might thus object strenuously to some and yet support others.

My final assumption concerns the ability of the states system to cope with change. In essence, the states system is seen as viable and able to accommodate territorial change and change in the status of its units without being thrown into crisis. The empirical evidence on this point is quite compelling. Since 1989, the states system has managed to cope with the dissolutions of Czechoslovakia, Ethiopia, the Soviet Union, and Yugoslavia, as well as with the reunifications of the two Germanys and the two Yemens. Going back even further, one could add the dissolution of Pakistan, the division of Korea, and the division and subsequent reunification of Vietnam. Perhaps even more impressive than all of this, however, was the ability of the states system to cope with the massive increase in the number of sovereign states which accompanied the decolonization process. Changes in territorial boundaries and in the status of its units have clearly not overwhelmed the states system before and there is no reason to expect them to do so now. Regardless of whether or not Somaliland achieves independence or the entire island of Cyprus is or is not reunited under one government, the institutions of the international society of states will continue to function more or less as they have in the past.

5 Outline for the Remainder of the Study

Looking ahead, chapter two defines the *de facto* state. It outlines the specific theoretical criteria used to distinguish the *de facto* state from other entities in international politics. It also delineates the ethical foundations and the political logic of the *de facto* state.

Chapters three and four offer more detailed information on the four case studies. Chapter three considers Eritrea and the LTTE-controlled areas of Sri Lanka. Chapter four examines Somaliland and the TRNC. General historical, geographic, and demographic background information will be provided for each. Additionally, I will assess how well each case study fits the various theoretical criteria outlined in chapter two.

Chapters five through eight essentially comprise a birth, life, and death or evolution look at the *de facto* state. Chapters five and six consider separate aspects of the birth phase. Chapter five examines the systemic or macro-level factors that contribute to the emergence of *de facto* states in general. Chapter six, on the other hand, analyzes the micro-level factors that lead to the emergence of specific *de facto* states. Chapter seven investigates the life phase of the *de facto* state. It examines questions such as what, if any, impact does the *de facto* state have on international society?; can international law successfully cope with the existence of *de facto* states?; and does the *de facto* state serve any useful purpose for the international society of sovereign states? Recognizing the inherent instability so characteristic of life as a *de facto* state, chapter eight assesses various possibilities for the future evolution or transformation of these entities. From the perspective of the *de facto* state itself, these range from the dismal (crushing military defeat) to the ultimately prized (successful 'graduation' to sovereign statehood), with many others in-between. Chapter eight scrutinizes all of these assorted potential transformations.

The ninth chapter explores the impact of *de facto* states on international theory. In particular, it assesses what explanations for these entities can be found in existing international theories and what challenges the existence of *de facto* states poses to those same theories. A variety of theoretical perspectives such as realism, rationalism, structural economic viewpoints, and post-modernism will be analyzed here. Further research agendas within each tradition will be delineated. This chapter also considers what, if any, changes would need to be made to existing international theories if the *de facto* state were to remain a permanent fixture in international politics with an indeterminate status. Chapter ten serves as a general conclusion to this work. Beyond that, it also evaluates the future prospects for the *de facto* state and answers the question what, if anything, can or should be done about this phenomenon?

Notes

[1] See, for example, Ayoob, 1991; Buzan, 1991b; Goldgeier and McFaul, 1992; Holsti, 1992; Holsti, 1996; and Sayigh, 1990.
[2] Herbst, 1990, p. 137. This line of thinking is also further developed in Herbst, 1996, pp. 151-172.
[3] Beitz, 1991, p. 243. This is also a major theme developed in Beitz, 1979.
[4] See, for example, Helman and Ratner, 1992-93, and the various contributions in Zartman, 1995a.
[5] Oakeshott, 1975, p. 323, my italics.
[6] 'Sri Lankan Forces Launch Heavy Assault on Tigers,' *The Guardian*, 10 July 1995, p. 8.
[7] The phrase 'a sprawling de facto state' is used in 'Sri Lankan Troops Take Two Towns, Reward on Tiger Chief Raised', *Agence France Presse*, 15 November 1995; and the phrase 'the former de facto state' is used in 'Roman Catholics Call for Sri Lanka Truce: Rebels', *Agence France Presse*, 28 April 1996.
[8] 'Africa's Bizarre Borders', *The Economist*, 25 January 1997.
[9] See, for example, the LTTE-friendly 'eelamweb' internet site which, in answering the question 'What is Tamil Eelam?', replies that it 'is a de facto state in [the] Indian Ocean'. This can be viewed at http://www.eelamweb.com/faq.html.
[10] U Thant, cited in Suzuki, 1976, p. 845.
[11] Buchheit, 1978. Two attempts to develop criteria for secession within the context of liberal democracy are Beran, 1984; and Birch, 1984.
[12] Buzan, 1991a, p. 441. See also Heraclides, 1992, p. 399.
[13] Buchanan, 1991; Eastwood, 1993, pp. 341-349; Heraclides, 1992, pp. 408-410; and McMullen, 1992, pp. 118-123.
[14] The volume of literature on Cyprus and Sri Lanka is clearly much greater than the volume of literature on Eritrea or Somaliland. Of the four case studies considered, it is Somaliland that suffers the most from having the fewest academic resources available.
[15] Compare, for example, Carroll and Rajagopal, 1992-93, which quite strongly sets out the case for Somaliland's independence with Minasse Haile, 1994, which quite strongly sets out the Ethiopian case against Eritrean independence.
[16] James, 1986b, p. 3. See also Inayatullah and Blaney, 1995, p. 3; and Thomson, 1995, p. 213.
[17] Rosenau, 1988, p. 21. See also Cassese, 1986, p. 125.
[18] Each case features two major nations in one state; the smaller of which views itself as a distinct co-founder of the country and desires to be treated as a confederal equal;

the larger of which views the national question in terms of majorities and minorities and believes that it can best be addressed through some form of federalism.

[19] Some of the most useful overviews of this tradition include Brown, 1995; Bull, 1966; Cutler, 1991; Dunne, 1995; Suganami, 1983; and P. Wilson, 1989. More critical perspectives can be found in Grader, 1988; Halliday, 1994, chapter five; and Wæver, 1992.

[20] James Rosenau, for example, refers to states as 'sovereignty-bound actors' in order to call attention 'to the ways in which states are limited by the very considerations that are usually regarded as the source of their strengths.' See Rosenau, 1990, p. 36.

[21] Buchanan, 1991, p. 102. See also Herbst, 1996-97, p. 137.

[22] See Beran, 1984, pp. 29-30; and Kamanu, 1974, pp. 366-367 for more on this.

[23] While self-determination is usually associated with full independence as a sovereign state, General Assembly Resolution 1541 of 15 December 1960 also included free association with an independent state and integration with an independent state as acceptable forms of self-determination. The International Court of Justice's advisory opinion in the *Western Sahara* case also makes reference to these other options. See Pomerance, 1984, p. 327; and White, 1981-82, p. 149 for more on this.

[24] See Heraclides, 1992, pp. 404-405; and Wiberg, 1983, p. 49 for more on these three categories.

[25] On some of these inconsistencies see Pomerance, 1984, pp. 322-327; and Hannum, 1990, pp. 36-37.

2   Defining the *De Facto* State

1 Introduction

This chapter is designed to answer the question 'What is the *de facto* state?'
Section 2 begins this task by offering a working definition.   This sets the
stage for the following section which elaborates various theoretical criteria
used to distinguish the *de facto* state from other entities in international
politics.   The fourth section of this chapter then considers the ethical and the
political logics behind the *de facto* state.   Our next section considers the
criteria and requirements for statehood.   In particular, it compares the
respective position of quasi-states and *de facto* states under these criteria.
This section also explains why the use of the term 'state' in *de facto* state is
justified and it explores what these entities have and lack in terms of the
contemporary requirements for statehood in the late twentieth century.
Section 6 evaluates the comparative limitations faced by quasi-states and *de
facto* states.   Finally, the last section summarizes this chapter and looks
forward to chapters three and four.

2 Defining the *De Facto* State

A *de facto* state exists where there is an organized political leadership which
has risen to power through some degree of indigenous capability; receives
popular support; and has achieved sufficient capacity to provide
governmental services to a given population in a specific territorial area, over
which effective control is maintained for a significant period of time.   The *de
facto* state views itself as capable of entering into relations with other states
and it seeks full constitutional independence and widespread international
recognition as a sovereign state.   It is, however, unable to achieve any degree
of substantive recognition and therefore remains illegitimate in the eyes of
international society.

This working definition obviously comprises a number of different
elements.   In part, it is derived from the traditional criteria for statehood in
international law—the most famous statement of which is probably Article 1

of the 1933 Montevideo Convention on Rights and Duties of States. According to this convention, 'The State as a person of international law should possess the following qualifications: (a) a permanent population; (b) a defined territory; (c) government; and (d) capacity to enter into relations with other states'.[1] Population and territory are clearly covered in the working definition of the *de facto* state. For government, I use the somewhat weaker formulation of 'organized political leadership'. Similarly, point (d) is also qualified to indicate that the *de facto* state leaders view themselves as having this capacity to enter into relations with other states; an opinion not necessarily shared by other states.

In terms of subject matter, some of the elements of this definition deal with the *de facto* state's capabilities: it has an organized leadership; it has reached such a level that it is able to provide a degree of governmental services; it is able to control a given territorial area for extended periods of time. Other elements focus on the logic, intent, or desired goals of the *de facto* state: it is territorially-based and in the business of providing governance; it sees itself as capable of entering into relations with other states; it seeks recognition as a sovereign state. Another set of elements delineates the *de facto* state's relationship with its society: it has arisen to power through a degree of indigenous ability and it receives popular support. Finally, the last part considers how the *de facto* state is received by the larger international society of sovereign states: it is unable to attain any degree of substantive recognition and thus is perceived to be illegitimate.

The working definition offered above and the theoretical criteria to follow below are intended to illustrate an ideal type of *de facto* state. One should not be surprised to see variations or deviations from this model. Just as the umbrella term 'capitalist state' can cover such a wide range of entities as France, Japan, Singapore, and the United States, so too can the term *de facto* state stretch to embrace a variety of situations. Some *de facto* states, for example, are larger or smaller, richer or poorer, more or less ethnically homogeneous than others. Adam Watson's warning is prescient here:

> while the division of reality into categories can assist our understanding of what actually happens, there is an inherent danger that our categories may come between us and reality. We may slip into the assumption that phenomena lumped together in a category are more alike than they really are, or that because some things are true about all of them, other things are true also (1992, p. 18).

This chapter's division of reality into the category '*de facto* state' is intended to assist our understanding of what actually happens. The reader has been forewarned so as not to slip into the assumption that *de facto* states are more alike than they really are.

3 Theoretical Criteria to Distinguish the *De Facto* State from Other Entities

In this section, ten separate criteria will be advanced to sharpen our focus on the *de facto* state and to distinguish it from other entities in international relations. In order to aid future references back to these criteria, they will be numbered from one to ten. The numbering system is used merely as an organizing device, not as an indication of relative importance. These ten criteria, which can be broken down into three or four larger sub-headings, are shown graphically in the table on the next page.

Criterion number one distinguishes the *de facto* state from a power vacuum or a state-less situation. Herbert Weiss, in his attempt to compare Zaire [now Congo] with other 'collapsed' African states, is helpful in illustrating this point. According to Weiss, Zaire [at least pre-Kabila] cannot be compared with Sudan because 'Although one cannot say that Kinshasa really controls the interior, it cannot be claimed that a substantial part of the state's territory is under the control of another authority. The same conclusion can be made regarding a comparison with Liberia' (1995, p. 158). In this regard, quasi-states and *de facto* states are not found in anything approaching a 1:1 ratio. Indeed, most quasi-states do not face *de facto* state challengers: one suspects that the ratio of quasi-states to *de facto* states would be somewhere in the range of 15:1 or 20:1. A *de facto* state requires some sort of viable, organized, functioning governing entity. The mere fact that a sovereign state's control does not run throughout its entire country should in no way be interpreted as indicating the presence of a *de facto* state. Power vacuums, unorganized polities, control by local strongmen, state-less situations, and the like would not qualify as *de facto* states.

Our second criterion also speaks to the *de facto* state's capabilities. This criterion distinguishes it from other groups and situations such as terrorists, riots, sporadic violence, or random banditry. This section uses a number of different lenses from such areas as traditional international law and the Geneva Conventions to try to bring these distinctions into clearer focus.

Table 2.1 Dimensions of *De Facto* Statehood

Criterion #	General Focus	Specific concern
One	Capacity/ability	*de facto* states vs. a power vacuum or state-less situation
Two	Capacity/ability	*de facto* states vs. riots, terrorists, sporadic violence and random banditry
Three	Capacity/ability	Perseverance, length of time
Four	Goals/motives	There is a goal; the goal is sovereignty as constitutional independence
Five	Goals/motives	Secession vs. emigration; the need for a territorial justification
Six	Distinction/difference	*de facto* states vs. puppet states
Seven	Distinction/difference	*de facto* states vs. peaceful secession movements
Eight	Distinction/difference	*de facto* states vs. other non-sovereign entities with greater international legitimacy
Nine	Distinction/difference	*de facto* states vs. the premature recognition of colonial liberation movements
Ten	Legitimacy/likelihood of success or acceptance	Democratic accountability

The easiest distinction to be made under this criterion concerns random banditry. The *de facto* state is a political animal. Its organized political leadership seeks to provide governmental services to a given population in a specific territory, with the ultimate aim of securing sovereignty. The *de facto* state is thus not to be confused with bandits, drug lords, or nominally-political groups whose main intent is to line their own pockets with profit, plunder, or taxes. It is distinguished from such groups by its goals (political versus monetary or non-political goals), its capabilities (providing some sort of governmental services versus solely parasitic extraction), and its degree of popular support (presumably much higher in the case of *de facto* states).

Separating the *de facto* state from terrorists, sporadic uprisings or other lesser forms of violence is not quite as clear-cut. In this case, all such groups may share similar political goals and may receive comparable levels of popular support. The main distinction here thus comes in the area of capabilities. Let us first consider the traditional international law distinction between the conditions of rebellion, insurgency, and belligerency. While these distinctions are imprecise, contested, and 'highly theoretical and devoid of practice in support of theory' (H.A. Wilson, 1988, p. 37), they may still be of use to us in conceptualizing the *de facto* state. Under this scheme, rebellion 'is understood to entail sporadic violence which is capable of containment by the national police or militia' (Higgins, 1971, p. 86). This is the lowest of the three conditions considered here. International law offers no protection to the rebels and international society is not required to take any formal notice of them. By contrast, 'certain traditional norms of international law are—or are said to be—relevant to internal hostilities which are deemed either insurgency or belligerency' (Higgins, 1971, p. 86). Insurgency is considered the next level up from rebellion. Its formal recognition can be seen as an international acknowledgment of internal war. While there are supposedly some international legal obligations concerning the ill-defined and elusive status of insurgency, 'recognition as an insurgent has comparatively few formal legal consequences' (Reisman and Suzuki, 1976, p. 426). As such, our focus will be on the distinction between rebellion and belligerency.

The recognition of belligerency is more than a mere international acknowledgment of an internal war; it imposes a duty of neutrality on outside parties. Our concern here is not with the alleged legal consequences of recognizing belligerency. Indeed, as Rosalyn Higgins notes, the near-total reluctance to accord this status in contemporary international relations means that this is 'a legal concept fast becoming irrelevant...' (1971, p. 94). Rather, our concern is with the criteria traditionally advanced to identify a state of belligerency. W. Michael Reisman and Eisuke Suzuki identify four such criteria which must be met for there to be a status of belligerency. As they see it, the concept 'belligerent'

> is a term of art referring cumulatively to (1) an organized group within a nation-state (2) which seeks control by force of arms within that state and (3) which has already acquired stable control over a significant segment of territory and (4) which has undertaken the operations of a regular government in that sector (1976, p. 426).

Regardless of this concept's declining legal relevance, the four points of Reisman and Suzuki's formulation can be used to help distinguish the *de facto* state from other lesser 'rebellions'.

Another lens which can be adapted for our purposes here comes from the 1949 Geneva Conventions. Among many other things, the Geneva Diplomatic Conference of 1949 recorded a number of 'convenient criteria' which are useful for 'distinguishing a genuine [internal] armed conflict from a mere act of banditry or an unorganized and short-lived insurrection'. The first criterion here is 'That the party in revolt against the *de jure* government possesses an organized military force, an authority responsible for its acts, acting within a determinate territory and having the means of respecting and ensuring respect for the Convention'. The fourth criterion expands on these requirements further so

> (a) That the insurgents have an organization purporting to have the characteristics of a state; (b) that the insurgent civil authority exercises *de facto* authority over persons within a determinate territory; (c) that the armed forces act under the direction of the organized civil authority and are prepared to observe the ordinary laws of war; (d) that the insurgent civil authority agrees to be bound by the terms of the Convention.[2]

Depending on the specific *de facto* state considered, points (c) and (d) above may be problematic. The first criterion and points (a) and (b) of the fourth criterion, however, do assist in distinguishing the *de facto* state from other less capable entities.

In 1977, the Diplomatic Conference on the Reaffirmation and Development of International Humanitarian Law Applicable in Armed Conflicts, meeting in Geneva, adopted two Protocols additional to the 1949 Geneva Conventions. Article 1 of Protocol II deals with the applicability of that Protocol. Five conditions are set forth which must be met before Protocol II becomes applicable. The fifth condition is that 'They[the dissident or separatist group] have control over a part of the territory of the High Contracting Party so as to enable them to carry out sustained and concerted military operations and to implement Protocol II'. Additionally, there is a negative qualification which, in the words of Thomas Fleiner-Gerster and Michael Meyer, 'provides that Protocol II does not apply to situations of internal disturbances and tensions, such as riots, isolated and sporadic acts of violence and other acts of a similar nature, as not being armed conflicts' (1985, p. 276). A *de facto* state would meet the fifth condition above and is therefore distinct from the other entities excluded by Article 1's negative qualification.

Criterion number three also speaks to the *de facto* state's capability. This is what might be called the perseverance or length-of-time criterion. Clearly, for it to make sense to speak of a *de facto* state, the entity so labeled must be more than something which is here today and gone tomorrow. Exactly where to set this criterion, however, is not readily apparent. Obviously, an entity like the TRNC which has existed for more than a decade in its present form (it was proclaimed on 15 November 1983) and for more than twenty years if its predecessor, the Turkish Federated State of Cyprus (TFSC, proclaimed on 13 February 1975), is considered would exceed whatever time threshold was set. Similarly, one can exclude an entity like the Democratic Republic of East Timor (DRET), which was proclaimed by the *Frente Revolucianaria de Timor Leste Independente* (FRETELIN) on 28 November 1975 after it had occupied a substantial part of the territory on East Timor. The DRET failed to secure any international recognition before it met its demise in December 1975 at the hands of the invading Indonesian army.[3] An entity in existence for less than one month definitely fails to qualify as a *de facto* state.

Between the two extremes of less than one month and more than twenty years, the exact point at which to set the perseverance criterion for the *de facto* state is somewhat arbitrary. Intuitively, a minimum perseverance criterion of one year seems to be necessary. Much more than that risks excluding potential *de facto* states such as Biafra (officially proclaimed on 30 May 1967 and officially disbanded on 12 January 1970) and the 'Republic of Serbian Krajina' (established in the fall of 1991 and militarily crushed in August 1995). The argument made here is that both Biafra and Krajina were substantial enough entities with large enough impacts on international relations to merit serious academic study. Therefore, this study arbitrarily will establish two years as the minimum time period necessary to qualify as a *de facto* state.

The fourth criterion for the *de facto* state addresses its goals. In regard to the existence or non-existence of a goal itself, this distinction has already been made above in criterion number two which separated the *de facto* state from bandits, drug lords, and others who either completely lack a goal or who have predominantly non-political goals. The *de facto* state, though, can also be distinguished from other politically-oriented groups with different goals. Here we come to Alan James's (1986b) notion of sovereignty as constitutional independence. For James, sovereignty 'consists of being constitutionally apart, of not being contained, however loosely, within a wider constitutional scheme' (1986b, p. 24). It is this constitutional independence which separates Tuvalu from Texas. While both have defined territories, populations, and governments, and Texas is the much more substantial entity, it is only Tuvalu that is considered sovereign in international relations. Why? Because Tuvalu is constitutionally independent and Texas is not. In terms of its goals, the *de facto* state seeks sovereignty as full constitutional independence. It does not seek a different role within a federal system (although, if unsuccessful, it may ultimately be compelled to accept such a role). Therefore, the *de facto* state can be distinguished from such sub-federal events as Jura splitting from the Berne Canton in Switzerland in the 1970s or Staten Island's proposed secession from New York City. Allen Buchanan refers to this distinction as being between national and local secession (1991, p. 15). In his terms, the *de facto* state seeks national secession; Jura and Staten Island only seek local secession. Obviously, the *de facto* state can be distinguished from Jura or Staten Island in a number of other ways; the point here is that it seeks sovereignty as constitutional independence, not a change in its position within an existing sovereign state.

More relevant perhaps than Jura or Staten Island is the distinction that can be made here between the *de facto* state and groups which have *de facto* territorial control of a given area but do not seek sovereign statehood. One example of the latter phenomenon might be the Eastern Kasai region of Zaire [now Congo], home of Mbuji-Mayi, the country's second-largest city. While this region's leaders are able to maintain a large amount of autonomy and *de facto* independence from the central government in Kinshasa, they do not advocate secession for fear of unnecessarily antagonizing the center and having more ethnic violence directed against the Luba people of the region. Many of these people were killed in or fled from earlier violence in neighboring Shaba province.[4] Thus, while the levels of territorial control, provision of governmental services, and degree of popular support may be similar to other *de facto* states, the lack of a secessionist goal distinguishes situations like Eastern Kasai from Northern Cyprus or Somaliland.

Another possible example here might be the parts of Liberia controlled by Charles Taylor before his election as president of the country in July 1997. At one time, Taylor's territory boasted its own currency and banking system, a television and radio network, a number of airfields, and a deep water port. In some ways, Taylor found his lack of international recognition advantageous as it freed him from legal entanglements and creditor demands arising from sovereign Liberia's US$ four billion debt. Ironically, as William Reno argues, 'Taylor's freedom from creditors and his access to foreign firms put him in a better position to generate foreign exchange quickly than the Monrovia enclave, with its international recognition' (1995, p. 113). As such, with their extremely limited political goals, 'Taylor the rebel leader and those like him do not seek or need immediate formal recognition as members of international society. They do need intermediaries who can be used to help exploit resources and gain access to international commercial networks' (Reno, 1995, p. 113). Again, an entity which might otherwise meet many of the criteria for a *de facto* state is excluded due to its different political goals.

Beyond situations like Eastern Kasai or Charles Taylor's Liberia, where the political goals are vague or unstated, we can also make the distinction here between the *de facto* state which seeks sovereignty for its part of an existing state and other explicitly political groups which do not seek independence. Thus, the distinction is made between a group seeking to secede and a group seeking to 'capture' the existing state or change its government. Buchanan (1991) conceptualizes this distinction in terms of secessionists and revolutionaries. As he puts it,

> Unlike the revolutionary, the secessionist's primary goal is not to overthrow the existing government, nor to make fundamental constitutional, economic or sociopolitical changes within the existing state. Instead, she wishes to restrict the jurisdiction of the state in question so as not to include her own group and the territory it occupies (1991, p. 10).

Peter Wallensteen and Karin Axell (1993) frame this same distinction in terms of governmental conflict versus territorial conflict. The former is characterized by an incompatibility 'concerning type of political system, the replacement of the central government or the change of its composition'. The latter is characterized by an incompatibility 'concerning the status of a territory, e.g. the change of the state in control of a certain territory (inter-state conflict), secession or autonomy (intra-state conflict)' (1993, p. 343).

Thus, the effect of this distinction is to separate *de facto* states from groups such as the *Sendero Luminoso* (Shining Path) in Peru or the Farabundo Martí National Liberation Front (FMLN) in El Salvador. At various times, the latter two groups, particularly the FMLN, have fit many of the characteristics of the *de facto* state. The fact that they did not, however, seek international recognition as a sovereign state distinguishes them from the *de facto* state.

Our fifth criterion also relates to the goals of the *de facto* state. The *de facto* state seeks to secede from the existing state and to take its territory with it. One thus comes here to the distinction between secession and emigration. Under the latter, disaffected people seek to leave an existing state, but they make no claim on its territory. Opting for secession places a higher burden on the *de facto* state's leadership. As Lea Brilmayer argues, 'By choosing secession rather than emigration, secessionists assume a duty of justification that refugees [emigrants] need not bear. Secessionists must somehow establish a claim to the territory on which they would found their new state' (1991, p. 188). Thus, our fifth criterion is that the *de facto* state, based as it is on territory, must provide a territorial justification to underpin its claim to recognition as a sovereign state. It is impossible to understand or to evaluate the relative merits of its claims without reference to territory. In seeking sovereign statehood as its goal, the *de facto* state 'is claiming a right to a particular piece of land, and one must necessarily inquire into why it is entitled to that particular piece of land, as opposed to some other piece of land -- or to no land at all' (Brilmayer, 1991, p. 201).

Criteria six through nine are all designed specifically to separate the *de facto* state from other entities in international relations with which it may be confused. Criterion number six focuses on the difference between *de facto* states and puppet states. According to James Crawford, 'The term "puppet State" is used to describe nominal sovereigns under effective foreign control, especially in cases where the establishment of the puppet State is intended as a cloak for manifest illegality' (1976-77, p. 130). Crawford argues that there is frequently a presumption of puppet character when regimes are constituted under belligerent occupation, or subsequent to illegal intervention or to the threat or use of force. Additionally, other factors that Crawford maintains should be taken into account when assessing whether or not an entity is a puppet state

> have included the following: that the entity concerned was established illegally, by the threat or use of external armed force; that it did not have the support of the vast majority of the population it claimed to govern; that in important matters it was subject to foreign direction or control; that it was staffed, especially in more important positions, by nationals of the dominant State (1976-77, pp. 132-133).

For Alan James, puppet states are defined as such 'because their relationship with another and more powerful state is regarded as so close that it justifies their treatment as mere appendages of the larger state, entities which move at its will and only at its will' (1986b, p. 139). He distinguishes here between puppet states and dependent states. The latter group might include countries such as Bhutan and Nepal which habitually avoid certain courses of action so as not to upset their much larger neighbor India, but which cannot properly be considered Indian puppet states. In James's scheme,

> The line between a dependent and a puppet state may not always be easy to draw.... The crucial element is the staffing of all the key positions in a state's decision-making apparatus by nationals of another state, those nationals being known to be there for the purpose of seeing that the will of their state is done (1986b, p. 140).

Crawford and James both offer Manchukuo and the Nazi-dominated states of Slovakia and Croatia during World War II as examples of puppet states. James also includes Egypt after its independence in 1922, Iraq after its independence in 1930, Cambodia after the Vietnamese invasion in 1978, and Afghanistan after the Soviet invasion in 1979 as other possible puppet states. Most interesting from the perspective of this study is his inclusion of the TRNC as a probable puppet state (James 1986b, pp. 140-142; Crawford, 1976-77, pp. 130-133). Whether this assessment is correct or not is a question that will be considered in chapter four.

As for the distinction between *de facto* states and puppet states, two parts of the working definition of the *de facto* state offered earlier speak to this question: its leadership has risen to power through some degree of indigenous capability, and it receives popular support. The *de facto* state has a much more organic and symbiotic relationship with its population than the puppet state does. An entity with an externally-imposed leadership that lacks strong indigenous roots and is bereft of all but the most minimal popular support would not qualify as a *de facto* state. Since both of these entities are somewhat imprecise constructions, this is a distinction based more on artful interpretation than it is on scientific evidence. Still, it is a distinction worth making. While Manchukuo and Biafra may both merit further study, they are clearly different entities.

Criterion number seven distinguishes the *de facto* state from peaceful secession movements. As Robert Young notes, in peaceful secessions, the declaration of one state or group to end the union or federation 'is accepted by the other government, in principle, a move that obviously distinguishes peaceful from contested secessions, since the only other alternative is to attempt violent repression' (1994, pp. 774-775). This acceptance of the idea in principle and the reluctance to undertake military countermeasures has not been the case with any of the *de facto* states considered here, although the situation in Northern Cyprus is somewhat anomalous in terms of the general lack of violence there since the Turkish military invasions of 1974.

Young has identified thirteen stages which are characteristic of peaceful secessions. His first two stages, which are: 1) 'secession follows protracted constitutional and political disputes', and 2) 'the secessor state declares its intent to withdraw', could be shared with any *de facto* state. His third stage, however, separates peaceful secessions from *de facto* states. That stage is 'the predecessor state accepts the principle of secession: negotiations follow'. This simply does not happen with *de facto* states. Additionally, Young's stages seven, ten, and thirteen (respectively 'the settlement is made quickly'; 'the secession is accomplished constitutionally'; and 'secession is irrevocable') also distinguish *de facto* state situations from peaceful secessions (1994, pp. 773-792).

In addition to the non-use of force from both sides, there are two additional factors which separate *de facto* states from peaceful secession movements. First, the types of devolved powers obtained by a group such as the Basques or the Catalans in a federal system and the consensual manner in which those powers are exercised are different from the types of power obtained by the *de facto* state and the manner in which it exercises them. Second, peaceful secession movements face a qualitatively different level of challenges than *de facto* states do. For example, while political uncertainty might have a diversionary or negative impact on foreign direct investment in Québec, that impact is of a substantially lower magnitude than the negative impact on investment in the illegal or juridically dubious areas of Somaliland and Northern Cyprus. Similarly, whatever happens in Québec, it is difficult to contemplate that province ever facing anything like the challenges Eritrea encountered at the end of its thirty-year war with Ethiopia.

Our eighth criterion distinguishes the *de facto* state from other non-sovereign or questionable/disputed-sovereign entities which have a much higher degree of international legitimacy. Although the *de facto* state seeks widespread recognition as a sovereign state, it is unable to achieve any degree of substantive recognition. The qualifier 'substantive' is used to indicate, for example, that an entity like the TRNC which has secured recognition from one state (Turkey) is still deemed illegitimate by the wider world. The question of where to draw the line between substantive and non-substantive recognition comes into play most clearly with the case of Taiwan or, as it is formally known, the Republic of China (ROC). At present, the ROC maintains formal diplomatic relations with 27 countries, most of which are located in Central America and the Caribbean.[5] It also maintains what it calls 'substantive relations'—economic, trade, technological and/or cultural ties—with over 140 countries and regional bodies. The ROC has 90 representative offices in 60 countries with which it does not have formal diplomatic relations and 37 of those countries have established representative offices in Taiwan (Republic of China, 1993, pp. 172-174). While this is clearly a higher degree of acceptance than that enjoyed by Somaliland or the TRNC, it does still make sense to speak of Taiwan as a *de facto* state.

To attain substantive recognition, an entity would need success in at least a majority of the following five areas. First, it would secure recognition from some of the major powers of the day—presently, for example, the United States, the other permanent members of the UN Security Council and the relevant regional great power(s). Second, it would secure recognition from the existing juridical state which it was seeking to leave, or at least no objections from them to others recognizing it—in other words, Ethiopia's consent for Eritrea, the Czech and Slovak mutual recognitions, and the like. Third, it would secure recognition from neighboring countries and countries with which it shares borders. Fourth, it would secure recognition from a majority of countries in the UN General Assembly. Fifth, it would be able to participate in global and regional international organizations. One could say that an entity which scored well in a majority of these categories (particularly the first two) had attained substantive recognition and thus should not be considered a *de facto* state. In the case of Taiwan, it completely fails the first four categories, albeit with the recognition of approximately 30 of the General Assembly's 185+ members. Though it has had partial success in the last category, one would still have to characterize Taiwan as a *de facto* state in this regard.

Where criterion number eight may be relevant is in relation to a few other entities in contemporary international relations. The Kurdish 'safe haven' in northern Iraq, for example, meets some of the criteria for inclusion as a *de facto* state. While there are serious questions as to the legality of establishing this safe haven against the expressed wishes of the Iraqi government (Duke, 1994, p. 41), the Kurdish safe haven does appear to have secured a much greater degree of international acceptance (due to its however tenuous origins in UN Security Council Resolution 688 of 1991) than any of the *de facto* states discussed here. Similarly, whatever its exact legal status and whether it ever achieves sovereign statehood or not, the Palestinian Authority also clearly has a degree of legitimacy not approached by the TRNC or the LTTE-controlled areas of Sri Lanka. In particular, it has a more secure legal basis as its status is now a part of international law after its incorporation into the treaties coming out of the Oslo peace process. Therefore, our consideration of *de facto* states will not include such entities as the Kurdish safe havens or the Palestinian Authority. Criterion number eight can also be used to distinguish the *de facto* state from other 'exceptions to sovereignty' such as the handful of remaining colonies, protectorates, trust territories, and possessions which have voluntarily chosen to remain constitutionally-associated with another state. Thus, unless they were to 1) begin demanding sovereignty as full constitutional independence, and 2) have this demand rejected by the parent state, entities such as Bermuda, the Cook Islands, Martinique, Puerto Rico, Tahiti, and the US Pacific Islands Trust Territory would not qualify as *de facto* states. Another such exception, albeit for different reasons, might be the Saharan Arab Democratic Republic (SADR)—which has been recognized by more than seventy states and admitted as a full member of the Organization for African Unity (OAU) even though Morocco effectively controls and occupies most of the Western Sahara (Fowler and Bunck, 1996, pp. 401-402).

A last distinction that is made in criterion number nine separates the *de facto* state from the historical phenomenon of prematurely recognizing colonial liberation movements. In the case of Algeria, for example, the Provisional Government of the Algerian Republic was recognized by 29 states even though its headquarters were not in Algeria itself, but in neighboring Tunisia. Another case that is of relevance here is Guinea-Bissau. In that situation, Amilcar Cabral's *Partido Africano da Independencia da Guine e Cabo Verde* (PAIGC) declared Guinea-Bissau's independence from Portugal on 26 September 1973. As Heather Wilson puts it,

> There is little doubt that the PAIGC did not have firm control in the territory. Under traditional international law, recognition of the State of Guinea-Bissau would probably have been premature. Nevertheless, by the end of 1973 forty States had recognized the Republic... (1988, p. 112).

On 2 November 1973, the UN General Assembly passed a resolution welcoming 'the recent accession to independence of the people of Guinea-Bissau thereby creating the sovereign State of the Republic of Guinea-Bissau....' by a vote of 93 in favor to 7 against with 30 abstentions. This vote took place almost a year before the new Portuguese government *de jure* recognized the Republic of Guinea-Bissau on 10 September 1974. In summarizing Algeria, Guinea-Bissau, and other cases, Wilson reaches the conclusion that the willingness of Third World states to recognize a State prematurely when the territory involved is or was a colony contrasts sharply with the practice of these States when a territory secedes which is part of a self-governing State as in Biafra or Katanga. In these cases, the principle of territorial integrity and fear for their own vulnerability determines their policies (1988, p. 117).

The fact that *de facto* states must contend with the latter practice while some colonial liberation movements have benefited from the former clearly illustrates that they are two distinct phenomena. Additionally, the liberation movements referred to above certainly had nowhere near the same level of empirical capabilities that *de facto* states do.

Our tenth criterion is not so much a standard for defining the *de facto* state as it is a means of evaluating its legitimacy and assessing its likely prospects for acceptance in international society. This is what might be called the democratic accountability criterion. In some ways, this is a forward-looking criterion—something that appears to be of increasing political and legal importance, rather than something that is a well-established canon of international law or something that has been consistently demonstrated by the actual practices of sovereign states.

Thomas Franck (1992) speaks here of what he calls 'the emerging right to democratic governance' (1992, pp. 46-91). Increasingly, as Franck sees it,

> governments recognize that their legitimacy depends on meeting a normative expectation of the community of states. This recognition has led to the emergence of a community expectation: that those who seek the validation of their empowerment patently govern with the consent of the governed. Democracy, thus, is on the way to becoming a global entitlement, one that increasingly will be promoted and protected by collective international processes (1992, p. 46).

Franck does not claim that this emerging global entitlement to democratic governance has yet become a fully-established international legal right. Rather, he concludes that the 'transformation of the democratic entitlement from moral prescription to international legal obligation has evolved gradually. In the past decade, however, the tendency has accelerated' (1992, p. 47).

This vision of an emerging right to democratic governance is clearly most advanced and codified in Europe. The Conference on Security and Cooperation in Europe's (CSCE, now the Organization on Security and

Cooperation in Europe, OSCE) Copenhagen Document of June 1990 and its Charter of Paris for a New Europe in November 1990 both specifically elaborate an assortment of democratic criteria that aspiring members must meet before they will be accepted into the European club. The result is that 'the legal principle of non-interference in the internal affairs of states is beginning to be eclipsed in Europe by a commitment to promote democratic pluralism, human rights, and fundamental freedoms' (Halperin and Scheffer with Small, 1992, p. 62). Additional evidence of this emerging democratic entitlement in Europe comes from the European Community's (EC, now European Union, EU) criteria for recognizing the former Yugoslavian republics during that country's dissolution. The first condition put forward by the EC for recognition was 'respect for the provisions of the Charter of the United Nations and the commitments subscribed to in the Final Act of Helsinki and in the Charter of Paris, especially with regard to the rule of law, democracy and human rights'. Guarantees for the rights of ethnic and national minorities also featured prominently in the EC's criteria (Weller, 1992, pp. 587-588).

        None of this should be taken to imply that there currently exists a global entitlement to democracy or that international recognition will objectively be accorded to groups with strong democratic credentials and denied to those without them. Indeed, the EC's criteria for the Yugoslav republics can be cited as a paradigmatic example of the continued importance of subjective political concerns in the recognition process. In that case, the EC appointed French lawyer Robert Badinter to adjudicate the various requests for recognition it received based on the criteria it had established. Badinter recommended that two republics, Macedonia and Slovenia, met the EC's criteria and should be recognized. He recommended against recognizing Croatia because its legal provisions for minorities were unsatisfactory. While it did recognize Slovenia, the EC gave into Greek pressure and declined to recognize Macedonia. It also gave into German pressure and went ahead and recognized Croatia despite Badinter's prescient objections (Gow and Freedman, 1992, pp. 124-126). Whatever the rhetoric to the contrary, politics clearly trumped principle in this case. As Inis Claude noted more than thirty years ago, 'the process of legitimization is ultimately a political phenomenon, a crystallization of judgment that may be influenced but is unlikely to be wholly determined by legal norms and moral principles'.[6]

        In spite of this patchy and nascent moral framework, the importance of democratic accountability for recognition should be noted. In a broad sense, the democratic accountability criterion addresses the *de facto* state's need for some form of popular support. It also has much to say about its likely acceptance or degree of toleration in international society. Quite simply, even if it still cannot attain widespread recognition, a *de facto* state with strong democratic credentials has a much better chance of achieving success (defined here as reluctant toleration or less than wholehearted opposition) in today's international society than one without such credentials.

4 The Ethical and Political Logics Behind the *De Facto* State

In regard to its ethical logic, David Mapel and Terry Nardin's (1992) distinction between rule-based and consequence-based ethical traditions can be brought to bear on the *de facto* state. In their view,

> Arguably, the most fundamental distinction between these traditions is whether they link judgments of right and wrong to consequences or to rules.... For the first group, an act, policy, or institution is right or just according to its causal contribution (actual or expected) to bringing about a desired state of affairs; for the second, its rightness depends on the interpretation of rules, the question being whether or not the act or practice in question falls under the rule (1992, p. 297).

While the *de facto* state may wish to act in accordance with international law and certain recognized rules, its ethical foundation is consequence-based. Acts, policies, and institutions are judged according to their expected causal contribution to maintaining the *de facto* state's existence and securing it widespread international acceptance. Within the various consequence-based ethical traditions, Mapel and Nardin argue that

> the most basic divergence is between realism, which reckons the value of consequences in terms of the survival and well-being of particular communities, and utilitarianism and Marxism, which reckon the value of consequences in terms of the well-being of humanity at large (1992, p. 298).

Utilizing this distinction, the *de facto* state's ethical logic is akin to realism's focus on the survival and well-being of particular communities. The TRNC, for example, was established to safeguard and promote the interests of Turkish Cypriots and Turkish Cypriots alone. Therefore, one can say that the *de facto* state's ethical foundations are consequence-based and focused only on particular communities.

As for the *de facto* state's political logic, this section will only focus on two elements of it. The first of those elements concerns the relative primacy of political and economic goals in the thinking of its leadership. Essentially, the *de facto* state is characterized by a willingness to trade economic benefits for political separation or survival. In other words, its primary focus is political; economic considerations play a subsidiary role. This is not to deny that economic considerations may constitute a major part of a *de facto* state's perceived grievances. It is to argue that the economic costs of non-recognition are quite substantial and that these costs are incurred because the positive economic benefits of integration are less important than the political goal of separation. Eritrea before independence and Somaliland today accept the denied or delayed international aid that comes along with their uncertain status in order to preserve their political freedom of action. Similarly, depending on which year is compared and whose figures are used, the Greek Cypriots now have a per capita income that is three to four times higher than that of the Turkish Cypriots. An overall Cypriot settlement would obviously alleviate many of their economic problems, yet 'economic factors have always been perceived by the political leadership of the Turkish Cypriots as being subservient to political considerations' (Lafrenière and Mitchell, 1990, p. 82). So it goes with other *de facto* states as well.

The second element considered under the political logic category is whether the *de facto* state is organized under what Anthony Smith terms the 'state principle' or the 'national principle' (1981, p. 192). Essentially, the state principle is primarily defined by a recognized territorial boundary. Under the state principle, everyone residing within the boundary is inclusively considered to be a part of the group regardless of their ethnic, linguistic, religious, or racial background. Under the national principle, communities are organized along cultural, linguistic, ethnic, religious, racial, or other such lines. One either is or is not a member of community x. Those who are not members are either expelled, discriminated against, ignored, or marginalized. The group is not organized by or for them; rather it is established solely for the benefit of community x. *De facto* states can and have been organized under both principles. Of the four cases considered here, two (Somaliland and Eritrea) illustrate the state principle while the other two (Northern Cyprus and Tamil Eelam) are examples of the national principle.

5 Sovereign States, *De Facto* States, and the Criteria for Statehood

At this point, we need to consider why the use of the term 'state' in *de facto* state is justified. For if this term is not warranted, then this study should be using a different term such as '*de facto* entity' or 'aspiring separatist group'. Since it is not, we must explain why the use of the term state is merited. This can be done in two very different ways. The first line of argument centers around the essential similarities of states. The second line of argument takes the almost polar opposite tack and focuses on the tremendous diversity of states.

Despite the essentially contested nature of the concept 'state', Robert Jackson and Alan James argue that 'The essential components of the generally accepted definition of a State in international law are population and territory along with an effective government' (1993, p. 17). They then go on to note that the legal definition of a State takes no notice of such things as its religious mix, ethnicity, economic system, and the like. While such factors may be crucial for understanding the behavior of a particular state, they are not essential to defining statehood itself.

Perhaps the most famous exponent of the viewpoint that states are essentially similar is Kenneth Waltz (1979). Waltz begins by assuming that states seek to ensure their own survival. This assumption is a radical simplification made to assist him in constructing a theory of international politics. As he acknowledges, 'Beyond the survival motive, the aims of states may be endlessly varied...' (1979, p. 91). From this starting point, Waltz argues that as long as the international system remains anarchical, states (whatever their vast differences in resources and capabilities) will remain 'like units'. In his conception,

> States vary widely in size, wealth, power, and form. And yet variations in these and in other respects are variations among like units.... States are alike in the tasks that they face, though not in their abilities to perform them. The differences are of capability, not of function. States perform or try to perform tasks, most of which are common to all of them; the ends they aspire to are similar (1979, p. 96).

One could argue that *de facto* states meet the criteria of population, territory, and effective government and that they are 'like units' in terms of the functional tasks they face. Therefore, they deserve to be classified as 'states'. This position would probably encounter strong objections from those who feel that international society's refusal to accept or recognize the *de facto* state should be interpreted as denying it the very use of the term 'state'. The refusal to recognize an entity like the TRNC, however, does not necessarily mean that it is not a state. Common sense tells us that the Soviet Union and the People's Republic of China were states long before they were recognized as such by most of the western world. Citing Article 19 of the Charter of the Organization of American States (OAS), Ahmed Sheikh maintains that 'the existence of a state or government under international law is generally a question independent of its recognition by one or more other countries' (1980, p. 324). Alan James is also helpful here. Discussing the near-universal shunning of UDI Rhodesia, Taiwan, and the TRNC, he concludes that these entities clearly are not members of international society. He goes on to note that many lawyers would deny the term 'state' to such entities and that this approach would be endorsed by all those who are politically opposed to the relevant entity in question. In James's view, however, 'This is going rather far, for the word "state" has a clear meaning which would appear to be entirely applicable to Taiwan and the rest. It could easily be qualified by "illegal" or some such word by those who wish to make that kind of point' (1986b, pp. 272-273). This study chooses to qualify 'state' with *de facto*, thus indicating that the entity in question has not achieved *de jure* acceptance. This is seen as a less charged or judgmental term than illegal. Having made such a qualification, there is no doubt that these entities merit the appellation 'state'.

The second way that the use of the term 'state' in *de facto* state may be justified is almost the exact opposite of the first line of argument discussed above. In contrast to the Jackson and James position, this perspective would start from James Crawford's view that there is 'no generally accepted and satisfactory contemporary legal definition of statehood' (1976-77, p. 107). It would then go on to highlight the tremendous variety and diversity of entities which are lumped together under the label 'state'. As Yale Ferguson and Richard Mansbach (1991) insist, 'by any standard—territory, ethnicity, GNP, industrialization, military capability, governing capacity—contemporary "states" have little in common. They are as different as persons, dogs, and whales in the "mammal" category' (1991, p. 381). This tremendous heterogeneity thus fundamentally limits the utility of the entire 'state' concept. Sabino Cassese argues that 'Since 1931, when 145 usages of it were found, the word "state," like all terms with too many meanings, has ceased to distinguish any concept useful for purposes of study' (1986, p. 120). Therefore, the term 'state', in and of itself, 'is almost useless. That is why it always takes a qualifying noun or adjective: "Rechtstaat," "Ständestaat,"

"Etat-providence," "welfare state," absolute state,... and so on' (1986, p. 125). Again, the qualifier of choice in this study is *de facto*. The argument advanced here is that the term *de facto* state is as useful or more useful than other widely-accepted academic terms such as capitalist state, developmental state, puppet state, weak state, or welfare state.

It might be helpful to compare *de facto* states and sovereign states here in terms of the traditional empirical criteria for statehood. Let us begin with the three Montevideo criteria singled out by Jackson and James: population, territory, and effective government. First, in regard to population, 'there must be people identifying themselves with the territory if it is to be regarded as a state' (Wallace-Bruce, 1985, p. 590). Crawford goes on to argue that the population under consideration must be permanent, though it need not be of any particular nationality (1976-77, p. 114). The popular support component of the *de facto* state's working definition addresses the people's identification with the state. The permanence requirement is also addressed by the perseverance criterion. Crucially, there is no longer any kind of minimum population size requirement here. Andorra, Liechtenstein, Nauru, San Marino, São Tomé and Principe, Tuvalu, and many others are widely recognized as sovereign states despite their small populations. Therefore, none of the *de facto* states considered in this study would have problems due to the respective size of their populations.

In terms of the territorial requirement, two points need to be made. First, there is no minimum size requirement for the territory concerned. Nauru is recognized as a sovereign state even though its entire territory comprises only about 21 square kilometers. San Marino and Tuvalu are other diminutive states. Again, *de facto* states do not have any problems qualifying as sovereign states merely because of the size of the territory they control.

The second point on territory is perhaps even more applicable to the *de facto* state. The extent of territory effectively controlled by most of these entities has varied over time. The lack of fixed or definite borders, however, has not traditionally been a suitable reason to exclude an entity from statehood. The most cited legal precedent here comes from the ruling of the German-Polish Mixed Arbitral Tribunal in the 1928 case of *Deutsche Continental Gas-Gesellschaft v. Polish State*. According to that ruling,

> In order to say that a state exists... it is enough that this territory has a significant consistency, even though its boundaries have not yet been accurately delimited and that the state actually exercises independent public authority over that territory.[7]

Practice in this area has been quite consistent. Albania was admitted to the League of Nations without fully delimited or defined boundaries. Yemen was similarly admitted to the United Nations in 1947. The Congo (Zaire) was admitted to the UN in 1960 although part of its territory, Katanga, was actively engaged in a secessionist attempt. Perhaps even more tellingly, Israel, Kuwait, and Mauritania have all been recognized as sovereign states even though disputed claims to their entire respective territories have been raised. In arguing for Israel's admission to the UN in 1949, the United States representative to the Security Council maintained that 'both reason and history demonstrate that the concept of territory does not necessarily include precise delimitation of the boundaries...'.[8] Crawford thus concludes 'that even a substantial boundary or territorial dispute with a new State is not enough to bring statehood into question. The only requirement is that the State must consist of a certain coherent territory effectively governed' (1976-77, p. 114). Thus, the mere fact that the territory controlled by a *de facto* state might shift over time does not, in and of itself, preclude it from sovereignty.

The effective government criterion is another one which does not pose insurmountable problems for the *de facto* state. Recent UN practice in this area is again quite clear and consistent. The Congo (Zaire) was admitted to the UN in 1960 even though a civil war was raging at the time and its governing structures were completely ineffective for a number of years. Rwanda and Burundi were admitted even though the General Assembly openly acknowledged that they did not fulfill the traditional criterion of effective government. In 1975, Angola was admitted to the UN in spite of the fact that the country was plagued by a civil war with three competing would-be governments all proclaiming their rule. Cambodia and Lebanon have kept their seats at the UN even during their periods of near-total collapse as viable entities. Again, arguments that the somewhat patchy forms of governance which may characterize particular *de facto* states should preclude them from recognition as sovereign states will not stand alone on their own merits. Indeed, a number of *de facto* states fare better under this criterion than many sovereign states do.

Another criterion that is sometimes postulated as a requirement for statehood is independence. The most famous definition of independence is that given by Judge Anzilotti in the 1931 *Austro-German Customs Union* case at the Permanent Court of International Justice. According to James Crawford, there are two main elements involved in this definition of independence: 'the separate existence of an entity within reasonably coherent frontiers; and the fact that the entity is "not subject to the authority of any other State or group of States", which is to say, that it has over it "no other authority than that of international law" ' (1976-77, p. 122). The *de facto* state clearly meets the first of these two elements. The second part, which is similar in form to James's notion of sovereignty as constitutional independence, is what the *de facto* state is denied by international society: *de jure* acceptance of not just its control, but its authority to exercise that control. In Crawford's interpretation, when an entity meets the first condition, 'the area concerned is potentially a "State-area", but as Judge Anzilotti made clear, some further element—the absence of subjection to the authority of another State or States—is necessary' (1976-77, pp. 122-123). Thus, here we have a clear difference between *de facto* states and sovereign states. While the *de facto* state positively may be free from 'subjection to the authority of another state', this empirical freedom is juridically negated by the international society of sovereign states.

It should be noted that not all authorities regard independence as an essential criterion for statehood. Adam Watson, for example, contends that 'it obscures our understanding of the nature of states to maintain dogmatically that to count as states they must be independent' (1992, p. 16). The dichotomizing of entities into 'independent' and 'dependent' is one that obviously is based on a considerable degree of subjectivity. Still, the point remains that this is one of the few traditional criteria for statehood that can be said to pose any sort of problem for most *de facto* states.

The problematic nature of the *de facto* state's independence leads us into the most substantive problem facing these entities when it comes to the criteria for statehood. This is the question of legality or illegality of origin. In essence, this question is simply part of the shift from empirical to juridical criteria for statehood. The fact that 'the juridical cart is now before the empirical horse' (Jackson, 1990, pp. 23-24) makes the *de facto* state's ability to meet the traditional criteria for statehood worthless in today's international society. The consensus seems to be that an entity which has emerged either (a) outside of the accepted rules of international law, particularly in regards to the use of force and the principle *ex injuria jus non oritur* ('a right cannot originate in an illegal act'); (b) in violation of a colonial entity's right to self-determination; (c) without the consent of the existing sovereign state; or (d) is based fundamentally on the denial of certain civil and political rights to the large majority of its population (i.e., *apartheid* regimes) will not be recognized juridically as a sovereign state.[9] The profound implications of this should not be minimized. For Jackson, the fact that the acquisition of territory by force or against the will of an existing sovereign government no longer has legal effect 'represents a fundamental change in international orthodoxy' which is 'underestimated by many students of contemporary international relations, who have perhaps not yet adjusted theories which are still based very considerably on historical power politics' (1993a, p. 350).

It is possible to argue against this position. Metin Tamkoç (1988), for example, maintains that the legality of a state's origin does not guarantee its future legitimacy, nor does the illegality of a state's origin preclude its future legitimacy. He goes on to argue that

> all States established as a consequence of the successful conclusion of a civil war initiated by 'nationalists' or 'revolutionaries' against the existing State and its legal order (whether that legal order is legitimate or not) must be considered to have 'illegal' origin. In fact the illegality of the origin of the State is not an exception but an established rule in international politics (1988, p. 29).

Indeed, the stricture against illegality of origin is far from universal. One can cite here the international community's recognition of Bangladesh despite the fact that its creation was substantially dependent upon Indian military intervention. More recent examples are the widespread recognition of Croatian and Slovenian independence without the consent of Belgrade.

Still, the post-1945 consensus on fixed territorial borders and the preservation of existing states is a fundamental sea change in the history of international relations. One of the products of this new normative framework is the *de facto* state. These entities are distinguished from sovereign states not by their population, territory, government, level of popular support, or military capability. Rather, they are distinguished by the existing international society's unwillingness to accept them into the club as new members with full juridical equality and the mutual recognition of legitimate authority which that implies. As this 'new sovereignty game' has only existed since 1945 and, most forcefully, since 1960, that is the time period from which this study begins to consider *de facto* states. While there have probably always been various groups throughout history which have maintained contested, yet effective *de facto* territorial control of a given area, the *de facto* state itself is a contemporary phenomenon of the postwar decolonization period.

6 Sovereign States, *De Facto* States, and Their Limitations

At this point, we need briefly to sum up what the *de facto* state has and lacks and how these limitations affect it. These entities do not lack much in terms of the traditional empirical criteria for statehood. They function, more or less, as effective governing authorities over particular territorial areas. They also have popular support and internal legitimacy. What the *de facto* state most lacks is international legitimacy. Whatever its successes in building internal legitimacy, that cannot overcome its external illegality.

The *de facto* state's lack of international acceptance affects it in a variety of ways. It limits the *de facto* state's ability to participate in international affairs. Most of these entities are not allowed membership in intergovernmental organizations. They generally cannot turn to the UN or any other international organization for verbal or material assistance in a time of crisis. Similarly, they are unlikely to benefit from bilateral or multilateral treaties and alliances. They are substantially limited in their ability to capitalize on the benefits offered by the international aid regime. Their uncertain legal status deters investment and may make it impossible for their products to be accepted in world export markets. A reluctance on the part of private firms to offend the *de jure* sovereign government may prevent *de facto* states from being able to capitalize on the natural resources under their control—although as examples from Angola, Cambodia, and Liberia show, this problem may be overcome if the *de facto* authority is in possession of sufficiently lucrative resources. All of this leads J. D. B. Miller (1986) to conclude that the prospects for what I am terming *de facto* states are dismal. Considering Taiwan, Biafra, and UDI Rhodesia, Miller argues that the fact that each of these three was able to establish a government which exercised full domestic control of a particular territory is

> unimportant in comparison with the refusal of large numbers of sovereign states, and through them of the United Nations, to acknowledge that a sovereign state exists. Without this acknowledgment, a government of a particular area... exists and may seem to possess the loyalty of groups of people, but its opportunities for intercourse with other communities are restricted, and the likelihood that it will retain its position is remote, unless influential states give it support (1986, pp. 79-80).

What of sovereign states faced with a *de facto* state challenge? These states obviously benefit from the normative consensus around fixed territorial borders and the preservation of existing states which serves as a kind of safety net to prop them up whatever their sundry other failings might be. Unlike the *de facto* state, these sovereign states can turn to the UN for assistance and they can draw upon whatever limited benefits are available to them from the international aid regime. Still, they have fundamentally lost control of a part of their territory.

It may be useful to conceptualize their dilemma in terms of the oft-made distinction between internal and external sovereignty. According to Martin Wight, internal sovereignty refers to 'a supreme law-making authority in each community' while external sovereignty is 'the claim to be politically and juridically independent of any superior' (1977, pp. 129-130). In essence, internal sovereignty is a claim to domestic supremacy whereas external sovereignty is a claim to juridical equality and independence from outside authorities. Sovereign states that are faced with a *de facto* state challenge still have full external sovereignty. Their internal sovereignty is also theoretically intact and internationally recognized, but in practice their writ has ceased to run over a part of their territory. The sustained and substantial benefits of international recognition, however, are such that their problems really pale in comparison to those faced by the *de facto* state. As Miller puts it, 'Sovereignty's role in providing vitality to a state has no parallel' (1986, p. 87).

Let us consider finally the respective arguments put forward by Janice Thomson (1995) and Robert Jackson (1993a) in this area. Looking at the historical example of the Soviet Union and the contemporary example of Taiwan, Thomson concludes that these states have been able to manage quite well without substantive international recognition. In her view, 'This suggests that power capabilities are equally as or more important than outside recognition' (1995, p. 220). Jackson distinguishes here between the sociological potential and the political prospects for would-be sovereign states. As he sees it,

> Even if governmental force is not sufficient to put down rebellions, and separatists become in effect a State within a State, the international community can thwart the inner State's international emergence by refusing to recognize it or enter into overt relations with it. In short, international recognition and participation can 'trump' sociological determination or armed force in the game of sovereign statehood (1993a, p. 353).

These positions are not necessarily divergent. Thomson's view can be sustainable, but only for a finite number of extremely successful *de facto* states—the only two examples which come to mind are Taiwan's tremendous economic success (which initially developed under a widely-recognized sovereignty and an American military umbrella) and Eritrea's arguably unparalleled military prowess and ability to mobilize a broad mass of popular support. These two cases might thus be seen as the exceptions which prove Jackson's rule. As for Jackson's position, his vision allows for the emergence of what he calls 'a State within a State' and what is referred to here as the *de facto* state. His argument that these entities will be trumped in the game of sovereign statehood does not necessarily preclude Thomson's possibility that some of these same groups might be able to succeed without outside recognition. Similarly, his vision can allow for the possibility of an entity like the TRNC which gets trumped in the game of sovereign statehood but grudgingly accepts this fate because its political logic places a higher value on freedom, survival, and independence than it does on the prestige and the profound economic, cultural, and diplomatic benefits associated with widely recognized sovereign statehood.

7 Conclusion

This chapter answers the question 'what is the *de facto* state?' It does so in four main ways. First, it advances a working definition of the *de facto* state. Second, it puts forward ten theoretical criteria designed to facilitate clearer academic analysis of this concept. Third, the chapter reviews the ethical and political logics behind the *de facto* state. Finally, it assesses these entities in terms of the traditional criteria for statehood and compares the *de facto* state here with the sovereign state. The chapter also evaluates the actual limitations and challenges facing both *de facto* states and their sovereign parents and it justifies the use of the term 'state' in *de facto* state.

      In the next two chapters, our discussion shifts from the theoretical to the empirical plane. Historical, geographic, demographic, and other such background information will be provided on the four case studies considered—Eritrea before independence; the LTTE-controlled areas of Sri Lanka; the Republic of Somaliland; and the Turkish Republic of Northern Cyprus. An attempt will also be made to analyze how each of these case studies fits into the general or ideal model of the *de facto* state advanced in this chapter.

Notes

[1] Cited in Crawford, 1976-77, p. 111.

[2] These criteria can be found in Higgins, 1971, pp. 86-87.

[3] For more on this situation see Blay, 1985, pp. 395-398; and Clark, 1980, pp. 2-44.

[4] For more on this situation, see 'Zaire: A Provincial Gem', *The Economist*, 27 April 1996.

[5] 'Taiwan and China: How Happy To Be With Either', *The Economist*, 2 May 1998.

[6] Claude, 1966, pp. 368-369. See also Shain, 1991, p. 219.

[7] Cited in Ijalaye, 1971, p. 552; and Crawford, 1976-77, p. 113.

[8] Cited in Wallace-Bruce, 1985, footnote # 1, p. 590.

[9] Compare in this regard Wallace-Bruce, 1985, p. 590; Crawford, 1976-77, pp. 164-165; and James, 1986b, p. 160.

3   Eritrea Before Independence and Tamil Eelam

1 Introduction

The next two chapters delve into our case studies. This chapter examines Eritrea before independence and Tamil Eelam, the LTTE-controlled areas of Sri Lanka, while chapter four assesses the Republic of Somaliland and the Turkish Republic of Northern Cyprus. This section provides the general introduction for both chapters. Chapter four includes a general conclusion summarizing the findings from both chapters.

Our analysis of each of the case studies will consist of two main parts: the provision of general geographic, demographic, and historical background information; and an assessment of how well each of these entities fits the various theoretical criteria for *de facto* statehood. To assist this evaluation, our theoretical criteria and a few of the other considerations from chapter two have been reorganized under four main headings. These headings are: territory; the organized political leadership's relations with its own society; its capabilities; and its relations with international society. The territory category incorporates the need for a territorial justification and assesses the extent of territory controlled by these entities at various points in time. The relations with its own society heading refers to popular support, democratic accountability, and also considers whether the *de facto* state is organized under the 'state' or the 'nation' principle. The capabilities category assesses governance capabilities, including policy initiatives and directions; military capabilities; the perseverance criterion; and the question of external dependency—i.e., whether the entity in question should more properly be labeled a puppet state. The relations with international society heading examines how these entities have been received by sovereign states and also analyzes whether they should more properly be considered as something other than *de facto* states. Each of the case studies will be evaluated following this same pattern of categories.

No reference is made to criteria four, seven, or nine in the above quadripartite scheme. While these criteria are helpful in distinguishing the *de facto* state from other entities in international relations, they are not germane to this detailed exploration of our four case studies. As will be made clear, none of these cases could be considered a peaceful secession movement. Similarly, none has benefited from the type of premature recognition that was given to some colonial liberation movements. All of them also share the ultimate goal of sovereignty as constitutional independence and thus need not be distinguished further in this regard.

2 Eritrea Before Independence

Background Information

Located in the Horn of Africa, Eritrea comprises approximately 50,000 square miles in area. It is bordered to the south by Ethiopia, to the east by Djibouti, to the west by the Sudan, and to the north by the Red Sea. The current population of Eritrea is usually thought to be somewhere above 3,000,000.[1] Religiously, the population is almost evenly split between Christians and Muslims. Geographically, a major division occurs between highland (mainly-Christian) and lowland (mainly-Muslim) regions. The EPLF, now renamed the People's Front for Democracy and Justice (PFDJ), officially recognizes nine nationalities. This particular scheme is contestable but, as Lionel Cliffe points out, the ethnic situation in Eritrea 'is complex and fluid enough for arbitrariness to occur with any classification' (1989, p. 132). The country's tremendous heterogeneity is aptly summarized by Paul Henze, who argues that 'Eritrea is Lebanon squared. It has more languages, more ethnic diversity, more religious differences' (1986, p. 34).

Eritrea first became a political-legal jurisdiction in 1890 when it was proclaimed an Italian colony. The Italians ruled Eritrea from 1890 until 1941, when they were militarily defeated in Africa during World War II. Britain then established a temporary wartime administration in Eritrea. At the end of the war, various options were proposed for Eritrea's future. The British favored partitioning Eritrea between Ethiopia and the Sudan. Italy wished to resume its colonial mission in Eritrea, while Ethiopia wanted to annex Eritrea. The matter was referred to the UN General Assembly in 1948. On 21 November 1949, the General Assembly established the UN Commission for Eritrea with a mandate to ascertain the wishes of the Eritrean people. Depending on whose account is accepted, one finds arguments that there was majority support for independence; majority support for a link with

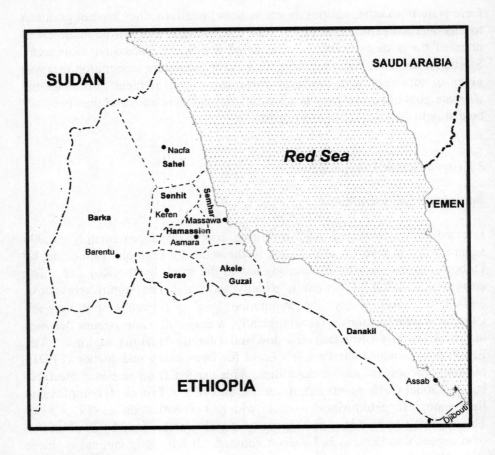

Map 3.1 Eritrea

Ethiopia; no clear majority support for any option; and/or that no adequate assessment of Eritrean popular opinion was ever undertaken.[2]

The outlines of a 'compromise' plan began to emerge in 1950. The compromise, seen as occupying a middle ground somewhere between independence and annexation, was for Eritrea to be linked with Ethiopia through an internationally-guaranteed federalism. The United States backed this plan in order to secure for itself a military base on the western shores of the Red Sea.[3] Resolution 390 A (V) was ultimately approved in 1952 by the General Assembly, the Eritrean assembly, and the Ethiopian government. This resolution contained a section known as the 'Federal Act', which provided the juridical basis for the Eritrean-Ethiopian federal relationship.

Under the resolution, Eritrea was characterized as 'an autonomous unit federated with Ethiopia under the sovereignty of the Ethiopian crown'. It was thus not considered a state in a federal union, but rather an autonomous region. Eritrea was to have its own constitution, budget, parliament, executive, and judiciary. It would handle all governmental functions except foreign affairs, defense, currency, communications, and trade. It would also have its own flag, police, and languages (Tigrinya and Arabic). Although it could not withdraw unilaterally from the federation, residual powers rested with Eritrea. The UN resolution did not provide for the creation of a 'federal' government—i.e., a government separate from those of Ethiopia and Eritrea. Rather, the Ethiopian emperor was the federal head of state, and the Ethiopian government ministries were the federal ministries. There were no provisions for future UN or other international involvement should Ethiopia violate Eritrea's autonomous status.[4]

The Eritrean-Ethiopian federation formally lasted a decade until 1962 when the Eritrean assembly voted to dissolve itself and Eritrea was annexed to Ethiopia as its fourteenth province, subject to direct rule under Ethiopia's 1955 constitution. However, as Mesfin Araya argues, Eritrean autonomy 'was gradually undermined by Haile Selassie, notably by banning its trade unions in 1953, by replacing its President in 1955, by suspending its Parliament in 1956, and by removing its flag in 1959, so that well before 1962 the "federation" had been *de facto* dismantled' (1990, p. 81). In the view of Tesfatsion Medhanie, 'The "federation" failed because it was designed to fail' (1994, p. 22).

Ethiopia's repressive actions against Eritrea's press, opposition parties, and trade-unions, along with its suspension of the Eritrean assembly in 1956 and its attempts to impose Amharic as the sole national language helped produce a growing backlash against the federation. The Eritrean

Liberation Front (ELF) launched its first military attack in September 1961. In the early 1970s, a number of different movements splintered off from the ELF. Christians dissatisfied with the ELF's Muslim dominance, Muslims upset at its limited progress, and a variety of more radical ideologues ultimately merged to form the Eritrean People's Liberation Front (EPLF). From 1972 - 1974, the ELF and the EPLF fought a vicious civil war against each other. In the mid-1970s, the EPLF emerged as the dominant Eritrean liberation movement and by 1981 the ELF was finished as a credible military force.[5]

In summarizing the Eritrean liberation struggle, Crawford Young (1983) maintains that

> there has been a short-term pattern of cyclical fluctuations in the nature and intensity of conflict and a long-term trend toward increasingly massive confrontation between the Ethiopian state and the Eritrean people.... The long-term trend was determined by the incorporation into the struggle of widening segments of the Eritrean population, transformation of the insurgency from quasi-shifta [bandit] skirmishes to a people's war, a progressive polarization and ideological radicalization at all levels..., and increasing violence (1983, pp. 215- 216).

This assessment is more or less echoed by Lionel Cliffe (1994). Militarily, he sees the Eritreans moving from 'bandit groups in the early 1960s, to a guerrilla movement fighting a people's war in the late 1970s..., to the emergence of a powerful conventional army able to win well-conceived campaigns in "positional warfare" by the late 1980s...'. In terms of popular mobilization, the initial support for the liberation struggle was predominantly limited to Muslims in the north and west of the country. From this small base evolved 'a broad mobilisation where peoples from all regions contributed taxes, conscripts, intelligence and no doubt enthusiasm to a liberation army which provided increasing numbers of them with some protection, social and administrative services and, eventually, food' (1994, p. 58).

In 1977, the Eritreans appeared to be on the brink of military victory against Ethiopia, but they were repulsed in a savage counter-attack by the Ethiopian forces of Mengistu Haile Mariam. Final military victory for the now EPLF-dominated forces would not come until 24 May 1991. On that date, following the collapse of Mengistu's regime, forces of the Eritrean People's Liberation Army (EPLA, the military wing of the EPLF) entered the capital city of Asmara. Upon entering Asmara, the EPLF did not immediately proclaim Eritrean independence. On 29 May 1991, Isaias

Afwerki,[6] the Secretary-General of the EPLF, announced the formation of the Provisional Government of Eritrea (PGE). The PGE was essentially an amalgamation of established EPLF departments along with former ministries of the Ethiopian-run administration. Its primary task was to prepare Eritrea for a referendum which would be held two years later to determine its ultimate political status. The decision not to declare independence immediately and to hold a referendum in two years was taken for two main reasons: 1) it was felt that the waiting period and the referendum itself would contribute substantially to Eritrea's legitimacy and greatly ease its future international acceptance and *de jure* recognition; and 2) it was felt that a precipitous declaration of independence might destabilize the transitional government in Ethiopia, lead to a resurgence of Ethiopian nationalism, and thus to renewed military conflict.[7]

The costs of Eritrea's thirty year war were tremendous. An estimated 50 - 60,000 Eritrean fighters were killed. The number of civilian deaths is uncertain, but estimates range into the hundreds of thousands. The combination of war damage and recurrent drought means that Eritrea is now only able to feed about 20 percent of its population. The country's annual per capita income is less than US$ 150. War casualties and land-mines have produced tens of thousands of disabled people. Estimates of the number of refugees produced range from 750,000 to upwards of 1,000,000. The country's bridges, roads, factories, and infrastructure were also devastated by the fighting.[8]

The UN-supervised referendum on independence was held from 23 - 25 April 1993. More than one million Eritreans registered to vote, and of those registered, 98.5 percent cast their ballots in the referendum. Of these, 99.8 percent voted for Eritrean independence; only 1,822 people voted against it. While the PGE was criticized for the electoral imagery associated with voting yes or no, the referendum was certified as free and fair by the UN and other outside observers. Independence was formally proclaimed on 24 May 1993, two years to the day after EPLA forces entered Asmara. Eritrea was admitted to the UN on 28 May 1993.[9]

Eritrea as a De Facto State

Territory The Eritrean territorial justification was based upon its former colonial borders. As this unit was administered separately from Ethiopia for more than 60 years (1890 - 1952), the Eritrean territorial justification is comparatively quite strong. Eritrea's borders were also accepted unaltered as the basis for its incorporation into a federation with Ethiopia in 1952. The fact that Eritrea was once a colony allowed the EPLF to argue that Eritrean independence would not violate the self-determination of a colonial entity, nor would it result in any change to existing frontiers. Thus, the precedent set by granting Eritrea independence would be quite limited and the Pandora's box of endlessly redrawing any and all African borders would remain unopened.

The extent of territory controlled by the Eritrean liberation forces varied quite substantially over the course of the thirty-year war. In the initial phases of the war, the Eritreans did not have anything like the kind of territorial control required of a *de facto* state. By September 1970, however, guerrilla activity in Barka, Sahel, and Senhit provinces had reached such a level that the Ethiopian government placed them under martial law. As the liberation movements grew in strength after 1974, so too did the amount of territory they controlled. By the end of 1977, the EPLF and the ELF controlled approximately 90 percent of Eritrea. The only areas remaining in Ethiopian hands at this time were four cities: Barentu, Asmara, and the ports of Massawa and Assab. During this period, separate administrations were established, the population was mobilized in mass organizations and what Crawford Young refers to as an 'embryonic state' was set up (1983, p. 216; Markakis, 1988, pp. 60-65). The Ethiopians launched a major counter-offensive in 1978. By May of that year, 95 percent of the land captured by the EPLF and the ELF had been retaken. The only area remaining firmly under Eritrean control was Sahel province; Nacfa was the only city remaining in Eritrean hands (Keller, 1994, p. 178; Markakis, 1988, p. 66).

From their low point after the Ethiopian counter-offensive of 1978, the Eritrean liberation movements (increasingly, only the EPLF) gradually built up the amount of territory under their control. Looking at Eritrea and the neighboring Ethiopian province of Tigre, Barbara Hendrie notes that by 1984, forces of the EPLF and the Tigrean People's Liberation Front (TPLF) 'were active in up to 85% of the countryside, while government troops were located in garrisoned towns along the main highway running north-south from Asmara to Addis Ababa' (1989, p. 352). By the late 1980s, the EPLA openly operated in vast areas of the countryside. Before 1991, the only two cities never to fall into Eritrean hands were Asmara (located at a height of some 6,000 feet in the central highlands) and Assab (Ethiopia's principal seaport). In regards to its level of territorial control before 1991, Roy Pateman (1990a) points out that

The EPLA has shown its ability to capture towns and hold them for long periods of time; however, as it cannot deny the Ethiopians control of the air, it rarely attempts to maintain permanent control of urban areas—not wanting to risk civilian lives or the lives of the fighters (1990a, pp. 83-84).

Learning from the devastating aerial bombardment of Massawa, the EPLF decided not to enter Asmara as soon as it could have for fear of bringing subsequent destruction upon that city. From 24 May 1991 until its declaration of independence two years later, the EPLF controlled all of Eritrea's territory.

Thus, the extent of territory controlled by the Eritrean forces ('liberated areas' in the EPLF's jargon) varied considerably during the thirty-year war. While some areas such as Nacfa have been controlled for most of this period, others such as Asmara only came under EPLF control in 1991. Certainly the period from 1991 - 1993 would count as the highest possible level of territorial control that a *de facto* state could ever hope to achieve. Similarly, the post-1977 rebel offensive period would also score quite highly on the possible scale of territorial achievement. During other periods, though, the extent to which one could speak of an Eritrean *de facto* state was limited.

Relations with Society In regard to the question of whether the de facto state is organized under the state or the nation principle, Eritrea is interesting in that its two leading liberation movements (the EPLF and the ELF) were fundamentally different here. The ELF was a predominantly-Muslim organization. Its chosen form of mobilization was akin to what we are calling the nation principle. The ELF initially organized itself into four autonomous zones, each under a local commander who in turn drew recruits from the area. According to Lionel Cliffe, 'There was no central recruitment or training, no common strategy—the zones acted like "competing fiefs controlled by rival ethnic groups" ' (1989, p. 136). The ELF's national conception failed to win broad support amongst Christians.

The EPLF, on the other hand, organized under the state principle. It officially recognized nine nationalities. In mobilizing this diverse population, the EPLF took a number of measures designed to make everyone feel as if they were part of a single, larger Eritrean project, rather than just an Afar, a Beni Amir, a Christian highlander, or a Muslim lowlander. So as not to elevate either Islam or Christianity, Wednesday was adopted as a common holiday instead of Friday or Sunday. To avoid Tigrinya language dominance, EPLF radio broadcast in a variety of languages and schools were taught (at considerable expense) in the local language. The EPLF consciously attempted to balance the number of Muslims and Christians in its Political Bureau and Central Committee (Cliffe, 1989, pp. 140-141). These practices have carried through to the present as the Eritrean government remains sensitive to keeping a balance in the cabinet and top government positions between Christians, Muslims, and various ethnic groups—all nine of which were represented in 1994.[10] The EPLF leadership thus chose to define and organize its polity on the basis of inclusive, non-ethnic 'state' territorial lines. As the EPLF ultimately became the dominant political leadership in Eritrea, one can thus cite this *de facto* state as a clear and successful example of organization under the state principle.

In terms of its popular support, there can be no doubt that the EPLF, the Eritrean *de facto* state, and the political goal of sovereignty as constitutional independence all had massive support. With the exception of the rabidly pro-Ethiopian author Minasse Haile,[11] one struggles to find any account of the Eritrean situation that disputes this fact. The EPLF could not have defeated one of the largest armies in Africa, nor could it have won such a huge yes vote in the 1993 referendum without sustained popular support. It is hard to envision any *de facto* state's organized political leadership receiving greater popular support than the EPLF did.

In terms of democratic accountability, Eritrea's draft constitution provides for such things as the rights of free assembly, free speech, and free association. The Eritreans' lack of discrimination against minority groups and their sensitive handling of the country's volatile ethnic mix certainly compares favorably to the vast majority of other governments in the world today. The EPLF's commitments to broad-based land reform and to advancing the status of women also deserve praise. During the 1984 - 1985 famine, the Eritrean *de facto* state leadership drew accolades for its organizational prowess, its fairness, and its lack of corruption in distributing relief supplies.[12] The general lack of major human rights violations should also count strongly in favor of Eritrea's democratic accountability. While the government has recently been criticized for its persecution of the small Jehovah's Witnesses community, there have been no reports of political or extrajudicial killings, disappearance, or torture.[13] While it is dangerous to extrapolate backwards from present behavior, one does not find accusations of disappearances, extrajudicial killings, torture, and the like in accounts of the Eritrean liberation struggle.

One big question remains to be answered as far as Eritrean democratic accountability goes. That question is whether or not the EPLF, now renamed the PFDJ, will ever put its leadership to the test in open, multi-party, democratic elections. The EPLF committed itself to multi-party democracy as far back as 1987. As Isaias Afwerki notes, this was at a time when the world-wide trend toward multi-party electoral democracy had not yet started.[14] Recently, however, tight government control of the media, vague allusions to the 'chaotic political situation', already-announced bans on the formation of any religious or ethnically-based political parties, and the fact that no election has yet been held have lead some observers to question the Eritrean leadership's democratic credentials. It should be noted that this question has arisen only in the period since Eritrea achieved its independence.

During its *de facto* state period, Pateman (1990b) characterized the EPLF's style of decision-making as being akin to 'democratic centralism'. While this Leninist phrase is usually dismissed as an oxymoron, in the case of the EPLF, there did appear to be both strong democratic elements and strong centralist elements. Though he warns against the potential dangers of authoritarianism, Pateman concludes that 'there is a well established and vigorous practice... of open and free discussion, including criticism of the leadership, by the rank-and-file' (1990b, p. 461). Along similar lines, Hussein Adam (1994b) characterizes the EPLF as a 'radical social democracy'. In his conception, radical social democracy tends toward one partyism and it often neglects the need to establish detailed systems of checks and balances. It does, however, merit the label 'democracy'. As Adam puts it, 'While radical social democracy neglects electoral competition and related mechanisms, it stresses the substantive issues — emancipation of women, combating poverty, broadly based participation and social transformation' (1994b, p. 34). Thus, one might conclude that while Eritrea is not yet a western-style, multi-party democracy, it did have a fairly high degree of democratic accountability during its period of *de facto* statehood.

Capabilities The EPLF's organizational prowess during the 1984 - 1985 famine has already been mentioned. Militarily, the Eritreans' achievements are arguably unparalleled. Pateman (1990a) contends that the Eritreans' ability to wage guerrilla war 'matches the achievements of the Chinese Red Army and the North Vietnamese.... The fighters of the EPLA can be compared only to the Israelis of the 1967 and 1973 campaigns for morale, brilliant improvisation, and dedication' (1990a, p. 95).

Politically, the Eritrean *de facto* state was also quite highly evolved. Based on a 1984 visit to the 'liberated areas', Mohammed Hassen (1994)

characterized the EPLF as 'a formidable organization, a *de facto* government
with ten or more pre-state departments'. He based this assessment on a
number of things, including the EPLF's 'growing industrial base in Sahel'; its
'sophisticated medical establishments (which have no parallel in the history
of liberation struggles in Africa)'; its 'progressive educational system'; and
'garages, which are as modern as any in Africa...'. Hassen concludes that by
1984, 'the EPLF was already stronger and better organized than many
governments in Africa' (1994, pp. 93-94). Probably the biggest limitation on
the EPLF's governance abilities was the necessity of directing its efforts
toward the armed struggle. The EPLF's construction commission, for
example, built, rehabilitated, and/or maintained over 4,000 kilometers of
roads during Eritrea's period of *de facto* statehood. However, as that
commission itself frankly acknowledges, 'given the general war situation, the
main aim... was to promote the armed struggle.... Thus, construction
programs implemented were specific and short-lived, with limited
contributions to the bases of infrastructure'.[15]

In 1983, the EPLF launched a widespread literacy campaign in the
areas under its control. Two of the other policies for which it was most noted
were land reform and efforts to improve the status of women. The EPLF
began instituting a program of land reform in 1975. By 1988, land reform
had been carried out in about one-third of Eritrea's 1,800 villages. As for
women's rights, in 1977, the EPLF decreed a marriage law banning dowry,
polygamy, child betrothal, and concubinage. Women and children were
given full legal equality with men and every people's assembly was required
to have women on its executive. During the liberation struggle, women
constituted some forty percent of the EPLF's total membership and they
comprised approximately one-quarter of its front-line fighting troops
(Markakis, 1988, p. 65; Pateman, 1990b, pp. 464-466). In 1991, the PGE
codified a broad range of rights for women that included guarantees of equal
educational opportunity, land ownership, legal sanctions against domestic
violence, and equal pay for equal work.[16] The Eritrean leadership has also
taken consistently strong stands against female genital mutilation.

Another subject considered under the capabilities sub-heading is the
degree of external dependency. The ELF and the EPLF certainly did receive
some external financial and materiel assistance from a variety of sources,
including China, Cuba, Egypt, Iraq, Kuwait, Libya, Saudi Arabia, the Soviet
Union, and the Sudan (Heraclides, 1990, p. 350; Markakis, 1988, pp. 56-62).
However, the EPLF was not dependent upon this aid, nor was it a significant
recipient of such aid. According to Veronica Rentmeesters (1993), 'the

Eritrean struggle, to a much greater extent than any other contemporary movement, was genuinely self-reliant. Foreign assistance was miniscule'.[17] Hassen argues that, in the area of self-reliance, 'the EPLF has made a truly remarkable achievement unsurpassed even by the Algerian revolution' (1994, pp. 93-94). Pateman also points out that, unique among African liberation movements, the entire infrastructure of the EPLF was located inside the 'liberated areas' (1990a, p. 82). Thus, the Eritrean *de facto* state cannot be considered an entity dependent upon outside support or one that lacks indigenous roots. If the question of excessive external dependency that detracts from domestic legitimacy is to be raised, it should be directed at Mengistu's Ethiopian regime, the beneficiaries of at least US$ 12 billion in military assistance from the Soviet Union (Henze, 1994, p. 71; Pateman, 1994, p. 228).

As for perseverance, an Eritrean *de facto* state can be said to have existed continuously in Sahel province since the early 1970s. Many other areas of the country also came under EPLF-control for a decade or more. While the extent of territory controlled by the Eritreans certainly ebbed and flowed over time, there can be no doubt that the Eritrean *de facto* state successfully demonstrated its perseverance.

Relations with International Society For the most part, the Eritrean situation did not figure high on international society's priority list. With this case, our main interest here is in whether or not this particular entity should more accurately be considered a legitimate 'exception to sovereignty', rather than an illegitimate de facto state. This question did not arise until the EPLA entered Asmara on 24 May 1991. One might, however, argue that from that point until the declaration of independence two years later, Eritrea ceased to be a de facto state and instead became something else. The evidence for this proposition is, however, scant. Unlike the Palestinians today, the Eritreans' status from May 1991 - May 1993 was not the subject of any international treaties. Similarly, unlike the Kurdish safe havens, their status in this period was not premised upon any UN Security Council resolutions. The closest thing one finds to a formal acceptance of the Eritreans' legitimacy to rule during this period comes from the May 1991 London Conference. This was a failed attempt at peace negotiations in the waning days of Mengistu's regime which, according to Okbazghi Yohannes, 'endorsed the formation of the Provisional Government of Eritrea and implicitly recognised the de facto independence of the territory' (1993, pp. 17-18). Needless to say, however, there is a huge difference between implicitly recognizing a territory's de facto independence and explicitly recognizing its de jure independence.

There are two other reasons for arguing that Eritrea still remained a *de facto* state during this period. The first concerns the existence of a scholarly consensus in this regard. Kidane Mengisteab, for example, refers to this period as being 'two years of *de facto* independence' (1994, p. 75). Andreas Escheté describes it as a period of '*de facto* separation' which would enable Eritrea to prepare itself for future *de jure* separation (1994, pp. 25-26). Lionel Cliffe refers to Eritrea's 'new status of *de facto* and unchallenged independence' (1994, p. 52). The second concerns international practice at this time. The PGE's ambiguous status prevented Eritrea from qualifying for bilateral aid or loans from the International Monetary Fund (IMF) or the World Bank. Eritrea was not allowed to join the International Telecommunications Union, something which greatly hindered the PGE's ability to establish telephone, postal, and other such links to the outside world. In June 1992, an Eritrean delegation was denied observer status at the OAU summit meeting in Senegal.[18] Also, foreign aid agencies were reluctant to commit money to Eritrea due to its uncertain status. From 1991 - 1993, the overall aid commitment for Ethiopia exceeded US$ 2 billion, while that for Eritrea in the same period amounted to less than US$ 200 million (Araia Tseggai, 1994, footnote #2, p. 65). Thus, while Eritrea may have moved up in the ranks of *de facto* states, its lack of juridical acceptance in this period still means that it should be considered a *de facto* state and not a more legitimate exception to sovereignty.

3 Tamil Eelam, the LTTE-Controlled Areas of Sri Lanka

Background Information

With a total area of 25,332 square miles, Sri Lanka lies in the Indian Ocean just off the southern tip of India. These two countries are separated by the narrow Palk Strait. In 1992, Sri Lanka had a population of approximately 17. 5 million people. This is composed of three main groups. About 74 percent of the population are Sinhalese Buddhists. Tamils, the majority of whom are Hindu, make up the next largest group at approximately 18 percent. The third major group are the Muslims, who comprise about 7 percent of the population. The Muslims use the Tamil language but are

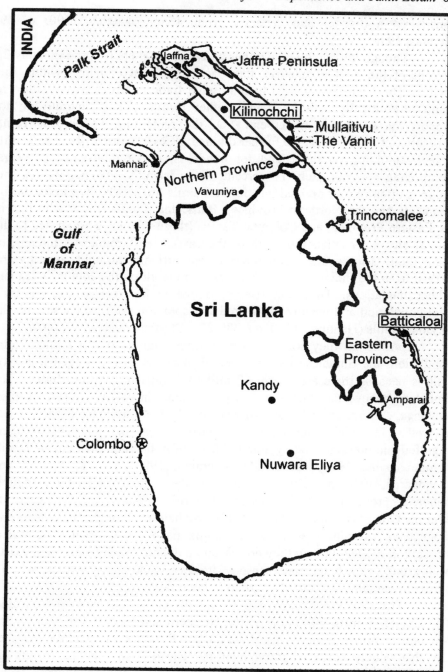

Map 3.2 Sri Lanka

considered a distinct and separate group (Samarasinghe, 1990, p. 49; Thomas, 1994, p. 95).

Though the combined number of Tamil-speakers is approximately 25 percent of the total population, there are significant divisions within this group. The Tamil-speaking Muslims have traditionally had very little in common politically with the island's other Tamils. They generally do not support the separatist movement. Of the remaining 18 percent Tamil population, this group is also further divided. 'Ceylon' or 'Sri Lanka' Tamils have been living on the island for hundreds, if not thousands, of years. Comprising approximately 11 percent of the island's total population, this group is often further divided into Jaffna Tamils (those who live in the Jaffna Peninsula and the Northern Province), Batticaloa Tamils (those who live in the Eastern Province) and Colombo Tamils (those who have emigrated to the capital city from either the north or the east). 'Hill country', 'Indian', or 'plantation' Tamils are much more recent arrivals, brought over by the British from the Indian state of Tamil Nadu to work on the country's tea and rubber plantations. They comprise approximately 8 percent of the country's total population and have rarely shared any common political cause with the Ceylon Tamils (Hannum, 1990, pp. 280-281; Pfaffenberger, 1994, pp. 6-7).

Although they comprise nearly three-quarters of Sri Lanka's total population, the Sinhalese tend to view themselves as a besieged minority. This is because there are nearly 60 million Tamils in southern India. The Sinhalese believe that they have only Sri Lanka in which to preserve their language, culture, and religion, whereas the Ceylon Tamils have Tamil Nadu as well. The Sinhalese genuinely appear to fear the prospect of being engulfed and marginalized by a united front of Indian and Sri Lankan Tamils (Samarasinghe, 1990, pp. 54-55; Sivarajah, 1990, p. 138; Wilson and Manogaran, 1994, p. 238). Sri Lanka is thus characterized by a 'double minority' problem. The Tamils are minorities because the Sinhalese are dominant in Sri Lanka itself. The Sinhalese, though, also perceive themselves as minorities because Tamils have much greater numerical strength in the region than they do. Where a double minority problem exists, each group has a heightened sense of its own vulnerability which makes it harder to bargain with the other group in good faith.

The Sinhalese are concentrated mainly in the southwest of the island. The Ceylon Tamils are mainly in the Northern and Eastern Provinces. The Muslims comprise a major part of the Eastern Province's population, but they are also widely scattered throughout the island. The Indian Tamils are concentrated in the central highlands, particularly around Nuwara Eliya.

Using figures from the 1981 census, Robert Kearney (1987-88) finds that the Sinhalese are a majority in all of Sri Lanka's 24 districts except Nuwara Eliya and the seven districts of the Northern and Eastern Provinces. Ceylon Tamils formed a majority of the populations in Jaffna, Mannar, Vavuniya, and Mullaitivu districts in the north and Batticaloa district in the east. They were also large minorities in the eastern districts of Trincomalee and Amparai. Almost three-quarters of all Ceylon Tamils live in the seven districts of the Northern and Eastern Provinces; their other major concentration of population occurs in the urbanized region around Colombo (1987-88, pp. 563-565). With the exception of larger numbers of Sinhalese in the eastern districts, one suspects that Kearney's assessment is accurate today.

Sri Lanka's ethnic conflict is a relatively recent phenomenon. The Tamils and Sinhalese did, as the British colonial official Cleghorn observed in 1799, live in separate territories. They were in sufficient proximity to each other, however, that each group influenced the other's language and caste system. Bryan Pfaffenberger (1994) maintains that Sri Lanka's colonial history 'is remarkable for the *absence* of ethnic conflict *qua* ethnic conflict, with the notable exception of the 1915 Buddhist-Muslim conflict—in which, to testify to the newly-constructed character of Sinhalese-Tamil conflict, the Tamil leadership took the side of the Sinhalese'. As such, 'it is reading history backwards to suppose that today's problems stem from yesterday's divisions. They are of recent origin' (1994, pp. 3-4).

At independence, the removal of external British control changed the political dynamics between the country's two principal ethnic groups. Under the British, the Tamils had done quite well in a number of areas such as higher education and civil service employment. They would soon find themselves to be a minority group constituted under a system of Sinhalese majority rule. While many factors played a role in fueling the Tamil-Sinhalese conflict, our account will focus on just four. These factors are: 1) the 'Sinhala only' language policy; 2) the 'standardization' policy for the country's universities; 3) the 1972 constitution; and 4) the Sinhalese 'colonization' of Sri Lanka's Eastern Province.

In 1956, S. W. R. D. Bandaranaike instituted the Sinhala Only Act. This was designed to make Sinhala the country's official language. Tamils responded to this act with civil disobedience and protest. Subsequently, a 1957 pact was signed between Bandaranaike and Tamil political leader S. J. V. Chelvanayakam. This pact provided for the use of the Tamil language in Tamil areas, but it was poorly implemented. It also produced a strong counter-reaction from Sinhalese extremists that ultimately led to the first major outbreak of communal violence in 1958.

The university 'standardization' policy gave preference to Sinhala-medium students over Tamil-medium students. It was seen by Sinhalese as a positive affirmative action measure designed to redress years of comparative disadvantages. To Tamils, it was seen as a discriminatory measure that denied meritorious students access to higher education. Whatever one's perception, the overall Tamil share of admissions to science-based university faculties fell from nearly 40 percent in 1969 on a merit system to less than 20 percent in 1974 - 1975 on the 'standardized' system (Wilson, 1988, p. 47; Samarasinghe, 1990, p. 52).

The country's 1972 constitution which established Sri Lanka as a republic was another major sore point for the Tamil community. Essentially, the Tamils had four main objections to this constitution. First, it constitutionally entrenched the Sinhala Only language policy, which until now had only been a piece of legislation. Second, it dropped Article 29 of the 1947 constitution which had specifically prohibited discrimination against Sri Lanka's minority communities. Third, in spite of Sri Lanka's professed secularism, it recognized 'the duty of the state to protect and foster Buddhism'. Finally, the Tamils feel that this constitution was imposed upon them without their consent. This claim is made for two main reasons. First, the Sri Lanka Freedom Party campaigned in the 1970 elections by asking the people for a mandate to end the dominion constitution and to establish Sri Lanka as a republic. They received only 14 percent of the combined vote in the Northern and Eastern Provinces. Thus, it is argued that these proposed changes received a mandate from the seven Sinhalese provinces, but not from the two Tamil provinces. Second, 15 out of 19 Tamil MPs boycotted the constituent assembly which ratified this constitution. Additionally, S. J. V. Chelvanayakam resigned his seat in parliament and challenged the government to contest him on the validity of the 1972 constitution. He was subsequently re-elected with the largest majority of his career (Hannum, 1990, pp. 283-284; Vanniasingham, 1989, pp. 19-20; Wilson, 1988, pp. 87-88).

Perhaps the most contentious issue of all has been the state-sponsored 'colonization' of the Northern and Eastern Provinces. The stated aims of this program were to alleviate the problems of landless peasants in the overcrowded southwestern wet zone and to increase food production by bringing marginal lands in the northern and eastern dry zone into greater usage. Ceylon Tamils, who were once a majority in each district of the

Northern and Eastern Provinces have now been reduced to minority status in Amparai and Trincomalee districts and to slim majorities in Mannar and Vavuniya districts. Of particular importance here is the Trincomalee district, which separates the large Tamil populations in Jaffna and Batticaloa from each other. In the sixty years from 1921 - 1981, the Tamil share of the population in Trincomalee declined from 53.2 percent to 33.8 percent. Over the same period, the Sinhalese share of the population grew from 4.4 percent to 33.6 percent. The vast majority of this change occurred after independence in 1947. To the Tamils, this 'colonization' is a deliberate program designed to make their concept of a Tamil homeland unworkable.[19]

In spite of these grievances, the Tamil political leadership did not advocate secession until nearly 30 years after Sri Lanka won its independence. Looking at this, K. M. de Silva (1990) contends that 'the striking feature of the emergence of Tamil separatism in Sri Lanka... is its late development' (1990, p. 32). Tamil aspirations initially centered around greater autonomy or the desire to shift from a unitary to a federal state. At first, the Tamils pushed for their goals through peaceful political pressure. Later, civil disobedience appeared, as did sporadic acts of violence. It was only in the late 1970s and early 1980s that the use of violence became more systemic and deliberately organized.[20]

In both 1965 and 1970, the leading Tamil political party, the Federal Party, contested elections on explicitly non-secessionist manifestos. In 1974, this party joined with a number of others to form the Tamil United Front. In 1976, this party formally adopted a resolution demanding the secession of the Northern and Eastern Provinces which would then be consolidated into a separate sovereign state called 'Tamil Eelam'. Subsequently changing its name to the Tamil United Liberation Front (TULF), this party asked the electorate to grant it a mandate for secession in the 1977 general election. The TULF won 72 percent of the vote and all eleven seats in the Jaffna district. It also won all three seats in the other two northern districts and 58 percent of the votes there. The TULF won four seats in the Eastern Province but captured only 32 percent of the vote. In the combined Northern and Eastern Provinces as a whole, it won 50 percent of the votes cast, but received the support of only 42 percent of the eligible electorate—the difference being due to absenteeism (Wilson, 1988, pp. 85-86; Kearney, 1987-88, pp. 569-571; Shastri, 1994, footnote # 11, p. 233).

At this point, civil war in Sri Lanka was far from inevitable. Unfortunately, though, the Sri Lankan government's response to the Tamil demand for separatism was to increase substantially the military presence in

Tamil areas and, in March 1982, to pass the Prevention of Terrorism Act, allowing, among other things, for suspects to be detained without charges for up to 18 months. By comparison, the legislation of the same name in Northern Ireland only allows suspects to be detained without charges for seven days. The result, according to Lakshmanan Sabaratnam (1987), was that 'Indiscriminate arrests and torture of prisoners followed this legislation and caused even more Tamil resentment.... Militant Tamil nationalism emerged as a response to entrenched Sinhala domination' (1987, p. 314). The government also passed the Sixth Amendment to the constitution in 1983. This required all members of parliament to take an oath against separatism and it ultimately led to the TULF's collective resignation from parliament.

July 1983 is the date generally used to refer to the start of the Sri Lankan civil war. The spark which set off the communal violence at that time came when LTTE forces ambushed and killed 13 Sinhalese soldiers on 23 July 1983. The anti-Tamil pogroms which followed were clearly state-directed. Between 140 (official figures) and 600 (unofficial estimates) Tamils were killed and thousands more were forced to flee their homes during five days of violence. During this entire period, the government did not broadcast one call for order. Two separate massacres of Tamil prisoners occurred in Welikade Prison in which more than 50 people were killed while guards failed to intervene. Organized gangs were allegedly provided with electoral lists and other lists of Tamil addresses and Tamil shops from government officials. Even the government press acknowledged that these events were centrally planned and coordinated.[21]

The Sri Lankan civil war can be seen as having gone through five phases so far. The first, from the early-mid 1970s until mid-1983, was characterized by sporadic or isolated incidents of violence and really should not be considered a civil war. The second, from July 1983 - July 1987, marks the initial phase of what one could call a civil war. Initially, the Sri Lankan government was faced with military threats from a variety of Tamil groups including the LTTE, the Tamil Eelam Liberation Organization (TELO), the People's Liberation Organization of Tamil Eelam (PLOTE), and the Eelam People's Revolutionary Liberation Front (EPRLF). In 1986, however, the LTTE under the leadership of Velupillai Prabhakaran began waging war against these other groups in a bid for supremacy. By early 1987, it had virtually succeeded in eliminating all rival groups, except the EPRLF which retained a strong base of support in the Eastern Province. Consensus estimates are that about 7,000 people were killed in the fighting that occurred between 1983 and 1987 (Singer, 1990, pp. 409-410 and 416-417).

The third phase of this civil war started in July 1987 when the Indo-Sri Lankan Accord was signed.[22] Among other things, this accord attempted to delineate a basis for a future resolution of this conflict within the framework of a united Sri Lanka and it also provided for the introduction of Indian 'peace-keeping' troops into Sri Lanka.[23] The Indian Peace-Keeping Force (IPKF), though, was soon seen as a military occupation force by the Tamils. Its initial deployment of 3,000 troops was ultimately increased to nearly 50,000 troops as fighting between the IPKF and the LTTE grew increasingly violent. By the time its forces withdrew from Sri Lanka in March 1990, the IPKF, on one account, had suffered 1,155 fatalities and 2,984 wounded. The LTTE suffered 2,220 fatalities and 1,220 wounded. Between 3 - 4,000 civilians were also killed in this fighting (Bullion, 1994, p. 155).

The IPKF intervention can also be blamed for sparking new violence in the Sinhalese southwest of the country. The Indian presence infuriated the extreme nationalist *Janatha Vimukti Peramuna* (JVP) which launched its own insurrection against the Sri Lankan government in the south. The government responded with death squads and terror tactics. Success was claimed as the JVP was ultimately defeated, but it came at an extremely high cost: some estimates place the number of people killed in the south between 1987 and 1990 at up to 60,000 people.[24]

After the withdrawal of the IPKF in March 1990, the government and the LTTE appeared to have reached some sort of agreement amongst themselves. For a time in April - May 1990, civilian life almost seemed to return to normal in the Northern and Eastern Provinces. This calmer state of affairs would, however, only last until June 1990. In that month, tensions between the LTTE and the police in the Eastern Province led to the start of what the Sri Lankan press called 'Tamil War II' and what we are calling the fourth phase of the civil war in Sri Lanka. This phase of the conflict was characterized by sharply higher levels of violence and more systemic human rights violations by all sides. Robert Oberst (1992) captures the war's increasing escalation in violence quite well:

> Before 1987 the conflict was small-scale, and caused relatively few casualties. After Indian troops arrived in 1987 the mortality level increased. And after the war between the Liberation Tigers and the government resumed in June 1990, the death toll rose to levels that made the Sri Lankan

conflict among the most violent worldwide in the last 20 years (1992, p. 130).

This phase of the war effectively ended the second week of January 1995 when a new cease-fire came into play.

The fifth phase of this civil war started on 19 April 1995 when the LTTE abrogated the cease-fire arrangement and launched an attack on a government naval base in Trincomalee. The government responded in July 1995 with the launch of Operation Leap Forward. This saw the massing of huge numbers of troops for an assault on the Tigers' stronghold, the Jaffna Peninsula. Operation *Rivirasa* (Sunshine) was then launched on 17 October 1995. On 2 December 1995, Sri Lankan troops succeeded in capturing the city of Jaffna, long the most-important LTTE stronghold. This renewed fighting has produced an estimated 480,000 new displaced persons. Though the loss of Jaffna was a major blow, the LTTE still has an extensive network of jungle bases in the Vanni region of northern Sri Lanka and it remains a formidable fighting force. Any premature thoughts of its demise were put to rest when a group of 2,000+ Tigers overran an army base at Mullaitivu in July 1996 after a surprise attack.[25]

The costs of Sri Lanka's civil war have been enormous. If one leaves aside the violence associated with the JVP insurrection, the Sinhalese-Tamil conflict is now estimated to have killed more than 50,000 people.[26] The number of refugees and displaced persons produced by this conflict could be more than 1,000,000.[27] The financial costs have also been huge: at various points in time, the Sri Lankan government has been spending about US$ 1,000,000 a day on the war.[28] The Sri Lankan civil war has also become one of the 'dirtiest' conflicts in the world today. For its part, the litany of LTTE human rights abuses includes such things as extrajudicial killings; terrorist bombings; the use of civilian shelter areas as munitions storage depots; the use of child soldiers; the forced expulsion of civilian populations; the use of civilians as 'human shields'; and rape. The government's ledger includes such things as indiscriminate shelling of civilian areas; torture; arbitrary arrest; disappearances; reprisal attacks on civilians that have included burning, looting, raping, and mass killings; and the use of so-called 'poor man's napalm'—drums of fuel with strips of rubber placed inside which are thrown from aircraft. Upon impact, the fuel explodes, sending forth burning pieces of rubber which can then attach themselves to a person's skin.[29]

There have been numerous unsuccessful attempts to find a solution to this conflict. The establishment of District Development Councils in 1981;

talks at Thimpu, Bhutan in 1985; the Indo-Sri Lankan Accord; the establishment of Provincial Councils by the Thirteenth Amendment to the constitution in 1987; and the present devolution schemes being proposed by Chandrika Kumaratunga's government—none of these has produced any kind of a lasting solution. As Marshall Singer (1992) notes, when it comes to a political solution, between the two extremes of a unitary state and total independence for Tamil Eelam, 'there exists an almost endless variety of options' (1992, p. 713). Unfortunately, agreement on any one of these options does not appear to be imminent.

Tamil Eelam as a De Facto State

Territory The Tamil territorial demand is for the secession of today's Northern and Eastern Provinces, united together to form an independent Tamil Eelam. This demand is formulated on the basis of centuries of Tamil occupation of these regions—the so-called 'traditional homelands' of the Tamils. In their conception, the Tamils have historically occupied the northern and eastern dry zone, while the Sinhalese have occupied the southwestern wet zone and the central highlands. These territories were physically separated from each other by jungle and abandoned irrigation works. As evidence, Tamil scholars point to the independent existence of the ancient Tamil kingdom of Jaffna; the 1799 'Cleghorn Minute' in which a British colonial official describes the existence of two separate nations on the island and details where each group lives; the predominance of ethnic Tamils in the Northern Province; and the fact that, at the time of independence, approximately 90 percent of the Eastern Province's population was Tamil-speaking (this includes Tamil-speaking Muslims). Subsequent changes in the Eastern Province's demographic mix are due to state colonization schemes and thus should not detract from the traditional homelands claim (Hannum, 1990, p. 297). In some versions, the Tamil territorial demand is postulated not as a secessionist claim, but as a direct 'reversion to sovereignty' based on the prior existence of the ancient Tamil kingdom of Jaffna.[30] For reasons of economic viability, the inclusion of the Eastern Province in Tamil Eelam is considered essential by the separatists.

The Sinhalese essentially raise four main objections to the Tamil traditional homelands concept. First, the proposed Tamil homeland includes nearly 30 percent of the country's land and 60 percent of its coastline while the Tamils only comprise 18 percent of the island's population. Second, they believe that while the Tamils have another homeland in south India, the

Sinhalese have only Sri Lanka in which to preserve their language, culture, and religion. Third, numerous objections are raised in regard to the Eastern Province. Much of the eastern seaboard was never part of the ancient Tamil kingdom of Jaffna. The ethnic heterogeneity of the Eastern Province is a contemporary reality and Tamil-speaking Muslims have not shown any desire to be a part of an independent Tamil Eelam. Fourth, the Tamil version of history is disputed. Much of the Eastern Province was an integral part of the Kandyan kingdom. The Tamil kingdom of Jaffna did exist, but its four centuries of life needs to be placed in the context of Sri Lanka's over 2,000 years of recorded history. There is no direct or unbroken link between that kingdom and the 'traditional homelands' today (de Silva, 1990, pp. 35-46). Perhaps even more important than these objections is the fact that the Tamil territorial justification, unlike those put forward in Eritrea and Somaliland, has no colonial basis from which to draw upon.

What about the extent of territory controlled by the LTTE's *de facto* state? As with Eritrea, this has varied over time. In the case of the LTTE, its level of territorial control has also differed quite substantially between the Northern Province (particularly the Jaffna Peninsula) and the Eastern Province—with its control generally being much higher in the former. By early-mid 1985, the LTTE effectively controlled almost the entire Jaffna Peninsula (including Jaffna city), with Sri Lankan troops there generally confined to barracks and forced to receive supplies by air. This situation prevailed throughout the rest of 1985 and 1986. During this time, though, the LTTE's control of the Eastern Province was contested and much less effective. The government generally controlled the main cities and roads there, while the LTTE and the EPRLF controlled much of the countryside, small villages, and jungle areas.[31]

During this 1985 - 1986 period, an interesting pattern of accommodation developed between the LTTE and the Sri Lankan government. Although the government was unable to exercise any authority or administrative control over the Jaffna Peninsula, its staff continued to work in various government offices and Colombo continued to pay their salaries. The LTTE encouraged these officials to remain on the job as their salaries were an economically beneficial influx of money. These government officials while nominally continuing to occupy their posts would either a) take direct instructions from the LTTE, or b) ensure that they did nothing to displease local LTTE officials (O'Ballance, 1989, p. 60; Vanniasingham, 1989, p. 7).

The LTTE now effectively operated as the *de facto* government of the Jaffna Peninsula and other parts of the Northern Province. On 27 October 1986, it announced that, from 1 January 1987, an LTTE civil administration would begin ruling the Jaffna Peninsula district. This administration was to be organized into 20 divisions, encompassing such things as education, health, transportation, and policing. The Sri Lankan government responded by announcing an embargo on all fuel shipments to the north. Cutting off electricity and food supplies was threatened later. These actions prevented the formal establishment of this LTTE civil administration, but the LTTE still maintained its *de facto* control of the Jaffna Peninsula (Hannum, 1990, p. 298; O'Ballance, 1989, p. 72).

The Sri Lankan government launched Operation Liberation against the LTTE in May 1987. The LTTE suffered a number of losses during this campaign, particularly in terms of its positions in the Northern Province outside of the Jaffna Peninsula. Just before the IPKF intervention, the LTTE-controlled area had effectively shrunk to most of the Jaffna Peninsula, including Jaffna city (O'Ballance, 1989, p. 83; Hoole, Somasundaram, Sritharan, and Thiranagama, 1990, pp. 350-51). With the launch of the IPKF's Operation Pawan against the LTTE in October 1987, further losses were suffered. Much of the LTTE's leadership and fighting forces withdrew from the Jaffna Peninsula to the jungles of the Vanni. The IPKF was gradually able to extend its control over most of the towns in the Jaffna Peninsula, but the LTTE remained in control of much of the countryside, villages, and outlying areas. Despite the IPKF's relative success, by order of the LTTE government offices, banks, and other institutions were only allowed to function three days of the week. This order was widely followed in the Jaffna Peninsula and in parts of the Northern Province while it was almost completely ignored in the Eastern Province (Rajanayagam, 1994, p. 183; Sardeshpande, 1992, pp. 71-72; O'Ballance, 1989, pp. 107-108).

With the withdrawal of the IPKF in March 1990, the LTTE assumed virtual control of most of the northeast. Its position was somewhat analogous to that which it enjoyed in the 1985 - 1986 period, except that it was stronger in the Eastern Province where the departure of the IPKF severely weakened the EPRLF. At the time hostilities resumed in June 1990, 'the government was limited to control of a few army outposts in the Jaffna peninsula and several cities south of the peninsula' (Oberst, 1992, p. 130). This situation would prevail for the next five years. During this period, Jaffna city served as the nerve-center of the LTTE's *de facto* state. The government continued to send food to the peninsula and to pay its civil servants there, but the Tigers effectively ran the administration—controlling the police force, appointing their own judges, regulating the economy, and the like.[32]

Things changed dramatically in late 1995 when the government captured Jaffna city on 2 December. While this was a severe blow to the LTTE, it does not necessarily mark the end of an LTTE-run *de facto* state in Sri Lanka. First, much of the civilian population fled Jaffna (some against their will) for Tiger-controlled territory in the Northern Province outside of the peninsula. Second, the Sri Lankan army's focus on recapturing Jaffna has forced them to shift troops out of the Eastern Province. This has allowed the LTTE to operate freely in the east—something it could not do before. Thus, even now the LTTE remains in control of large areas in Sri Lanka's north and east. Third, the government's control of the main road connecting Jaffna to the south is extremely tenuous. Until this road can be secured (thus obviating the very-costly need to air-lift supplies to Jaffna), the government's long-term control of the entire Jaffna Peninsula will remain questionable. Finally, though sustained losses have been suffered, the LTTE's military apparatus appears more or less intact, with its primary base of operations now in the Vanni jungles.[33]

Relations with Society The LTTE has organized its de facto state under what we are calling the nation principle. While a territorial demand has been made in terms of merging the country's existing Northern and Eastern Provinces, the LTTE's focus is not so much on borders as it is on a particular sub-set of ethnic Tamils. The LTTE's national principle is drawn so exclusively that it has generated little support amongst either the Indian Tamils or the Tamil-speaking Muslims, let alone amongst any Sinhalese who live in the Northern or Eastern Provinces of Sri Lanka.

Thus, unlike the EPLF which tried inclusively to integrate a variety of groups under a broad Eritrean state umbrella, the LTTE has vilified Sinhalese as the ethnic enemy; ignored the Indian Tamils and the Colombo Tamils; marginalized the Batticaloa Tamils; and expelled tens of thousands of Tamil-speaking Muslims from their homes. Four Tamil critics of the LTTE have described its guiding ideology as 'a nationalism of extreme narrowness, deriving its energies from primitive instinctive loyalties - in our case to language and race'. These authors go on to note that this ideology 'leads to fanaticism, since the imagery is in absolutes - the Nation, the Language, and the Movement' (Hoole, Somasundaram, Sritharan, and Thiranagama, 1990, pp. 360-361). The LTTE is thus a paradigmatic example of a particularly narrow form of organization based on the national principle.

Considering its intolerance of dissenting views and its violent practices, one might suspect that the LTTE does not have much in the way of popular support. This appears to be wrong. The LTTE's 1985 - 1987 *de facto* administration appeared popular and found widespread acceptance.[34] The IPKF's Lieutenant General Sardeshpande believes that '90 percent' of the population of the Jaffna Peninsula is 'pro-LTTE'. While he attributes this support to a combination of brainwashing, terror, and helplessness, he does see it as a solid reality (Sardeshpande, 1992, pp. 17-18, 27 and 160-161). Sardeshpande's 90 percent figure is more or less confirmed by Marshall Singer (1990). In his view, 'perhaps 80% to 90% of the population of the north supports the LTTE'. Singer explains that

> The people admit that the LTTE is ruthless, authoritarian, and completely ideological, but they also believe its members to be honest, incorruptible, and true nationalists; they respect the Tigers for having protected them from the excesses of both the Sri Lankan and Indian armies' (1990, p. 417).

The situation in the east is dramatically different—the LTTE has far less support there than it does in the north.

In terms of democratic accountability, the LTTE has none. It is not a democratic organization and its leadership is philosophically opposed to the idea of multi-party democracy. Its persistent pattern of massive human rights abuses clearly violates any possible construction of democratic accountability. The LTTE has not only brutally eliminated rival Tamil militant groups, it has also suppressed dissent within its own ranks through extrajudicial executions. Print and broadcast media are tightly restricted in areas under the LTTE's control and freedom of expression is not tolerated. Academic freedom is not respected and many intellectuals who have criticized the LTTE have been killed.[35] It would be hard to envision another *de facto* state with a worse record in terms of democratic accountability.

Capabilities   In terms of the provision of governance services, Dagmar-Hellmann Rajanayagam maintains that,

> Wherever the LTTE is in control, it has set up people's committees, people's law courts, etc., and the grassroots infrastructure that it established is alive and efficient. Since 1985, the LTTE had virtually taken over the administration in Jaffna, down to petty justice and traffic regulations (1994, p. 182).

This is more or less echoed by the IPKF's Sardeshpande. According to him, no government agency, public service, or financial activity functioned outside of the LTTE's control. The leaders of the LTTE 'held court, dispensed justice, awarded punishment, collected taxes, managed farms and small industries... and ran transport' (1992, p. 26). Although they had to pay taxes and reach agreements with the LTTE, business leaders generally found its administration acceptable because 'people could make money unmolested' (Hoole, Somasundaram, Sritharan, and Thiranagama, 1990, p. 107). The LTTE's capabilities in the 1990 - 1995 period appear broadly similar to those it exercised in the 1985 - 1987 period.

The LTTE's military capabilities are also quite well-developed. LTTE cadres are renowned for their dedication and motivation. The LTTE operates its own munitions factories and repair facilities, and it maintains a sophisticated network of bases and supply caches in the Vanni jungles. It has engaged in naval warfare and brought down Sri Lankan army helicopters. Its capacity for surprise attacks is great. In terms of logistics, IPKF General Sardeshpande argues that the LTTE has 'enviable expertise in flexible, innovative, reliable and effective communications systems including codes and ciphers, rarely matched by any other insurgent group the world over' (1992, p. 28). To date, neither rival Tamil militant groups, the Sri Lankan government, or the 40,000+ soldiers of the IPKF have been able militarily to eradicate the LTTE.

We now come to the question of dependence on external support. All of the various Tamil militant groups, including the LTTE, did receive some external support from India in the 1983 - 1986 period. Though exact figures are unavailable, Singer (1990) concludes that after 1983, there is no doubt that 'the Indian central government, Indian intelligence... and the Tamil Nadu state government in South India all were supporting one or another of these militant groups with arms, money, training, and most important of all for a time, safe sanctuary' (1990, p. 419). Such support dried up after 1986. With the exception of this three-year period of Indian support, the LTTE has relied primarily on the Tamil community for its sustenance. Essentially this support has come in two main ways. The first is from fund-raising efforts among expatriate Tamil communities in western countries. The second is from its own direct economic activity, as well as levies, taxes, and other fees assessed on domestic Tamils in the areas under its control. Tamils who wish to leave LTTE-controlled areas are charged large 'exit taxes'. The LTTE has also made a number of mutually beneficial arrangements with the Tamil business community. It levies taxes on some goods arriving from the south and it also directly operates a number of its own businesses.[36] Thus, while the LTTE has received some external support from India, it would be difficult to label it an Indian puppet state.

The last question considered under the capabilities section is the perseverance or time criterion. The LTTE has survived 15 years of civil war against a variety of opponents. Its perseverance, resourcefulness, and ability to adjust to changing situations are impressive. While it might not equal the longevity of the Eritrean or Turkish Cypriot examples, it is certainly plausible to talk about the existence of an LTTE *de facto* state in parts of Sri Lanka for more than a decade.

Relations with International Society For the most part, international society has been content to view the question of the LTTE de facto state as an internal matter for Sri Lanka. Should any international action ever be considered, the wishes of India as the regional great power are likely to be deferred to.[37] While some aid donors such as Norway have cut funding to Sri Lanka to express their displeasure with its human rights record and its inability to find a political solution to the conflict, there is no evidence of any support for the LTTE in these decisions. Unlike the Eritrean case, there is no question as to whether or not the LTTE de facto state has attained some sort of higher standing in international society. Rather, there is clearly a perception in some quarters of international society that the LTTE is nothing more than a group of outlaw terrorists. While they do engage in terrorism, this viewpoint neglects the governance provided by the LTTE, particularly in the Jaffna Peninsula. It also neglects the fact that the LTTE easily meet most of the criteria that would once have accorded them the legal status of belligerency.[38] This status, though, is generally not accorded on a de jure basis in the modern era. Certainly, there is no sense in the international community that the LTTE and the Sri Lankan government are to be treated as equals with a strict duty of neutrality imposed on outside parties in regard to the conflict—as would be required under traditional international law if the LTTE had belligerent status.[39] Considering their atrocious human rights record, it is unlikely that the LTTE can ever hope to attain any higher status in international society other than passive neglect of its de facto statehood.

Notes

[1] Zarembo (1995) estimates Eritrea's population to be 3.2 million people. The US Department of State believes it to be 3.6 million people. See United States Department of State, 'Eritrea Country Report on Human Rights Practices for 1996' (Washington, D.C., February 1997).

[2] Various perspectives on Eritrean history from 1890-1950 can be found in Hannum, 1990, pp. 337-341; Minasse Haile, 1994, pp. 484-486; and C. Young, 1983, pp. 211-215.

[3] See Keller, 1994, p. 173; and Okbazghi Yohannes, 1993, pp. 8-10 for more on this.

[4] Tesfatsion Medhanie, 1994, pp. 19-22; C. Young, 1983, pp. 214-215; and Hannum, 1990, pp. 340-341.

[5] Markakis, 1988, pp. 51-70; C. Young, 1983, pp. 215-216; Henze, 1986, pp. 23-27; and Cliffe, 1994, pp. 52-69.

[6] This gentleman's name is variously spelled as Isayas Afeworq, Isayas Afeworki, Isaias Afwerki, Issayas Afewerki and various permutations thereof. This study will standardize his name to Isaias Afwerki.

[7] Compare, for example, Pool, 1993, p. 392; Okbazghi Yohannes, 1993, p. 19; and Cliffe, 1994, pp. 55-61.

[8] For more on the costs of the war and the problems of reconstruction, see Pool, 1993, pp. 389-402; Pateman, 1994, pp. 229-230; 'Drought, Landmines, Greet Refugees Returning Home', *The Christian Science Monitor*, 15 January 1992, p. 11; and the various contributions in Gebre Hiwet Tesfagiorgis, 1993. The per capita income figure comes from United States Department of State, 'Eritrea Country Report on Human Rights Practices for 1996'.

[9] General information on the referendum can be found in Pateman, 1994, pp. 228-230; and Pool, 1993, footnote # 23, p. 401. Criticisms of the PGE's handling of the referendum can be found in Biles, 1993, p. 17; and Minasse Haile, 1994, pp. 526-528.

[10] United States Department of State Dispatch, 'Eritrea Human Rights Practices, 1994' (Washington, D.C., March 1995).

[11] See Haile, 1994, pp. 525-526 for an argument that neither the EPLF nor the goal of independence had widespread support.

[12] For more on the famine-relief effort, see Cliffe, 1994, p. 59; and Hendrie, 1989, p. 355.

[13] See the annual United States Department of State reports on Eritrean Human Rights Practices.

[14] See Isaias' remarks in 'Eritrean Leader Answers Public's Questions on Occasion of Takeover Anniversary', *BBC Summary of World Broadcasts*, 22 May 1992.

[15] The Construction Commission, EPLF, 1993, p. 254. Similar assessments can also be found in The Commerce Commission, EPLF, 1993, and in The Manufacturing Commission, EPLF, 1993.

[16] United States Department of State Dispatch, 'Eritrea Human Rights Practices, 1993' (Washington, D.C., February 1994).

[17] Rentmeesters, 1993, p. 79. See also Pool, 1993, p. 391.

[18] Cliffe, 1994, pp. 62-64; and 'Eritrea: Africa's Longest Struggle Creeping to an End?' *Inter Press Service*, 12 September 1992.

[19] Samarasinghe, 1990, p. 53; Kearney, 1987-88, pp. 572-576; Wilson, 1988, pp. 219-220; Manogaran, 1994, pp. 99-116; and Shastri, 1994, pp. 215-224.

[20] On the various phases of the Tamil separatist movement, see Samarasinghe, 1990, p. 48; and de Silva, 1990, p. 32.

[21] For more on the July 1983 violence, see Rupesinghe, 1988, pp. 344-345; Singer, 1990, p. 413; and O'Ballance, 1989, pp. 23-28.

[22] For more on the events leading up to the accord, see Bullion, 1994, p. 149; Samarasinghe, 1990, pp. 56-59; Kodikara, 1990b, pp. 163-165; and Bastiampillai, 1990, pp. 97-101.

[23] Samarasinghe, 1990, pp. 60-61; O'Ballance, 1989, p. 91; Bastiampillai, 1990, pp. 101-106; and Saravanamuttu, 1989, p. 314.

[24] The up to 60,000 figure comes from 'Murder and Mystery in Sri Lanka', *The Economist*, 29 October 1994. For more on the JVP insurrection, see also Hoole, Somasundaram, Sritharan, and Thiranagama, 1990, pp. 414-421; and Oberst, 1992, pp. 128-129.

[25] Taken from a variety of media reports in *Agence France Presse*, *The Economist*, *The Guardian*, and *The New York Times*. The displaced persons figures come from United States Department of State, 'Sri Lanka Country Report on Human Rights Practices for 1996' (Washington, D.C., February 1997). The Mullaitivu attack information comes from 'Sri Lanka: On the Warpath', *The Economist*, 27 July 1996.

[26] This figure is cited in 'Army-Rebel Fighting Kills 140 in Sri Lanka', *The New York Times*, 29 June 1995; 'Colombo to Offer Devolution Package to Tamils', *Financial Times* 25 July 1995; and 'Free Trade and the Tigers', *The Economist*, 26 August 1995.

[27] The US State Department estimates 600,000 displaced persons had been produced before the October 1995 offensive with another 480,000 since that offensive. See United States Department of State, 'Sri Lanka Country Report on Human Rights Practices for 1996'.

[28] Singer, 1992, p. 716; 'Truce With the Tigers', *Far Eastern Economic Review*, 19 January 1995.

[29] See any of the annual Amnesty International, Human Rights Watch or US State Department human rights reports. One recent report is Human Rights Watch/Asia, 1995. O'Ballance, 1989; and Oberst, 1992 are also good here.

[30] See, for example, the arguments put forward by the LTTE-friendly 'eelam.com' internet site. Their claims to a 'reversion to sovereignty' can be viewed at http://www.eelam.com/introducton/reversion.html. See Alexandrowicz, 1969, pp. 465-480 for an academic introduction to this concept.

[31] Samarasinghe, 1990, p. 59; Pfaffenberger, 1994, pp. 14-15; and Hoole, Somasundaram, Sritharan, and Thiranagama, 1990, p. 72.

[32] 'No Kite Flying in Jaffna', *The Economist*, 2 July 1994; and 'Sri Lanka: The Victory Still to Come', *The Economist*, 9 December 1995.

[33] 'Sri Lankan Military Worried by Lull in Fighting', *Agence France Presse*, 15 December 1995; 'Sri Lanka: People Power', *The Economist*, 11 May 1996; and 'Sri Lanka's Civil War: What Chance for Peace?' *The Straits Times*, 16 April 1997. See section 2 in chapter 8 for more on the LTTE's potential evolution here.

[34] Vanniasingham, 1989, p. 182; Hoole, Somasundaram, Sritharan, and Thiranagama, 1990, p. 107; and Rajanayagam, 1994, p. 182.

[35] For more on these areas, see Pfaffenberger, 1994, pp. 16-17; Hoole, Somasundaram, Sritharan, and Thiranagama, 1990, pp. xi, xiv, 17, 73, and 349; and United States Department of State Dispatch, 'Sri Lanka Human Rights Practices, 1995'.

[36] Sivarajah, 1990, p. 154; O'Ballance, 1989, p. 71; Hoole, Somasundaram, Sritharan, and Thiranagama, 1990, pp. 85-86; and United States Department of State Dispatch, 'Sri Lanka Human Rights Practices, 1995'.

[37] This can be seen from the international community's total unwillingness to condemn India's unilateral humanitarian airdrop of relief supplies to the Jaffna Peninsula against the expressed wishes of the Sri Lankan government. See Bastiampillai, 1990, pp. 110-111; and Singer, 1990, p. 420 for more on this.

[38] Of the four criteria postulated by Reisman & Suzuki (1976, p. 426), the LTTE meet or partially meet all of them.

[39] For more on the legal duties imposed by the recognition of belligerency, see Higgins, 1972, p. 171; Vincent, 1974, pp. 286-287; and Walzer, 1992, p. 96.

4 The Republic of Somaliland and the Turkish Republic of Northern Cyprus

1 The Republic of Somaliland

Background Information

A former British colony located in the Horn of Africa, Somaliland comprises a total area of approximately 68,000 square miles. It is bordered to the west by Djibouti, to the south by Ethiopia, to the east by Somalia, and to the north by the Gulf of Aden. The current population of Somaliland is usually thought to be somewhere in the two to three million range.[1] According to Hussein Adam, 'The people are homogeneous in language, religion (Islam) and customs: social pluralism manifests itself in clan rather than ethnic cleavages' (1994b, p. 22). Approximately two-thirds of the population belongs to the Isaaq[2] clan. The Isaaq's traditional land comprises all of Somaliland except the extreme eastern and western reaches. Toward the western border with Djibouti, the Dir clan predominates. This clan itself comprises two main sub-clans: the Gadabursi and the Issa. These two groups account for approximately 15 percent of Somaliland's total population. Toward the eastern border with Somalia, the Darod clan predominates. This clan is also divided into two main sub-clans: the Dulbahantes and the Warsangelis. These two groups account for approximately 20 percent of the population (McMullen, 1993, p. 428; Adam, 1994b, p. 22). Somaliland's economy is based primarily on nomadic pastoralism. Its major source of income derives from the export of livestock to Saudi Arabia and the Gulf States through the port of Berbera.

Somaliland first became a legal and political jurisdiction in the late nineteenth century when the European colonial powers divided the Somali peninsula into five separate zones. The French established the colony of Djibouti. The British established the Protectorate of Somaliland in the north and they also occupied the Northern Frontier District of Kenya, which is now

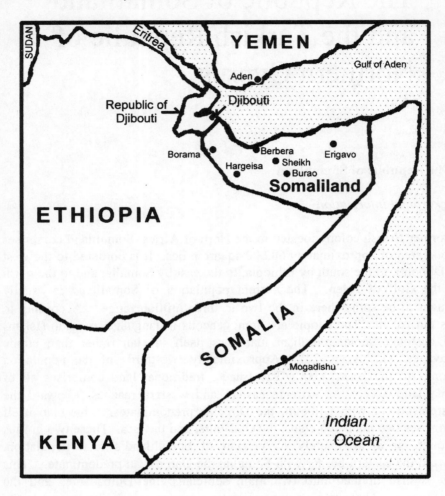

Map 4.1 The Republic of Somaliland

the northern province of Kenya. The Ethiopians ruled the Ogaden region and the Italians established their colony of Somalia along the remainder of the southern coast (Omaar, 1994, p. 232). Somaliland would remain a British protectorate until 1960.

As independence approached, all of the parties participating in Somaliland's pre-independence legislative elections advocated union with Somalia, then a UN trust territory and itself about to be granted independence. Ronald McMullen observes that 'The contending Somaliland parties differed on the issue of unification only in the speed and timing of the merger, but unification was nearly universally favored by party leaders and the man-in-the-street alike' (1993, p. 423). While the proposed unification initially had widespread support in Somaliland, it soon ran into problems. Foremost among these problems was the decision to advance the dates of independence for both Somaliland and Somalia due to UN pressure. This put severe pressure on the internal administrations of both territories, particularly as no one had yet been given the responsibility for drafting the legal basis of this proposed union. The UN voted to move up Somalia's independence date from 2 December to 1 July 1960. The British government subsequently announced that Somaliland would be granted its independence on 26 June 1960. Somaliland's five days of sovereign statehood (26 June - 1 July 1960) would later feature prominently in its attempt to formulate a justification for secession.

Originally, the plan was for delegates from Somaliland and Somalia to sign an international treaty between the two states to form a union. On 27 June 1960, Somaliland's legislative assembly passed the Union of Somaliland and Somalia Law. This was sent to Mogadishu, but it was never signed. Instead, on 30 June 1960, the legislative assembly of Somalia passed its own, substantially different, *Atto di Unione* (Act of Union). Then, on 31 January 1961, the Somali assembly repealed the Union of Somaliland and Somalia Law and proclaimed a new Act of Union, retroactive as from 1 July 1960.

The validity of the union between Somaliland and Somalia is brought into question for three main reasons. First, both parties never gave their consent to the same agreement. Second, the new Act of Union was subject to approval in a referendum. In the June 1961 referendum on the unified country's new constitution, the north's leading party, the Somali National League (SNL), campaigned against ratification and called for a boycott of the referendum. More than half of the eligible electorate heeded this boycott call. Of the 100,000 people who did vote, well over one-half voted against the constitution. Third, a subsequent court case held that the Act of Union was not valid in Somaliland. In that case, the judge acquitted a group of military officers implicated in a coup attempt because, in the absence of a valid Act of Union, the court had no jurisdiction over Somaliland (Drysdale, 1992, pp. 11-12; Carroll and Rajagopal, 1992-93, pp. 660-661; Adam, 1994b, pp. 23-26).

Somaliland's union with Somalia did go ahead, though. Northern grievances against southern domination began appearing almost immediately. A key northern complaint was that the south monopolized all the key political posts. Southern Somalia provided the new country's president, prime minister, commander of the army, head of the police, and ten out of its fourteen cabinet ministers. The centralization of government in Mogadishu (1,500 miles from Hargeisa, the north's former capital) meant that economic and political opportunities also became concentrated there. Additionally, the south provided the country's flag, its constitution, and its national anthem. Popular resentment of this southern domination was manifested in the north's decisive rejection of the constitutional referendum and in a failed coup attempt led by northern officers in 1961 (Adam, 1994b, p. 24; Drysdale, 1992, pp. 13-18; Adam, 1995, p. 74).

Events took a dramatic turn for the worse in 1969 when Mohamed Siad Barre came to power in a military coup. Siad Barre's military dictatorship intensified the politicization of clan identities. His government's misdirected interventions in the economy also contributed to the impoverishment of all Somalis. The Isaaq came in for particularly bad treatment from his regime. Hussein Adam argues that under his rule, the country's 'inequality in power-sharing exploded and reached neofascist proportions with Siad treating the majority clan-family in the north, the Isaaq, as if they were aliens...' (1994c, p. 122). Isaaq grievances intensified following the conclusion of Somalia's 1977 - 1978 Ogaden war with Ethiopia. After that war, hundreds of thousands of ethnic Somalis fled Ethiopia for Somalia. Siad Barre's regime organized them into militia units and then resettled them in the north where they terrorized the local population. The refugees' preferential treatment in terms of jobs, land, and allocation of services reduced the Isaaq 'to the status of second-class citizens in their own region' (Omaar, 1994, p. 233).

In 1981, Isaaq opponents of Siad Barre's regime formed the Somali National Movement (SNM) in London. Shortly thereafter, the SNM moved its base of operations to Ethiopia. The SNM was not much of a military threat to the Siad Barre regime until 1988. In that year, Ethiopian leader

Mengistu told the SNM to cease its military activities from Ethiopian soil. This led to the SNM's decision to take all of its forces and launch surprise military attacks against the northern Somaliland cities of Hargeisa and Burao in May 1988 (Adam, 1994a, pp. 150-151).

Siad Barre's forces responded to these SNM attacks with a brutal counter-offensive. Hargeisa and Burao were subjected to intense and indiscriminate artillery shelling and aerial bombardment. Most estimates are that between 70 and 80 percent of Hargeisa was razed by this shelling. Between 50 - 60,000 people were killed and another 400 - 500,000 refugees fled to Ethiopia. As these people fled, their property was looted and destroyed by government troops. The Siad Barre regime's myriad human rights violations in former Somaliland also included summary executions, rape, torture, imprisonment without charges, and the laying of more than one million unmarked land-mines in the region. Some refugees were even strafed by Somali planes after they had already crossed into Ethiopia.[3]

The May 1988 SNM offensive and the brutal retaliation it provoked marked a turning point in Somaliland's history in two ways. First, by producing hundreds of thousands of refugees, Siad Barre inadvertently brought the SNM into a much more direct relationship with the people it claimed to represent than anything it had previously experienced. Second, the sheer brutality of the human rights violations led to a dramatic hardening of attitudes among the northern population. Throughout the 1980s, the leadership of the SNM had consistently maintained that it was not advocating secession. In part, this was a tactical decision designed to placate the fears of Mengistu who, in February 1982, had explicitly warned the SNM that a secessionist movement would not receive support from Ethiopia (Bryden, 1994b, p. 37). In larger part, though, this non-secessionist stance was taken because it was genuinely felt that northern grievances could be addressed within a reformed Somalia under a new leader. All of this changed after 1988. As Rakiya Omaar put it, Somaliland's population 'crossed the Rubicon of secession in May 1988. The scale and ferocity of the war in the north had nurtured a visceral hatred not only of the regime but of everything it represented, including the union' (1994, pp. 233-234).

As in the Ethiopian case, it was not one guerrilla movement that defeated Siad Barre, but rather a loose coalition of groups, foremost among whom were the SNM, the United Somali Congress (USC), and the Somali Patriotic Movement (SPM). In January 1991, USC forces under the leadership of General Mohamed Farah Aideed scored a major victory against the government. Their gains ultimately led to Siad Barre's flight from

Mogadishu on 27 January 1991. Before his fall, the SNM, USC, and SPM had all agreed to cooperate with each other in the formation of a provisional government. However, while General Aideed was in pursuit of Siad Barre's retreating forces, another USC faction, under the leadership of Ali Mahdi Mohamed, declared itself to be the new government of all of Somalia. This decision would ultimately prove to be the straw that broke the Somaliland camel's back in terms of secession (Drysdale, 1992, pp. 19-23; Bryden, 1994b, p. 39; Omaar, 1993, p. 45).

Even as late as early 1991, the SNM was not advocating secession. In a series of documents in early 1991, it proposed a sort of devolved regionalism for Somalia. Similarly, no mention of secession was made at a conference of four northern political parties held in Berbera from 15 - 27 February 1991. After witnessing the total devastation of their cities and hearing of Ali Mahdi's unilateral decision to declare himself president, however, Somaliland's general population wanted nothing to do with the south. The SNM called a popular congress in Burao, which started in May 1991. When radio reports suggested that SNM leaders would attend reconciliation meetings with political leaders in the south, crowds of civilians and soldiers surrounded the congress hall in Burao to demand secession. The SNM's formal declaration of Somaliland's independence was issued on 18 May 1991. The measure passed without abstention or dissent.[4]

SNM chairman Abdiraham Ahmed Ali 'Tur' (Tur is a *nom de guerre* which translates as the hunchback) became Somaliland's first president on 26 May 1991. His administration soon came under severe criticism. Rakiya Omaar (1994) referred to it as 'a haphazard creation without coherent administrative structures', while Julie Flint argued that Tur's 'political leadership was both inert and incompetent' (Omaar, 1994, p. 234; Flint, 1994, p. 37). Foremost among Tur's problems was the inter-clan fighting which took place in 1992. The fighting which broke out in Berbera in March of that year led a group of clan elders to embark upon a series of local and regional conferences that ultimately culminated in a grand national conference, held in Borama from January - May 1993. This conference not only sought to find solutions to the inter-clan fighting; it also developed a constitutional format for Somaliland and led to a change of government. Mohamed Ibrahim Egal, Somaliland's former prime minister, was elected by a group of clan elders to replace Tur as president in May 1993 (Adam, 1994b, p. 33; Omaar, 1994, pp. 234-235).

While much of the world's attention at this point was devoted to the chaos, famine, and banditry of southern Somalia, Somaliland itself was a comparative picture of stability and good governance. Anthony Carroll and B. Rajagopal (1992-93) characterized it as 'the most stable region in the Horn....' while Peter Biles (1992) noted that 'the peace and stability which has been restored in Somaliland... is a stark contrast to the continuing chaos in Mogadishu' (Carroll and Rajagopal, 1992-93, p. 680; Biles, 1992, p. 58). In spite of its relative success, though, Somaliland has failed to secure any international recognition. Indeed, it has had a variety of clashes with the United Nations Operation in Somalia (UNOSOM). UNOSOM has been accused of focusing all of its attention on Mogadishu; not offering any assistance to Somaliland; and working to undermine its independence bid by bankrolling disaffected forces loyal to Abdirahman Ahmed Ali Tur, who now campaigns for a united Somalia. In August 1994, the Egal administration expelled UNOSOM from Somaliland territory (Bryden, 1994a, p. 42; Bryden, 1994b, p. 40; Flint, 1994, pp. 37-38). In spite of its lack of international recognition, the Republic of Somaliland continues to survive, having recently celebrated the seventh anniversary of its declaration of independence. The Egal administration does not have unchallenged authority over the entire country, but the writ of Mogadishu is nowhere to be felt in Somaliland.

Somaliland as a De Facto State

Territory The Somaliland territorial justification, like Eritrea's, is based on its former colonial borders. As this unit was administered separately from Somalia for more than 70 years (1887 - 1960), the Somaliland territorial justification is comparatively quite strong. Unlike the Eritrean case, Somaliland was even a sovereign state, albeit only for five days. Thus, in addition to arguing that a reversion to colonial borders would not violate the self-determination of a colonial entity, nor result in any change to existing frontiers, Somaliland can also argue that its independence would not be secession, but rather a reversion to sovereignty.[5] Granting Somaliland independence would thus not create much of a precedent for other ethnonationalist movements. Still, as McMullen argues, 'This narrower "reestablishment" window... might still provide rationale for potential separatist conflicts in south Yemen, Zanzibar, northwestern Cameroon, the Hejaz, and elsewhere' (1993, p. 430).

The extent of territory controlled by the SNM has varied considerably in the years since 1988. Prior to its May 1988 offensive, the SNM did not have any substantive territorial control. Its initial high point in terms of territorial control probably came in 1989 and 1990, in the aftermath of its surprise invasion in 1988. During that time period, only the main cities such as Hargeisa, Burao, and Berbera remained under Siad Barre's control. The SNM controlled virtually the entire countryside outside of these few cities (Adam, 1994c, p. 117; Drysdale, 1992, p. 12). According to Hussein Adam, 'After 1988 the SNM, for all practical purposes, came to constitute a counter-government with all the responsibilities that go with that transformation' (1994b, p. 29). One can see parallels here between the 1989 - 1990 SNM and the 1977 - 1978 EPLF.

Though ferocious, from a military perspective, Siad Barre's counter-offensive was not nearly as effective as the 1978 Ethiopian counter-offensive against the EPLF. The SNM remained in control of most of the countryside. In 1991, as Siad Barre's regime was collapsing, the SNM captured Hargeisa on 31 January, and controlled all of Somaliland's major cities by 5 February (Drysdale, 1992, p. 20). At the time it declared independence in May 1991, the SNM either controlled or faced no effective opposition in all of Somaliland.

This situation was not, however, to last for long. The decision of clan elders to replace Somaliland's first president, Abdirahman Ahmed Ali Tur, with Mohamed Ibrahim Egal in May 1993 plunged Somaliland's fledgling administration into deep trouble. Tur aligned himself with Mohamed Farah Aideed and began fighting for a unified Somalia. In November 1994, troops loyal to Tur and to Egal fought a pitched battle in the streets of Hargeisa. This and other subsequent fighting sent up to 90,000 refugees fleeing from Somaliland to Ethiopia.[6] It is difficult to state with any exact certainty how much of Somaliland the Egal administration now controls. Certainly, Egal controls Hargeisa, the port city of Berbera, and the road connecting them. Areas in the far east of Somaliland are apparently not hostile to Egal's government, but are presently unadministered. Tur's opposition forces are now based around Burao, to the south-east of Hargeisa.[7] One of Tur's lieutenants has boasted that Egal's administration only controls one-third of the country's area,[8] while the US State Department believes that the Republic of Somaliland has 'created functional administrative institutions, albeit in only a small portion of the territory it claims to rule'.[9] Against this, however, a number of aid officials and government ministers dismiss the threat from Tur's forces as a mere nuisance. His forces are, in this conception, not seen as capable of posing any real threat to the Egal administration. They can, however, harass it and hinder its campaign for international recognition.[10] While the exact extent of the administration's territorial control in Somaliland is a matter of dispute, it is certain that the government does not control all of Somaliland and that its rule is contested.

Relations with Society   The SNM has chosen to organize Somaliland according to what we are calling the state principle. This can be shown in a number of ways. First, the SNM bases its territorial claim on Somaliland's colonial frontiers; it is not seeking to achieve independence for an 'Isaaq homeland', nor does it want to redraw Somaliland's borders to exclude non-Isaaq groups. Second, upon achieving its military victories in 1991, the SNM carefully pursued a policy of non-retaliation against other clans, some of whom (especially the Dulbahante, Gadabursi, and Warsangeli) had been quite friendly with the Siad Barre regime. Its decision not to seek vengeance may have been taken merely on the basis of its own rational self-interest. It did, however, help Somaliland avoid the factional fighting and internecine warfare that so devastated southern Somalia (Omaar, 1994, p. 236; Drysdale, 1992, p. 24).   Third, the SNM leadership has practiced a version of consociational democracy (discussed below) which places a premium on the use of clan elders in mediation efforts and which seeks to ensure that all clans are represented in government. The 1993 grand national conference was deliberately held in Borama (a non-Isaaq town) to emphasize inclusivity. The Guurti (council of elders) which elected Mohamed Ibrahim Egal president also elected Abdirahman Ali Farah (a Gadabursi) as his vice-president. The speaker of Somaliland's parliament is a Dulbahante. President Egal has promised that any referendum on secession would require at least 70 percent approval to ensure that there was minority support for independence. Somaliland has given up the fiction of pretending that clan loyalties no longer matter. In acknowledging the reality of clans, however, the SNM's leadership has gone some way toward ensuring that all clans are represented within its de facto state.[11]

On the question of popular support, the Republic of Somaliland has a mixed record. On the one hand, there was clear popular support for the declaration of independence. The skillful use of clan elders and traditional methods of mediation has also given the Somaliland regime a legitimate historical continuity with its own society's practices that many governments in the so-called Third World manifestly lack. The continuing conflict in southern Somalia also provides Somaliland with a negative form of popular support. On the other hand, the SNM has failed to establish its authority over all of its purported sovereign state. The tens of thousands of refugees produced by the inter-clan fighting in Somaliland can be seen as tens of thousands of people voting against the Egal administration with their feet. In addition to Abdirahman Ahmed Ali Tur, the SNM also faces small, but well-organized Islamic fundamentalist opposition to its rule (McMullen, 1993, pp. 429-430; Adam, 1994b, p. 38). President Egal's introduction of a new currency, the Somaliland shilling, and his attempt to make it the country's sole currency have also drawn widespread opposition from businessmen and aid groups. The Somaliland shilling, which was introduced at an official rate of 80 Somaliland shillings to one US dollar was soon trading in the markets at a rate of 480 shillings to the dollar. It currently trades at a rate of more than 500 shillings to the dollar.[12] The Somaliland regime does, however, appear to have made substantial progress recently in mollifying the opposition to its rule. The government has made peace with a number of armed opposition groups and the relative calm thus produced has led to thousands of refugees voluntarily returning from Ethiopia.[13] Perhaps at this point the most that one can say is that the Somaliland *de facto* state has secured broad popular support but also generated some opposition.

We now come to the question of democratic accountability. The Somaliland *de facto* state does have a number of accomplishments here. First, its lack of retaliation against clans that supported the Siad Barre regime and its attempt to include all clan groups in the workings of its government both count strongly in its favor. Second, its constitutional structure of government has evolved in a democratic manner. The 1993 Borama conference formally endorsed a structure which separates executive, legislative, and judicial powers from one another. It also adopted a president/vice-president style of executive branch and a bicameral legislature with the upper house being a Council of Elders and the lower house being an elected Chamber of Representatives (Adam, 1994b, p. 33). The National Communities Conference in Hargeisa formally adopted a new constitution in February 1997 which maintains these features and provides for future presidential elections to be carried out by universal suffrage. The same conference, acting as an electoral college, also re-elected President Mohamed Ibrahim Egal for a five-year term. Egal won what his leading opponent termed a 'fair and open' election by securing 223 votes from the 315 delegates present.[14]

Finally, Somaliland's use of traditional clan elders in what Hussein Adam (1994b) terms a 'consociational or power-sharing democracy' deserves mention. Unlike the EPLF, the SNM has not attempted to initiate any broad-based policy reforms. Whereas the EPLF attempted to transform its society, 'The SNM tends to accept its own civil society and to rely on its elders and its politics of compromise' (Adam, 1994b, p. 30). The SNM's use of neo-traditional structures involving religious and clan elders is most apparent at its national conferences, such as those held in Berbera, Burao, Borama, and Hargeisa. The search for consensus dictates that 'SNM congresses be open, at times chaotic, always full of surprises, because they are full of compromises' (Adam, 1994b, p. 30). Unlike Eritrea's radical social democracy which concentrates on substantive issues at the expense of electoral competition, Somaliland's consociational democracy 'concentrates on procedures and mechanisms, as well as elaborate traditional protocol... at the expense of democratic content' (Adam, 1994b, p. 34).

Capabilities Of the four cases considered here, the Somaliland de facto state arguably has the least governing capabilities of all. As this entity is trying to break away from one of the poorest and most war-devastated countries in the world, this lack of resources should not come as a great surprise. It is acknowledged forthrightly by the SNM leadership. According to President Egal, if Somaliland establishes an effective administration that can collect revenue, 'then we will be able to sustain at least our recurrent expenses, in a skeletal form, for several years. We will not develop the country, we will not rebuild our ruined infrastructure, but I think we can subsist as a government' (Bryden, 1994a, p. 42). Presently, most government employees are still unsalaried, relying on outside sources of income for their sustenance.

In spite of its many limitations, it does still make sense to speak of Somaliland as a *de facto* state in the sense of an organized political leadership that provides some degree of governmental services to a given population in a specific territorial area. In addition to its grand national conferences and constitutional structure, Hussein Adam argues that whatever ultimately happens, 'the independent administration in former British Somaliland would have served a useful purpose: it has facilitated relief efforts and the renewal of the formerly vital private sector' (Adam, 1994c, p. 121). To these two main achievements, one might also add a third: the government's initiatives in the areas of security and demobilization.

The Somaliland leadership are strong supporters of free market economics. This belief in the free market is not simply because the government's limited capabilities prevent it from doing anything else. Rather, it stems from the capitalist orientation of the Somali people themselves and a genuine belief 'that the "self-correction", incentive-promoting mechanism of the profit motive can assist the new nation in its recovery/rehabilitation and propel it forward towards meaningful development' (Adam, 1994a, p. 158). The results of this commitment to the free market have been impressive. Livestock exports have more than tripled in the past two years and, in one twelve-month period from 1994 - 1995, the port of Berbera exported some US$ 100 million worth of livestock. The Somaliland *de facto* state derives its main source of revenue from taxes levied on these livestock exports. Recently these taxes have amounted to about US$ 30,000 a day.[15] The main exception to the government's free market policy has been the attempt to force traders to use the new currency, the Somaliland shilling, as the country's exclusive currency.

In terms of security, the SNM is attempting to demobilize the country's clan-based militias so it can retrain them and reorganize them into mixed-clan or multi-clan units. The SNM hopes to demobilize 50,000 militia members. Unfortunately, this is a costly process as work and training needs to be provided for the demobilized soldiers. Also, moving from a clan-based system to a mixed-clan system of organization increases costs as mixed-clan units will no longer be able to depend upon their home regions for food and other necessities. The Somaliland regime does not have sufficient funding to cover its needs and the response from the international community has been disappointing. As Julie Flint (1994) notes, 'The United Nations, which is spending $1.5 billion on the forcible disarming of the rest of Somalia, has so far promised much but delivered little'.[16] The lack of progress on demobilization is arguably the greatest single threat to Somaliland's stability.

In terms of its military capabilities, the SNM never really advanced beyond the stage of guerrilla warfare to the type of open, conventional warfare seen periodically in Eritrea from the mid-1980s onward and, more recently, in Sri Lanka. Even today, the government is not in complete control of all its territory. This may, however, have something to do with Somaliland's consensus-based politics. According to *The Economist*, 'Ill-armed gangs of no more than a few hundred should be little match for Somaliland's army of 15,000. But Mr Egal says he does not want to humiliate his opponents and so ruin any chance of political reconciliation'.[17] Exactly how much of this is a lack of desire to humiliate and how much is a lack of ability to humiliate remains unclear.

Our capabilities section also considers the question of external dependency. In this regard, Somaliland clearly cannot be labeled a puppet state. The SNM was dependent upon Ethiopia for bases from 1982 - 1988. Its primary funding came from expatriate Somali Isaaq communities in Saudi Arabia, the Gulf states, the Middle East, East Africa, and assorted Western countries (Adam, 1995, p. 76). After 1988, the SNM ceased depending on

Ethiopia for bases. The movement received comparatively little outside assistance and is noted for its self-reliance. Since 1991, the Somaliland *de facto* state has suffered from a distinct lack of external assistance. The fact that it remains unrecognized makes it ineligible to receive government-to-government loans and grants. As Rakiya Omaar (1994) explains,

> Neither the government nor the public can comprehend the refusal of the UN and donor countries to assist Somaliland. The folly of spending millions to wage a military conflict in Mogadishu while withholding the thousands that could sustain peace in Somaliland has given their criticism a sharper edge (1994, p. 236).

The Republic of Somaliland has received some external assistance—the European Union, for example, is providing about US$ 1.5 million to help upgrade Berbera's port—but the sums involved are quite small.

We now come to the question of perseverance. Formally proclaimed in May 1991, the Republic of Somaliland has now been in existence for seven years. If one considers particular areas or regions of Somaliland, then one might say that parts of this *de facto* state have been in existence since 1988. Considering its chaotic surrounding environment, its limited resources, and its lack of outside recognition, seven years of *de facto* statehood for the Republic of Somaliland is no small accomplishment.

Relations with International Society Unlike the Eritreans from 1991 - 1993, there is really no question of Somaliland having any other status more advanced or accepted than de facto statehood. One could, however, argue that some of the initial hostility directed at the Somaliland secessionist bid has now given way to a more neutral viewpoint. According to John Drysdale, 'The understandable international impetus, initially, for Somaliland to reunite with southern Somalia... appears to have faded' (1992, p. 31). Non-governmental and governmental aid agencies are increasingly willing to deal with the Egal administration. The United Nations Development Program (UNDP) now maintains a representative office in Hargeisa. In the fall of 1995, the US sent a fact-finding mission to Somaliland that included State Department officials, the American ambassador to Djibouti, and the head of the United States Agency for International Development (USAID). The subtle shift in US policy appeared to be related to bellicose statements made at the time by now-deceased Somali warlord Mohamed Farah Aideed. Aideed, who wanted forcibly to reunite Somaliland to Somalia, had been in alliance with Abdirahman Ahmed Ali Tur. Both leaders were reportedly being funded by Libya. When put in the context of potential domination by Libyan-financed warlords from the anarchical south, Somaliland's de facto statehood apparently no longer seemed so offensive.[18] The US now deals with the Egal administration through the American embassy in Djibouti and, for aid projects, through the USAID office in Nairobi.[19] The Republic of Somaliland remains largely ignored and it has not advanced beyond de facto statehood. It does seem, however, to have won for itself a degree of toleration from the members of international society.

2 The Turkish Republic of Northern Cyprus

Background Information

The third largest island in the Mediterranean Sea, Cyprus has a total area of 3,572 square miles. It lies some 40 miles south of Turkey, 77 miles west of Syria, and 650 miles south-east of Greece. Today, the UN-patrolled 'Green Line' which separates the island into the areas controlled by the (Greek) Republic of Cyprus and the TRNC comprises approximately 3 percent of Cyprus's total area. Depending upon whether one includes that land or not, the amount of territory controlled by the TRNC is between 34 and 37 percent of the island's total area.

Demography is one of the most contentious issues in the entire Cyprus conflict. Greek and Turkish Cypriots comprise over 95 percent of the entire population, with the remainder being made up of Armenians, Maronites, British, and others. At the time of the Turkish invasion in 1974, Turkish Cypriots were thought to have numbered some 120,000—about 18 percent of the island's total population of 650,000. The TRNC's 1992 census estimated the population in Northern Cyprus to be 176,127 and the residents of Northern Cyprus may now account for almost 25 percent of the island's population. Like Sri Lanka, Cyprus is an example of the 'double minority' problem—Greeks are a majority on the island itself, but there are far more Turks in the region than there are Greeks.

There are two major arguments over Cypriot demography today. The first concerns refugees. Estimates of the number of Greek Cypriot refugees who left the north for the south range from 140,000 to 250,000. If it could be called that, a consensus view seems to put the number of Greek Cypriot refugees at around 160,000. Estimates of the number of Turkish Cypriot refugees who fled to the north range from 'as many as 37,000' to 'possibly

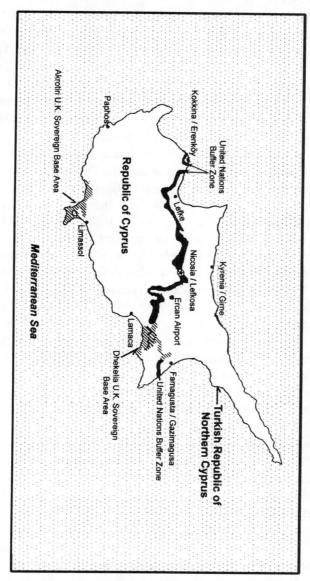

Map 4.2 Cyprus

65,000', with a sort of consensus again emerging around a figure of about 45,000. The second major point of contention concerns the number of mainland Turks who have now settled in the TRNC. The Turkish Cypriot leadership does not acknowledge the presence of even 20,000 Turkish immigrants (*Turkiyeli*) in Northern Cyprus. The Republic of Cyprus, on the other hand, now claims that 'more than 85,000 Turkish colonists' live in Northern Cyprus. A consensus figure on the number of *Turkiyeli* does not exist, but 40 - 45,000 would probably be a good estimate.[20]

At various times Cyprus has come under the rule of Egyptians, Persians, Romans, Greeks, Venetians, and the French. In 1571, the Ottomans conquered Cyprus and the first Turkish settlers arrived on the island—before, as the Turkish Cypriots like to point out, the Pilgrims landed at Plymouth Rock. The Ottomans ruled Cyprus for over 300 years. In 1878, the British took over running Cyprus with the consent of the Ottoman government. Though administered by the British, Cyprus still remained under the nominal suzerainty of the Ottoman empire at this time. With the outbreak of World War I, the British formally annexed Cyprus in 1914. In 1925, it was made a crown colony (Dodd, 1993e, pp. 1-2; Oberling, 1982, pp. 2, 7 and 29).

Turkish Cypriots find the roots of the island's pre-independence violence in the British decision to establish municipal councils in 1944. The manner in which these councils were run led the Turkish Cypriots to fear that the ultimate Greek Cypriot goal was *enosis* (union with Greece) and the elimination of all vestiges of Turkish culture from Cyprus. The demand for *enosis* gained strength in the 1950s under the leadership of Archbishop Makarios. During this time, the nationalist Greek Cypriot organization *Ethnikí Orgánosis Kipriakoú Agónos* (National Organization of Cypriot Fighters, EOKA) began militarily pursuing independence from Britain. EOKA also began targeting Turkish Cypriots, who established the *Türk Mukavemet Teskilati* (Turkish Resistance Organization, TMT) in November 1957 to defend themselves. Greek Cypriots date the start of the communal violence from 7 June 1958. In their view, the Turkish Cypriots started the communal violence by exploding a bomb at the Turkish consulate in Nicosia—an act which they then falsely blamed on Greek Cypriots. This gave them the excuse to burn and loot Greek Cypriot homes. The Greek Cypriots responded and fighting spread throughout the island (Rossides, 1991, p. 31). Whichever view one subscribes to, intercommunal violence was an established part of Cypriot life during its crown colony period.

Cyprus became an independent republic on 16 August 1960. Unlike the vast majority of other colonies, Cyprus did not receive its independence by a unilateral act of the colonial power. Rather, its independence was the result of a series of negotiations between Greece, Turkey, and the UK carried out at two conferences in February 1959. These conferences produced three main documents. The first was the 'Basic Structure of the Republic of Cyprus'—an outline of the essential provisions of the constitution. The second was the Treaty of Guarantee between the Republic of Cyprus on the one hand and Greece, Turkey, and the UK on the other. The third was the Treaty of Alliance between the Republic of Cyprus, Greece, and Turkey. The basic articles of the Cypriot constitution were unamendable and the constitution itself, as well as the independence, security, and territorial integrity of the island were guaranteed by Greece, Turkey, and the UK. Britain was allowed to retain sovereignty over two military bases and Greece and Turkey were each allowed to station limited numbers of troops on the island. Partition and union with any other state were prohibited. These documents were signed by representatives from the Greek and Turkish Cypriot communities, as well as by officials from the three guarantor countries.

The 199-article 1960 constitution of the Republic of Cyprus contained a number of *sui generis* provisions. It provided for separate elections in each of the two main communities. Greek Cypriots would elect the president as well as 35 of the 50 members of the legislature (70 percent). The Turkish Cypriot community would elect the vice-president and the other 15 (30 percent) members of the legislature. Each community would also elect its own Communal Chamber which would be empowered to deal with cultural, religious, and educational affairs. There would also be separate municipal administrations (the Turkish Cypriots originally established their own municipal administrations in June 1958) for the island's five largest cities. The Council of Ministers was to be composed of seven Greek Cypriots and three Turkish Cypriots, with at least one of the key posts of defense, finance, or foreign affairs allocated to a Turkish Cypriot. In legislative matters dealing with changes to the electoral law, taxes, and municipal affairs, separate majorities from both communities are needed. Posts in the judiciary, civil service, and police were to be allotted between the two communities on the basis of a 7:3 ratio and the army was to be formed on the basis of a 6:4 ratio.[21]

The Greek Cypriots argue that this constitution was imposed upon Cyprus from outside and that its provisions were inherently unworkable. They also believe that it was undemocratic in that it provided for minority veto government. The Turkish Cypriots, on the other hand, see the 1960 constitution not as a dictated settlement, but rather as the product of mutual concessions and compromises. It was an innovative document which could have worked had there been sufficient cooperation between the two communities.[22]

A number of major controversies struck Cyprus soon after its independence. Greek and Turkish Cypriots had strong differences of opinions over such things as the composition of the civil service and the armed forces, the proper structuring of municipal government, the constitutional court, and taxes. Things came to a head on 30 November 1963, when President Makarios proposed 13 amendments to the constitution. These amendments would have deprived the president and vice-president of their veto powers; abolished the requirement of separate majorities for the passage of certain laws; established unified municipalities; and modified the stipulated ratios of Greek to Turkish Cypriots in the civil service, army, and security forces to reflect the island's actual ethnic composition. Seven of these proposed amendments involved changing the constitution's basic, supposedly unamendable, articles.[23]

The Turkish Cypriots refused to go along with these proposed constitutional changes. Their three ministers withdrew from the council of ministers and their 15 deputies left the legislature. The Greek Cypriots now refused to recognize Dr. Fazil Küçük as the country's vice-president. Violence between the two communities broke out on 21 December 1963. Four days later, three Turkish fighter planes flew over Nicosia as a warning. By 30 December, a neutral zone (the so-called green line) had been agreed upon in Nicosia and was being patrolled by British troops from the UK's two sovereign base areas on the island. Between 20 - 25,000 Turkish Cypriots fled their homes and villages during this initial fighting to seek safety in the larger Turkish enclaves.

On 4 March 1964, the UN Security Council unanimously passed Resolution 186 authorizing the deployment of the United Nations Peace-keeping Force in Cyprus (UNFICYP). This force became operational on 27 March 1964. UNFICYP could not, however, stop the intercommunal violence. In 1964, the now exclusively Greek Cypriot government of President Makarios launched blockades against the Turkish Cypriot enclaves in Nicosia, Lefke, Limnitis, Kokkina, Famagusta, and Larnaca. Twice that year, the Turkish military threatened to invade Cyprus unless all attacks against the Turkish Cypriot community stopped. Also in 1964, the Cyprus Supreme Court approved the actions taken by the Greek Cypriot members of the House of Representatives in the absence of the Turkish Cypriot members to amend unilaterally the country's constitution. This was justified on the basis of the 'doctrine of necessity'.[24] Similarly offensive to the Turkish Cypriots was Resolution 186 referring to the 'Cyprus Government' in such a way as to recognize the now exclusively Greek Cypriot administration as constituting the legitimate government of the bi-communal Republic of Cyprus. From the Turkish Cypriot point of view, the Republic of Cyprus ceased to exist after December 1963 (Dodd, 1993e, p. 8; Alemdar, 1993, p. 81; Denktash, 1988, p. 13).

The next ten years were characterized by continued intercommunal tensions. One of the more serious crises occurred in 1967 when the presence of Greek troops well in excess of what was permitted under the 1960 Treaty of Alliance led Turkey again to threaten an invasion of Cyprus if the violence continued. By this point, the Turkish Cypriots had largely withdrawn from isolated positions or mixed villages to their own enclaves. From December 1963 forward, they had been governing themselves under the leadership of a 13-member General Committee headed by vice-president Küçük. On 28 December 1967, this Committee was transformed into the Provisional Cyprus Turkish Administration, complete with its own constitution, legislative assembly, and communal chamber drawn from those established under the 1960 constitution. The Turkish Cypriots dissolved their legislature to hold elections for new members on 5 July 1970 (McDonald, 1988-89, pp. 15-16; Necatigil, 1993, p. 56; Dodd, 1993d, pp. 103-104).

In July 1974, a Greek-backed coup attempt was launched against the government of President Makarios. Though Makarios escaped, his government was deposed. Nicos Sampson, a former EOKA assassin, was installed as president on 15 July 1974. The Turkish government then invited the British to join them in intervening under the Treaty of Guarantee. The British declined and the Turkish army launched its initial invasion of Cyprus on 20 July 1974. After establishing a beachhead on the island, the Turkish forces agreed to a cease-fire on 22 July 1974. Under the Geneva Declaration of 30 July 1974, the two sides were to exchange prisoners and hostages and Greek and Greek Cypriot forces were supposed to evacuate the Turkish Cypriot enclaves that they had occupied. Numerous Turkish Cypriot villages remained under siege, though, and attacks continued to be launched against the enclaves. The Turkish army then launched a second invasion of Cyprus from 14 - 16 August 1974. This second invasion dramatically expanded the amount of territory under Turkish control and led to the partition of Cyprus which exists today.[25]

The Turkish attempt to justify their military invasions of Cyprus is composed of a number of elements. First, citing a letter that President Makarios wrote to the president of Greece on 2 July 1974 and an appearance that he made before the UN Security Council on 19 July 1974, the Turks argue that the Greek-backed coup was an invasion of Cyprus, a flagrant violation of its independence, and an attempt to abolish the state. Therefore, the Turkish interventions were in response to prior Greek interventions. Second, the grave condition of the Turkish Cypriot community is used to provide a humanitarian justification. Third, the legal claim is based on Article IV of the Treaty of Guarantee which gives each contracting party the unilateral 'right to take action' if the other parties do not agree to undertake joint action. In the Turkish view, the procedural requirements of Article IV were met in their consultations with the British, which the Greeks refused to attend. Fourth, the Greeks and Greek Cypriots failed to implement the provisions of the Geneva Declaration (Necatigil, 1989, pp. 74-123).

The Greek Cypriot objections to the Turkish invasions are also composed of a number of different parts. First, the Sampson coup was overturned on 23 July 1974 and the legitimate constitutional order in Cyprus was reestablished. Second, Article IV's use of the word 'action' does not authorize the use of 'force' or 'military action'. Even if it did, the Treaty of Guarantee could not take precedence over Article 2 (4) of the UN Charter. If Article IV is construed as authorizing the use of 'force' (a word not mentioned in the entire Treaty) it is inconsistent with the UN Charter and consequently void *ab initio* under Article 103 of the Charter. Third, Turkey consulted with the UK, but not with Greece. Therefore, the procedural requirements of Article IV were not met. Fourth, the Treaty of Guarantee specifically prohibits partition—which is what the second invasion imposed upon Cyprus. Fifth, the Treaty of Guarantee only provides for action to restore the *status quo ante*. This had been done by 23 July 1974. The second invasion clearly established a new situation (Jacovides, 1995, p. 1227; Rossides, 1991, pp. 48-60).

Following a series of population exchange agreements, nearly all of the Turkish Cypriots remaining in the south moved north and most Greek Cypriots left for the south. In February 1975, the Provisional Cyprus Turkish Administration declared itself the Turkish Federated State of Cyprus (TFSC). A fifty-member constituent assembly drew up a constitution for the TFSC which was overwhelmingly approved in a popular referendum held on 8 June 1975. Rauf Denktash[26] was elected president of the TFSC the following year. The TFSC was presented by the Turkish Cypriots not as a breakaway state, but rather as a constituent member of a future federated Cyprus. It did not ask for international recognition. UN Security Council Resolution 376 of 12 March 1975 noted that this proclamation was not intended to prejudge a final settlement. The establishment of the TFSC was not seen as a UDI and Resolution 376 did not call on states to withhold recognition as the relevant resolutions on UDI Rhodesia had done (McDonald, 1988-89, pp. 21-22; Necatigil, 1989, pp. 89-92; Dodd, 1993d, pp. 104-106).

On 17 June 1983, the TFSC assembly passed a declaration asserting the Turkish Cypriots' right to self-determination. In November 1983, President Denktash decided to declare independence. In his opinion, nothing short of a declaration of independence would make the world see that there were two nations in Cyprus. The decision was taken at this time because it was the interim period in Turkey between the election and the taking of office of Prime Minister Turgut Ozal. Denktash felt that the outgoing military administration would be unable to stop the declaration while the incoming government would be presented with a *fait accompli*. He told all of the party leaders that if they did not vote for independence they would automatically exclude themselves from participation in the future republic. This was interpreted by some opposition leaders as a threat to exile them if they voted against independence. On 15 November 1983, the TFSC assembly unanimously approved a declaration of independence and the establishment of the Turkish Republic of Northern Cyprus. This decision was later ratified by 70.16 percent of the electorate in a referendum held on 5 May 1985.[27]

The Turkish Cypriots tried to formulate their declaration of independence in such a way that the establishment of the TRNC would not be seen as precluding a bi-communal settlement of the Cyprus problem. The declaration stipulates that the TRNC will not unite with any other state, except with the southern part of Cyprus, to form a federal union. While it is presented as an exercise of the Turkish Cypriots' right of self-determination, it also reserves for them the right to exercise that same right once more to establish a federal republic of Cyprus. As the declaration itself puts it, 'The proclamation of the new State will not hinder, but facilitate the establishment of a genuine federation'.[28]

The UN Security Council responded by passing Resolution 541 on 18 November 1983 with 13 votes in favor, one against (Pakistan) and one abstention (Jordan). Resolution 541 deplores 'the purported secession of part of the Republic of Cyprus..., Considers the declaration... as legally invalid and calls for its withdrawal'. It also 'Calls upon all states not to recognise any Cypriot state other than the Republic of Cyprus'. The language of this resolution was much stronger than the comparable language of Resolution 376 on the formation of the TFSC. Only one state, Turkey, recognized the new entity.

A variety of international negotiations aimed at finding an overall solution to the Cyprus conflict have failed to produce any comprehensive settlement. The first face to face summit meeting between the two presidents took place in 1977. Major negotiating efforts also took place in 1979, from 1984 - 1986, and from 1988 - 1989. UN Secretary-General Boutros Boutros-Ghali produced a multi-faceted 'Set of Ideas' which was endorsed by the Security Council in Resolution 750 of 1992 'as an appropriate basis for reaching an overall framework agreement'. Unfortunately, the Set of Ideas has not produced a settlement nor has agreement even been reached on its modest 'Confidence Building Mechanisms' (Groom, 1993, pp. 15-45; McDonald, 1988-89, pp. 24 and 76-77; Coughlan, 1991, pp. 80-100).

Though both communities have committed themselves to a bi-communal and bi-regional federal republic, wide disparities still characterize each side's position. Essentially, the Greek Cypriots seek a strong federal government with substantial and residual authority over most matters of importance. In their vision, the regional governments would only cover such specifically defined matters as education and social services. The implementation of the so-called 'three freedoms'—the rights to own property, to settle, and to have freedom of movement—throughout the entire island are crucial for the Greek Cypriots. Confederal solutions, borders between the two federated units, and any restrictions on the three freedoms are unacceptable. Greek Cypriots also insist on the immediate withdrawal of all Turkish troops and they refuse to countenance any form of future Turkish military guarantee. The Turkish Cypriots accuse the Greek Cypriots of seeking a centralized, unitary state that is federal in name alone.

In contrast, the Turkish Cypriots believe that the regional governments should be paramount with the powers of the federal government sharply limited to a few specific areas. Residual powers would belong to the federated states. If this weak federation proved itself to be effective, then future powers could be devolved to it by the regional units—a sort of federation by accretion. The implementation of the three freedoms would be qualified for fear of their federated unit being overwhelmed by the more numerous Greek Cypriots. The Turkish Cypriots insist on some sort of continued Turkish military guarantee and they believe that a settlement should precede any withdrawal of Turkish troops. The Greek Cypriots accuse the Turkish Cypriots of seeking a confederation of two partitioned independent states that is genuinely federal in name alone.[29]

Northern Cyprus as a De Facto State

Territory Of the four cases considered here, the Turkish Cypriots clearly have the weakest territorial justification of all. Their territorial claim is based neither on historical occupancy (as with the Tamils), on former colonial status, or on pre-existing internal boundaries (i.e., the northern and eastern provinces for the Tamils). Historically, one can argue that the island's two communities maintained their own separate religions, cultures, languages, and local governing institutions in spite of more than four centuries of shared coexistence on Cyprus (Doob, 1986, pp. 386-387; Alemdar, 1993, p. 76; Branthwaite, 1993, p. 56). The Turkish Cypriots, though, cannot point to distinct parts of the island that they have historically occupied. Nor can they base their claim on any internal boundaries. The two communities lived interspersed throughout the whole island and approximately 80 percent of the original inhabitants of what is now Northern Cyprus were Greek Cypriots.

In essence, the Turkish Cypriot territorial claim is based on two main factors—one theoretical and the other factual. The theoretical basis for the territorial claim is the belief that Greek Cypriots and Turkish Cypriots cannot live together peacefully. Therefore, to ensure their communal security, the Turkish Cypriots require a separate territory of their own. The factual part of this territorial justification is that the Turkish Cypriots have indeed had their own territory in Northern Cyprus since 1974. However illegitimate the existence of the TRNC is deemed to be, this actual possession of territory is a hard cold reality which cannot be ignored. As Pierre Oberling (1982) puts it, 'Inasmuch as they already occupy the area being contested and have the full military and political backing of Turkey, the Turkish Cypriots have been in the enviable position of arguing from strength'.[30]

In terms of the extent of territory that they have controlled at various periods of time, the Turkish Cypriots are somewhat of an anomaly when compared to other *de facto* states. Whereas the other three case studies considered here (with the exception of Eritrea from 1991 - 1993) have all been characterized by fluctuating levels of territorial control, the extent of territory controlled by the Turkish Cypriot *de facto* state has remained constant for more than twenty years now. Prior to the second Turkish invasion in August 1974, though, the Turkish Cypriot case can be seen as somewhat more similar to the other *de facto* states considered here.

The historical etiology of the TRNC does not date from 1983 or even from 1975; rather it goes back at least to the General Committee in 1963 and to the Provisional Cyprus Turkish Administration in 1967. Certainly from at least 1963 forward, when some twenty thousand Turkish Cypriots left their smaller villages for the security of enclaves in the larger cities, one can speak of the Turkish Cypriots as having *de facto* territorial control over parts of Cyprus. While these areas of control were small, non-contiguous enclaves, they did exist. Indeed, their existence has been recognized internationally at least twice. In his report to the Security Council, S/6228 of 11 March 1965, UN Secretary-General U Thant noted that the writ of the Greek Cypriot government had not run in the areas under Turkish Cypriot control since December 1963. Similarly, the 1974 Geneva Agreement, signed by the foreign ministers of Greece, Turkey, and the UK in the period between the two Turkish invasions, 'noted the existence in practice in the Republic of Cyprus of two autonomous administrations, that of the Greek Cypriot community and that of the Turkish Cypriot community' (Necatigil, 1989, p. 60; Oberling, 1982, p. 175).

Relations with Society   The Turkish Cypriot de facto state is clearly organized under what we are calling the national principle. The 200,000+ Cypriots from both communities who fled either from or to the Turkish-controlled areas are clear illustrations of the national orientation upon which the Turkish Cypriot de facto state is based. The identity basis of the TRNC is Turkish Cypriot and no attempts are made to integrate the remaining Greek Cypriot and Maronite minority communities into any larger, more inclusive conception of identity.

There is no doubt that the TRNC has the support of the vast majority of Turkish Cypriots. All of the major political parties support a bi-zonal, bi-communal federal solution to the Cyprus problem and there is a strong consensus around the need for a Turkish security guarantee in any future settlement. The electorate has also consistently demonstrated its support for Rauf Denktash as their chosen representative to the outside world and their chief negotiator on the Cyprus issue.[31]

We now come to the question of democratic accountability. From a larger perspective, the facts that: 1) the Turkish Cypriot *de facto* state's territory was created after an outside military invasion and is maintained by tens of thousands of foreign troops; 2) its creation produced more than 100,000 Greek Cypriot refugees; and 3) its poor treatment of the small minority Greek Cypriot and Maronite populations leaves much to be desired all militate against its democratic accountability. From an internal perspective, however, the TRNC does quite well in this regard. The TRNC's internal democratic accountability can be demonstrated by focusing on three areas: constitutional provisions; actual democratic practice; and human rights.

First, in terms of its constitution, with the exception of its disenfranchised Greek Cypriot and Maronite minorities, the TRNC's basic law grants its citizens an extensive range of civil and political liberties. According to Article 1, the state is a secular republic based on the principles of democracy, social justice, and the supremacy of law. Citizens are guaranteed the right to liberty and security of person; the right to a fair and public trial within a reasonable time; the right to form associations; freedom of religion, conscience, thought, speech, and expression; and the right to a free press. Citizens can freely form political parties, although those parties must not 'violate the indivisibility or the integrity of the State....' and they must not act against 'the principles of a democratic and secular republic and the principles of Atatürk'. The rights to establish trade unions, to collective agreement, and to strike are also provided for, although these rights may be restricted for purposes of national security or public order (Yesilada, 1989, pp. 105-108; Dodd, 1993f, pp. 167-192; Necatigil, 1989, pp. 259-270).

Second, in terms of the actual practice of democracy, general and presidential elections have been held in the Turkish Cypriot *de facto* state every five years or less since 1976. At one point, there were 12 political parties in existence and several parties of differing ideologies have been represented in the TRNC national assembly. The political spectrum includes the far-right New Dawn Party, the center-right Democratic Party and National Unity Party, the center-left Communal Liberation Party, and the far-left Republican Turkish Party. Voter turnout is consistently high and compares favorably to many western democracies. While President Denktash's five electoral victories often lead to allegations of strong-man rule, one can see his percentage share of the vote fluctuating from a high of 76.4 percent in 1976 to 51.3 percent in 1981, 70.5 percent in 1985, 66.7 percent in 1990, and then down to 40.4 percent in 1995, thus forcing a second round of voting in which he was reelected with just over 62 percent of the vote. The most serious threat to democracy in the TRNC probably came in 1990 when changes in the electoral law designed to produce stronger coalitions led to a decision by two major parties to boycott the national assembly. While this had a noticeable effect on the level of debate in the assembly, each of these parties' newspapers continued to air their views and the trade unions remained politically active. Jonathan Warner (1993) argues that while democracy itself seems entrenched in the TRNC, its final form has not yet taken shape. C. H. Dodd (1993c) concludes that 'Elections in the North are in fact free, the press is not muzzled, and there is a good deal of informed political discussion in what is a politically aware society...'.[32]

Third, in terms of its actual human rights record, the US State Department finds that 'there is a generally strong regard for democratic principles' in the Turkish Cypriot community. There were no reports of political prisoners and no public allegations of police brutality in the TRNC. Representatives from international human rights groups have access to the TRNC, international broadcasts are available without interference, academic freedom is respected, opinions circulate freely, and independent trade unions regularly take stands on public policy issues.[33] In its 1995 annual report on human rights, Amnesty International makes only one mention of the TRNC and that is in reference to Salih Askerogul, a conscientious objector who was imprisoned in 1993 (Amnesty International, 1995, p. 113). Its 1997 annual report is, however, more critical of the TRNC's human rights record, particularly in relation to the deaths of two Greek Cypriots in incidents along the green line (Amnesty International, 1997, pp. 135-136). Every year Freedom House ranks countries and territories in the two categories of political rights and civil liberties. This is done on a scale from one to seven, with one being the best and seven being the worst. These two ratings are then combined into an overall 'Combined Average Rating' which leads to a freedom rating. The three options for the freedom rating are 'free', 'partly free', and 'not free'. In 1995, 1996, and 1997, Freedom House gave the TRNC a four for political rights and a two for civil liberties. This leads to a combined average rating of three, which is the highest possible score for countries and territories whose freedom rating is 'partly free'. For comparative purposes, other countries which also received a combined average rating of three for those three years include Brazil, El Salvador, Madagascar, and Papua New Guinea.[34]

Capabilities In terms of its governing capability, the TRNC has reached an advanced level well beyond that attained by many sovereign states. It clearly meets or exceeds any plausible criteria for effective governance. The TRNC is characterized by a mixed parliamentary and presidential system where the president is head of state. The Council of Ministers is formed by ten ministers and the prime minister and is responsible to the national assembly. The judiciary is independent from any military or executive influence. In addition to the ten ministries, there are also extra-departmental organizations such as the State Planning Organization, the Public Service Commission, and the Radio and Television Authority. The TRNC also operates a number of economic enterprises including a tobacco monopoly, the state airline, and a citrus fruit exporter. Locally, there are 26 municipalities and 186 villages divided amongst three districts. Local government is run by popularly elected mayors and councils. In 1990, the entire public service (central and local government as well as state-owned enterprises) employed nearly 16,000 people—approximately 22 percent of the TRNC's total workforce (Dodd, 1993f, pp. 170-174).

In terms of military capabilities, the TRNC's own indigenous capabilities are quite limited. While it maintains its own police and security forces, the entire area of military security has essentially been sub-contracted out to the Turkish army. The TRNC's limited military capabilities stand in sharp contrast to its more developed political infrastructure.

More than any of the other *de facto* states considered in this study, the TRNC is characterized by a substantial degree of external dependence— in this case, dependence on Turkey. This raises the salient question of whether or not the TRNC should be considered a puppet state. Alan James (1986b), for example, thinks that it should. In his view, the TRNC effectively 'depends on Turkey in almost every respect, and it may therefore be assumed that Turkey will have a very big say in its government. It is therefore reasonable to categorize it as a puppet state' (1986b, p. 142). Recalling our discussion in chapter two, the factors identified by James Crawford and Alan James in distinguishing puppet states from other entities include such things as: 1) whether the entity was established illegally, by military occupation or the threat or use of external armed force; 2) evidence that the entity does not have the support of the vast majority of the population it claims to govern; 3) evidence that the entity is subject to foreign control or direction in important matters of policy; and 4) the staffing of important government positions by foreign nationals.[35]

The argument that the TRNC should be considered a puppet state starts from point number one above and emphasizes its complete military dependence on external forces. It was along these lines that the European Court of Human Rights found in a December 1996 ruling that 'It was obvious from the large number of troops engaged in active duties in northern Cyprus that the Turkish Army exercised effective overall control there'.[36] The TRNC as puppet state argument also points to such things as the use of the Turkish lira as its currency, Turkish control over the postal service and passports, the TRNC's dependence on Turkey for air and shipping links to the outside world, and its dependence on Turkish economic assistance.

The argument for the TRNC as a puppet state also focuses on point number three above. Perhaps the best example of the TRNC being subject to foreign direction or control in important matters of policy comes from its changing economic policies in 1980. In line with a Turkish policy of import substitution, the TRNC government announced a list of 108 major items that could no longer be imported. Then, in April 1980, following the fall of the Ecevit government in Turkey, a more open economic policy was implemented that promoted freer trade and virtually abolished the list of 108 items that were previously prohibited. As C. H. Dodd (1993d) puts it, 'The well-nigh inevitable reliance of Northern Cyprus on Turkish economic policy could not be better demonstrated' (1993d, p. 117).

The argument against the TRNC as a puppet state starts from point two above. Unlike Manchukuo and the Nazi regimes in Slovakia and Croatia during World War II, the TRNC actually does have the support of the vast majority of the population it claims to govern. It is not an alien entity imposed from abroad on an unwilling civilian population. A second component of this argument points to the fact that the TRNC does not always march in step with Turkey. The TRNC's constitution, for example, has many more liberal democratic principles in it than the Turkish constitution has. The TRNC has also shown a far more tolerant attitude toward the activities of left-wing trade unions and political parties than the mainland Turks have. Birol Ali Yesilada (1989) argues that 'If the TRNC was indeed a puppet state of Turkey, then these extensive individual civil and political rights would have been far more restricted in Northern Cyprus -- especially the activities of the leftist political parties and trade unions'.[37]

Another plank in the argument against the TRNC as a puppet state places the TRNC's dependence on foreign aid in comparative perspective. Foreign aid has accounted for some 40 percent of Sri Lanka's government budget and an even greater percentage of some African countries' budgets. Neither these countries, nor Israel, which annually receives about US$ 3 billion in aid from the United States, are referred to as puppet states. A related component of this argument asks why is the TRNC so dependent on Turkey? The Greek Cypriots have waged an intensive and successful international embargo campaign against the TRNC. They have, for example, succeeded in getting the 1979 Universal Postal Union Congress to declare Turkish Cypriot postage stamps as 'illegal and of no validity'. The International Civil Aviation Organization does not allow Cyprus Turkish

Airlines to fly to any of its member states, nor are those states' carriers allowed to fly to the TRNC. Similarly, the International Air Transport Association 'does not recognize the Ercan airport, as it operates unofficially and poses safety hazards...'. Similar restrictions are applied to TRNC maritime ports (Martin, 1993, pp. 362-363; Lockhart, 1994, p. 371; McDonald, 1988-89, p. 22). From a functional perspective, Ercan airport operates efficiently and has a good safety record. Similarly, the TRNC is quite capable of adhering to any international standards on the safety of its ports or the mutual recognition of postal services. Thus, it is disingenuous to cite the TRNC's reliance on Turkish postage and airports as evidence of puppet statehood when that course of action is forced upon it by international embargoes. As Mustafa Ergün Olgun (1993) observes,

> at a time when Turkish Cypriots have been isolated and effectively prevented from integrating with the rest of the world, they cannot be blamed for taking steps that would improve their economic and cultural well-being through integration with friendly countries (1993, p. 284).

A final key part of the argument against the TRNC being a puppet state focuses on the fourth point above. In James's own scheme, in making the distinction between dependent states and puppet states, 'The crucial element is the staffing of all the key positions in a state's decision-making apparatus by nationals of another state...' (1986b, p. 140). This 'crucial element' is simply not present in the case of the TRNC. TRNC officials consult closely with their Turkish counterparts on a number of matters and the Turks maintain a large embassy staff in Lefkosa (Nicosia), but all of the key positions in the TRNC's decision-making apparatus are staffed by Turkish Cypriots. Thus, according to his own scheme, James should not have classified the TRNC as a puppet state.

Clearly, the TRNC has a greater level of external dependency than any of the other *de facto* states considered in this study. The case for dismissing it as a puppet state, though, is far from self-evident. Some of the logic of the TRNC differs from that which one would find in, say, Somaliland or Chechnya. In broad terms, though, the TRNC does maintain effective territorial control of a given area over which it provides governance services and receives popular support. Its effectiveness, though, has failed to translate into widespread international recognition and it can thus be considered a *de facto* state.

The last consideration under the capabilities section is the perseverance criterion. The TRNC itself has been in existence for more than

14 years now. Its immediate predecessor, the TFSC, goes back more than 20 years. One can also trace the roots of the Turkish Cypriot *de facto* state back to the movement of Turkish Cypriots into enclaves following the communal violence that broke out in December 1963.

Relations with International Society Of all the cases considered here, the Turkish Cypriots have clearly received the most attention from the rest of international society. Of even greater importance than the active embargo campaign is the international community's recognition of the Greek Cypriot government as being the sole legitimate sovereign authority over the entire island. The Cyprus situation has been the subject of dozens of UN resolutions and it has also been discussed in a variety of other fora ranging from the Non-Aligned Movement to the Commonwealth. UN peacekeepers have been patrolling the green line for more than thirty years now and the Secretary-General's office has been leading negotiating efforts in Cyprus for more than twenty years. While the international negotiations have consistently dealt with the two communities on an 'equal footing',[38] the overwhelming thrust of international society's involvement in Cyprus has been to condemn the TRNC as illegal, to call for its dissolution, and to call upon all UN member-states not to recognize it. Therefore, there is no question of the TRNC having attained some higher or more legitimate status than de facto statehood. Indeed, the TRNC is a paradigmatic example of the de facto state remaining illegitimate no matter how effective it is.

3 Conclusion

The detailed review of four case studies in chapters three and four serves three purposes. First, it has provided detailed empirical background information on each of the case studies concerned. Second, by subjecting each of these case studies to the same type of analysis, our theoretical criteria from chapter two have been operationalized and a system has been established by which other cases can be assessed using the same criteria. Finally, this exercise has shown the tremendous diversity inherent within the category *'de facto* state'. We have seen *de facto* states that have formulated strong (Eritrea, Somaliland), moderate or questionable (Tamil Eelam) and weak (the TRNC) territorial justifications. Two of our cases (Eritrea, Somaliland) are organized under what we are calling the state principle; two (Tamil Eelam, the TRNC) are organized under the national principle. Some *de facto* states (Eritrea) have pursued activist, even revolutionary policies while others (Somaliland) have been content to accept the traditional structures of their societies and to work within them. In terms of democratic accountability, the spread of *de facto* states considered here runs from very high (the TRNC) to completely non-existent (Tamil Eelam). Much of this diversity is shown graphically in the table on the following page.

The next four chapters of this study comprise a birth, life, and death or evolution look at the *de facto* state. Chapters five and six together examine the factors that produce *de facto* states. Chapter seven analyzes how international law and international society cope with the existence of these entities. Chapter eight explores various possibilities for the future evolution or transformation of the *de facto* state.

Table 4.1 The Diversity of *De Facto* States

Consideration	Eritrea	Tamil Eelam	Somaliland	TRNC
Territorial justification	colonial borders	Northern & Eastern provinces of Sri Lanka	colonial borders	existing areas of control
Extent of territory	Varied	varies	varies	stable
Popular support	Extremely high	high with some opposition	moderate to high with some opposition	high
Democratic account-ability	high with some question marks	none	high	extremely high for Turkish Cypriots, low for minorities
Organization principle	state principle	nation principle	state principle	nation principle
Governance services	Extremely high	moderate	moderate	extremely high
Military capabilities	Extremely high	high	moderate to high	low for TRNC, extremely high for Turkey
Perseverance	16 years[#]	15 years[*]	7 years	23 years[@]
External dependency	Low	low	very low	very high

[#] 1977 – 1993. This figure could be revised in either direction depending on the area in question.

[*] 1983 – 1998. This figure could perhaps be revised down somewhat.

[@] 1975 – 1983 as the TFSC; 1983 – 1998 as the TRNC.

Notes

[1] McMullen (1993, p. 428) estimates 2.7 million people; Drysdale (1992, p. 1) figures 'two million or so'; and Adam (1994b, p. 22) refers to 'approximately three million'.

[2] This clan's name is variously spelled Isaak, Isaaq, and Isaq. This study will standardize its spelling to Isaaq unless it appears inside a quotation. Note: the Issa are a completely separate group.

[3] Carroll and Rajagopal, 1992-93, pp. 665-666; Omaar, 1994, p. 233; Adam, 1994b, p. 29; Drysdale, 1992, pp. 15-18; and Bryden, 1994b, p. 39.

[4] Drysdale, 1992, pp. 24-26; Omaar, 1993, p. 45; Bryden, 1994b, pp. 38-39; and Adam, 1994c, pp. 117-119.

[5] For more on the concept of reversion to sovereignty, see Alexandrowicz, 1969, pp. 465-480.

[6] The 90,000 refugees estimate comes from United States Department of State Dispatch, 'Somalia Human Rights Practices, 1995' (Washington, D.C., March 1996).

[7] 'Somalia: Somaliland They Call It', *The Economist*, 8 April 1995; and 'Somaliland: Another Country', *The Economist*, 18 May 1996.

[8] 'Rival Somaliland Group Scorns Ceasefire Call', *Reuters World Service*, 21 May 1995.

[9] United States Department of State Dispatch, 'Somalia Human Rights Practices, 1995'.

[10] 'Rebels Attack Government Forces in Somaliland', *Reuters World Service*, 20 January 1996; and 'In Somaliland, a New State Rises From the Ruins', *Reuters World Service*, 27 January 1996.

[11] Bryden, 1994a, p. 42; McMullen, 1993, p. 429; Adam, 1994b, pp. 32-33; and Bryden, 1994b, p. 40.

[12] 'Agencies Warn Over Northwest Somali Currency Law', *Reuters World Service*, 12 January 1996; 'Somaliland: New Currency Law', *The Indian Ocean Newsletter*, # 702, 20 January 1996; 'European Aid for Berbera', *The Indian Ocean Newsletter*, # 706, 17 February 1996; and 'Somaliland: Another Country', *The Economist*, 18 May 1996.

[13] 'Somaliland: All Eyes on Egal', *The Indian Ocean Newsletter*, # 765, 17 May 1997; and ' "Somaliland" Leader Says a Nation Is Being Built', *Agence France Presse*, 15 June 1997.

[14] 'Somaliland President Re-Elected in Landslide Vote', *Reuters World Service*, 23 February 1997; and 'Egal Re-Elected', *The Indian Ocean Newsletter*, # 755, 1 March 1997.

[15] 'Somalia: Somaliland They Call It', *The Economist*, 8 April 1995; and 'Somaliland: Another Country', *The Economist*, 18 May 1996.

[16] Flint, 1994, pp. 36-37. See also Drysdale, 1992, p. 30; and 'Somalia: Drifting', *The Economist* 16 April 1994.

17 'Somaliland: Another Country', *The Economist*, 18 May 1996.
18 On the UNDP, see 'Somaliland; President Tells UN Official Aid Agencies Doing More Harm Than Good', *BBC Summary of World Broadcasts*, 6 June 1995. On the American visit, see 'Somalia Breakthrough as Americans Visit Somaliland', *Africa News*, September 1995; and 'Somalia; Somaliland: Egal Receives Visiting US Delegation', *BBC Summary of World Broadcasts*, 11 November 1995.
19 Telephone interview with Mr. Ken Shivers, US State Department desk officer for Djibouti and Somalia, 10 April 1997.
20 The above two paragraphs are based on a variety of sources including: McDonald, 1988-89, pp. 20-21; Christofinis, 1984, p. 85; Morvaridi, 1993b, pp. 219-220; Doob, 1986, p. 385; Coughlan, 1991, p. 82; and *Cyprus Newsletter* (Washington, D. C.: Embassy of Cyprus Press and Information Office), 6 July 1994, p. 1.
21 The above two paragraphs draw from a variety of sources including: Alemdar, 1993, p. 79; Cooper and Berdal, 1993, p. 120; McDonald, 1988-89, pp. 10-11; Necatigil, 1993, p. 47; and Oberling, 1982, pp. 63-65.
22 Lafrenière and Mitchell, 1990, p. 12. For the Greek view, see Rossides, 1991, p. 86. For the Turkish view, see Tamkoç, 1988, p. 57; and Alemdar, 1993, p. 79.
23 For more on this, see Dodd, 1993e, p. 7; Necatigil, 1989, pp. 17-24; Oberling, 1982, pp. 71-84; and Rossides, 1991, pp. 31-32.
24 The above two paragraphs are drawn from a variety of sources including: Cooper and Berdal, 1993, p. 120; Dodd, 1993e, pp. 7-9; Necatigil, 1989, pp. 35-37 and 52-56; McDonald, 1988-89, pp. 12-14; and Oberling, 1982, pp. 98-127.
25 Cooper and Berdal, 1993, pp. 120-121; McDonald, 1988-89, pp. 18-19; Oberling, 1982, pp. 168-181; Dodd, 1993e, pp. 10-11; and Denktash, 1988, pp. 72-74.
26 This gentleman's last name is also spelled Denktas or Denktas with a cedilla on the s. This study will standardize the spelling to Denktash.
27 Dodd, 1993d, pp. 125-132; McDonald, 1988-89, p. 43; Denktash, 1988, pp. 116-121; and Warner, 1993, pp. 203-204.
28 The TRNC's declaration of independence is reproduced in appendix 16 of Denktash, 1988. See also Necatigil, 1989, pp. 174-175, 197-198, and 279.
29 The above two paragraphs are drawn from: Rothman, 1991, pp. 98-105; McDonald, 1988-89, pp. 22-23; Lafrenière and Mitchell, 1990, pp. 15-16, 40 and 70; Jacovides, 1995, pp. 1223 and 1229; Necatigil, 1989, pp. 147-151; and McDonald, 1984, pp. 421-423.
30 Oberling, 1982, pp. 195-196. See also McDonald, 1988-89, pp. 30-31.
31 Denktash has now won five presidential elections in 1976, 1981, 1985, 1990, and 1995.
32 Dodd, 1993c, p. 377. See also Warner, 1993, pp. 193-217; McDonald, 1988-89, pp. 41-42; Dodd, 1993d, pp. 106-135; Yesilada, 1989, pp. 105-108; and Dodd, 1993b, pp. 136-154.
33 United States Department of State, 'Cyprus Country Report on Human Rights Practices for 1996' (Washington, D. C., February 1997).

[34] See Freedom House's annual *Comparative Survey of Freedom.* This account is based on the summaries of this provided in *Freedom Review* 26 (January-February 1995); *Freedom Review* 27 (January-February 1996); and *Freedom Review* 28 (January-February 1997).

[35] See the discussion of criterion number six in chapter two. The references are to Crawford, 1976-77, pp. 130-133; and James, 1986b, pp. 139-140.

[36] See 'Court's Cyprus Verdict Stuns Turkey', *The Independent,* 19 December 1996; 'Cyprus Pleased by European Court Verdict Against Turkey', *Agence France Presse,* 18 December 1996; and United States Department of State, 'Cyprus Country Report on Human Rights Practices for 1996'.

[37] Yesilada, 1989, pp. 107-109. The specific quote is found on p. 109.

[38] See McDonald, 1988-89, p. 23; Necatigil, 1989, pp. 64-65; and Dodd, 1993b, p. 155.

5 Macro-Level Factors Implicated in the Birth of *De Facto* States

1 Introduction

This chapter examines the various systemic or macro-level factors that contribute to or allow for the emergence of *de facto* states in contemporary international society. The discussion here is concerned with why these entities (plural) arise, not with the factors leading to the emergence of any one specific entity. The chapter comprises six main sections, each of which explores a feature of the contemporary international system that in some way contributes to the emergence or continued existence of *de facto* states. These six factors are the new normative environment on territory; changing conceptions of sovereignty; the shift from empirical to juridical statehood; state recognition policies; the 'weak state' security problematic; and the principle of self-determination. Obviously, a number of these factors are interrelated. It would be impossible, for example, to understand the dynamics involved in the weak state security problematic without considering the changing normative environment on territory. Therefore, these six features should be viewed as interrelated parts of a larger whole.

2 The Changing Normative Environment on Territory

From the Peace of Westphalia through to at least World War I, territorial change was seen as a normal, indeed inevitable, part of international relations. The cut and thrust of international politics required that some states be created, swallowed, or partitioned in order to preserve the larger balance of power. In this regard, Friedrich Kratochwil (1986) argues that there are two different ways that territorial boundaries can be used to minimize conflict. These are the 'management of the *types* of exchanges mediated by boundaries, and manipulation of the *location* of the boundaries'. The second of these types, to which we are referring above,

> was characteristic of the European balance-of-power system that attempted to 'preserve the equilibrium in Europe' through territorial gains and divisions such as the division of Poland and the territorial adjustments at the Congress of Vienna (1986, p. 37).

In James Mayall's (1990) view, this 'traditional model' of international relations was based on a legal settlement and a political dispensation. The legal settlement was premised upon the sovereign equality of all states. The political dispensation, in contrast, was an acknowledgment by the major powers of the day that they had special responsibilities for maintaining international order. Should these two ever come into conflict, 'in the final analysis, the legal settlement is subordinated to the requirements of the balance of power.... Thus was Poland partitioned... and Africa divided...'.[1] William Coplin (1965) goes even further in asserting that the international legal settlement itself supported the fluidity of territorial borders. As he sees it, territorial boundaries served three functions in classical international law. First, they demarcated a state's territory. Second, they were essential for preserving the states system itself in that revised boundaries could provide the foundation for a new international order following the conclusion of major wars. Third, boundaries afforded a means through which the expansion and contraction of international power could be measured. Coplin concludes that 'Since the boundary law was a legal means of measuring territorial changes, international law in effect reinforced the idea that the struggle for power was an essential and accepted part of international politics' (1965, pp. 620-621).

This accepted inevitability of territorial change stands in sharp contrast to the post-World War II era's attempt, in Mayall's phrase, to 'freeze the map' and sanctify the existing distribution of territorial boundaries as permanent and inviolable. Post-1945 international society is more fundamentally conservative on the need to preserve the existing territorial map and more adverse to secessionist aspirations than anything witnessed before in the history of international relations.[2] The profound theoretical implications of this change are well captured by Peter Willets, who notes 'that Morgenthau has specifically ruled as impossible that there could ever be universal acceptance of the territorial status quo, yet we are now very near to that situation' (1981, p. 115).

A major vehicle used in shifting international society from a fluid to a fixed territorial conception was the legal principle *uti possidetis* (as you now possess). This principle first emerged in Latin America in the nineteenth century in an attempt to forestall any potential territorial disputes between the newly independent former Spanish colonies of the region. Essentially, *uti possidetis* was designed to confirm the sanctity of the colonially-inherited borders so as to remove a potential source of inter-state conflict. From its initial use in Latin America, this principle has subsequently been adopted by post-colonial African states and invoked in disputes between Asian states. In a 1986 case involving Burkina Faso and Mali, the International Court of Justice declared *uti possidetis* to be of universal applicability (Naldi, 1987, pp. 893-903; Lapidoth, 1992, p. 341).

In addition to expanding beyond its original geographic confines, the principle of *uti possidetis* has also seen its content and subject matter expanded. Originally designed to prevent inter-state conflicts, the principle has been enlarged and 'is now expected to proscribe not only irredentist demands at the level of inter-state relations, but also secessionist attempts by purely domestic groups' (Kamanu, 1974, p. 355). In the post-Cold War period, international society has also extended *uti possidetis* to include internal boundaries. This was done in the case of the former Soviet republics and, more explicitly (by the EC's Badinter Commission), in the case of the Yugoslav successor republics (Jackson and James, 1993, pp. 9-10; Weller, 1992, pp. 589-590). One can thus see the international boundary regime moving progressively from general fluidity to fixed inter-state borders in one region to fixed inter- and intra-state borders globally.

From the standpoint of the *de facto* state, what is important is not the mere existence of this conservative consensus on territory but its continued strength and effectiveness. One could, for example, argue that although *apartheid* was universally condemned, the actions taken against the South African regime were often weak and ineffective. In the case of fixed territorial borders, though, the moral consensus has been backed up by effective action. Albeit with a small number of exceptions, the consensus against changing borders has prevailed against both external and internal challenges to the sanctity of existing frontiers. As Robert Jackson puts it, 'International legitimacy and law is revealed, perhaps surprisingly, as a normative framework capable of withstanding the pressures of armed force and indigenous culture' (1990, p. 154).

Why does this consensus on fixed territorial borders prevail? First, as most states face some sort of national or minority problem within their own borders, they all have a self-interested incentive to ensure the general sanctity of existing boundaries. This mutual reciprocity of interest in preserving borders can be accepted as reasonable or it can be lambasted cynically as, to use Ken Booth's phrase, 'the diplomatic equivalent of honour among thieves' (1995, p. 121). Either way, it is arguably the closest thing to a universal consensus there is in today's diverse international society. Second, from a purely logistical standpoint, secession is a poor solution to many state problems. It is fraught with potential dangers ranging from concerns over unviable entities to trapped minorities to the subversion of majority rule and the fear of unlimited 'Balkanization'. Third, the fixed territorial borders regime has a wonderful simplicity about it. Whereas national identification necessarily remains subjective, juridical borders can be delimited precisely.

The future prospects for this fixed territorial regime necessarily remain uncertain. Though his overall assessment is quite cautious, James Mayall (1990) argues that 'Intuitively, this unprecedented attempt to bring history to an end, at least so far as the territorial division of the world is concerned, seems unlikely to succeed'.[3] Crawford Young (1983), on the other hand, maintains that 'Whatever else may lie ahead, "respect for the sovereignty and territorial integrity of each State" appears to be one of the safer political forecasts'.[4] As this normative regime on territory is based on shared understandings it can be seen as socially constructed. Therefore, it could be deconstructed or reconstructed in a different manner. Unless and until that happens, however, the post-1945 normative environment on territory will remain one of the leading causes of *de facto* statehood in contemporary international society. The main effect of this regime on *de facto* states is not so much in actively causing their creation as it is on preventing them from realizing their ultimate goal of sovereignty as constitutional independence. No matter how effective or internally legitimate they are, the normative regime of fixed territorial borders operates to ensure that *de facto* states remain just that: *de facto* states and not sovereign states.

3 Changing Conceptions of Sovereignty

One cannot speak of a states system in the sense of distinct and formally equal units that regularly interact in the absence of a hierarchical authority without some conception of sovereignty. It is in this regard that Alan James (1986b) describes sovereignty as 'the organizing principle of inter-state relations', and Jackson and Rosberg (1982) label it 'the central principle of international society' (James, 1986b, pp. 268-269; Jackson and Rosberg, 1982, pp. 12-13). The corollary to sovereignty as the exclusive legitimate authority to rule in a specific territorial area (which says nothing about the actual degree of control exercised) is some sort of general non-intervention principle. As one state's claim to exercise final and legitimate authority within its own exclusive jurisdictional domain necessarily depends on extending similar consideration to others, Barry Buzan (1993) identifies the mutual recognition of sovereignty as being the defining boundary whose crossing marks the coming into existence of an international society of states. In his conception, it is the mutual recognition of sovereignty and the legal equality of all states that 'denies the possibility of suzerain, dominion, and imperial relations (though not hegemonic ones) and sets the minimum conditions for societal relations among culturally diverse units' (1993, p. 345).

The fact that the states system is necessarily premised upon some sort of mutually recognized sovereignty combined with a generalized non-intervention principle, however, says little about the specific form which that sovereignty may take. Indeed, sovereignty has taken a variety of forms over different historical periods. Perhaps its largest shift was from earlier notions of sovereignty based on dynastic legitimacy to more contemporary notions based on popular legitimacy. As Martin Wight (1977) puts it,

> Until the French Revolution, the principle of international legitimacy was *dynastic*, being concerned with the status and claims of rulers. Since then, dynasticism has been superseded by a *popular* principle, concerned with the claims and consent of the governed. The sovereignty of the individual prince passed into the sovereignty of the nation he ruled.[5]

Changes in the prevalent standards of sovereign legitimacy substantively affect state practice and favor or facilitate certain practices while marginalizing or excluding others. As Rob Walker argues, 'The patterns of inclusion and exclusion we now take for granted are historical innovations' (1993, p. 179). They are neither natural nor inevitable. Thus, while a resort to national self-determination may seem commonplace today, it would have appeared bizarre and incomprehensible in the age of absolute monarchs. Similarly, long-established dynastic practices now appear fatally anachronistic in an age of popular sovereignty.

The implications of this are well captured by Cynthia Weber, who maintains that 'the meanings attached to sovereignty and the practices which follow from them are historically and geographically variable' (1992, p. 204). A similar point is made by J. Samuel Barkin and Bruce Cronin (1994). As they see it, most scholars err in focusing on sovereignty's legal content. As this changes little, sovereignty is mistakenly seen as fixed. This is because the 'institutionalization of authority within mutually exclusive domains is... as much a function of its legitimacy as of its legal content...'. And, as 'understandings of legitimacy tend to change from era to era.... the rules of sovereignty are neither fixed nor constant, but rather are subject to changing interpretations' (1994, pp. 107-108). Sovereignty is thus a social construct characterized by changing intersubjective understandings.

There is one particular change in how sovereignty is interpreted that has a significant impact on the likelihood of *de facto* states being present in the international system or not. That is the oscillation between what Barkin and Cronin term 'state sovereignty' and 'national sovereignty'. In their conception, state sovereignty 'stresses the link between sovereign authority and a defined territory...' while national sovereignty 'emphasizes a link between sovereign authority and a defined population' (1994, p. 108). Though these two types of sovereignty are institutionally and structurally alike, they differ fundamentally in the source of their legitimation—one based on people, the other on territory. Barkin and Cronin do not believe that the tension between state legitimation and national legitimation can ever be fully resolved. Rather, in a somewhat dialectical fashion, 'When an international order focuses legitimacy on one, tensions often arise in the other. Thus, postwar settlements will tend to favor one over the other, and the emphasis is often reevaluated during the creation of a new international order' (1994, p. 115). Historically, they see the post-Napoleonic war era as favoring the state over the nation; the post-World War I era as favoring the nation; the post-World War II era favoring the state; and no definitive statement yet emerging from the post-Cold War era, although there seems to be a shift in the direction of national legitimacy again.

Which sovereignty norm prevails clearly affects the prospects for successful secession. During periods when state sovereignty predominates, international society 'will tend to defend the rights of established states against nationalist claims of domestic ethnic groups'. However, during periods when national sovereignty predominates, 'the international community will be more sympathetic to pleas for national self-determination, often at the expense of established states' (Barkin and Cronin, 1994, p. 108). The *de facto* state's ultimate goal of sovereignty as constitutional independence makes it a challenge to the existing state order. Therefore, following Barkin and Cronin's scheme, one could argue that any such challenge would be more likely to succeed during a period when sovereignty is ascribed to national entities. Conversely, *de facto* state challengers would be less likely to succeed during periods when sovereignty is conceived along state lines.

Thus, while the oscillation between state sovereignty and national sovereignty might not have any specific impact on the likely creation of *de facto* states, one suspects that there would be a much greater likelihood of encountering such entities in the international system during periods when understandings of state sovereignty prevailed. This is because state sovereignty norms act as a kind of ceiling that prevents the *de facto* state from attaining juridical recognition of its empirical success. The argument here is not that such periods necessarily create or give birth to *de facto* states. Rather, it is that such entities are more likely to be found during these periods because their prospects for successfully joining the international club of sovereign states are so low.

4 From Empirical to Juridical Statehood

Another major factor behind the emergence and continued existence of *de facto* states is the shift from sovereign statehood based on empirical capabilities to sovereign statehood based on juridical rights. For nearly three centuries of international relations, sovereignty was accorded on the basis of demonstrated empirical capabilities, particularly effective governance. As Robert Jackson put it, 'Demonstrated capacity for self-government created capability and respect which warranted recognition: sovereigns preceded sovereignty...' (1990, p. 34). How such capability was acquired did not matter; the only concern was that it was present.

This normative framework outlasted the end of World War II by a little more than one decade. This can be seen in such things as Italy's desire to resume its colonizing mission in Eritrea and the British and French desire to prepare their colonies for independence gradually, if at all. Things changed, however, with the wave of decolonization that swept the international system in the late 1950s and early 1960s. As Peter Lyon notes, 'decolonization led to the acquisition of formal independence by a number of states and mini-states, many of whose substantive claims and qualifications for independence would not have been taken seriously by the governments of most other independent states only a decade earlier' (1973, p. 47). Perhaps the signal defining moment here was the passage of UN General Assembly Resolution 1514 (entitled 'A Declaration on the Granting of Independence to Colonial Countries and Peoples') by 89 votes in favor, zero against, with nine abstentions on 14 December 1960. According to that resolution, 'All peoples have the right to self-determination; by virtue of that right they freely determine their political status and freely pursue their economic, social and cultural development'. Within this context, requiring prospective states first to clear the substantive hurdles of the traditional empirical criteria for statehood would no longer be acceptable. Therefore, Resolution 1514 mandated that 'inadequacy of political, economic, social or educational preparedness should never serve as a pretext for delaying independence'.

Nii Lante Wallace-Bruce (1985) incorrectly ascertains that this shift in international practice signifies that the traditional Montevideo criteria for statehood now require an additional fifth criterion of legality of state origin. After referencing the four Montevideo criteria of a permanent population, a defined territory, a government, and the capacity to enter into relations with other states, Wallace-Bruce argues 'It appears that in recent times an additional criteria [sic] has emerged — that of legality. This requires that in achieving the traditional criteria, the entity must do so in conformity with the rules of international law' (1985, p. 589). Yet, as chapter two showed, the argument that any of the traditional criteria for statehood in terms of population, territory, or government remain valid is not supported by post-1945 state practice. Legality of origin and conformity with accepted international norms is not an additional criterion, but rather is now *the only* criterion for statehood. In Robert Jackson's poignant phrasing, 'To be a sovereign state today one needs only to have been a formal colony yesterday. All other considerations are irrelevant' (1990, p. 17).

A more detailed exposition of Jackson's basic point above is that an entity which has emerged either (a) outside of the accepted rules of international law, particularly Article 2 (4)'s prohibition on the use or threat of force; (b) in violation of a colonial entity's right to self-determination; (c) without the consent of the existing sovereign state; or (d) is an *apartheid* regime will generally not attain juridical recognition as a sovereign state. The main objections to most contemporary *de facto* states will come from points (a), (b) and/or (c) above. The expansive, catch-all nature of those three points trumps whatever legitimate grievances the *de facto* state may have and whatever other successes it may obtain in terms of military capabilities, popular support, territorial control, and the like. Indeed, the *de facto* state's efforts at securing effective territorial control of a given area, building up an efficient governing apparatus, and winning popular support (i.e., state-building) can be seen as playing yesterday's game in violation of today's rules. As with the argument on state-based sovereignty, the point here is not that the shift from empirical to juridical statehood has directly created *de facto* states. Rather, it is that the normative consensus around this juridical statehood prevents the *de facto* state from ever successfully resolving its own situation through the acquisition of sovereign statehood. Therefore, as long as it does not give up trying, it will be condemned to the juridical never-never land of *de facto* statehood.

5 Recognition Policies

The question of recognition simply did not arise in the earliest writings on international law. The reason for this, according to James Crawford, was that 'sovereignty, in its origin merely the location of supreme power within a particular territorial unit, necessarily came from within and therefore did not require the recognition of other States or princes' (1976-77, p. 96). The recognition of states first became an issue in international law around the middle of the eighteenth century. Later, in the nineteenth century, international legal positivists linked sovereignty to a constitutive theory of recognition whereby new states acquired international personality only after they had been recognized by existing states. At this point, international law was seen as the law between 'civilized' nations and recognition came to serve as one's entry ticket of admission into this 'civilized' group—'a sort of juristic baptism', in Crawford's phrasing. Recognition was generally extended to new states once they had successfully demonstrated their empirical capabilities, particularly in regard to effective control. As such, 'how a State *became* a State was a matter of no importance to traditional international law...' (Crawford, 1976-77, p. 98). This situation prevailed until the end of World War I. The concern with the causes of war and the conditions for peace at that point, especially in relation to Woodrow Wilson's views on the contributions of democratic states to world peace, led to recognition then becoming 'imbued with ideological considerations' as governments increasingly tried to withhold recognition from states and governments whose politics they found distasteful (Shain, 1991, p. 224). This increasing 'politicization' of recognition policies is a trend that has continued throughout the twentieth century. Where recognition was once based on 'objective' criteria such as effective control, it is now based on more subjective judgments about a state's policies and its legality or illegality of origin. Much to the dismay of many international lawyers, recognition today is more discretionary and political than it is objective and legal.

In regard to the *de facto* state, two main topics need to be canvassed here. These are: first, the distinction between constitutive and declaratory theories of recognition and, second, the concept of collective non-recognition. On the first point, according to the constitutive theory, it is the act of recognition itself that creates statehood and international personality. In other words, a state does not exist until it is recognized as such by other states. The declaratory theory, on the other hand, sees statehood as being independent of recognition—i.e., something that objectively can exist prior to its recognition or formal acknowledgment by others. In this view, the recognition of a state is a political act independent of that state's actual existence in international law. Thus, recognition is merely a declaratory acknowledgment of a state's existence.[6]

Each of these two main theories of recognition is problematic and Crawford concludes that 'neither theory of recognition satisfactorily explains modern State practice in this area' (1976-77, p. 95). Be that as it might, the relevant question for our purposes is whether or not recognition under either theory substantively affects the prospects for or the existence of *de facto* states.

Suzanne Palmer (1986), in a policy-oriented analysis of the TRNC directed at US decision-makers, seems to suggest that it would. In her view,

> Under the declaratory theory, the Turkish Republic of Northern Cyprus would qualify as a state under international law, since it has a population, territory, government and the capacity to enter into relations with other states. Under the constitutive theory, the Turkish Republic of Northern Cyprus would not qualify as a state since Turkey is the only state which recognizes it... (1986, p. 447).

Following Palmer's logic, one would conclude that the *de facto* state would clearly prefer the declaratory to the constitutive tradition as it would satisfy the demands of the former while falling short of the requirements of the latter. This viewpoint, however, fails to emphasize adequately the fact that recognition under the declaratory theory is discretionary. As Alan James notes, 'the declaratory doctrine accords well with the abundantly evident fact that most states regard recognition as a political act. Thus they will refuse to recognize entities of whose existence or policies they strongly disapprove' (1986b, p. 148). As such, the *de facto* state comes up short under either tradition—self-evidently under the constitutive theory and less obviously under the declaratory theory where its existence in international law is overshadowed by the refusal of existing sovereign states to have anything to do with it.

This brings us to the issue of collective non-recognition. As a principle of international law, collective non-recognition first appeared in the so-called 'Stimson Doctrine' in the 1930s in connection with the Japanese attempt to establish the state of Manchukuo. The juridical basis of collective non-recognition is the principle *ex injuria jus non oritur*—a right cannot originate in an illegal act or, as Wallace-Bruce puts it, 'a wrong-doer cannot derive rights from an illegality created by him or her' (1985, p. 595). Perhaps the two most famous cases of collective non-recognition involved UDI Rhodesia and the four South African 'Bantustans' of Bophuthatswana, Ciskei, Transkei, and Venda. In each of these cases, a series of UN resolutions were passed which, like the subsequent Security Council Resolution 541 on the TRNC, called upon all states not to recognize these entities. There can be no question of these entities, especially UDI Rhodesia, meeting the traditional criteria for statehood in terms of such things as defined territories, permanent populations, and effective governments. The Bantustans could be accused of puppet statehood, but UDI Rhodesia was clearly a viable or potentially viable stand-alone entity. Alan James argues that the collective non-recognition of UDI Rhodesia shows 'the viewing of sovereignty not just as the concomitant of certain facts but also as a kind of moral accolade, which must therefore be refused to those who fall short' (1986b, p. 160).

One could argue that each of the cases mentioned above is somewhat exceptional as they fall afoul of international society's specific condemnation of *apartheid* regimes. While true, this argument obscures the fact that collective non-recognition has also proven quite effective in a number of other cases ranging from Katanga (recognized by no one) and Biafra (recognized by Gabon, Haiti, the Ivory Coast, Tanzania, and Zambia) to the TRNC (recognized by Turkey) and Somaliland (recognized by no one) where *apartheid* was not involved. The latter two cases are particularly interesting. The notion of an 'Islamic bloc' within the international system is certainly put to question by the TRNC's failure to secure any recognition from its Islamic brethren. This case lends credence to the argument that the functional norms of international society ('practical association' in Nardin's terms) can override cultural affinities. In the Somaliland case, the chaos of Mogadishu stands in stark contrast to the relative peace and security of

Hargeisa. Yet, even with its former colonial status, no one has recognized the Republic of Somaliland.

Two other points on collective non-recognition also need to be made. The first concerns the importance of prior sovereign consent for recognition. When such consent is granted by the former sovereign, be it in a colonial or non-colonial (Czechoslovakia, the Soviet Union) situation, the right of the breakaway entity to sovereignty as constitutional independence is widely recognized throughout the international community. As Ronald McMullen notes,

> The key member of the international community for secessionists is, ironically, the government of the mother state. Unless secessionists can vitiate the active opposition of the central government, other states will be extremely hesitant to recognize the breakaway region in all but the most egregious of circumstances (1992, p. 116).

The main recent exception to this has been the widespread recognition of the former Yugoslav republics without the consent of Belgrade. The special circumstance of German insistence on recognizing Slovenia and Croatia and the fact that these recognitions have not led to any widespread change of practice, however, leads one to conclude that this may be the exception which proves the rule. As Lawrence Eastwood observes, the recent secessionist violence in former Yugoslavia 'will likely cool some of the enthusiasm for recognition of a secession right under international law and could encourage a return to the historical disapproval of secession in state practice' (1993, p. 348).

The second point to be made is that 'In the absence of a supranational entity exercising supreme authority, the act of recognition is still by and large political in nature and the prerogative of an independent sovereign state' (Ijalaye, 1971, pp. 556-557). Therefore, decisions on whether or not to recognize a secessionist entity are often not principled, but rather based on pure self-interest. Thus, one finds abundant hypocrisy in contemporary state practice. The Soviet Union, for example, offered military support to crush secessionist attempts in the Congo and Nigeria, yet strongly supported Bangladesh's demand for self-determination. The Bangladeshis received the bulk of their support from India, a state which fails to extend similar support to the Kashmiris. While Croatia steadfastly insisted on the need for its own independence from Yugoslavia, it refused to countenance similar demands from Krajina Serbs for their own independence from Croatia. Thus, one should not be surprised to see some variance in state practice. That variance must, however, be put in the context of a strong general refusal to recognize any secessionist entity that does not receive consent from its existing sovereign. Somaliland and the TRNC are clear examples of the power of collective non-recognition. So long as international practice remains united behind such a policy, the prospects for *de facto* states are bleak.

6 Weak State Security Dynamics

Our previous four sections have examined factors which prevent *de facto* states from graduating to sovereign statehood. These factors thus explain the existence of *de facto* states by reference to the figurative ceilings that serve to hold them down. In contrast, this section and the one that follows it both assess factors that inspire or motivate the attempt to seek sovereignty in the first place. The focus here is on a variety of phenomena grouped together under the rubric of 'weak state security dynamics'.

In this context, the term 'weak states' refers to states that are lacking in legitimacy and socio-political cohesion, not states that are lacking in power. A weak state may or may not be a weak power—despite their formidable military power, Nigeria and Pakistan can still be considered weak states due to their lack of domestic legitimacy and cohesion.[7] In Michael Mann's (1988) terminology, a weak state may or may not have high levels of despotic power. What it certainly lacks is a high level of infrastructural power (1988, pp. 5-8). Our comments here will be limited to four main areas: the location and types of security threats; the state-making process; the state-nation disjunction; and the changing nature of conflict.

In regard to our first main area, Barry Buzan argues that 'Security as a concept clearly requires a referent object, for without an answer to the question "The security of what?" the idea makes no sense' (1991b, p. 26). Thus, one can distinguish between such things as national security, state security, regime security, and individual security. Out of this larger insight come a number of more specific points. One of the most significant is that the various levels of individual, national, state, and regime security are not necessarily congruent. What the leadership of, say, the Sri Lankan government does to preserve its own existence may not contribute to individual, national, or state security. Similarly, Turkish Cypriot attempts at national self-determination do not necessarily further individual, state, or regime security. Another major insight here concerns the fact that the leadership of the state (i.e., the regime) and not the state itself may be the appropriate level of analysis in attempting to understand why certain decisions are taken. As Steven David puts it, understanding why political leaders make certain decisions 'requires an understanding of what is in the best interests of the leaders and not of what is in the best interests of the state' (1991, p. 243). A third insight concerns the location and etiology of security threats. While traditional international theory highlights the danger of external threats in an anarchic environment, the focus on weak state security shows that the primary threats to most contemporary states are internally-generated. Finally, in contrast to the Hobbesian notion of individuals banding together in states to ensure their own security, this analysis shows that, for many people, security threats from within their *own* state are the biggest threat to their existence. None of this has much to say about why *de facto* states emerge. It does, however, provide a general backdrop that can help put into context why so many groups fear their own governments and seek to protect themselves from its machinations. Similarly, it also helps to explain why so many governments respond so negatively to any challenges to their leadership of the state's entire territory.

In terms of the state-making process, while the western industrialized states of today are often held up as models of peaceful, consolidated, and well-developed nation-states, their formation was characterized by a vicious and highly-contested process of enforced centralization.[8] In a competitive international environment, would-be states in Europe effectively faced two choices: 1) become viable and effective entities, or 2) fail and be incorporated into other more viable jurisdictions. The weak states of today have been denied the second choice. Juridical sovereignty that props up manifestly unviable states thus prevents a more efficient consolidation of empirical statehood and contributes to the weak state's security problematic by forcing it to exist within arbitrarily drawn borders that often make no logical sense from any geographic, economic, ethnic, religious, or linguistic point of view. Many would-be European states failed,[9] but those which succeeded are now held up as models to which others should aspire. States in the post-1945 Third World have not been allowed to fail; perversely, this has prevented many of them from succeeding.

The negative effects of juridical sovereignty on empirical state viability are also compounded by the demonstration effect of industrialized states. These states set a standard of human rights, mass consumerism, and democratic participation that is difficult to match. As Mohammed Ayoob (1992) points out, the norms of juridical sovereignty and the demonstration effect of successful states work at cross-purposes. The first insists on the juridical existence of even the most unviable states, while the second demands standards of effective and humane performance from fragile and weak polities that cannot even maintain basic order. The interaction of these two factors 'thus exacerbates the security predicament of the Third World state by not permitting it to exit from the system of states and by enforcing on it standards of "civilized" behavior that it is unable to meet' (1992, p. 78).

The creation of strong, unified states requires a tremendous concentration of social control. For state-making to succeed, the center must overcome traditional loyalties to tribes, clans, and other sub-state or trans-state groups. Traditional centers of authority, though, will seek to maintain their prerogatives against encroaching state centralization. During the historical emergence of the European states, this concentration of social control (and the development of effective state institutions) was often achieved through war—as summarized in Charles Tilly's famous quote that 'war made the state, and the state made war' (1975a, p. 42). Although the recent historical record of countries such as Afghanistan, Angola, Cambodia, Mozambique, and Nicaragua certainly calls into question the efficacy of war as a means of successful state-building, the prospects for peaceful state-making are not great.

The difficulties of state-making and nation-state building are a major part of what K. J. Holsti (1995) calls the 'conundrum of weak states'. In effect, this is a sort of perpetual Catch-22 that these states must face. As Holsti puts it, 'Without a nation, a state is fundamentally weak. But in attempting to build strength, usually under the leadership of an ethnic core, minorities become threatened or excluded from power. This is the foundation of the "insecurity dilemma" of most new states' (1995, p. 30). In essence, the measures designed to create a strong state only end up perpetuating the state's weakness. In a similar vein, Yezid Sayigh (1990) notes how the reform of existing state structures can entail substantial risks for the government leadership. In his view, 'without reforms, some Third World governments may suffer loss of legitimacy, damaged social consensus and economic viability, but paradoxically the process of instituting fundamental change may be just as threatening in the short term to security and stability' (1990, p. 21). Facing extremely slim margins of error, it is not surprising that many weak state leaders frequently decide to forego long-term benefits to avoid the short-term costs of instability.

In regard to the subject matter of this study, the argument is not that the problems and process of state-making produce *de facto* states. Indeed, for an entity to be considered a *de facto* state, it must itself undergo some sort of state-making process as well, with all the difficulties and dangers that implies. Rather, the argument is that the strenuous requirements of the state-making process, particularly when combined with internationally-guaranteed juridical sovereignty, fixed territorial borders, and the demonstration effect of successful states produce an environment in which challenges to the existing sovereign state are likely to arise. Within that environment, a small number of those challengers evolve into what we are calling *de facto* states.

The third factor considered under the weak state security heading is what may be termed the state-nation disjunction. Contemporary international parlance has become quite sloppy in applying the term 'nation-state' indiscriminately to any sovereign state regardless of its ethnic composition. As Walker Connor notes, however, the term nation-state

> was designed to describe a territorial-political unit (a state) whose borders coincided or nearly coincided with the territorial distribution of a national group. More concisely, it described a situation in which a nation had its own state (1978, p. 382).

While the nation-state in this sense is held out to be the international ideal, in fact very few numbers of real nation-states exist. A study in the early 1980s by Gunnar P. Nielsson, for example, found that out of the 164 states examined, only 45 (27.4%) could be classified as single group nation-states. Even this, however, may be too generous. A 1971 survey of 132 states by Walker Connor found that only 12 (9.1%) could justifiably be described as nation-states.[10] Whether these or other figures are used, the larger point remains: the vast majority of the world's sovereign states are multi-national and the true nation-state is the exception, not the rule. Thus, it is surprising that it is the nation and not the territorial state which serves as the exemplar in international politics. Though his own usage of the term nation-state is inaccurate, the irony of this situation is nicely captured by Adeno Addis:

> Even though it is Yugoslavia rather than Iceland, India rather than Japan, Ethiopia rather than Djibouti, that typically represent the nature of the current nation state, it is surprisingly the latter of each of the pairs that has formed the basis for political theorization, both on the domestic and international level (1991, pp. 1226-1227).

The disjunction between state and nation(s) can take a variety of forms. A nation may be dispersed over the territory of more than one state (the Kurds) or may simply lack a state of its own (the Palestinians). A nation with its own state may still find some of its brethren residing as minorities in other neighboring states (Hungary, the Serbs). The state may contain a small number of conflicting nationalities within its boundaries (Cyprus, Sri Lanka) or it may contain multiple nationalities within its boundaries (Eritrea, Ethiopia, India, Nigeria, former Yugoslavia). Some states that are ethnically, linguistically, and religiously homogeneous may still be sharply divided in other ways (Somalia with its clan-based politics). Other states do not face the problem of strong national movements, yet are still weakened by the lack of a coherent national identity (Saudi Arabia).

Conflict between different groups within the same state is far from inevitable. Enlightened leadership and successful nation-state building are distinct possibilities. The connection between the various forms of state-nation disjunctions and conflict should not, however, be dismissed lightly. K. J. Holsti, for example, argues that 'The poor fit between state and nation... is the essential source of wars in the Third World and, more recently, in the residues of collapsed communism' (1995, p. 330). This position is supported by Ted Robert Gurr who found in one recent study that 'All but five of the twenty-three wars being fought in 1994 are based on communal rivalries and ethnic challenges to states' (1994, p. 350). Gurr believes that communal conflict has increased more or less steadily since the 1950s. For a variety of reasons including increased refugee flows, democratization, and the effects of the break-ups of the Soviet, Yugoslav, and Ethiopian states, he concludes that 'The upward trends are almost sure to continue during the 1990s and beyond...' (1993, p. 190).

The link between ethnic conflict and the *de facto* state is problematic for a number of reasons. First, not all *de facto* states are ethnically-based. Organizing under the state principle is a viable possibility as shown by the Eritrean and Somaliland examples. Somalia certainly shows that ethnic homogeneity is no guarantee against the creation of a *de facto* state. Conversely, the large number of multi-ethnic states which have failed to produce *de facto* state challengers show that: 1) multi-ethnic states need not degenerate into conflictual situations, and 2) even if they do, they will not necessarily produce *de facto* states. The argument again is not that state-nation disjunctions produce *de facto* states. Rather, it is that these disjunctions produce an environment which is characterized by frequent challenges to the legitimacy of rule of existing sovereign states. Within that environment, one or more of those challenges may evolve into a *de facto* state situation.

The final factor considered here is the changing nature of conflict. Perhaps most important in this regard is the pronounced shift away from traditional interstate conflict and toward intrastate civil wars. Interstate wars featuring the regular armies of two or more states are no longer common; indeed, they are the exception. Guerrilla wars and civil wars are now far more typical. Along these lines, K. J. Holsti finds in a study of 164 wars that have taken place since 1945 that almost 77 percent of them were internal wars while only about 18 percent were purely state versus state wars (1996, pp. 21-25). In terms of the issues that lead to war, Holsti maintains that 'More than one-half (52 percent) of the wars of the post-1945 period were manifestations of the state-creation enterprise' (1992, p. 311).

The near-absence of interstate conflict, the increasing prevalence of intrastate conflict, and the growing importance of the search for statehood as a cause of war are all part and parcel of the same post-World War II international environment that has produced the fixed territorial borders regime, state-based sovereignty, and the shift from empirical to juridical statehood. The changing nature of conflict in and of itself does not lead to *de facto* statehood. It does, however, produce an environment in which *de facto* statehood is one of the roads which relatively successful would-be state creators may find themselves traveling down.

7 Self-Determination

As entire separate books are written on self-determination, the aims of this section are necessarily more limited. Here we wish merely to assess self-determination from the perspective of non-sovereign challengers to the existing states system. In other words, the goal is to view this concept from the vantage point of those who wish to self-determine—whether or not the larger international society views them as eligible to exercise that right.

Though the idea of self-determination is closely associated with Woodrow Wilson, its intellectual roots go back to such things as the Hebrew exodus from Egypt, the Greek city-states, the American Declaration of Independence, the French Declaration of the Rights of Man and of the Citizen, and Napoleon III. V. I. Lenin also had much to do with the popularizing of the idea.[11] When viewed in abstract terms, the essence of this concept is actually quite simple. Dov Ronen (1979) refers to self-determination as 'an expression, in succinct form, of the aspiration to rule one's self and not to be ruled by others' while David Knight (1984) argues that it 'refers to the right of a group with a distinctive politico-territorial identity to determine its own destiny' (Ronen, 1979, p. 7; Knight, 1984, p. 168).

Woodrow Wilson's own thoughts on self-determination shifted over the years, but he appears to have come to an ethnically-based version of the concept in the belief that it would: 1) promote democratic government (self government = democratic government), thereby assuring a peaceful world through the democratic control of foreign policy decision-making, and 2) remove a number of contentious nationalist or minority problems from the European political agenda. Michla Pomerance (1976) argues that the Wilsonian vision of self-determination

> reveals a fusion and confusion of several ideas. Uniting the various disparate elements is a pervasive and genuine, if amorphous, belief in the democratic ideal as a desideratum worth attaining for its own sake and as a means to achieve the ultimate goal of universal peace (1976, p. 20).

She goes on to note that whether it is conceived in terms of one nation-one state, freedom to select one's own form of government (internal self-determination), a form of continuing self-government (democracy), or freedom from 'alien' sovereignty (external self-determination), the principle of self-determination initially presents itself 'as eminently just and worthy of implementation' (1976, p. 20).

The devil, of course, is in the details. The fundamental problem here being the question of who is the 'self' that is eligible to determine. Wilson's own Secretary of State Robert Lansing recognized the inherent difficulties in identifying a coherent self and argued that self-determination 'is simply loaded with dynamite'. He felt that without a definite and practical unit to which the concept would adhere, its application would be dangerous to peace and stability (Lansing, cited in Pomerance, 1976, p. 10). This problem was perhaps put most famously by Sir Ivor Jennings: 'On the surface it seemed reasonable: let the people decide. It was in fact ridiculous because the people cannot decide until someone decides who are the people' (Jennings, cited in Mayall, 1990, p. 41).

In spite of its potentially revolutionary impact, the principle of self-determination was incorporated into Articles 1 (2) and 55 of the UN Charter. The subsequent history of self-determination since 1945 essentially can be summarized in two parts: 1) the attempt to extend the principle to all colonies and thus facilitate their speedy independence; and 2) the attempt to delimit sharply the number of eligible 'selves' to just colonies and a few small exceptions so as to minimize its potential disruption. Article 2 of Resolution 1514, for example, specifies that 'All peoples have the right to self-determination...'. Article 6 of that same declaration, however, qualifies this right by stating that 'Any attempt aimed at the partial or total disruption of the national unity and the territorial integrity of a country is incompatible with the purposes and principles of the Charter of the United Nations'. As Rupert Emerson (1971) put it, 'what is stated in big print—as in the reiterated United Nations injunction: All peoples have the right to self-determination— is drastically modified by what follows in small print' (1971, p. 459).

The form of the 'small print' (Article 6 above) changed somewhat in 1970. In that year, the General Assembly passed Resolution 2625—the so-called Declaration on Friendly Relations. After reaffirming the right of all peoples to self-determination, Resolution 2625's safeguard clause appears in Article 7:

> Nothing in the foregoing paragraphs shall be construed as authorising or encouraging any action which would dismember or impair, totally or in part, the territorial integrity or political unity of sovereign and independent states conducting themselves in compliance with the principle of equal rights and self-determination of peoples as described above *and thus possessed of a government representing the whole people belonging to the territory without distinction as to race, creed or colour* (my italics).

In the post-1945 era, the 'selves' eligible for self-determination essentially came to comprise three main groups: former colonies or other similar non-self-governing territories; territories under military occupation; and territories where majority colored populations were victims of institutionalized *apartheid* at the hands of Europeans. The first category was defined quite narrowly so as to only include cases of 'salt-water' or 'blue-water' colonialism under the category of non-self-governing territories. General Assembly Resolution 1541 of 1960 essentially defined non-self-governing territories as those which were both 'geographically separate' and 'distinct ethnically and/or culturally from the country administering it'. This was an explicit rejection of an argument put forward by Belgium that disenfranchised groups which did not enjoy self-government could be found in all parts of the world and not just in colonial situations.[12] Ibos might find rule by Hausas to be just as 'alien' as rule by the British, but it was not salt-water colonialism and therefore not a problem remediable by a resort to self-determination. The second category essentially comprised the Palestinians and perhaps East Timor, Western Sahara, and the Baltic states before the collapse of the Soviet Union. The third category was also defined quite narrowly so as to exclude all forms of institutionalized racism or discrimination by one non-European group against another non-European group. While black South Africans and black Rhodesians were entitled to self-determination, black southern Sudanese and black Mauritanians who suffered from institutionalized discrimination at the hands of Arabs were not.[13]

The main point to be made, though, is that no matter how carefully they are crafted or how forcefully they are stated, the safeguard clauses and the attempts to constrict severely those eligible for self-determination simply do not get through to the supposedly non-eligible selves. While an international lawyer or a political scientist might see the safeguard clause in Article 6 of Resolution 1514 trumping the general statement made in Article 2 of that same resolution, a would-be secessionist does not. Similarly, in the 1970 Declaration on Friendly Relations, the academic community might correctly interpret Article 7 of that resolution as only implicating the two *apartheid* regimes of Rhodesia and South Africa, but other putative 'selves' do not see it that way. Most Tamils and Turkish Cypriots sincerely believe that they live in states that are not 'possessed of a government representing the whole people belonging to a territory without distinction as to race, creed or colour'. One can also point in vain to the tenuous position of self-determination in the UN Charter and argue that it is listed merely as a 'purpose' of the organization and not incorporated into Article 2 which lists the 'principles' in accordance with which the organization 'shall act'. Thus Yehuda Blum (1975) concludes that in contrast to sovereignty and all that flows from it, self-determination 'was not originally perceived as an *operative* principle of the Charter. It was regarded as a goal to be attained at some indeterminate date in the future; it was one of the *desiderata* of the Charter rather than a legal right that could be invoked as such'.[14] Blum is correct, but the relevant point for secessionists is that the principle of 'equal rights and self-determination of peoples' appears twice in the UN Charter.

In defense of the secessionists, it should be noted that their interpretation of self-determination is not just the whining of special interest groups or faulty thinking produced by selective amnesia. Rather, secession and decolonization are based on the same principle. Instead of focusing on the common logic that underlies both principles, the international community has chosen to focus on the geographic distinction between the two—i.e., saltwater decolonization versus territorially-contiguous secession. Yet, as Debra Valentine (1980) notes, 'the discriminatory treatment of a population living in a contiguous area is no more justified than the subjugation of a population living in a different part of the globe' (1980, p. 808). In view of the rational self-interest of all existing states in avoiding dismemberment, the utility of the distinction between secession and decolonization is apparent on the grounds of political expediency. As Lee Buchheit (1978) points out,

> One searches in vain, however, for any principled justification of why a colonial people wishing to cast off the domination of its governors has every moral and legal right to do so, but a manifestly distinguishable minority which happens to find itself, pursuant to a paragraph in some medieval territorial settlement or through a fiat of the cartographers, annexed to an independent State must forever remain without the scope of the principle of self-determination (1978, p. 17).

The secessionists' view of self-determination is thus more intellectually consistent and arguably less hypocritical than the international community's view.

In attempting to understand the secessionists' viewpoint, it is helpful to envision self-determination, like sovereignty, as a socially constructed concept which has changed over the years. Self-determination has evolved in at least three ways: 1) in the extent of its application; 2) on what basis the 'self' is defined; and 3) in the inconsistent manner in which it has been put into practice. In all three of these areas, the secessionist's belief is that self-determination has evolved in the past and that it may evolve again in the future. In particular, it may evolve in such a manner as to benefit their own particular claims.

First, in terms of the extent of its application, Wilsonian self-determination after World War I was presented in universal terms but applied only to the territories of the defeated European powers in that war. It was not applied to the victorious allies or to their overseas colonies. The post-1945 version of self-determination was again presented in universal terms but applied only to cases of salt-water colonization. Though it is far from self-evident, one could argue that the inclusion of self-determination in the two 1966 International Covenants on Civil and Political Rights and on Economic, Social and Cultural Rights, as well as its inclusion in the 1970 Declaration on Friendly Relations, also advances its application beyond the colonial context. As the secessionist sees it, what is important is that self-determination has evolved from being of merely regional application to being of nearly global application. The number of people covered by the principle has also expanded over time. Therefore, secessionists keep trying in the hope that the scope of application will evolve again in a manner favorable to their own cause.

Second, the basis on which the 'self' is determined has also shifted dramatically over time. In the Wilsonian conception, the 'self' was the historical or ethnic nation, defined in terms of its people and their ethnic, religious, linguistic, and/or cultural affiliation to one another. In the post-1945 conception, the 'self' became the ex-colonial territorial jurisdiction, regardless of whatever disparate or incongruous mix of peoples it contained within it. Whereas it was people who drove the earlier conception, it is now territory that drives the contemporary conception.[15] Thus Robert Jackson concludes that 'Self-determination no longer means the same as previously and almost means the opposite' (1990, p. 77). Again, from the point of view of the secessionist, if self-determination could evolve from being based on people to being based on territory there is no reason to assume it can not evolve back again to a more popular conception. Indeed, David Knight (1985) argues that 'What we are seeing today... is pressure to return to a people over territory ranking' (1985, p. 269).[16]

Third, would-be secessionists derive much comfort from the totally inconsistent manner in which self-determination has been applied. In the contemporary era, the supposedly sacrosanct principle of territorial integrity has been disregarded on a number of occasions. Thus, Ruanda-Urundi emerged from its exercise of self-determination as the two separate countries of Rwanda and Burundi. Similarly, British India was partitioned into India and Pakistan. The Gilbert and Ellice Islands, a single colony, were granted independence separately: the Gilberts as Kiribati and the Ellice Islands as Tuvalu. The UN acceded to the division of the British Cameroons into north and south for the purposes of holding a referendum. The north decided to join Nigeria while the south became the state of Cameroon. In each case, a partition that redefined the 'selves' was accepted by the international community. Another set of exceptions concerns the number of colonies and possessions which were either annexed or forcibly incorporated into neighboring states. Ifni was incorporated into Morocco and India annexed Hyderabad, Sikkim, Goa, and part of Kashmir. In no case were the wishes of the local population ascertained in any meaningful way. Similarly, the people of West Irian and East Timor were incorporated into Indonesia—in the case of the East Timorese with much bloodshed and against the expressed wishes of the local population. The people of the former Spanish Western Sahara are still waiting for their wishes to be ascertained (Pomerance, 1984, pp. 322-327; Hannum, 1990, pp. 36-37; Knight, 1984, p. 175). As Yehuda

Blum puts it, 'even if one recoils from using strong expressions, it is difficult to refrain from noting that what stands out here is the utter insincerity with which the principle of self-determination has been manipulated by the international community to suit changing political needs' (1975, p. 514).

Secessionists also note that while Biafra and Katanga failed in their attempts to win independence, Bangladesh and Eritrea ultimately succeeded in theirs. It is certainly not lost on the Turkish Cypriots that the Bangladeshis' independence came only with the backing of a massive military intervention from India. Thus, inconsistent international practice affords hope that one's own situation might benefit someday from such fluctuating treatment.

Once again, the argument in terms of this study is not that self-determination produces *de facto* states. Rather, it is that self-determination shines like a beacon in the night and attracts adherents from would-be selves around the world. In doing so, it spurs challenges to existing states that, in some cases, may eventually produce *de facto* states. While most of the other factors considered in this chapter are in effect ceilings that serve to hold the *de facto* state down, the principle of self-determination is arguably the leading spark that spurs would-be secessionists on in their quest for sovereignty. In the words of Ralph Premdas (1990),

> Without a recognised and widely accepted doctrine of self-determination, few secessionist movements would arise. It is the availability of this doctrine and its enshrinement in the international moral order that has facilitated, if not created, many separatist movements (1990, pp. 15-16).

8 Conclusion

This chapter has assessed a number of systemic or macro-level factors that influence the creation and/or continued presence of *de facto* states in the international system. While these factors have been broken down and addressed in six separate sections, many of them are interrelated. Thus, they should not be considered as stand-alone explanations, but rather as component parts of an integrated whole.

For two main reasons the analysis presented in this chapter constitutes only a partial assessment of the factors responsible for *de facto* statehood. First, this chapter focuses on the macro-level of explanation. Thus, it is concerned with the *de facto* state phenomenon as a whole, not with any specific examples of it. As such, it needs to be considered in conjunction with chapter six which assesses the more micro-level reasons individual *de facto* states emerge. Second, the analysis and explanation offered here is at a certain degree of abstraction. The six features considered here are intended to act as constraints on the creation of *de facto* states in the sense that they are designed to discourage would-be 'selves' from ever attempting to 'determine' in the first place. Their purpose is to discourage attempts at secession by indicating that the chances of attaining sovereign statehood are next to nil. Yet, this message never fully gets across to those dissatisfied groups that seek to exercise their right to self-determination. Thus, in some ways, these six features unintentionally contribute to an environment where the emergence and continued existence of *de facto* states is possible. This is because they do not succeed in stopping the attempts at secession, yet they generally serve to prevent such attempts from succeeding juridically. They might thus be considered permissive or enabling conditions, perhaps even necessary conditions for the creation and maintenance of *de facto* states in the international system. They are certainly not sufficient conditions, though, and these factors do not, individually or collectively, actually produce *de facto* states. No evidence of direct causality in the form of 'if fixed territorial borders, then *de facto* states' has been presented here.

The six factors considered here are all part of a new normative framework that has characterized post-1945 international relations. The strong international consensus that has emerged around such things as fixed territorial borders, juridical statehood, state-based sovereignty, and extremely limited eligibility for self-determination marks a fundamental shift in international relations. The *de facto* state can be seen as one of the unintended by-products of this new normative framework. While groups maintaining effective *de facto* control of a given territorial area have probably always existed, the *de facto* state as such is a product of the postwar decolonization era.

The question then becomes what, if any, impact has the post-Cold War period had on this larger normative framework. For if that period has ruptured the consensus on fixed territorial borders or led to a shift back to nation-based sovereignty, then we should expect the prospects for new or continued *de facto* states to change as well. It appears, though, that the post-Cold War changes may not be quite as dramatic as originally feared or hoped, depending upon one's perspective. First, there has not been an explosion of ethnopolitical conflict in the post-Cold War era. Ted Robert Gurr (1994) finds the increase in ethnopolitical conflict since the late 1980s to be a continuation of a trend that first became evident in the 1960s. The breaking-up of the Soviet bloc nudged the trend upward, but did not create it. Similarly, there has not been any global explosion of secessionist demands in the post-Cold War era—in spite of the Czechoslovak, Ethiopian, Soviet, and Yugoslav state dissolutions, the dreaded Pandora's Box of never-ending secessionist attempts remains unopened. As Gurr argues,

> tendencies toward ethnic fragmentation have characterized world politics since the 1960s and have long been evident to observers who were not preoccupied by Cold War issues.... Serious new conflicts generated by aspirations for independence and autonomy have thus far been confined almost entirely to the Soviet and Yugoslav successor states (1994, pp. 363-364).

Along these lines, Milica Zarkovic Bookman points out that 'Instead of asking why there are so many secessionist movements in the 1990s, it may be more appropriate to ask why there are so few' (1992, p. 17).

Second, in terms of state practice, while a number of observers such as Alexis Heraclides and Ronald McMullin detect a slight weakening in the international community's innate hostility to secession,[17] none argues that secession has achieved widespread acceptance in the society of states. Whatever initial enthusiasm there may once have been for a looser secession regime has been dampened by the events in former Yugoslavia. Lawrence Eastwood concludes that despite some evidence of a shift in recent state practice toward secessionist movements, 'the establishment of a right of secession as an accepted norm under customary international law is not imminent' (1993, p. 348).

Third, the creation of more than twenty new states since 1989 certainly did open the question of territorial revisionism in a way in which it had not been aired in at least the past forty years. Still, one would be hard-pressed to argue that there has been any fundamental shift in the international consensus on the desirability of fixed territorial borders. The international community still refuses to accept the reality of the Turkish Cypriot state and it continues to maintain the fiction that Somalia actually exists.

Finally, in terms of sovereignty and self-determination, a number of observers detect some shift in the direction of an increasingly national-based legitimacy. Ole Wæver (1992), for example, maintains that we are

> in a period of transition, where the very strict state and stability-oriented interpretation of national self-determination prevailing since 1945 has started to give way to more *national* (or popular) self-determination; only partly,

146 International Society and the De Facto State

but enough to make the situation unclear and open (1992, pp. 122-123, italics in original).

He goes on to emphasize the tentative nature of this shift by arguing that the Soviet, Yugoslav, and Kurdish examples 'have placed question marks in the system, but hardly exclamation marks' (1992, p. 123). There is a huge difference between halting and tentative moves in the general direction of greater national legitimacy and a wholesale abandonment of the sovereign state as the fundamental basis of international relations. The post-Cold War period does not offer any evidence of movement in the latter direction.

In the post-Cold War era, one can detect a slight lessening of the instinctive hostility toward secession and a greater willingness to consider matters such as the prospects for territorial revisionism which were once kept firmly off the international agenda. The recent experiences of Somaliland and the TRNC, though, show that the international environment for the *de facto* state has by no means changed beyond recognition. More substantive change can not be ruled out, but for the moment the factors identified in this chapter as producing an environment conducive to the formation and maintenance of *de facto* states appear likely to persist.

Chapter six continues our look at the factors responsible for the *de facto* state in international relations. In contrast to this chapter's focus on the systemic or macro-level, chapter six addresses more specific or micro-level concerns and offers an assessment of the various ways in which specific *de facto* states are created. Examples from our four case studies and from other cases will be analyzed here. This chapter also seeks to evaluate possible sources of these entities in the future.

Notes

[1] Mayall, 1990, pp. 18-25. The specific quote is from p. 25.
[2] On the strength of this consensus, compare Buchheit, 1978, p. 105; Heraclides, 1992, p. 407; Jackson, 1990, p. 190; and Mayall, 1990, p. 123.
[3] Mayall, 1990, p. 56. See also Knight, 1983, pp. 129-130; and Ronen, 1979, pp. 114-115.
[4] Young, 1983, p. 229. See also Jackson and James, 1993, p. 23.
[5] Wight, 1977, p. 153, italics in original. See also Jackson, 1986, pp. 247-248.
[6] See the various discussions in Ijalaye, 1971, pp. 557-559; Reisman and Suzuki, 1976, p. 413; Wallace-Bruce, 1985, p. 594; Necatigil, 1989, p. 272; and Crawford, 1976-77, pp. 100-107.

[7] The distinction between weak states and weak powers is set out clearly in Buzan, 1991b, pp. 97-98.

[8] The classic statements here come from Charles Tilly. See Tilly, 1975a, and Tilly, 1975b.

[9] Cohen, Brown, and Organski argue that 'by 1900 there were around 20 times fewer independent polities in Europe than there had been in 1500'. See Cohen, Brown, and Organski, 1981, p. 902.

[10] The Nielsson data is cited in Ryan, 1988, pp. 161-162. The Connor data is from Connor, 1972, p. 320.

[11] See Friedlander, 1980, pp. 309-310; Pomerance, 1976, pp. 1-2; and Franck, 1992, p. 53 for more on this history.

[12] For more on salt-water colonialism, see Thornberry, 1989, pp. 873-875; Halperin and Scheffer with Small, 1992, p. 22; and Wight, 1977, p. 171.

[13] For more on this, see Vincent, 1984, pp. 252-253; Jackson, 1986, pp. 251-252; and Emerson, 1971, p. 467.

[14] Blum, 1975, p. 511. Similar points are also made in Pomerance, 1984, p. 316; and H. A. Wilson, 1988, p. 60.

[15] For more on this, see Valentine, 1980, pp. 804-805; Emerson, 1971, pp. 463-464; and Knight, 1985, p. 252.

[16] An explicit argument that international society should move decisively in the direction of a people over territory ranking here is made in Hannum, 1998. A counter-argument against this position can be found in Etzioni, 1992-93.

[17] See Heraclides, 1992, p. 399; and McMullin, 1992, pp. 113-115.

6 Micro-Level Factors Implicated in the Birth of *De Facto* States

1 Introduction

This chapter continues our look at the various factors responsible for the emergence and continued existence of *de facto* states in the contemporary international system. Whereas chapter five focused on the systemic or macro-level factors which contributed to this phenomenon as a whole, this chapter shifts our attention toward the micro-level factors that are responsible for the emergence of individual *de facto* states. The chapter begins with a brief discussion of the different etiologies characteristic of quasi-states and *de facto* states. It then considers seven factors that either have been or, in some cases, may potentially be implicated in the birth of *de facto* states. These seven factors are foreign invasions; external political involvement; external humanitarian involvement; indigenous secession attempts; state collapse; the role of UN peacekeepers in separating warring parties; and the demonstration effect of already-existing *de facto* states. As was the case with the macro-level factors analyzed in chapter five, these seven factors should not be seen as rigidly separate or distinct. They are often interrelated and a number of them may appear together in the same situation. The Republic of Somaliland, for example, can be seen as the product of both an indigenous secession attempt and a collapsed state. Northern Cyprus has featured foreign invasions, external political involvement, and the presence of an interpositionary UN peacekeeping force for more than thirty years. The final section of this chapter summarizes our findings and looks forward to chapter seven.

2 The Different Etiologies of Quasi-States and *De Facto* States

Statehood and international personality used to be contingent upon the demonstration of certain empirical capabilities, particularly effective governance. The *de facto* state is in many ways an anachronistic entity trying

148

to follow this classical (and now outdated) pattern. It seeks to secure and maintain effective territorial control over a given area and population. Within this territory, the leadership goes about constructing institutions that will enable it to provide some sort of governmental services to the population in question, thereby securing their loyalty and garnering popular support for this state-creation enterprise. Over time it is hoped that the *de facto* state's proven empirical capabilities and its solid base of popular support will earn for it widespread international recognition. The etiology of the *de facto* state is thus: 1) the construction of effective state institutions which demonstrate empirical capabilities and, hopefully, 2) lead to subsequent juridical recognition and acceptance of those capabilities.

This stands in sharp contrast to the etiology of the quasi-state. As mandated by General Assembly Resolution 1514, the granting of juridical statehood is now no longer contingent upon any prior demonstration of empirical capabilities. The etiology of the quasi-state is thus: 1) a normative grant of juridical statehood from international society, which 2) is not contingent on either previously-demonstrated or subsequently-developed empirical capabilities. We now examine the various factors which may be responsible for the emergence of specific *de facto* states.

3 Foreign Invasions

While the Serbian Republic of Krajina in Croatia is the most recent example, it is the Turkish Republic of Northern Cyprus which provides the classic example of a *de facto* state being established in the aftermath of a foreign invasion by one sovereign state against the territory of another. As chapter four pointed out, the roots of Turkish Cypriot *de facto* territorial control and effective political organization certainly go back further than 1974. Thus, to allege that the Northern Cypriot *de facto* state is solely the product of a foreign invasion would be historically myopic. That said, however, it is the foreign invasions alone which provided the Turkish Cypriots with the territorial base necessary for the creation and subsequent fuller development of their *de facto* state. Had those invasions never taken place one could easily have envisioned the assorted Turkish Cypriot enclaves furthering their development and consolidating themselves into a handful of isolated mini- or proto-*de facto* states. It would, however, be difficult to imagine them evolving into such a sophisticated, secure, and functionally-differentiated entity as the TRNC in the absence of those invasions.

While the TRNC and the Serbian Republic of Krajina are perhaps the only 'pure' or 'classic' cases where the emergence of a *de facto* state has been facilitated by a foreign invasion, there are two other cases also worthy of consideration here. The first concerns the role of the Indian army in the establishment of an independent Bangladesh in 1971. This is a case much beloved by the Turkish Cypriots, for they believe it clearly shows that massive foreign military assistance need not preclude a state's legality of origin. Contrary to the presumption of puppet statehood that supposedly comes with foreign military interventions, Bangladesh has received widespread international acceptance of its sovereign statehood—in spite of the fact that its establishment was clearly dependent upon massive military assistance from India.

How does one explain this supposed anomaly? One broad school of thought focuses on the 'special circumstances' of the Bangladeshi case. Ved P. Nanda (1972), for example, emphasizes such factors as Bangladesh's geographic separation from the rest of Pakistan; its linguistic, ethnic, and cultural differences from the rest of the country; the economic disparities between the two halves of the country; the Awami League's overwhelming electoral mandate for East Pakistani autonomy; and the excessive brutality of the Pakistani response to this secession attempt as being decisive in explaining Bangladesh's recognition (1972, pp. 328-334). James Crawford also points out that East Pakistan did, in 1971, meet the criteria set out for non-self-governing territories in General Assembly Resolution 1541 (1960) in terms of it being both geographically separate and ethnically distinct from the 'country administering it'. It might therefore be considered eligible to exercise the right to self-determination (1976-77, pp. 171-172). The second broad school of thought rejects the 'special circumstances' explanations and instead emphasizes the fact that India's military intervention created a *fait accompli* which Pakistan and the rest of the world could not ignore. Along these lines, Robert Friedlander (1980) argues that 'It was not the "right" of a national self-determination which triumphed in East Pakistan but Indian military might. Bangladesh succeeded where Biafra failed because it had the strong support of an effective political ally' (1980, p. 318). Clearly, the international community prefers the special circumstances explanation as it helps to minimize the precedent set by the Bangladeshi example. Whichever explanation is accepted, though, Bangladesh's ultimate success still affords hope to the Turkish Cypriots.

The second case worthy of consideration is the possible *de facto* state example found in the Trans-Dniester (or Transdniestria) region of Moldova.

This is not technically a foreign invasion because the 6,000-some Russian troops which have helped prop up the Trans-Dniester 'republic' under the leadership of Igor Smirnov were originally sent to Moldova when it was still a part of the Soviet Union and hence an internal region of the same country. That said, however, there can be no doubt that the republic of Trans-Dniester has been substantially dependent upon the support of those now foreign troops of the 14th Russian Army. Trans-Dniester may not meet all of the criteria established for *de facto* statehood in chapter two and the Russian troops there did not technically invade the country. Still, this case does illustrate the potential role foreign troops may play in supporting a secessionist bid.[1]

The role of foreign invasions in the creation of *de facto* states is problematic for three reasons. First, to be considered a *de facto* state, an entity must demonstrate some degree of indigenous capability and it must secure popular support. The Turkish Cypriot example shows that these two things are not necessarily incompatible with the presence of foreign troops, but the burden of proof here is clearly on the would-be *de facto* state to show that it is not an artificial puppet state imposed from outside against the expressed wishes of the local population. Second, due to the strictures of Article 2 (4) of the UN Charter and the general presumption of puppet statehood that comes along with any foreign military presence, this sort of assistance is likely to be a double-edged sword for the *de facto* state. While foreign troops may initially be quite effective in establishing the territorial base needed for *de facto* statehood, their long-run impact is likely to be substantially negative on the entity's bid for international acceptance. As Ronald McMullen notes, 'secessionists must strike a delicate balance between ties to external backers and international perceptions of the movement's internal viability' (1992, p. 117). Third, there are really only two pure examples of this phenomenon in relation to *de facto* statehood— Krajina and Northern Cyprus. As such, the soundness of the conclusions that can be drawn from such a limited sample necessarily remains limited.

4 External Political Interest in Creating a *De Facto* State

The 'external political interest' referred to in this section is every form of external support to the secessionist that falls short of actually committing one's own troops to come to their aid. This can take a broad variety of forms ranging from quiet diplomatic support to the provision of training facilities to direct financial and materiel assistance. Examples of such support can be found in each of our four case studies. They include Turkey 'holding the diplomatic ring' for the TRNC at the UN; India providing the assorted Tamil militant groups with sanctuary and training facilities in Tamil Nadu; Ethiopia allowing the SNM to set up rear base areas on its territory; and the various forms of financial and materiel assistance provided to the Eritreans by the Gulf states. In spite of the general stricture against intervention, other research suggests that the provision of such assistance is by no means unique to our four case studies. In a study of seven post-1945 secessionist movements (only one of which, Eritrea, is considered here), Alexis Heraclides found that 'no fewer than seventy-two states (roughly half of the states at the time) became involved or showed some interest. And if a margin of error due to the inability to glean every act of assistance, particularly minor ones, is taken into account, the figure is even higher' (1992, p. 352).

External involvement in secessionist conflicts, though, is not necessarily beneficial to the secessionists. Incumbent governments will generally attract much more support than rebels ever will. As Hurst Hannum points out, 'Although intervention may occasionally greatly influence (or even determine) the outcome of struggles for autonomy, it has more frequently repressed than encouraged minority or secessionist movements' (1990, p. 456). The amount of external assistance received by the Eritreans, for example, paled in comparison to the at least US$ 12 billion in military assistance Ethiopia received from the Soviet Union. Similarly, though the sanctuary and training facilities provided to the LTTE in Tamil Nadu were no doubt beneficial, the Sri Lankan government annually receives hundreds of millions of dollars of foreign aid—aid which has, at times, accounted for some 40 percent of the total government budget (O'Ballance, 1989, p. 92). Even the Northern Cypriot *de facto* state, an entity that is far more dependent on external assistance than any of our other case studies, receives strong competition here from the (Greek) Republic of Cyprus. In a 1979 article in *Maclean's*, Martin Woollacott argued that

> Greek Cyprus must rank as one of the most subsidized nations in the world. With a population of only half a million people, it receives something like $54 million annually in grant aid from the United States, Greece, the United Nations, Britain, Germany and other countries, as well as an average $12 million a year in soft loans.... Foreign aid and loans approach a fifth of all government revenues, and the over-all contribution to the economy, including military spending, may be of the same order.[2]

In addition to the fact that external assistance to secessionists is often dwarfed by the much larger flows of such assistance to the sovereign government, one must also keep in mind the fact that such aid is seldom of the magnitude that, say, India provided to Bangladesh or of the duration that Turkey has provided to Northern Cyprus (Cooper and Berdal, 1993, p. 135). Without other conditions present that make for a viable and popularly-supported indigenous secession movement, external assistance in and of itself is unlikely to lead to the creation of any *de facto* states. The role of external assistance, in other words, is much more likely to be facilitative than it is to be determinative. As Alexis Heraclides puts it, 'while support by external parties is one factor influencing the feasibility of a secessionist bid, it is not the sine qua non and is certainly not the crucial element that would "galvanize the masses" to become separatists' (1992, p. 376).

Our discussion thus far has been concerned with external assistance to secessionist movements as a whole. We must now ask is there any external political interest in specifically creating or maintaining *de facto* states? The evidence on this point is much more speculative than it is conclusive, but it does point to a number of interesting possibilities—three of which will be considered here. First, there may be an external interest in having a partially, though not ultimately, successful opponent with which to harass one's enemies. The *de facto* state, in the sense that it is a relatively successful and long-term serious challenger to the existing sovereign state, may be an ideal vehicle to support here. As long as it does not receive widespread international recognition, the *de facto* state can act as a continual parasite draining its host state. Though it probably did not meet our criteria for *de facto* statehood, one possible example here was the US and Iranian support for the Iraqi Kurdish opposition in the 1970s. According to a leaked Congressional document, rather than hoping for a complete Kurdish victory, the US 'preferred instead that the insurgents simply continue a level of hostilities sufficient to sap the resources of our ally's [Iran] neighboring country [Iraq]. This policy was not imparted to our clients [the Kurds]...'.[3]

Another potential example here concerns India's relations vis-à-vis the LTTE. A number of observers have suggested that India has used the Tamil insurgency for its own purposes and that it has an interest in maintaining the LTTE's position. A large segment of Sinhalese popular opinion also believes that the only reason the LTTE survived its war with the dramatically-superior forces of the IPKF is because India wanted them to. In other words, the LTTE's survival was not due to its own prowess or to Indian military incompetence but to deliberate Indian strategic calculations. Along these lines, Shelton Kodikara (1990b) maintains 'that the IPKF was in no mood to... eradicate the Tamil Tiger insurgency from Sri Lanka'. In large part, this decision was 'connected with India's realisation that a military solution of Sri Lanka's ethnic crisis under the aegis of the Indian army... would deprive it of its most potent weapon to pressure Sri Lanka into India's own regional security orbit'.[4] Marshall Singer (1992), on the other hand, believes the idea that India wishes to maintain the LTTE's position so as to perpetuate Sri Lanka's ethnic conflict and destabilize its government 'is conspiracy theory, and there is a better reason to believe that the Indians see their best interests served by having a peaceful Sri Lanka as their southern neighbor' (1992, p. 717). It is not claimed here that either the Tamil or the Kurdish case argues convincingly for an external political interest in creating *de facto* states. They do, however, highlight one way in which such an external interest might be seen to exist.

A second possible external political interest in creating or maintaining a *de facto* state may be to neutralize irredentist sentiment. In this regard, Donald Horowitz (1991) argues that above and beyond all of its other reasons for intervening, the main reason India got involved in East Pakistan in 1971 was to neutralize 'incipient claims in West Bengal for the unification of all Bengalis, east and west'. Such a unification would have had two undesirable consequences for India: first, it would have permanently altered the country's Hindu-Muslim balance and, second, it would have forced India to assume the burden of supporting one of the world's poorest and most densely-populated regions. As such, for the Indian state leadership, 'An independent Bangladesh was far preferable to a growing demand for a Bengali irredenta...' (1991, pp. 19-20). Horowitz believes that the same logic can be used to explain Turkish actions in Northern Cyprus. In his view, there are a number of similarities between Northern Cyprus and Bangladesh, 'especially the external invasion from a state that, had it not helped to set up an autonomous Turkish state on Cyprus, might have come under pressure to annex the Turkish areas of the island' (1991, footnote # 16, p. 22). The evidence here is again more potentially illustrative than conclusive, but we can see a second specific external interest in establishing a *de facto* state: it may be easier and cheaper to deal indirectly with a neighboring *de facto* state than to deal directly with the pressures for irredentism.

The third specific area where there may be some external interest in utilizing *de facto* states is in regard to conflict resolution. Northern Cyprus is again the most relevant example here. However unjust its creation may have been, the establishment of the Turkish Cypriot *de facto* state did, more or less, remove a contentious issue from the international agenda. The creation of this entity transformed a volatile situation into one where a mostly stable peace (however noxious its foundation) has prevailed. Along these lines, François Lafrenière and Robert Mitchell (1990) point out that a general consensus exists

> that the superpowers -- as well as NATO and the EC -- had directed interest in Cyprus largely towards management of the problem rather than its resolution. Cyprus was not regarded as a major issue but rather as a situation under control. The practical concern... was, therefore, to see that it remained low profile... (1990, pp. 48-49).

None of this is to argue that any country consciously sought a *de facto* state solution to the communal violence in Cyprus or that the Republic of Somaliland is seen as the international community's preferred solution to the domestic chaos of Somalia. It is, however, to argue that the establishment of *de facto* states may provide certain benefits to external parties and that those parties thus have some interest in the existence of these entities. Chapter seven will examine this issue at greater length.

5 External Humanitarian Interest in Creating a *De Facto* State

The 'external humanitarian interest' referred to in this section essentially refers to the prospect of a humanitarian intervention leading to the creation of a *de facto* state. To date, there has not been a single case of a *de facto* state being created from such an intervention. Indeed, even the future prospects for this happening are not great. Therefore, this section should be viewed as a speculative look at what *might* happen rather than as an examination of what has already happened.

The whole concept of an external humanitarian interest being involved in the birth of one of these entities is problematic to our understanding of *de facto* statehood. Theoretical criterion number eight in chapter two specifically distinguishes the *de facto* state from other non-sovereign or questionable/disputed sovereign entities which have a much higher degree of international legitimacy. The underlying rationale behind this criterion is that international society clearly treats entities such as the Palestinian Authority or the Kurdish safe havens differently than it treats *de facto* states like the TRNC or Tamil Eelam. Whatever question marks or disputes revolve around the former pair of entities, they have a higher juridical and moral standing in international society than do the latter two entities. The argument here is thus not that the Kurdish safe haven is or is destined to become a *de facto* state. Rather, the argument is that something like the Kurdish safe haven or the UN-authorized French 'safe zone' established in southwestern Rwanda in the summer of 1994 could perhaps evolve into a *de facto* state situation.[5]

In spite of the recent scholarly and media attention lavished on the concept of humanitarian intervention, the prospects that it will facilitate the creation of more *de facto* states are quite remote. There are two main reasons for this. The first concerns the general limits to what humanitarian intervention is designed to do. As Simon Duke argues, 'Humanitarian intervention is not designed to secure the overthrow of a state or the establishment of democratic regimes...; it is primarily concerned with the protection and upholding of human rights within an *existing* state' (1994, p. 29). The limited aims of humanitarian intervention are often matched by correspondingly limited resources. In essence, it can often be seen as a sort of last-minute, band-aid solution to complicated and deep-seated problems. The need to be seen to be doing something in the face of massive televised human suffering often overrides any principled or long-term concern for the welfare of the targeted group. As such, most real or claimed humanitarian interventions are of an extremely short duration—lasting for only a few months and leaving nothing of substance behind when they exit. The multi-year commitment to the Kurdish safe havens (which may or may not be considered a genuine humanitarian intervention) is an exception. Even here, though, very little has taken place that would facilitate the future creation of a *de facto* state.

Even more important as a limiting factor is our second reason—the extremely limited standing of humanitarian intervention in the international society of sovereign states. Notwithstanding recent UN interventions in Iraq and Somalia, the fact remains that there is very little support for humanitarian intervention in international law or in state practice. Though it was written more than twenty years ago, Thomas Franck and Nigel Rodley's (1973) conclusion remains valid today:

> Neither the historic nor the contemporary practice of nations in the least sustains the proposition that there is a general right or conventional practice on the part of a state to use military force to intervene for genuinely humanitarian purposes. Similarly, none of the resolutions, declarations, or conventions on human rights in any way purports to extend this right (1973, p. 299).

Even taking into account the post-Cold War era, it is not sustainable to argue that either custom or treaty recognizes a right to humanitarian intervention in international law. In regard to state practice, Jack Donnelly (1984) notes that 'Most major post-war instances of genocidal violations of human rights have met with inaction, for reasons ranging from "security interests" to simple lack of interest'.[6] Examples here include the non-responses to such things as the systematic killings of indigenous people in Guatemala, genocide in East Timor, India's repression of the Kashmiri and Naga populations, the various atrocities committed against Hutus and Tutsis in Burundi and Rwanda, and the decades-long violence against the southern Sudanese. As Donnelly argues, 'a single case of action every decade or two, in the face of literally dozens of instances of inaction, in no way establishes humanitarian intervention as state practice' (1984, p. 317). International society's condemnation of Tanzania's actions against Idi Amin in Uganda and Vietnam's invasion to depose Pol Pot's genocidal regime in Cambodia are also telling here.

In spite of the limited and tenuous position of humanitarian intervention, domestic human rights violations are now a legitimate topic of concern in international society. In John Vincent's (1990) phrasing,

> The absence of a well-established doctrine of humanitarian intervention does not evaporate international concern, and now each state is quite legitimately exposed to the scrutiny and criticism of the international community on the relationship between government and governed within it (1990, p. 255).

Though they do not share equal status with sovereign states, individuals and non-state groups have put themselves and their issues onto the international agenda. Additionally, through their willingness to sign human rights treaties and proclamations, states themselves have facilitated the growth of international human rights law in a process that Dorothy Jones refers to as 'the declaratory tradition in modern international law' (1992, pp. 42-61). In spite of these developments, however, no general license for intervention in defense of human rights has been issued. As Vincent points out, though, the fact that the internal regimes of sovereign states have now been opened to legitimate scrutiny by their peers 'may turn out not to have been a negligible change in international society' (1986, p. 152). It is for this reason that we consider the possibility of an external humanitarian interest in creating a *de facto* state—even though the present prospects of this happening appear so distinctly remote.

6 Indigenous Secession Attempts

Of all the factors considered here, indigenous secession attempts are clearly the one most frequently implicated in the creation and formation of *de facto* states. As there probably is no such thing as a purely indigenous secession movement which receives no external support of any kind, what we are referring to in this section are secessionist movements that are substantially self-reliant and not dependent upon external sources for their very survival. Eritrea is arguably the classic example of this in regards to *de facto* statehood. Other examples might include Chechnya, Somaliland, and Tamil Eelam.

In considering what qualifies as an indigenous secession movement it is helpful to examine one aspect of the distinction between secession and irredentism. That aspect is where the organizational impetus for each movement comes from. According to James Mayall, irredentist demands 'are mostly claims by what may loosely be called the national core, which already has its own independent government, to peripheral lands...' (1990, p. 59). As such, they may be used as diversions or as mobilization tools to secure support for unpopular governments of the already existing state. Secession, on the other hand, 'depends on group sentiment and loyalty — not just on a disputed title to land or a doctrine of prescriptive right. In the final analysis, it is a form of mass politics organised from below rather than imposed from above through propaganda and the apparatus of the state' (Mayall, 1990, p. 61). Thus, while the Somali irredentist claims were not contingent upon substantial popular support from ethnic Somalis living in the Ogaden, there could not have been an Eritrean secessionist movement without massive popular support from below.

The relative frequency of secessionist and irredentist movements is also interesting. As Donald Horowitz (1991) notes, secession and irredentism are both abundantly plausible possibilities in the contemporary states system. Yet, 'the two phenomena are by no means proportionately represented in relation to the possibility of their occurrence. In spite of predictions to the contrary, there have been remarkably few irredentas in the postcolonial states, but there have been a great many secessionist movements' (1991, p. 11). Horowitz advances a number of explanations for this state of affairs. From the perspective of external states, aiding secessionist movements is often preferred to aiding irredentist movements because this support can be easily reversed. Iran could cut off aid to the Iraqi Kurds in 1975 without fearing any domestic reprisals for this decision.

Somalia, however, would not have been able to cut off support to its irredentist ethnic brethren with the same ease. From the perspective of the dissatisfied group itself, secession is often seen as preferable to irredentism. Perhaps even more important here is the perspective of the dissatisfied group's political leadership. They often prefer being leaders of smaller, less viable entities to being mere supporting actors in larger states—i.e., Radovan Karadzic would rather be a bigger fish in the smaller Bosnian Serb pond than a smaller fish in the larger Serbian pond. The sum of all this, according to Horowitz, 'is a powerful structural bias against the incidence of irredentism'. As there is no reason to expect the constraints on irredentism to decline, 'secession is likely to remain by far the most common movement'.[7]

The preconditions for secession in terms of such things as state-nation disjunctions; corrupt, mismanaged, and brutally repressive governments; economic disparities within states; the availability of external assistance; motivated sub-state political leaderships; and the principle of national self-determination are certainly widespread in today's international society. Yet, in spite of this and Horowitz's observations above, secession is somewhat rarely resorted to in the contemporary states system. To take the case of Africa, what might be seen as striking is not the fact that secessionist movements have arisen in Biafra, Katanga, Eritrea, Somaliland, the Southern Sudan, and amongst the Oromo and other groups in Ethiopia. Rather, when one considers the large number of countries in Africa, their tremendous ethnic heterogeneity, and the prevalence of ineffective and repressive governments, what might be seen as striking is that secessionist movements have *only* erupted in those limited numbers of cases. As Allen Buchanan observes, 'in spite of the fact that both the potential number of secessionist movements is extremely high and the moral slogans for justifying them are readily available, there have been relatively few serious secessionist movements' (1991, p. 103).

A number of reasons can be advanced to explain this apparent paradox. First, many would-be secessionists are aware of international society's presumption against secession and in favor of less drastic solutions. In the American Declaration of Independence, for example, immediately preceding the 18 point indictment of the British government is the following sentence: 'Prudence indeed will dictate that governments long established should not be changed for light and transient causes'. A more contemporary manifestation of this sentiment comes from Morton Halperin, David Scheffer and Patricia Small (1992): 'Good faith efforts at accommodating self-determination claims within federal or other multiethnic structures should be supported before new states are created and international boundaries redrawn'.[8]   Second, secession frequently brings about a harsh and brutal response from the existing state government.   While a few enlightened governments may seek to negotiate peaceful solutions with dissatisfied groups, a large number choose instead to send in the tanks and heavy artillery.   The result, as Ralph Premdas puts it, is that 'a secessionist struggle is usually prolonged, punishing and prohibitively costly' (1990, p. 12). Third, the odds against a successful secession are quite long.   K. J. Holsti finds that since 1945, excluding the collapse of the Soviet Union, there have been only four peaceful secessions (Anguilla, Singapore, Mayotte, and the Slovak Republic) and four successful violent secessions (Bangladesh, Eritrea, Slovenia, and Croatia).[9]   In other words, Eritrea is the exception while Biafra and Katanga are the rule.

The tremendous empirical diversity so characteristic of secessionist movements makes generalizing about the phenomenon difficult. Secessionist movements have arisen in ethnically homogenous regions (Slovenia) and ethnically heterogeneous regions (Eritrea).   They are found in relatively prosperous areas (Biafra, Catalonia, northern Italy) and in relatively disadvantaged areas (Southern Sudan, Tamil Eelam)—sometimes even within the same country (Slovenia and Kosovo in Yugoslavia, Punjab and Kashmir in India).   Some secessions are widely supported (Eritrea) while others receive little popular support (Katanga). Secessionist movements also vary in terms of such things as the level of violence employed, the duration of the struggle, the type of state they are attempting to secede from, and the degree of external support they receive.[10]

From the standpoint of this study, the main point that needs to be made is that most secession attempts will not result in the creation of *de facto* states. Put another way, secession is a much broader phenomenon than *de facto* statehood is. There are two main reasons for this. First, a large number of secessionist movements such as those found in Catalonia, northern Italy, Québec, Scotland, and Wales are peaceful in nature. Criterion number seven in chapter two specifically distinguishes the *de facto* state from peaceful secession movements for a number of reasons, including the different logics they follow and the different level of challenges they face. Second, many of the violent secessionist movements never reach such an advanced level in terms of territory controlled, governing institutions, popular support, and the like so as to qualify as a *de facto* state. While the exact line of demarcation between what qualifies as a *de facto* state and what should be relegated to a lesser category such as terrorism or rebellion may be difficult to locate, it is clear that one can not speak of Baluchistan, Corsica, or Irian Jaya as *de facto* states in the same sense that one can speak of Chechnya, Somaliland, and Tamil Eelam as being these same entities. Those qualifications made, however, the fact remains that one of the best and most frequent routes to *de facto* statehood is through an indigenous secession attempt. In particular, *de facto* states result from secessions that are empirically successful on the ground yet juridical failures in international society.

7 State Collapse

The media and the academic community have both devoted much attention recently to the phenomenon of 'failed' or 'collapsed' states. While some failed states such as Afghanistan and Lebanon have been around for decades, the renewed focus on these entities owes much to the highly publicized post-Cold War UN peacekeeping efforts in Cambodia and Somalia. Of these two operations, the one in Cambodia was definitely the most ambitious. Yet, it was the Somalia operation which arguably brought the phenomenon of state collapse to a mass audience. In this section, we consider three elements of state collapse: its relation to secession; what exactly it entails; and what the likely prospects for the emergence of *de facto* states from conditions of state collapse are.

      Secession and state collapse are not the same thing and they are not necessarily coterminous phenomena. As Allen Buchanan points out, 'Conceptual clarity requires that we distinguish between withdrawal from an existing state, on the one hand, and the creation of a new state under conditions of anarchy, on the other. The term "secession" is better reserved for the former, not the latter' (1991, p. 22). In terms of their interrelationship, secession is clearly a much broader phenomenon than state collapse and one that does not require any kind of substantive state failure as a precondition for its appearance. Some cases of state collapse have featured secessionist movements (Somalia) while others have not (Afghanistan, Lebanon). The question as to whether or not a secession attempt in one area can bring about a collapse of the entire state apparatus is one that needs to be evaluated on an individual case-by-case basis. As Milica Zarkovic Bookman observes, 'there are numerous cases of ongoing secessionist attempts that have not shaken the political union at the center (such as in Indonesia), leading to the conclusion that secessions are neither a sufficient nor necessary condition for state unraveling' (1992, pp. 8-9).

What exactly is state collapse? According to I. William Zartman, it 'is a deeper phenomenon than mere rebellion, coup, or riot. It refers to a situation where the structure, authority (legitimate power), law, and political order have fallen apart and must be reconstituted in some form, old or new' (1995b, p. 1). State collapse is not a short-term phenomenon, but rather 'a long-term degenerative disease...' (Zartman, 1995b, p. 8). In a collapsed state, the most basic functions of the state are no longer performed. The state's decisionmaking apparatus is paralyzed. It has lost its hold over the population as a symbol of identity. It can no longer provide security for its territorial base. It has lost its legitimacy to govern as an authoritative political institution. The end result is that

> it no longer receives support from nor exercises control over its people, and it no longer is even the target of demands, because its people know that it is incapable of providing supplies. No longer functioning, with neither traditional nor charismatic nor institutional sources of legitimacy, it has lost the right to rule (Zartman, 1995b, p. 5).

The question then becomes what are the prospects for state collapse leading to the emergence of *de facto* states. As was the case with foreign invasions, the conclusions that can be drawn firmly here are limited due to the small number of cases. The Republic of Somaliland is the closest thing to a pure example here and even in this case the actual secession attempt preceded the final collapse of the Somali state rather than following on from it. However, if one accepts Zartman's view of state collapse as a long-term phenomenon and dates its beginnings from the start of the Siad Barre era in 1969, then a better case can be made for viewing Somaliland as an example of state collapse leading to the formation of a *de facto* state. Conceivably one could also include Chechnya, Trans-Dniester, Krajina, and/or the Bosnian Serb Republic as examples here if they are viewed as resulting from the collapse of the Soviet Union and Yugoslavia. This, however, is a bit of a stretch.

That said, the theoretical prospects for future *de facto* states emerging out of situations of state collapse appear mixed. Working against this possibility is the level of devastation and breakdown that usually accompanies state collapse. The substantive requirements for the *de facto* state in terms of such things as popular support, effective control of a given territorial area, and the provision of governance services are not easy to attain in any circumstances. That is why there will always be both more quasi-states and more secessionist movements than there will be *de facto* states. It may be especially difficult, however, to engage in the type of state-making process required here in conditions of general state collapse. As Zartman argues, as the collapsing state 'implodes, it saps the vital functions of society. State collapse involves the breakdown not only of the governmental superstructure but also that of the societal infrastructure' (1995b, p. 7). That breakdown of the societal infrastructure cannot be conducive to the creation of an organized and effective entity like the *de facto* state.

There are, however, a number of reasons for believing that *de facto* states can emerge from situations of state collapse. K. J. Holsti (1995), for example, argues that states fail or collapse when one or more of four characteristics prevail. Two of his four characteristics—external powers wielding effective authority within the territory of the state and communities warring against each other with the state unable to stop the violence—do not offer much in the way of circumstances conducive to the growth and development of *de facto* states. His other two characteristics do, however, provide a favorable environment for the creation of *de facto* states. The first of these is that 'There are one or more armed "mini-sovereigns" within the state'. These mini-sovereigns 'have effective rule-making capacity and are armed sufficiently to resist central authorities'. Holsti uses the examples of clan chiefs in Somalia and the Palestinian Liberation Organization (PLO) in Lebanon before 1982, but one can easily see how this scenario could produce a *de facto* state like Eritrea or Tamil Eelam. The other characteristic is that the 'state is incapable of providing minimal security for the ordinary tasks of life...'. The performance of these tasks then falls to outsiders such as UN peacekeepers or to 'local warlords' (1995, p. 333). Focusing on the latter part of this scenario, one can envision the emergence of *de facto* states should those local warlords develop sufficient governmental and administrative capability of their own, secure substantial popular support for their efforts, and begin actively seeking sovereignty as constitutional independence.

It is thus the inability of collapsing states to maintain law and order and to perform basic governmental functions that opens the door for other aspiring power-seekers. These would-be leaders emerge because, as Zartman puts it, the 'maimed pieces into which the contracting regime has cut society do not come back together under a common identity, working together, sharing resources'. As such, 'Organization, participation, security, and allocation fall into the hands of those who will fight for it...' (1995b, p. 8). Most of these aspirants will fall far short of the requirements for *de facto* statehood. A few, however, may reach that level. Thus, while our limited number of actual cases leads to a cautious overall assessment here, the possible emergence of future *de facto* states through state collapse is not something that can be dismissed lightly.

8 The Role of the UN in Freezing the Status Quo[11]

Since its initial application in the 1956 Suez crisis, the use of UN blue helmets as an interpositionary force to separate combatants has been a hallmark of the vast majority of peacekeeping operations undertaken. One reason for this is that the territorial separation of combatants has proven successful at a number of tasks including providing a face-saving means of withdrawal for the warring parties, minimizing conflict, and monitoring tense border areas. One unintended consequence of the use of UN peacekeepers in this regard, however, may be the creation or the maintenance of *de facto* states. The classic example here is Northern Cyprus, whose borders have been patrolled by UN peacekeepers since Turkey declared a second cease-fire on 16 August 1974. The Serbian Republic of Krajina and, to a lesser degree, the Bosnian Serb Republic are two other examples where the use of UN peacekeepers as an interpositionary force has had a major impact on the viability of the respective *de facto* states concerned.

As an organization of sovereign states, it is frequently noted that the UN can generally be counted on not to support any course of action designed to dismember one of its member states. Along these lines, one of the 'first principles' of UN peacekeeping has traditionally been that no such operations will take place without the consent of the sovereign government(s) on whose territory the blue helmets will be stationed. More emphatically, in the Congo, UN peacekeepers were explicitly used to preserve the sovereignty and territorial integrity of a member state and to eradicate the Katangan secessionist movement. In this regard, Rosalyn Higgins (1972) argues that 'In situations such as the Congo and Cyprus, it is inevitable that UN intervention will lessen the chances of success of rebelling minorities'. The reason for this is that the UN peacekeeping intervention 'freezes the possibility of change, and encourages the continuation of the *status quo*' (1972, p. 180). Higgins is correct in her argument if the 'success of rebelling minorities' is defined in terms of sovereignty as constitutional independence. Her point does not hold, however, if the lesser goal of *de facto* statehood will suffice as 'success' or if the continuation of the *status quo* is seen as positive by the secessionists.

There are two main reasons for this. First, one unintended consequence of territorially separating the warring parties may be the legitimization of advantages gained through aggression. Barry Posen (1993) points out here that UN peacekeepers generally do not make peace. Rather, they negotiate and preserve cease-fires. Because cease-fires favor the party that has had the most military success, UN peacekeeping 'protects, and to some extent legitimates, the military gains of the winning side...' (1993, pp. 33-34). Thus a cease-fire that preserves the current *status quo* may be quite favorable to a secessionist group that is satisfied with its present level of territorial control. In regards to Cyprus, Robert Cooper and Mats Berdal maintain that 'by freezing a particular *status quo*, UNFICYP has favored one side — in this case, the Turkish Cypriots who have shown a consistent preference for a divided Cyprus' (1993, p. 122). Obviously, UNFICYP must provide a number of specific benefits to the Greek Cypriot side or their government would not so consistently support extending its mandate. The point is, though, that the specific *status quo* that UNFICYP has helped to freeze is a *status quo* that the Turkish Cypriot political leadership is quite comfortable with. Thus, whatever its stated objectives may be, one can in some ways view UNFICYP as a midwife present at the birth of the Turkish Cypriot *de facto* state and as a guardian who helps make its continued existence possible.

The second, more general reason, is that by its very nature peacekeeping is better suited to some tasks than others. It is easier to separate groups (as in Cyprus or Bosnia) than it is to bring them together. The dual roles of the UN in Cyprus are illustrative here. In essence, the organization has attempted to facilitate a negotiated settlement to the conflict through the good offices mission of the Secretary-General while simultaneously maintaining the peace on the island through the peacekeeping presence of UNFICYP. François Lafrenière and Robert Mitchell (1990) conceptualize the distinction between these two roles in terms of conflict resolution versus conflict management. The requirements for successful conflict resolution are not necessarily the same as those for successful conflict management. As they see it, Cyprus has been managed successfully but not resolved. UNFICYP is implicated here for the reason that 'Because the UN has been instrumental in providing security, there has not been pressure on the parties to reach the compromises needed for a lasting resolution' (1990, p. 69). Somewhat similarly, Leonard Doob (1986) differentiates between these two functions in terms of peacemaking versus peacekeeping. He also believes that while UNFICYP has helped keep the peace, its very presence has weakened the incentives for peacemaking. As he puts it, 'Given that the status quo was not without its advantages to both sides, why hurry along an effort for a more permanent peace.... Peacekeeping that benefits two communities in conflict may hinder peacemaking' (1986, p. 385).

UNFICYP deserves widespread praise for its humanitarian efforts, its dedication, and its success in maintaining a delicate peace on Cyprus. Its efforts, however, may inadvertently help preserve the Turkish Cypriot *de facto* state. The preservation of peace at the price of a *de facto* state is far from the worst option available. Indeed, one can easily argue that it is preferable to renewed conflict and bloodshed. It is beyond the scope of this section to evaluate whether it is morally preferable to stop the violence in, say, Bosnia at the expense of creating a *de facto* state, or to let the bloodshed continue in the name of preserving existing territorial boundaries and not rewarding aggression. The point to be made is that the role of the UN in freezing a particular *status quo* and facilitating *de facto* statehood should be acknowledged and openly debated.

To date, UN peacekeeping has only been implicated in the creation or maintenance of three *de facto* states—those in Northern Cyprus, Krajina, and the Bosnian Serb Republic. What of the future prospects for *de facto* statehood through this route? On the one hand, there is the possibility that secessionist groups may come to see peacekeeping as a means of facilitating their separatist goals. These groups would then try to use the traditional peacekeeping function of separating the warring parties to legitimate their own *de facto* territorial gains. After securing their territorial goals, these groups would then call for the introduction of UN peacekeepers to separate the combatants and patrol a cease-fire line. The longer the peacekeepers remain in this role, the more solidified their own *de facto* boundaries would become. Bosnian Serb proposals for a general cease-fire in the spring of 1994 and the corresponding Muslim reluctance to agree to these proposals can be seen in this light.[12] Although not technically a *de facto* state because they do not seek sovereignty as constitutional independence, one can also interpret some of the actions of Jonas Savimbi's *União Nacional para a Independencia Total de Angola* (National Union for the Total Independence of Angola, UNITA) in regards to UN peacekeepers in Angola in a similar fashion.[13]

On the other hand, there is now a growing awareness of this potential problem which should, in and of itself, serve to limit its impact in the future. The increasingly common belief that the UN is now part of the Cyprus problem rather than part of its solution has led to what A. J. R. Groom refers to as 'the near collapse of donor participation in UNFICYP' (1993, p. 41). Though they may only be rhetorical and quickly followed by qualifications, one can also hear questions being raised from within the academy as to whether the international community might be better served by withdrawing its peacekeepers from Cyprus and coming to grips with the reality of a sovereign Turkish Cypriot state.[14] A second factor limiting UN involvement as a source of future *de facto* states is the current pronounced reluctance to engage in peacekeeping missions at all. In the initial euphoria of the post-Cold War period, the UN Security Council voted to authorize more than a dozen new peacekeeping operations, many of which were larger and more ambitious than anything which had come before then. This burst of enthusiasm has now given way to a more sober reluctance to enter into new undertakings. Empirically, this decline can be seen in the number of UN blue helmets active in the field. The estimated 78,111 peacekeepers serving on 30 September 1994 declined by more than two-thirds to an estimated 24,952 serving on 31 January 1997.[15] Fewer new peacekeeping missions should translate into fewer opportunities to use peacekeepers in constructing new *de facto* states. Finally, despite the voluminous rhetoric on peace-enforcement and forcible intervention, most states remain reluctant to commit forces to potentially bloody peacekeeping operations. The success of most peacekeeping missions still depends (in part) on the cooperation and consent of the governments on whose territory they are stationed. Third World leaders will be unlikely to offer that cooperation if they feel they may end up getting a *de facto* partitioned country in return. There is thus a tangible incentive to see that this does not happen.

9 The Demonstration Effect of Other *De Facto* States

This section considers the impact that already-existing *de facto* states may have on other would-be separatist entities. Specifically, it asks whether or not the presence of *de facto* states in the international system acts as an impetus to the creation of more such entities in the future. The evidence here is mostly anecdotal, but it does appear that there is some sort of demonstration effect at work in this regard. Correspondingly, sovereign governments faced with potential *de facto* state challengers also seem to be aware of the effects these entities have had in the past.

Perhaps the two *de facto* states that have the most in common with each other are Somaliland and Eritrea. Both are located in the Horn of Africa, both had separate juridical existence as colonies, and both were federated to other states at the time of decolonization. Eritrea was already fairly well established as a *de facto* state at the time the SNM launched its surprise attacks against Somalia in the summer of 1988. Perhaps even more importantly, the SNM's actual declaration of secession was issued on 18 May 1991—just one week before the EPLF entered Asmara on 24 May 1991 and took control over all of Eritrea. The first two years of the Republic of Somaliland's *de facto* statehood thus coincided almost exactly with the period when Eritrea's *de facto* statehood reached its maximum level of power, effectiveness, and international acceptance. In answer to the question of whether or not Eritrea served as any kind of exemplar for Somaliland, Hussein Adam argues that 'the Somaliland Republic looks upon Eritrea as a model and hopes that international recognition of Eritrea may pave the way to its own recognition' (1994a, p. 154). President Egal's expressed willingness to hold a referendum on Somaliland's independence can be seen in this regard as an attempt to follow the Eritrean path to sovereign statehood.

The one other case where the Eritrean example may have had some sort of demonstration effect is Chechnya. Here the Eritrean impact shows up in the response of the existing sovereign state (Russia) to its secessionist challenger. The recent peace treaties signed between the Chechen rebels and former Russian security advisor Alexander Lebed provide for a five-year transition period leading to a referendum on Chechen independence.[16] Though it has not been explicitly stated by either of the parties, this idea of a transition period leading to a referendum almost exactly mirrors the Eritrean experience from 1991 - 1993. This does not implicate Eritrea in the creation of the Chechen *de facto* state. It does, however, highlight the potential demonstration effect that existing *de facto* states may have.

Perhaps due to its extended life-span, the *de facto* state that seems to have the greatest demonstration effect is the TRNC. The TRNC example has been looked to by both government and insurgent leaders in Sri Lanka. According to A. Jeyaratnam Wilson, in 1983, Tamil political leaders in the TULF 'expected Mrs Gandhi to intervene militarily in Ceylon, emulating the Turkish invasion of northern Cyprus in 1974...' (1988, pp. 202-203). For his part, Sri Lankan President Jayewardene considered the potential consequences of a prolonged war against a disciplined and well-organized insurrection and 'said publicly that his island state might be divided like

Cyprus, or be partitioned with United Nations troops guarding the frontiers of the new states' (A.J. Wilson, 1988, p. 205).

Another *de facto* state situation that Northern Cyprus has influenced is Chechnya. In 1993, the now-deceased Chechen rebel leader Jokar Dudaev announced that his breakaway republic was recognizing the sovereign independence of the TRNC.[17] A number of wounded Chechen fighters were also reportedly given medical treatment in the TRNC.[18] Perhaps most interestingly, reports even circulated that Chechen emissaries were for a time in 1995 trying to arrange political asylum for Dudaev in the TRNC.[19] None of this necessarily shows any Northern Cypriot influence on the formation of the Chechen separatist movement. It does, however, indicate that the Chechen leadership clearly devoted both attention and effort to the TRNC.

The demonstration effect of the TRNC has arguably been strongest amongst the Bosnian Serbs. In his memoirs, Canadian Major General Lewis MacKenzie (1993) discusses a proposal that Bosnian Serb leader Radovan Karadzic made to UN headquarters in New York for peacekeepers to take over all of Sarajevo with a 'green line' running down the middle of the Miljacka River which bisects the city from east to west. In Karadzic's proposed solution, the Serbs would be to the south of the river while the Muslims and Croats were to the north of it. MacKenzie wryly observes that 'Dr. Karadzic must have visited Cyprus at some time, because he always brought up the subject of a UN Green Line' (1993, p. 11). The long shadow of Northern Cyprus also entered into the Bosnian government's calculations. One of the reasons President Izetbegovic wanted outside military involvement was to prevent just such a green line situation from occurring. As MacKenzie argues, there were two separate agendas at work in this regard. In his words, the 'Bosnian Serbs wanted their own state with a Green Line, manned by the UN, separating them from the rest of the Bosnians; whereas there were strong indicators that he, the President, wanted international military intervention' (1993, p. 230). At this point, whether the Dayton Accords ultimately prove to resemble more closely Karadzic's Green Line vision or Izetbegovic's unified Bosnian state vision remains to be seen.

At a broader level, Cypriot diplomat Andreas Jacovides (1995) makes the case for a Northern Cypriot demonstration effect in different and much stronger terms. He believes that

> There is a solid basis for the proposition that if the international community had taken effective steps in 1974 not to allow the victimization of Cyprus through its forcible division and deliberate massive 'ethnic cleansing,'

similar deplorable actions in the former Yugoslavia and elsewhere would not have taken place (1995, p. 1222).

Whether one accepts Jacovides's proposition or not, the fact that the Northern Cypriot *de facto* state has influenced other governments and secessionist movements appears clear.

The argument here is not that the demonstration effect of already-existing *de facto* states leads directly to the creation of new *de facto* states. Rather, it is that the existence of these entities is noted by both other secessionist entities and other sovereign governments who then consider these situations in deciding what types of strategies they wish to pursue in their own struggles. The demonstration effect of existing *de facto* states is limited and should be seen as a supplemental or secondary factor in the emergence of other *de facto* states. Eritrea, for example, may offer modest encouragement to Somaliland, and the TRNC may do the same for the Bosnian Serbs. Eritrea did not, however, create the SNM nor did the Turkish Cypriots ethnically cleanse Gorazde. Additionally, neither one of these examples has led to the wholesale redrawing of political maps in either Africa or Europe. The demonstration effect of other *de facto* states is not a primary factor, for without political leadership, keenly-felt grievances against their government, indigenous military capabilities, and a sense of their own distinct nationhood, there would be no Chechen secessionist movement regardless of how many TRNCs existed in the larger outside world.

10 Conclusion

This chapter has analyzed a number of specific micro-level factors that may be involved in the creation and/or maintenance of *de facto* states. While these various factors have been considered separately, many of them are interrelated and they often appear together in the same case. Depending on one's perspective, for example, the Bosnian Serb Republic could be seen as the product of a combination of factors including foreign invasion, an indigenous secession attempt, external political involvement, state collapse, the role of the UN in freezing the *status quo,* and the demonstration effect of other *de facto* states. The focus of this chapter has thus been on identifying these various factors and assessing the circumstances which make them more or less likely sources of *de facto* statehood. As such, the conclusions that can be drawn are more illustrative than they are empirically definitive. No evidence in the form of 'state collapse is involved in the birth of 37 percent of all *de facto* states' has been presented here.

As was the case with chapter five, this chapter constitutes only a partial look at the factors involved in the birth of *de facto* states. Its examination of the more specific or micro-level of analysis needs to be viewed in conjunction with the preceding chapter's examination of the systemic level of analysis. The assorted factors identified in both of these chapters interact with each other in a symbiotic fashion and help to produce both the general phenomenon of *de facto* statehood and its individual manifestations. No single factor is ever likely to be responsible for the creation of one of these entities. Rather, multiple macro- and micro-level factors are likely to be involved in each case. In some ways, the macro-level factors considered in chapter five frame the picture and provide the permissive conditions for the emergence of *de facto* states in general, while the micro-level factors considered here are more directly related to the actual events leading up to the birth of specific entities.

Chapter seven continues our birth, life, and death or evolution look at the *de facto* state by focusing on how international society and international law deal with the actual existence of these entities. This chapter's examination of the life phase seeks to evaluate both the problems posed by, and the opportunities created by the presence of *de facto* states in the contemporary international system. Whether or not the *de facto* state serves any useful purpose for international society is also considered here.

Notes

[1] On Trans-Dniester, see 'Russian Troops to Quit Moldova Hot Spot', *The New York Times*, 28 October 1994; 'Moldova: Yes, a Country', *The Economist*, 26 August 1995; 'Moldova Holds Its Breath, Too', *The Economist* 9 March 1996; and 'Moldova: River Dance', *The Economist*, 5 October 1996.

[2] Martin Woollacott, 'Cyprus: Dealing for Dollars', *Maclean's*, 25 June 1979, p. 29, cited in Oberling, 1982, p. 196.

[3] Cited in Buchheit, 1978, p. 158.

[4] Kodikara, 1990b, p. 170. See also Samarasinghe, 1990, pp. 60-62.

[5] On the French safe zone in Rwanda, see 'U.N. Accepts French Offer to Send Troops to Rwanda', *The New York Times*, 23 June 1994; 'France is Sending Force to Rwanda to Help Civilians', *The New York Times*, 23 June 1994; 'Hutus See France as Their Saviour', *Financial Times*, 27 June 1994; and 'The French in Rwanda', *The Economist*, 2 July 1994.

[6] Donnelly, 1984, p. 320. See also Franck and Rodley, 1973, pp. 294-296.

[7] Horowitz, 1991, pp. 15-18. The specific quote is from p. 18.

[8] Halperin and Scheffer with Small, 1992, p. 74. See also Buchheit, 1978, pp. 214-215.

[9] Holsti, 1995, p. 337. Slovenia is an extremely marginal case of 'violent' secession and could, arguably, be included in the peaceful secession category.

[10] For more on this see Bookman, 1992, pp. 19-24; and Wiberg, 1983, pp. 59-60.

[11] This section is partially based on earlier work I did operating with a much looser conception of *de facto* statehood. See Pegg, 1994, pp. 4-5.

[12] See 'Darkness at Dawn', *The Economist*, 16 April 1994 for more on this.

[13] 'Angola: The Ruins of Rebellion', *The Economist*, 26 February 1994.

[14] See, for example, Holsti, 1995, p. 336.

[15] These figures come from unofficial tabulations made by the journal *Peacekeeping and International Relations*. The 30 September 1994 figure comes from Volume 23 (6) of that journal, November/December 1994. The 31 January 1997 figure comes from Volume 26 (1), January/February 1997.

[16] 'A Way Out of Chechnya', *The Economist*, 31 August 1996.

[17] 'Rivals Become Enemies in Rebel Conflict', *The Daily Telegraph*, 17 January 1996.

[18] 'Russian General Staff Figures on Separatist Losses Throughout the Chechen War', *BBC Summary of World Broadcasts*, 31 July 1996.

[19] 'Dudayev Will Find Shelter in Turkey', *Russian Press Digest*, 12 July 1995; and 'Russia Pauses for Peace in Chechnya', *The Daily Telegraph*, 7 March 1995.

7   The *De Facto* State in International Society

1 Introduction

This chapter continues our birth, life, and death or evolution examination of the *de facto* state. The focus here is on the life phase—in particular, the impact that these entities have on international society and international law and how they are dealt with by those two bodies. The next section seeks to ascertain the *de facto* state's impact on international society. This is followed by an examination of how the members of the states system choose to deal (or not to deal) with specific *de facto* states. Another section also evaluates three possible alternative methods for dealing with these entities. Our fifth section considers the international legal ramifications of *de facto* statehood, while the sixth section asks whether or not these entities serve any useful purpose for international society. The chapter's final section summarizes our findings and looks forward to chapter eight.

2 The *De Facto* State's Impact on International Society

The *de facto* state has had substantive impact on international politics in two main areas: conflict and political economy. Of these two areas, its impact has clearly been the most apparent in the area of conflict and war. Limiting ourselves to just the four cases considered in this study, one finds that they have been implicated in somewhere between 160 - 275,000 fatalities and that they have produced somewhere between 2,345,000 - 2,795,000 refugees and internally displaced persons.[1]   While even approximate figures are unavailable for the number of those wounded or disabled, that figure must number in the hundreds of thousands. The number of land-mines deployed in these four areas certainly counts in the millions. As two of these cases—Somaliland and, especially, Tamil Eelam—continue to produce new fatalities and refugees today, these figures can be expected to rise. Were one to include other *de facto* states such as Biafra, Chechnya, and the Bosnian Serb

Republic, they would clearly go much higher still. Additionally, the fact that *de facto* state situations are involved in three of the world's most serious conflicts today—Chechnya, Sri Lanka, and the former Yugoslavia—illustrates the contemporary relevance of this phenomenon to conflict and war in the international system.

Beyond the sheer numbers of those killed, wounded, and displaced, Zeev Maoz (1989) highlights another reason why the international community should be concerned with the *de facto* state. In a study of the ways in which state formation processes affect international conflict involvement, Maoz distinguishes between evolutionary and revolutionary types of state formation. He finds that

> State formation processes affect patterns of post-independence involvement in interstate disputes. States that emerge out of a violent struggle for independence tend to be involved in a considerably larger number of interstate disputes than states that become independent as a result of an evolutionary process (1989, p. 226).

There are two main problems in applying Maoz's findings to the *de facto* state. First, his work focuses on states that have actually won their independence or, in his phrase, 'joined the club of nations'. Most *de facto* states never reach this level. Second, the distinction between evolutionary and revolutionary state formation is not always clear. Where, for instance, would the TRNC fall in this dichotomized distinction? Additionally, Eritrea would have appeared to be a classic case of revolutionary state formation until its 1991 - 1993 transition period brought it much closer to an evolutionary process. Indeed, one suspects that Maoz would be a strong supporter of the type of extended transition process that Eritrea went through and which has been proposed for Chechnya.[2] This is because of the two reasons why evolutionary state formation leads to reduced levels of subsequent involvement in interstate conflicts. First, evolutionary state formation is 'characterized by stable expectations of the indigenous national elites regarding their acceptance into the system by other states'. Second, these same evolutionary processes also create 'stable expectations by other states regarding the upcoming expansion of the club of nations...' (Maoz, 1989, p. 226). While Maoz's findings may not exactly translate to all *de facto* state situations, they do highlight one more reason these entities may have substantial impact upon international society.

As for political economy, the *de facto* state's impact is relatively modest. This can be explained by a combination of factors including their limited numbers, their generally small size, their often impoverished conditions, and their lack of juridical standing—which acts as a substantial deterrent to foreign investment and international economic integration. That qualification aside, however, these entities do affect the global political economy. Two main points need to be made in this regard. First, in spite of their lack of juridical status, business is done with *de facto* states and similar entities and this business may produce negative consequences. When looking at this issue from the perspective of sovereign governments which lose control of resource-rich regions, Jackson and Rosberg (1986) argue that 'international bodies, foreign powers, and even private firms are likely to respect their *de jure* claim to such regions...'. As such, 'non-sovereigns who are in *de facto* control of them may be prevented from benefitting fully from their material exploitation' (1986, p. 15). While the first part of this claim holds, the evidence is increasingly against the second part. In 1991, for example, Charles Taylor's 'Greater Liberia' was France's third-largest source of tropical timber. Taylor earned an estimated US$ 8 - 10 million a month from a consortium of multinational companies interested in extracting diamonds, gold, iron ore, timber, and rubber from the areas he controlled. Taylor's forces also allegedly reached an agreement with Firestone to cooperate in rubber production and marketing (Lowenkopf, 1995, p. 94; Reno, 1995, pp. 113-115). The Khmer Rouge in Cambodia and UNITA in Angola are two other examples of non-sovereign groups exercising effective territorial control which have been able to finance their operations through the sale of mineral resources they control—diamonds in UNITA's case and an assortment of gems and hardwood forest products for the Khmer Rouge.

In all three of these cases, no one challenged Angola, Cambodia, or Liberia's *de jure* claim to the regions in question. And yet, millions of dollars in business is regularly conducted by an assortment of public and private firms from around the world with the non-sovereigns who are in *de facto* control of those regions. Indeed, one suspects, based on the long-standing ability of these groups to finance themselves, that Charles Taylor, UNITA, and the Khmer Rouge must all make fairly good business partners. This type of business can negatively impact upon international society in a number of ways. First, the respective sovereign governments lose millions of dollars of lucrative revenues—often from non-renewable resources. Second, this loss of revenues indirectly leads to increased demands on other members of international society for greater assistance and, perhaps, for some sort of interventionary force. Third, such groups are unlikely to be the best respecters of trade regulations or the best protectors of the environment.

Finally, their very illegitimacy encourages illegal activities. *The New York Times*, for example, refers to the Kurdish safe haven in northern Iraq as 'the largest black market clearing house for cigarettes in the Middle East'.[3] Christopher Clapham also points out that the international trade in narcotics is one 'in which *not* being a formally recognized state confers substantial market advantages' (1998, p. 151, italics in original).

The second main point to be made, though, is that *de facto* political status does not necessarily produce bad economic outcomes. The classic example here is Taiwan. At a minimum, Taiwan shows that a lack of formal diplomatic relations with the vast majority of sovereign states in the world today does not preclude economic success. In 1996, Taiwan was the world's fifteenth largest trading power with a trade volume in excess of US$ 218 billion. Its foreign reserves are the third largest in the world at more than US$ 88 billion and its per capita GNP is in excess of US$ 12,800.[4]

The Taiwan example is unique in terms of the magnitude of its economic success, but it is far from the only *de facto* state that can claim some degree of economic prowess. As noted in chapter three, the LTTE has been able to reach a number of mutually acceptable arrangements with local businessmen. Under the SNM's leadership, livestock exports (the mainstay of the Somaliland economy) have more than tripled. This can be attributed both to the SNM's commitment to free market economics and to its comparative efficiency in providing governmental services and maintaining order. Though the per capita GNP in the TRNC is perhaps only one-fourth that of the Republic of Cyprus, even this case shows that *de facto* statehood does not rule out economic development. The TRNC's external trade volume has consistently risen and hit US$ 447 million in 1990. Despite the consistent accusations of puppet statehood, only about 14 percent of Northern Cypriot exports in that year went to Turkey. Approximately 78 percent of them were destined for the EU (primarily the UK). The TRNC currently has trade links with over 80 countries and it annually attracts approximately double its population in tourist arrivals. There is one automobile for every 2.5 persons—a level comparable to Greek Cyprus and higher than in some EU countries. Life expectancy is 71 years and the literacy rate stands at 97 percent (Olgun, 1993, pp. 273-288; Yesilada, 1989, pp. 99-100). Obviously, its lack of juridical standing has hindered the TRNC in a myriad of ways. Its economy also has serious structural problems (such as an over-dependence on tourist revenues and a specific over-dependence on Turkish tourists). Still, as the above examples show, *de facto* states and other related entities do impact the global political economy and they often manage to participate in it quite successfully.

3 How Does International Society Deal With the *De Facto* State?

Within the general context of its strong diplomatic and financial support for existing sovereign states, international society has traditionally chosen to respond to the existence of *de facto* states in three main ways: actively opposing them through the use of embargoes and sanctions; generally ignoring them; and coming to some sort of limited acceptance of their presence. Each of these three approaches has a different set of costs and benefits for the international community and for the *de facto* state itself.

The classic example of actively opposing the *de facto* state's existence through the use of international embargoes and sanctions comes from Northern Cyprus. The Greek Cypriot embargo campaign against the TRNC has been quite successful. A variety of international organizations including the Universal Postal Union, the International Civil Aviation Organization, and the International Air Transport Association have refused to recognize or deal with the Turkish Cypriots in their respective areas of competence. As such, TRNC maritime ports and airports have been declared illegal and TRNC postage stamps have been proclaimed 'illegal and of no validity'. The international embargo against Northern Cyprus was strengthened dramatically in 1994 when the European Court of Justice (ECJ, the judicial wing of the EU) ruled that EU member-states could no longer accept movement and phyto-sanitary certificates[5] from TRNC authorities. Under the 1972 association agreement between Cyprus and the then EC, Cypriot goods received preferential access to the EC marketplace. Until this 1994 ruling, the UK had been accepting certificates from TRNC authorities to ensure that the entire population of Cyprus benefited from the association agreement. In essence, the ECJ ruling held that movement and phyto-sanitary certificates could only be issued by authorities from the Republic of Cyprus. Produce and citrus exports from the TRNC are now banned from EU markets, although in practice many of them will probably be rerouted through Turkey.[6]

The international embargo has hurt the TRNC economy. The fact that no country other than Turkey maintains direct air links with the TRNC substantially increases both the costs and the inconvenience of traveling to Northern Cyprus and is a serious impediment to the development of the tourist industry there. The impact of this measure alone on the TRNC's fragile economy is enormous—in 1992 tourist receipts accounted for 30 percent of the TRNC's entire GNP and were equivalent in value to more than 320 percent of its total exports (Lockhart, 1994, p. 374). The overall effects of the embargo also show up in per capita income statistics. In 1995, Greek Cypriot per capita income stood at US\$ 12,500, while the comparable Turkish Cypriot figure was just US\$ 3,300.[7]

The isolate and embargo strategy obviously has substantial costs for the *de facto* state. It also, however, affects international society. Sticking with the TRNC example, in May 1993, Asil Nadir, the former head of Polly Peck International fled from London to the TRNC in order to avoid serious fraud charges in the UK. Because the UK does not recognize the TRNC, there is no extradition treaty between them. As such, Nadir is effectively beyond the reach of British justice in the TRNC. In a related incident, Elizabeth Forsyth, one of Nadir's aides who fled with him, asked to provide statements for her own trial from the TRNC. The British judge in the case would not allow as admissible any witness statements she made to a TRNC court because the UK did not recognize this entity. Nor would he allow evidence to be heard from the TRNC via a satellite television link.[8] The TRNC's status as a juridical black-hole in the international system may also appeal to organized criminals. Its lack of taxation and extradition agreements with other countries led one member of the Russian mafia to describe it as a perfect setting because 'No one can touch you in the Turkish sector'.[9]

Far more typical than deliberate campaigns against the *de facto* state is the second option of generally ignoring their existence and refusing to engage them in any manner. An example here is the OAU's refusal to allow the Provisional Government of Eritrea observer status at its June 1992 summit meeting in Dakar, Senegal. The OAU did not call for actions to be taken against the PGE; it merely refused to grant it any status at its own deliberations. More costly to the *de facto* state is the general inability of most intergovernmental organizations and non-governmental aid agencies to deal with non-sovereign entities. As Alan James (1986b) points out, it 'deserves emphasis that the acquisition of sovereign status does, in itself, constitute a material, and not just a nominal, change in a territory's position. For this alteration in its status is not simply a matter of words but has some practical implications, which can be of considerable significance' (1986b, p. 276). Eritrea, for example, was unable to qualify for any bilateral aid or loans from the IMF or the World Bank until after the conclusion of its independence referendum. The Republic of Somaliland's President Egal was particularly embittered over the UN's refusal to assist Somaliland in rebuilding its legal infrastructure. In his words,

> They were supposed to have repaired our courts and paid our justices. They were promising that for so long, and then… they came up with another brilliant excuse. They said 'You call yourselves "chief justices" and "supreme courts" and if we pay for them, it will be an act of recognition of Somaliland'. That's after six months of reneging on their promises (Bryden, 1994a, p. 42).

Besides the active embargo, the TRNC also suffers from this general neglect. Its diplomatic isolation prevents it from receiving nearly all non-Turkish external development assistance. One major problem here has been the growing salinization of its limited water supplies. This situation could have been avoided had the TRNC undertaken a large-scale irrigation program. Unfortunately, dams and irrigation systems require massive investments—which, in the case of the (Greek) Republic of Cyprus, were carried out only with major development funding from the World Bank, the EC, and other international institutions (Morvaridi, 1993a, p. 246). Another revealing example comes from Chechnya. In February 1996, the IMF negotiated a US$ 10.1 billion three-year loan agreement with the government of Russia. As it does not appear as an identifiable item in Russia's budget, the costs of the war in Chechnya have not been an issue between Russia and the IMF. Yet, under IMF pressure, the Russian government recently announced a series of spending cutbacks which included money earmarked for the rebuilding of Chechnya's devastated infrastructure. As *The Economist* put it, 'The perverse result is to leave the Russian government acknowledging a need to cut back on the cost of reconstructing Chechnya, but not on the cost of destroying it first'.[10]

For the *de facto* state, the costs of this second option are measured primarily in terms of potential aid and investment dollars lost. Looking at Eritrea from 1991 - 1993, David Pool observes that 'The costs of a smooth political transition to independence have been borne in the economic sphere, at least in the short run' (1993, p. 392). Unfortunately, for some extremely poor *de facto* states with slim margins of error such as Somaliland, these short run costs may make the difference between long run survival or not. For international society as a whole, however, the costs of this second option are only felt in the long run. After all, it costs nothing to ignore or neglect a *de facto* state today. If, however, to take one example, external assistance to develop Somaliland's legal infrastructure will show a positive long-term return on investment in terms of improved local (and hence regional) stability, then the short-term savings on not providing that assistance may be overwhelmed by the increased costs of future long-term instability. Similarly, not taking Chechnya into its calculations may benefit the IMF in terms of its short-term loan repayments schedule. One might suspect, however, that such neglect will come back to haunt international society in the not-too-distant future.

The third major option for international society in regard to *de facto* states is what might be termed the limited acceptance approach. This option is best exemplified by the international community's attitudes toward Eritrea in its 1991 - 1993 period and by its most recent attitudes toward Somaliland. Though it was denied access to international organizations and many forms of external assistance, the UN did open a permanent representative's office in Eritrea in November 1991. In February 1992, a USAID delegation visited Eritrea and held discussions with senior PGE officials. They ultimately promised to present proposals to the American government to give Eritrea US\$ 55 million worth of aid over a two-year period.[11] The PGE in some ways made their own situation more difficult by steadfastly refusing to deal with the outside world through Addis Ababa. They refused to receive officials from embassies in Addis Ababa and would not consent to their aid needs being considered as part of an Ethiopian country program. Still, Lionel Cliffe maintains that by 1992 'most governments had adjusted to the realities of Eritrea's *de facto* separation and to the inevitability of its eventual independence: external communications and most diplomatic relations had been normalised, and long-term aid was in the planning stage' (1994, p. 63). In the case of Somaliland, the evidence is somewhat more tentative. The US sent a fact-finding mission to Hargeisa in the fall of 1995 and the UNDP now maintains a representative office there. In June 1995, the UNDP representative, Earl Dyson, told the Somaliland government that UN agencies were prepared to work with it and that the government had the right to be informed about the budgets and projects of every agency. The US now deals with the Egal administration through the American embassy in Djibouti and, for aid projects, through the USAID office in Nairobi.[12]

Another example of the limited acceptance approach comes from the TRNC. In this case, though most countries support the isolate and embargo strategy, they realize that there can be no overall settlement of the Cyprus problem without the Turkish Cypriots. For this reason, the TRNC is allowed to maintain non-diplomatic representative offices in such cities as Brussels, London, Washington, New York, Islamabad, and Abu Dhabi. The UN's recognition of the two Cypriot communities participating in negotiations on an 'equal footing' also allows TRNC officials to have full, albeit non-diplomatic, access to the UN.[13] For some countries, contacts with TRNC officials are limited to resolving the Cyprus dispute. The US, for example, engages TRNC representatives on the issue of a negotiated settlement in a variety of locations. It will not, however, discuss with them any other matters. Should an American businessman have a commercial dispute or should an American tourist have a problem, there is no mechanism for US government involvement in such a manner. The political officer at the US embassy in Nicosia maintains a small office in the Turkish sector to facilitate his contacts with the Turkish Cypriots on the overall settlement issue but this is not a US consulate and it does not offer other services.[14] The fact that the TRNC can be cited in all three of our categories shows that they are not necessarily mutually exclusive.

Obviously, of the three choices presented above, this last option is the one that is most advantageous to the *de facto* state. While it might not contribute to success toward the ultimate goal of sovereignty as constitutional independence, this type of limited acceptance can potentially ease a number of pressing problems facing the *de facto* state. While greater international involvement will likely limit the *de facto* state leadership's autonomy through pressures to follow certain courses of action and avoid others, on balance the benefits should outweigh the costs as far as these entities are concerned. For international society, the greatest potential cost to this approach is angering the existing sovereign state. There is also the potential problem of not wanting to be seen to be encouraging these types of rebellions in the future. Indeed, the members of international society may fear that even such a non-juridical accommodation of the *de facto* state will only serve to undermine their normative position against secession. In the short-term, the costs of this approach (in terms of aid expenditures and diplomatic time spent) will probably exceed those of doing nothing. In the long-term, international society must hope that the investment in dealing with pressing humanitarian problems today will reap dividends tomorrow in terms of improved stability and less threatened or isolated political leaderships.

4 Three Potential Alternatives

Beyond these three main approaches, there are also a number of possible alternative methods for modeling future relations. We consider three here.

The first is what might be called 'the Ethiopian model' or 'the Meles formula'. Essentially, this is a variant on the third 'limited acceptance' model discussed above that seeks to reassure aid agencies, investors, and outside governments by proactively removing the existing sovereign state's objections to contacts with the *de facto* entity. These objections are removed without affecting or determining the course of future events. In the Ethiopian case, in October 1991, President Meles Zenawi explicitly invited foreign governments to deal directly with the PGE on economic matters without granting it full diplomatic recognition. Meles acknowledged the complexities that such a situation might entail but maintained that these complexities need not hold up investment or relief assistance in Eritrea. He explained to diplomats that 'The future of Eritrea will be determined by a referendum within two years and relations which any country maintains with the provisional government of Eritrea should not be viewed as determining future events there'.[15] Though it was never explicitly stated (and probably never considered), the Meles formula has the advantage of being consistent with a number of UN resolutions on Northern Cyprus. UN General Assembly resolution 37/253 of 13 May 1983, for example, 'stipulated that the *de facto* situation should not be allowed to influence or affect the solution of the problem...'.[16] In effect, the Meles formula removes the 'solution of the problem' from the agenda and considerations of all other parties and allows them to deal freely with the *de facto* state leadership in the meantime. This model has the same advantages as the limited acceptance model discussed above, with the additional advantage that it does not risk angering the sovereign state on whose territory the *de facto* state exists. Its major disadvantage is the fact that few sovereign states are willing to consider, let alone implement, such a model. As such, it is likely to remain mostly in the realm of theory for some time.

The second alternative model is what might be called 'the international economic organization membership model'. There are two main examples here: the Asia-Pacific Economic Cooperation (APEC) membership model and the General Agreement On Tariffs and Trade (GATT, now the World Trade Organization, WTO) membership model. Unlike the UN and most other international organizations, these groupings do not base their membership requirements upon juridical statehood. In the case of APEC, members are not sovereign states, but rather 'economies'. This formula was devised so that Hong Kong and Taiwan could participate in the organization's activities along with the People's Republic of China (PRC). As APEC has a much looser institutional structure than most international organizations, our primary focus here will be on the GATT/WTO. From its inception, GATT members have been 'contracting parties'—defined in article XXXIII of the General Agreement as 'governments which are applying the provisions of the Agreement...'. A drafting document of the General Agreement makes it clear that contracting parties were defined as 'governments' and not as 'states' or 'nations' specifically so that 'governments with less than complete sovereignty could be a contracting party to GATT'. Indeed, three of the original 22 contracting parties (Burma, Sri Lanka, and Southern Rhodesia) to the GATT were not sovereign states at the time the General Agreement was drafted. More recently, Hong Kong became a GATT contracting party in 1986. According to Ya Qin (1992), there are essentially two main qualifications that a government must meet in order to qualify as a GATT contracting party. First, it must represent a customs territory that maintains its own tariffs, non-tariff barriers, and other trade restrictions. Second, that same government must be responsible for those tariff and non-tariff trade restrictions so that it is in the position to remove or reduce them in accordance with GATT obligations (1992, pp. 1074-1076).

In essence, the hallmark of the GATT membership model is that it is based on functional competence rather than juridical standing. Applied to other international organizations, it would, for example, ask whether or not TRNC authorities were competent to run a safe airport or to meet postal obligations, not what their state's juridical standing was. The main advantage of such a model is that it accords well with the complex contemporary reality of international politics which often goes beyond the simple dichotomy of sovereign statehood or nothing. Whatever one thinks of their current or ultimate status, there is no doubt that the governments of Hong Kong and Taiwan are eminently capable of meeting their obligations under the GATT or the WTO. Similarly, there is no doubt that the TRNC could meet whatever international obligations there are on operating maritime ports. The main disadvantage of such a system is that most sovereign governments are likely to resist any sign of movement away from international participation based on juridical standing to international participation based on functional competence. As with the Meles formula, this alternative is also likely to remain mostly in the theoretical realm for the foreseeable future.

The third potential alternative is what might be called 'the Taiwan model'. As relations between the Republic of China and the 20-some countries which recognize it are conducted along standard diplomatic lines, our focus here is on what the Taiwanese term 'substantive relations'—the economic, trade, technological, and cultural ties that the ROC maintains with countries that do not have formal diplomatic relations with it.[17] In essence, the Taiwan model can be summarized in three main areas: 1) Taiwanese pragmatism, particularly in regard to nomenclature; 2) active cooperation from states that do not recognize the ROC; and 3) the 'privatization' of official relations.

The first component of this model is a flexible pragmatism on the part of the Taiwanese in regard to nomenclature. Taiwan's official name is the Republic of China. After the US switched recognition from Taipei to Beijing in 1979, however, the Beijing leadership formulated a policy that any Taiwanese presence in international affairs, be it official or unofficial, should be in the name of 'Taiwan, China' or 'Taipei, China' so that no one would be confused as to the existence of 'two Chinas' or 'one China, one Taiwan'. The name 'Taipei, China' is sometimes referred to as the 'Olympic formula' since it was first adopted by the International Olympic Committee in 1979. After some initial resistance to the use of this formula, Taiwan accepted it in 1981. This name is also now used by the Asian Development Bank (ADB). In February 1986, the board of governors of the ADB (of which Taiwan was a founding member under the name Republic of China) admitted the PRC as a member and voted to change Taiwan's designation from ROC to 'Taipei, China'. The Taiwanese boycotted the ADB's annual meetings in 1986 and 1987 in protest, but retained their membership and returned to full cooperation with the organization in 1988.   The ADB is the first intergovernmental organization in which Taiwan and the PRC have both participated. APEC became the second such organization in 1991 when it simultaneously admitted Hong Kong, the PRC, and 'Chinese Taipei' to its membership (Ya Qin, 1992, pp. 1065-1067). On January 1, 1990, Taiwan formally applied to join the GATT as 'The Separate Customs Territory of Taiwan, P'enghu, Kinmen and Matsu' under Article XXXIII of the General Agreement. This name was chosen in the hopes 'that by using the term "customs territory," the application would meet with fewer "unnecessary disturbances" '.[18] Many of the ROC's overseas missions go by the name of 'Taipei Economic and Cultural Office'. Though Taiwan has yet to be successful in its quest for GATT/WTO membership, its flexibility in nomenclature certainly eases its participation in international relations.

The second component in the Taiwan model is the active cooperation of its non-diplomatic partners. This cooperation has been most apparent in the case of the United States. In an attempt to minimize the consequences of derecognition, the US Congress passed the Taiwan Relations Act (TRA). Except for the use of diplomatic license plates and passports, under this act the US extends essentially the same privileges to Taiwanese representatives as it does to diplomats from officially recognized states. The TRA also provides for the capacity of Taiwan to sue and be sued in US courts. Typically, only a recognized government would have the capacity to sue in the courts of another state. Similarly, the act provides that the absence of diplomatic relations shall not affect the application of any US laws with respect to Taiwan and that US laws shall apply to Taiwan exactly as they did prior to derecognition on 1 January 1979. As President Carter explained in an official memorandum, 'Whenever any law, regulation, or order of the United States refers to a foreign country, nation, state, government, or similar entity, departments and agencies shall construe those terms and apply those laws, regulations or orders to include Taiwan'.[19]

The final component of the Taiwan model is the 'privatization' of diplomatic relations. In the case of the US, the TRA provided for the establishment of a new body called the American Institute in Taiwan (AIT) to handle relations in the absence of diplomatic recognition. The AIT is a private non-profit corporation which has entered into a contract with the US State Department to provide certain services in return for the reimbursement of its costs within defined limits. In theory, all AIT personnel are not government employees during the course of their tenure—even though many of them are seconded from the State Department and other governmental agencies. Section 7 of the TRA authorizes AIT employees to perform the functions and services of US consular officials and, in practice, the AIT performs most of the same functions which were previously carried out by the US Embassy in Taipei. Funding for the AIT comes from the annual State Department appropriation. The Taiwanese equivalent of the AIT is called the Coordination Council for North American Affairs (CCNAA). Under the TRA, all dealings between Taiwan and the US are to be handled exclusively through these two bodies. Therefore, should the US Department of Agriculture wish to liaison with its counterparts in Taiwan for some reason, it cannot make direct contact as it could with, say, similar officials in Mexico. Rather, it must transmit its request through the AIT-CCNAA framework.[20] R. Sean Randolph concludes that 'Unique in both form and function, the AIT is without precedent in United States diplomatic experience' (1981, p. 252).

In addition to the AIT-CCNAA framework, the Taiwanese have also worked out similar 'non-governmental' arrangements with the PRC. The Taiwanese equivalent of the CCNAA is in this case called the Straits

Exchange Foundation (SEF). The SEF was set up in 1991 because commercial contacts with the PRC had reached such a level that some type of regular forum was needed to handle such issues as fishing disputes, investment protection matters, litigation questions, and illegal PRC emigrants to Taiwan. The PRC's equivalent body to the SEF is called the Taiwan Affairs Office.

Whatever else one may say about it, this 'privatization' of official relations has certainly not appreciably hindered economic contacts between the parties concerned. In the case of the US, annual two-way trade between it and Taiwan has increased from US$ nine billion to more than 35 billion since the enactment of the TRA. Taiwan is now the US's fifth largest trading partner (Mangelson, 1992, p. 236). As for the PRC, Taiwan is now the second largest foreign investor in that country. According to the PRC's own statistics, some 20,000 Taiwanese companies had invested or were committed to invest US$ 22.6 billion in China by 1995. In 1994, two-way trade between Taiwan and the PRC was in excess of US$ 14 billion.[21]

At first glance, the Taiwan model would appear to be quite attractive to other *de facto* states. There is one major drawback, however. Most *de facto* states would probably be unwilling to show the same type of flexible pragmatism in terms of nomenclature that the Taiwanese have. Turkish Cypriots, for example, have often accused Greek Cypriots of blocking mutually beneficial joint economic projects over questions of recognition. The Greek Cypriots reply that the Turkish Cypriots use the bait of joint economic projects as part of a deliberate strategy to achieve *de facto* recognition and then accuse them of 'backing off' when they do not agree to nomenclature that, in their view, implies a degree of recognition of the TRNC (Lafrenière and Mitchell, 1990, p. 83). The internal logic of most *de facto* states advances political considerations over economic ones. Thus, maintaining official TRNC nomenclature without a mutually beneficial economic project is preferable to securing that project at the cost of being called 'Lefkosa, Cyprus' or some such name.[22] When it comes to *de facto* statehood, the Taiwanese are thus somewhat exceptional in elevating the economic over the political in recent times.[23]

The leading reason that this model is unlikely to see widespread application, however, is that most sovereign states lack the compelling economic incentive to cooperate with other *de facto* states that they have with Taiwan. Taiwan's rapidly growing market of 20 million people with a per capita GNP of more than US$ 12,800, its manufacturing prowess, and its leadership in a number of high-tech industries argue strongly for finding a way to accommodate it through such ruses as the 'privatization' of official relations. Such incentives are simply not present in the case of the 170-some thousand Turkish Cypriots with a per capita GNP of around US$ 3,000 in a tourism-based economy or in the case of the three million Somalilanders with a per capita GNP of only a few hundred dollars a year in an agriculturally-based economy.

5 International Law and the *De Facto* State

By definition the *de facto* state lacks juridical standing in the society of states. This fact, along with its imprecise and more fluid status might at first glance be seen as presenting fundamental problems to international law. On closer inspection, however, the international legal system appears quite capable of dealing with the presence of these entities. The first point to be made here concerns the applicability of international law to unrecognized bodies such as the TRNC or Somaliland. It might be thought, as James Crawford (1976-77) puts it, that 'if international law withholds legal status from effective illegal entities, the result is a legal vacuum undesirable both in practice and principle'. However, this view 'assumes that international law does not apply to *de facto* illegal entities; and this is simply not so'. The example Crawford uses here is Taiwan, which 'whether or not a State, is not free to act contrary to international law, nor does it claim such a liberty' (1976-77, p. 145). What Taiwan is not free to act contrary to in this regard is *jus cogens*—defined by one scholar as 'peremptory norms from which no derogation can be allowed by agreement or otherwise' (Jacovides, 1995, p. 1221). This idea has been incorporated into Article 53 of the 1969 Vienna Convention on the Law of Treaties.[24] Though far from unanimous, modern legal opinion is also strongly in favor of the notion of *jus cogens*. Where the consensus on *jus cogens* falls apart is in identifying exactly which principles are and are not subsumed under it. The point to be made in regard to the *de facto* state, though, is a simple one: if one accepts that such things as the prohibitions on genocide and on the use of force except for self-defense have attained the status of *jus cogens*, then these standards apply to *de facto* states in the same way that they apply to sovereign states.

      Beyond the realm of *jus cogens*, it can be shown both historically and in case law that unrecognized entities do have a juridically significant existence in international law. Historically, European states frequently entered into treaties with non-sovereign entities. Ian Brownlie (1984), for example, points out that until about the middle of the nineteenth century,

> it was perfectly possible to conclude treaties with various types of social structure which had a territorial base: but there had to be some definable and unified social structure. Basutos and Zulus qualified whilst Australian aboriginals and Fuegian Indians did not (1984, p. 362).

In regard to case law, both US and international court decisions hold that the actions of *de facto* states may be given legal recognition in spite of the lack of formal diplomatic relations. In the absence of specific enabling legislation such as the TRA, the lack of diplomatic relations prevents *de facto* states from bringing suits in US courts. It does not, however, deny them any juridical existence. In *Wulfsohn v. Russian Socialist Federated Soviet Republic* [1923], for example, a US court granted the unrecognized Soviet government sovereign immunity on the basis that, even if unrecognized by the US, the Soviet government did exist and hence was a foreign sovereign that could not be sued in an American court without its consent. In *M. Salimoff & Co. v. Standard Oil Co. of New York* [1933], another US court applied the act of state doctrine to a confiscatory decree of the still-unrecognized Soviet government. This doctrine, which holds in part that 'the courts of one country will not sit in judgment of the acts of the government of another done within its territory', was applied because, in the court's judgment,

> We all know that it is a government. The State Department knows it, the courts, the nations, and the man in the street. If it is a government in fact, its decrees have force within its own borders and over its nationals.... The courts may not recognize the Soviet government as the de jure government until the State Department gives the word. They may, however, say that it is a government.[25]

Another leading US court case in this regard involved East Germany. In *Upright v. Mercury Business Machines* [1961], the court allowed an American assignee of a corporation controlled by the unrecognized East German government to sue in US courts. In doing so, the court rejected the defendant's argument that the lack of *de jure* relations with the East German government should be determinative of whether or not transactions with it could be enforced in US courts. The court's ruling held that

A foreign government, although not recognized by the political arm of the United States government, may nevertheless have a de facto existence which is juridically cognizable.... The lack of jural status for such government or its creature corporation is not determinative of whether transactions with it will be denied enforcement in American courts, so long as the government is not the suitor....[26]

Internationally, this idea that unrecognized governments may still be 'juridically cognizable' had previously been put forth in the 1924 *Tinoco Claims Arbitration (Great Britain v. Costa Rica)*. In this case, it was the unrecognized Costa Rican government of Federico Tinoco whose *de facto* existence was deemed juridically cognizable (Randolph, 1981, p. 258).

Contemporary state practice also supports the idea that unrecognized *de facto* entities may conduct foreign relations with sovereign states which have not extended *de jure* recognition to them. Section 107 of the Restatement (Second) of Foreign Relations Law of the United States [1965], for example, specifies that

An entity not recognized as a state but meeting the requirements for recognition specified in § 100 [of controlling a territory and population and engaging in foreign relations], or an entity recognized as a state whose regime is not recognized as its government, has the rights of a state under international law in relation to a non-recognizing state....[27]

Based on this, Victor Li concludes that 'From an *international law perspective*, a *de facto* entity may clearly conduct foreign relations with countries which have not extended *de jure* recognition to it...' (1979, p. 139). Such a conclusion is supported by Article 74 of the Vienna Convention on the Law of Treaties which states that 'The severance or absence of diplomatic or consular relations between two or more States does not prevent the conclusion of treaties between those States...'.[28]

One objection might be that most of the examples in the above paragraphs deal with unrecognized *governments* (such as those in East Germany and the Soviet Union) and not with unrecognized *states* (which would be the case for Taiwan, Chechnya, and our four case studies) and that there is a distinction between these two phenomena. Yet, the first part of section 107 quoted above specifically deals with unrecognized states. Similarly, there is no logical reason that the privileges extended to the unrecognized Soviet government in the *Wulfsohn* and *Salimoff* cases would not also apply to the governments of Taiwan, the TRNC, or Eritrea from

1991 - 1993.   One might object that the LTTE's administration in Tamil
Eelam could not meet the same 'We all know that it is a government' test put
forward in the *Salimoff* judgment, but this would only be a reason to argue
that *de facto* states below a certain level are not 'juridically cognizable'.   It
would not be a compelling argument that all such entities are juridically
unrecognizable.

In all of this, M. J. Peterson (1982) finds a serious decline in the
importance of the distinction between recognition and non-recognition.
Recognized and non-recognized governments were, in her view, treated in
dramatically different ways in the nineteenth century. Today, the end result
of this blurring of status is

> a situation in which nonrecognition is not unlike recognition in that it
> presupposes, but does not assure, relations of a certain character.
> Recognition always meant that extensive, formal and political relations
> could begin, but did not guarantee their establishment or continuation.
> Today, it may be argued, nonrecognition means, but does not guarantee, a
> lack of relations (1982, pp. 349-350).

Another lens from which to view the *de facto* state and international
law comes from Common Article 3 of the 1949 Geneva Conventions.   The
historical significance of Common Article 3 is that it was the first attempt to
regulate civil wars through international law.[29]   The article itself defines its
scope in terms of 'armed conflict not of an international character'.   In
essence, it attempts to ensure a certain minimum humanitarian code of
conduct for internal conflicts irrespective of the legal status of the parties
involved.   According to paragraph two, the application of the article's
provisions 'shall not affect the legal status of the Parties to the conflict'.
Further, as the International Committee of the Red Cross (ICRC) emphasizes,
'applying Article 3 does not in itself constitute any recognition by the *de jure*
Government that the adverse Party has authority of any kind'.[30]

Sovereign governments, however, consistently refuse to acknowledge
the applicability of Article 3 to conflicts which take place on their territory.
Thomas Fleiner-Gerster and Michael Meyer (1985) point out that, in applying
Article 3, the sovereign government

> must accept that, notwithstanding the declaration that the application of that
> provision does not change the status of the parties, the revolutionary forces
> then take part in the conflict as a party with responsibilities under Article 3

of the Geneva Conventions of 1949 which are part of international law...
(1985, p. 274).

Sovereign governments would also have to accept allowing the ICRC to have
access to the territory controlled by the rebels without their consent. At least
implicitly, this acknowledges the sovereign's own lack of control over such
territory. As such, there is little incentive to apply Article 3. Rebel groups,
on the other hand, 'which may be considered to be criminal by a State's
internal law and without any international status, will try very hard to get
Article 3 applied because it can give them a quasi-international status...'
(Fleiner-Gerster and Meyer, 1985, p. 274).

Extrapolating from these contrasting positions, one might surmise
that while sovereign states have reasons to exclude *de facto* states from the
international legal system, those entities themselves do not create any
insurmountable problems for international law. Indeed, far from being an
unrepentant outlaw, the *de facto* state actively seeks its own further
incorporation into the international legal system. Thus, international society
can choose to keep Taiwan out of the WTO. The problem, though, is not that
Taiwan cannot or will not meet its obligations under world trade law. The *de
facto* state already has some recognizable international legal presence. It
bears emphasis that its logic and motives do not pose any substantive
problems to its further incorporation into the international legal system.

What of international law's ability to deal with the existence of *de
facto* states? Theoretically, there is not a problem here. International law is
by no means unfamiliar with non-sovereign entities. Historically, it has
found room to accept a wide variety of designations such as associated states,
mandates, trusteeships, colonies, protectorates, free cities, condominia, and
internationalized territories.[31] There is no compelling theoretical reason why
international law could not accommodate the *de facto* state or other such
territorially-based entities which had varying degrees of international
competence. The present system of sovereign states and nothing else could
mutate into a system of sovereign states plus a number of other entities.[32] As
Alan James observes, 'Such a mixed system could not claim to be based on
the equality of all its participants...'. Rather, its 'organizing principle would
therefore be that of accepted international competence' (1986b, p. 267). In
such a system, *de facto* states would have certain rights and responsibilities
and be excluded from others. One can even envision such a system evolving
to the point where finer distinctions are made within the category of *de facto*
statehood. The caveat to all such speculation, however, is that these

theoretical possibilities do not equate with contemporary realities. As James puts it, 'At the practical level, developments moved decisively, a long while ago, in the direction of an international system in which the regular territorial participants were all of the same kind' (1986b, p. 268).

While the practical prospects for such a mixed system are remote and states have shown a marked reluctance to apply the provisions of Article 3, there are a number of reasons why international society might wish to bring *de facto* states further under the authority of its legal system. As W. Michael Reisman and Eisuke Suzuki point out, 'Groups which have not yet been formally recognized as states but whose activities may have significant impacts on the international system are subjected to claims by others for conformity to critical international standards' (1976, p. 442). Commonsense leads one to think that the best way to ensure compliance with such standards is not to cast the *de facto* state as far as possible into the juridical equivalent of outer darkness.

In addition to the interests of the states system as a whole, individual sovereign states will, for example, want to ensure that proper controls are placed on the transfer of dangerous substances such as agricultural pests or toxic wastes regardless of their foreign origin or destination. They may also want to ensure that *de facto* states and other such entities are incorporated into their own domestic legal systems. Looking at the matter from an American perspective, Victor Li (1979) argues that

> the United States should be protected against certain harmful actions taken abroad whether or not they occur in *de jure* recognized countries.... Similarly, statutes that produce beneficial results for the United States or facilitate the operation of American activities abroad should be interpreted to apply to both *de jure* and *de facto* recognized entities (1979, p. 140).

De facto states already have some degree of 'juridically cognizable' existence. There is no theoretical reason why they cannot be further incorporated into the international legal system. While there are some understandable political reasons for sovereign states to oppose such a move, there are also some strong practical reasons for them to support it.

6 Does the *De Facto* State Have Utility for International Society?

Traditionally, the *de facto* state and other secessionist challengers to existing sovereign states have been viewed in extremely negative terms. International society's hostility to secession is based on a number of factors. Foremost among these is the domino theory and the fear of never-ending secession. While extreme versions of this theory should be rejected, the structural nature of the state-nation disjunction and the potential instability that would characterize any move away from the fixed territorial borders regime are legitimate concerns. International society's general conservatism here manifests itself as a fear of the unknown and a presumption in favor of the devil you know (the existing system) as opposed to the devil you do not know (any new regime allowing for secession). Thus, the standard view that secession should only be seen as a remedy of last resort. As Charles Beitz (1979) puts it, since secession involves a redistribution of personal, political, and property rights, 'it requires a justification against the general presumption that existing arrangements should not be interfered with without good reasons'.[33] The extent of economic and other issues to be worked out in any secession—including such things as the division of public assets and debts, treaty obligations, disentangling or maintaining monetary linkages, and the like—also counsels against secession (Bookman, 1992, pp. 119-143).

A variety of other concerns also inform international society's bias against secession. There is the question of mineral resources and the fear that allowing mineral-rich regions to secede may impoverish the remainder of the parent state. The inverse of this concern is the fear that the new states created by any secession will not be economically viable. In both of these arguments, secession is opposed because of the fear that it will produce a new group of mendicant states that drain the resources of international society. The only difference is that, in the first case, it is the secessionists impoverishing the existing state while, in the second, it is the secessionists themselves ending up impoverished. Both arguments suffer from the confused notion of equating economic viability with economic self-sufficiency or autarky (Schroeder, 1992, p. 549), yet they do raise legitimate points. There is also the problem of 'trapped minorities'—essentially the fear that secession will create new minorities. One recent example of this was Croatia's secession creating the 'trapped' Serb minority in Krajina. Secession is also opposed because it is seen as contrary to majority rule. How can majority rule work if minorities can opt out whenever they do not like something? Finally, secession is often seen as an inappropriate solution. The evidence from countries such as India and Pakistan indicates that separatist groups can successfully be reabsorbed into a larger pluralistic state. The logic of secession undermines this and therefore undermines the entire concept of the civic, multi-national state. Secession is often justified on the grounds of an inability to participate in political life. Yet, as Lea Brilmayer (1991) argues, participatory rights do not suggest secession as a remedy. Rather, 'they suggest that the appropriate solution for dissatisfied groups rests in their full inclusion in the polity, with full participation in its decision-making processes' (1991, p. 185).

There are, thus, a number of reasons why international society is hostile to secession and, by extension, to the *de facto* state. In contrast to this prevailing hostility, we now consider the question of whether or not the *de facto* state may, in some cases, actually serve a useful purpose for international society. While the evidence presented is much more potentially illustrative than it is definitive, a good case can be made that the *de facto* state is indeed a useful entity for the society of states.

The first way in which the *de facto* state may have utility is as a messy solution to a messy problem. The classic example here is Northern Cyprus. While few would argue that the TRNC represents a just, fair, legal, or pareto-optimal settlement to the Cyprus dispute, its effectiveness in terms of reducing tension, violence, and human suffering is hard to question. It is noteworthy that Cyprus registered as a blip on the world's media screens in 1996 when *two* Greek Cypriots were killed in incidents along the green line. The dramatic coverage given to these two unfortunate deaths only serves to highlight the fact that Cyprus has generally been an extremely stable place since 1974. A grand total of six people were killed along the green line from 1988 - 1994 and *The Economist* described the 900-some incidents noted by UN peacekeepers in one year as being 'mostly footling'.[34] In 1992, Security Council Resolution 774 reaffirmed the UN's view that the present *status quo* on Cyprus is unacceptable. Yet, the fact remains that the *status quo* on Cyprus has been quite viable for more than twenty years. The Greek Cypriot economy has developed rapidly and the Turkish Cypriots are willing to trade the costs of economic embargo for the benefits of political security. The TRNC *de facto* state is a messy solution because it exists in defiance of numerous international legal norms and UN resolutions, but it is a solution nonetheless. While it is easy to envision potentially better scenarios for Cyprus without the TRNC, it is also easy to envision dramatically worse scenarios than the present *status quo*.

The work of Chaim Kaufmann (1996) on how ethnic wars end provides some theoretical context from which to view the TRNC's 'messy solution' option. Kaufmann distinguishes between ethnic wars and ideological wars and argues that 'Stable resolutions of ethnic civil wars are possible, but only when the opposing groups are demographically separated into defensible enclaves'. In making this point, he emphasizes the fact that 'Sovereignty is secondary: defensible ethnic enclaves reduce violence with or without independent sovereignty...' (1996, p. 137). Kaufmann bases his argument on two main insights. First, through hypernationalist mobilizations and real atrocities, ethnic wars lead to a hardening of identity which means that cross-ethnic political appeals are unlikely to succeed. Second, intermingled populations create real security dilemmas that escalate the incentives for offensive combat. Solutions that aim to avoid partition and population transfers through power-sharing or state re-building will not work because they do nothing to minimize the security dilemma created by the existence of intermingled populations. Kaufmann readily acknowledges the fact that partition is considered anathema but paraphrases Winston Churchill to argue that 'separation is the worst solution, except for all the others'.[35] The choice for the international community may thus be quite stark: uphold international sovereignty norms at the cost of continued ethnic violence or save lives at the expense of ignoring the state-centric legal regime.

The potential utility of the *de facto* state as a messy solution is limited here for three main reasons. First, not all *de facto* states are ethnically-based, nor do all conflicts revolve around an ethnic axis. Second, partition along ethnic lines undermines the entire concept of the civic state and is therefore unlikely to garner widespread support. Another problem with partition, seen in both the Cypriot and Bosnian cases, is that it generally cannot produce ethnic homogeneity unless it is accompanied by massive population transfers. As Aaron Klieman observes, 'the flaw of partition lies in the necessary process by which an abstract concept is converted into a specific concrete proposal' (1980, p. 283). Third, the international community has a natural preference for solutions such as federalism or regional autonomy that fall far short of *de facto* statehood. The main problem with this preference, as Barbara Thomas-Woolley and Edmond Keller point out, is that 'The successful federation of deeply divided societies requires sincere political will and a determination to remain true to the terms establishing the new system of government and administration' (1994, p. 424). Such determination and political will, though, have been manifestly lacking in each of our four case studies.

Still, Ted Robert Gurr (1994) sees modest prospects for negotiated regional autonomy as a solution to ethnonational wars of secession. Eight of the 27 ethnic civil wars that have concluded in his data-set were ended with a negotiated solution that did not involve partition. Yet, each of these cases involved a regionally concentrated minority whose ethnic role in politics was reinforced through some sort of autonomy arrangement. Additionally, the violence involved in these eight cases was of a much lower order of magnitude than in the other cases which ended in either outright military victory for one side; suppression by a third party; or *de jure* or *de facto* partition. Kaufmann concludes that 'There is not a single case where non-ethnic civil politics were created or restored by reconstruction of ethnic identities, power-sharing coalitions, or state-building'.[36]

Thus, while one can always hope for and work toward a negotiated federal settlement, when push comes to shove, a *de facto* state solution may not be the worst option available to international society. Indeed, there are a few distinct advantages to using the *de facto* state in this way. First, because international society refuses to recognize the *de facto* state or grant it juridical legitimacy, aggression is not seen to be rewarded and future would-be secessionists are not provided with any encouragement. The rules and norms of existing sovereign legitimacy are thus upheld even though the *de facto* state functions as a sort of unacknowledged solution to the problem at hand. Second, because of their illegitimacy, *de facto* states are ineligible to make claims on the resources of international society. They are thus not likely to be extremely burdensome on the rest of the world. Third, and perhaps most importantly, the existence of *de facto* states does not preclude other future settlement possibilities. There is no reason why, for example, the existence of the Republic of Somaliland need preclude any future union, federation, confederation, or specific cooperative agreements with southern Somalia should the political will and popular support exist on both sides to enter into such arrangements. In regard to Taiwan, Victor Li points out that the '*de facto* entity concept deals with present political realities and does not require or preclude eventual reunification' (1979, p. 138). The extensive cooperation which took place between the PGE and Ethiopia is also illustrative here. One of the main concerns with granting Eritrea independence was that Ethiopia would become landlocked. As such, it is quite significant that one of the first official acts of the PGE was to enter into an agreement which declared Assab a free port of Ethiopia. A further agreement was signed giving Massawa the same status a few months later. Additionally, the two governments agreed to share a common currency and to provide for the free movement of citizens and trade across their borders.[37]

Another major way in which the *de facto* state may be seen as having utility is as a pragmatic and ad hoc way of reconciling irreconcilable principles. While there may be other examples, our consideration here is limited to two areas: self-determination short of full independence and the attempt to formulate criteria for 'just' secessions. The phrase 'self-determination short of full independence' is essentially shorthand for the belief that self-determination should embody a greater variety of choices than just sovereign statehood. In and of itself this idea is not controversial. Indeed, the International Court of Justice's advisory opinion in the *Western Sahara* case as well as General Assembly Resolutions 1541 (15 December 1960) and 2625 (the Declaration on Friendly Relations, 24 October 1970) all acknowledge that an act of self-determination need not result in sovereign independence. Free association or integration with an independent state are also deemed to be 'acceptable' forms of self-determination (Emerson, 1971, p. 470; Pomerance, 1984, p. 327; White, 1981-82, p. 149). Yet, in spite of this, actual UN practice has narrowly interpreted self-determination through a dichotomous lens that presents only two choices: sovereign statehood for the chosen few and absolutely nothing for the rest. As Michla Pomerance (1984) puts it, in the UN's vision of self-determination,

> the 'all-or-nothing' principle obtains, and it revolves around the 'colonial-racist' appellation. Those groups subjected to 'colonialism' and 'racism' are accorded plenary rights—*full* 'external' self-determination in the form of independence; but other groups may be accorded *no* rights, the sovereign gates barring secession from within and intervention from without... (1984, p. 333).

The UN's all-or-nothing conception of self-determination reflects the near-universal triumph of the sovereign state over all other forms of political organization. F. H. Hinsley (1986) dates the complete victory of sovereignty from the Concert of Europe period in the 1820s. As he sees it, sovereignty at that time was adopted as a 'fundamental idea' and, as such, 'the solution of all problems and the adjustment to all new developments were made to conform to it' (1986, pp. 204-205). One of the examples Hinsley cites here is the fact that the international status of the Holy See could not be settled without resorting to the device of establishing a sovereign Vatican city-state. Such rigidity affects our political choices today. As Stephen Krasner points out, 'the sovereign state is the only universally recognized way of organizing political life in the contemporary international system. It is now difficult to even conceive of alternatives' (1988, p. 90).

The argument here is not that the *de facto* state is an ideal solution to the need for more alternatives than just sovereignty or, from the perspective of the affected groups themselves, the vastly inferior concept of minority rights within existing states.[38] Rather, the argument is that in some cases the *de facto* state may serve as a functional 'non-solution' to this problem. The international community might, for example, determine that the people of Somaliland deserve better than forced reincorporation into Somalia's warlord-based politics and that the consociational rule of the Egal administration is far from the worst option available. At the same time, however, there is no desire to encourage other would-be secessionists or to 'unfreeze' the existing territorial map. As such, a strategy of either benignly ignoring the Somaliland *de facto* state or reaching some sort of limited accommodation with it may be in the best interests of all parties. Such a solution is not ideal, but it does have the important advantages of leaving future options open; preserving existing international norms; and requiring little in the way of monetary or diplomatic expenditures from international society.

Another major area where the *de facto* state may be seen as an ad hoc or pragmatic method of reconciling irreconcilable principles concerns the whole question of establishing criteria to distinguish legitimate from illegitimate secession attempts. There are a number of potential benefits to establishing criteria for 'legitimate' or 'just' secessions. Such criteria could help the international community balance its concerns for order between states and order within states. The existence of established criteria might also encourage moderation, both on the part of secessionists themselves and on the part of sovereign governments. Established criteria would also bring some degree of order and rationality to an area that has to date been ruled by inconsistency, hypocrisy, and unpredictability. As Lee Buchheit argues, 'Surely it is wiser, and in the end safer, to raise secessionist claims above the present "force of arms" test into a sphere in which rational discussion can illuminate the legitimate interests of all concerned' (1978, p. 245).

Along these lines, a number of attempts have been made at devising criteria for secession. Still, nothing even beginning to approach a consensus on the 'standards of legitimacy' for secession has been reached. In part, this is due to the difficulties in reconciling incompatible principles—how to balance self-determination with territorial integrity, for example. In part, this is also due to the unavoidable subjectivity involved in ascertaining such things as the degree of popular support for a secessionist movement or the existence of a separate nation. Finally, much of the problem results from the inability to translate vague theoretical premises into clear and concise guidelines. Eisuke Suzuki (1976), for example, bases his criteria on the need 'to approximate a public order of human dignity...'. Along these lines, 'the test of reasonableness is the determining factor in deciding how to respond to the claim of self-determination' (1976, p. 784). How such a vague notion as 'the test of reasonableness' can be any guide to achieving the equally vague goal of 'a public order of human dignity' is not mentioned. Similarly, for Lung-Chu Chen, the critical test in assessing a claim of self-determination 'is to evaluate the aggregate value consequences of honoring or rejecting the claim for all affected communities, potential as well as existing' (1991, pp. 1294 and 1296). Needless to say, one's perception of the 'aggregate value consequences' of honoring the TRNC's claim to self-determination varies dramatically depending upon which side of the green line one stands on.

As was the case with self-determination short of full independence, the *de facto* state may be an adequate (if not ideal) non-solution to this inability to reach consensus on the criteria for legitimate secession. Following this logic, one might argue that there will never be any commonly-accepted criteria for determining the legitimacy of secession because international society can never accept the prospect of secession as legitimate. As such, preserving the existing norms against secession and territorial revision is of paramount importance. Yet, forcing highly-mobilized populations with legitimate grievances and responsible leaderships to remain yoked to the likes of a Mengistu or a Siad Barre is extremely difficult to justify, even on the basis of international order. In this regard, international society can ignore or accept a *de facto* state on a limited basis without compromising its norms on fixed territorial borders or preserving the juridical existence of all current states. Under such a scenario, the secessionists are not offered any support or encouragement to reach the level of *de facto* statehood. Once there, however, they are allowed, more or less, to go about their business—with the one huge caveat that they must nominally remain a part of the state which they are trying so hard to leave.

The final way in which to view the question of the *de facto* state's utility is to compare it to Robert Jackson's (1990) arguments on the utility of the quasi-state. Jackson finds three main reasons why 'the negative sovereignty game' will likely have continued utility in the future (1990, pp. 189-202). The first reason is instrumental—essentially a powerful conservatism that is part inertia, part lack of imagination, and part fear that the costs of alternative arrangements may exceed their benefits. In the words of Alan James, the international community continues to recognize quasi-states and collapsed states because of its fear 'that abandoning what is little more than a pretence may open up a far more alarming prospect than continuing to connive at an unreality' (1986b, p. 117). This first reason poses no problem for the *de facto* state in that conniving at the unreality that

Northern Cyprus does not exist allows international society to maintain the illusion that a unified Republic of Cyprus does exist. Jackson's second reason is normative—international relations cannot be based on power and interest alone and must include not only law, but also respect, consideration, decorum, and courtesy. Again, this does not pose a problem for the utility of *de facto* states. Somalia's ambassador to the UN can be treated with sympathy, wined, dined, and fêted with the best of them all the while Somaliland continues to collect its tax revenues on the export of livestock to the Gulf states. Jackson's third reason is institutional—once the negative sovereignty regime was adopted, other options were precluded and set institutional arrangements are highly impervious to change. Nothing about the *de facto* state necessitates fundamental or even moderate institutional change in the present international system. As such, the potential utility of these entities to international society is in no way incompatible with the benefits of the negative sovereignty regime.

7 Conclusion

This chapter has analyzed the impact of *de facto* states on both international law and international society. While the limited numbers of these entities relegate the *de facto* state to a somewhat peripheral role in international relations, their impact on such things as conflict and political economy is far from negligible. International society has traditionally chosen to deal with this phenomenon in one of three main ways—actively trying to undermine them; more or less ignoring them; and reaching some sort of limited working accommodation with them. Each of these various methods has a different set of costs and benefits both for the *de facto* state and for the society of states as a whole. An implicit theme running throughout this chapter is that these entities matter and that the members of international society need to devote more attention to the question of how best to cope with their existence.

In terms of international law, the *de facto* state's lack of sovereignty does not prevent it from having a juridically cognizable existence. Perhaps surprisingly, international law is revealed to be quite capable of accommodating the *de facto* state—at least theoretically. There are obvious political reasons why existing sovereign states will likely continue to resist such an accommodation within the international legal system. Yet, there are also compelling practical reasons why sovereign states should want to see these entities further incorporated both into international law and into their own national legal systems. Intuitively, barring the legal gates and denying the *de facto* state even an extremely limited legal competence does not seem to be the way to encourage compliance with the fundamental norms, let alone the *desiderata* of international law.

Finally, in contrast to the prevailing negativity and disparaging judgments usually leveled against such entities, the argument put forth here is that the *de facto* state may, in some cases and in some regards, actually serve useful purposes. It is not claimed that the members of international society have consciously turned to these entities in an attempt to find the proverbial 'lesser of two evils' when faced with particularly difficult choices. Nor is it argued that these entities provide ideal solutions to most problems. Rather, the much more limited claim is that the existence of *de facto* states produces not only costs, but also benefits for the society of states. The evidence presented for the *de facto* state's utility is more speculative than it is conclusive but it does suggest that the prevailing view of these entities in solely negative terms obscures as much as it reveals. By its very nature, the *de facto* state is well suited to situations where the international community needs to be seen to be upholding cherished norms, while at the same time it finds creative or ad hoc ways to get around those very same norms. Its inherently nebulous status has the additional benefit of not precluding any other future settlement arrangements. If the *de facto* state did not exist, it might not need to be invented. Its very existence does, however, potentially offer a number of benefits to the society of sovereign states.

The next chapter concludes our birth, life, and death or evolution examination of the *de facto* state. Whereas this chapter considered the life phase, chapter eight examines the various possible transformations that these entities may go through. From the perspective of the *de facto* state itself, these options range from the terrible (military eradication) to the outstanding (graduation to sovereign statehood). Continued *de facto* statehood is also a real possibility. Their lack of juridical acceptance, however, creates a certain instability in status that necessitates an examination of the various ways in which these entities can evolve. Such an examination is the focus of chapter eight.

Notes

[1]   Note: These figures are composite calculations by the author based on the information provided in chapters three and four of this study. As many of these

figures are themselves contested and/or best guess estimates, these numbers should be seen as illustrative approximations rather than as definitive facts.

[2] For more on the Chechens' proposed five-year transition period to a referendum on independence, see 'A Way Out of Chechnya', *The Economist*, 31 August 1996.

[3] 'Kurds Blow Smoke Rings Across Iraq', *The New York Times*, 17 August 1994.

[4] Telephone interview with Ms. Cathy Hsu, Taipei Economic and Cultural Office in Seattle, 17 December 1997. See also 'Beware of Squirrels', *The Economist*, 11 January 1997.

[5] Movement certificates establish a good's place of origin. Phyto-sanitary certificates guarantee plant health.

[6] 'Ruling on Cypriot Import Certificates', *Financial Times*, 12 July 1994; and 'Cyprus: As Divided As Ever', *The Economist*, 6 August 1994.

[7] United States Department of State, 'Cyprus Country Report on Human Rights Practices for 1996'.

[8] 'PPI Case Judge Says No to Defence', *The Times*, 6 March 1996; and 'Asil Nadir's Aide is Brought to Book', *The Guardian*, 27 April 1996.

[9] 'Russian Syndicates Gain Hold in Israel; Political Influence Latest Crime Threat', *The Washington Times*, 29 April 1996.

[10] 'Russia's Budget: Another Battle to Fight', *The Economist*, 24 August 1996.

[11] 'Horn of Africa in Brief; Eritrea UN Permanent Representative to Open Office in Asmera', *BBC Summary of World Broadcasts*, 15 November 1991; 'Ethiopia; USAID Proposes Aid Worth 55m Dollars', *BBC Summary of World Broadcasts*, 18 February 1992.

[12] 'Somaliland; President Tells UN Officials Aid Agencies Doing More Harm Than Good', *BBC Summary of World Broadcasts*, 6 June 1995; telephone interview with Mr. Ken Shivers, US State Department desk officer for Djibouti and Somalia, 10 April 1997.

[13] Telephone interview with Dr. Sazil Korküt, TRNC representative in New York, 15 April 1997.

[14] Telephone interview with Ms. Siria Lopez, US State Department desk officer for Cyprus, 15 April 1997.

[15] 'Ethiopia Agrees Foreign Contact With Separatist Eritrea', *The Reuter Library Report*, 29 October 1991. See also 'Ethiopia: Eritrean [incorrect heading] President Invites Foreign States to Deal With Provisional Government', *African Business*, 1 December 1991.

[16] Necatigil, 1989, p. 165. Drysdale, 1992, p. 35 also advocates the use of such an approach for Somaliland.

[17] For more on this, see Republic of China, 1993, p. 174.

[18] Ya Qin, 1992, p. 1073. See also Republic of China, 1993, pp. 178-179.

[19] The Carter quote is cited in Li, 1979, p. 137. On the significance of the TRA, see Ling, 1983, pp. 163-184; Mangelson, 1992, pp. 231-251; Randolph, 1981, pp. 249-262; and Sheikh, 1980, pp. 323-341.

20 For more on the AIT, see Ling, 1983, pp. 173-174; Randolph, 1981, pp. 251-253; and Sheikh, 1980, p. 339.

21 'Taiwan Investors Unaffected by Chinese Sabre-Rattling', *Financial Times*, 25 July 1995; and 'Taiwan: The Outsider', *The Economist*, 2 July 1994.

22 Lefkosa (sometimes spelled with a cedilla on the s) is the Turkish name for Nicosia. As such, this formula would be the TRNC equivalent of 'Taipei, China'. Dr. Sazil Korküt, the TRNC representative in New York, is somewhat dismissive of Taiwanese pragmatism in this regard. What good would it do, he asks, for the TRNC to change its name in order to be admitted to an international organization that deals with Latin America. Telephone interview, 15 April 1997.

23 Initially, it can be argued that the Taiwanese did elevate political factors over economic ones in order to cement their security relationship with America. Once the American military umbrella was in place, however, the economic began to assert itself as the most important factor. At present, one can see signs that the political is beginning to reemerge and reassert itself in Taiwan. Taiwanese exceptionalism in this regard is thus somewhat historically bounded.

24 Reproduced in Crawford, 1976-77, p. 146.

25 Cited on pp. 257-258 of Randolph, 1981.

26 Cited on p. 258 of Randolph, 1981.

27 Cited in footnote #16, p. 139 of Li, 1979.

28 Cited on p. 259 of Randolph, 1981.

29 For a variety of perspectives on both the significance of Common Article 3 and its limitations, see Fleiner-Gerster and Meyer, 1985, pp. 269-271; Røling, 1976, p. 151; Higgins, 1972, pp. 182-183; and H.A. Wilson, 1988, pp. 43-48.

30 ICRC Commentary, cited on p. 3 of Human Rights Watch/Asia, 1995.

31 See Buchheit, 1978, p. 233; and Hannum, 1990, pp. 16-18 for more on this.

32 For an argument that international law needs to move in this direction, see Buchanan, 1991, pp. 20-21.

33 Beitz, 1979, pp. 111-112. Similar sentiments are also expressed in the American Declaration of Independence; Buchheit, 1978, pp. 214-215; Halperin and Scheffer with Small, 1992, p. 74; and Zartman, 1995c, p. 268.

34 'Cyprus: As Divided as Ever', *The Economist*, 6 August 1994.

35 The specific quote is from Kaufmann, 1996, p. 170. The general discussion comes from pp. 136-175.

36 Kaufmann, 1996, p. 161; and Gurr, 1994, p. 366.

37 Kidane Mengisteab, 1994, p. 73; Pateman, 1994, p. 231; Araia Tseggai, 1994, footnote #8, p. 66; and Tekie Fessehatzion, 1994, pp. 42 and 50.

38 The prospects for and the problems with the concept of minority rights are canvassed in chapter ten.

8   Potential Transformations of the *De Facto* State

1 Introduction

This chapter concludes our birth, life, and death or evolution examination of the *de facto* state by focusing on the ways in which these entities may ultimately develop or be transformed.   Transformation is by no means preordained and continued existence as a *de facto* state is certainly one possibility we might expect to see. Yet, compared to the legal stability and extremely low death rate so characteristic of contemporary sovereign states, the *de facto* state is a volatile entity. The general unwillingness of sovereign states to participate peacefully in their own dismemberment, combined with international society's refusal to accept these entities as legitimate are strong reasons one might expect to see their future demise or metamorphosis. From the perspective of the *de facto* state itself, its various possible transformations range from the dismal (complete military eradication) to the triumphal (successful graduation to sovereign statehood), with a host of other options in between. All of these possibilities are considered below. Methodologically, the limited number of cases available prevents us from predicting the likelihood of each outcome with any degree of precision. Therefore, the specific examples used are designed to illustrate possibilities, not to predict outcomes. The chapter concludes with an examination of the various factors which determine success or failure in securing sovereign recognition.

2 Three Different Types of Military Defeat

In theory, a *de facto* state might peacefully collapse on its own accord due to some combination of poor leadership, declining popular support, harsh economic conditions, inter-group fighting, and the like. The most likely route, however, to *de facto* state collapse is through some form of military defeat. Within that realm, there are a number of potentially different outcomes. Here we consider three: a complete military defeat that is coupled with an expulsion or mass flight of the civilian population; a complete military defeat which leads to a more or less successful reincorporation into the existing sovereign state; and a partial military defeat that transforms the *de facto* state into something more akin to isolated enclaves of rebellion or a terrorist threat.

The first option is obviously the worst fate which can befall a *de facto* state. Whereas lesser forms of military defeat may only lead to its destruction as a viable political institution, this option in effect leads to its complete eradication as both the political infrastructure and the popular support base are eliminated. The one classic example here comes from Krajina. This is the crescent-shaped region of Croatia where fighting first broke out between Serbs and Croats in the summer of 1991. Before the war, around 400,000 people lived in the region. The Croatian residents of Krajina (approximately one-half of the original population) fled or were expelled in 1991 following the initial fighting. For just over four years, the 'Republic of Serbian Krajina', with its capital at Knin, functioned as a *de facto* state for the remaining ethnic Serb population under the leadership of President Milan Martic. For much of this time UN peacekeepers patrolled the cease-fire line separating the Krajina *de facto* state from the rest of Croatia.

On 4 August 1995, Croatian forces launched 'Operation Storm' against Krajina. This region's unusual shape meant that the estimated 30 - 50,000 Krajina Serb soldiers defending it had to cover a frontier that was more than 700 miles long. With no help forthcoming from Serbia itself, the Krajina Serbs were overrun in just three days. Along with the retreating soldiers, approximately 150,000 Krajina Serb civilians also left the region. Only about 3,500 people remained behind—most of whom were either too sick or too old to join those who fled to Serb-held territory in Bosnia.[1] Minus the vast majority of its ethnic Serb population, Krajina has now been fully reintegrated into Croatia. Whereas moderates in the former *de facto* state might once have sought some sort of negotiated regional autonomy within Croatia, nothing whatsoever now remains of the Republic of Serbian Krajina. From the perspective of the *de facto* state itself, it is hard to imagine a worse fate than that which befell Krajina.

The best example of a complete military defeat leading to successful reincorporation into the existing sovereign state comes from Biafra. In this case, the Biafran secession was formally proclaimed on 30 May 1967. Nigerian federal troops subsequently invaded Biafra on 5 July 1967. Under the leadership of Odumegwu Ojukwu, the Biafrans essentially sought to fight a prolonged defensive war against the vastly superior Nigerian forces. As

Crawford Young points out, the hope was that 'if Biafra could hold out long enough, world opinion would force Nigeria into negotiations which would result in de facto independence, or that the pressures of the war would bring about the disintegration of Nigeria' (1983, p. 210). The Biafrans were at least partially successful in their attempt to swing world opinion behind their cause. Tanzania became the first country to extend Biafra *de jure* recognition on 13 April 1968. Subsequently, Gabon (8 May 1968), Ivory Coast (14 May 1968), Zambia (20 May 1968) and Haiti (May 1969) also extended *de jure* recognition to Biafra. France was instrumental in providing the Biafrans with arms and other forms of financial assistance. A variety of other countries including Israel, the PRC, Portugal, Senegal, Sierra Leone, and Uganda also provided the Biafrans with various forms of assistance. Many others expressed concern at the humanitarian plight of those involved in the civil war (Heraclides, 1990, p. 348; Ijalaye, 1971, pp. 553-554; C. Young, 1983, pp. 209-210).

The Biafrans were ultimately unsuccessful in their secession attempt for a variety of reasons. The strain of the war did not lead to a general collapse of the Nigerian state and the federal forces received substantial military assistance from the UK and the Soviet Union. Despite the four African states that recognized it, the OAU's orthodox interpretation of the need to preserve existing territorial boundaries prevailed. The Biafrans also failed to secure the support of many of the non-Ibo minorities located within the Eastern Region of Nigeria. On 12 January 1970, the Biafran forces formally surrendered and brought their secessionist bid to an end. Unlike the situation in Krajina, there was no mass popular exodus following this military defeat.

In spite of the fears of the Biafran leadership and much of the Ibo population, there was no wholesale settling of scores with those who had tried to secede from Nigeria. The federal forces are generally credited with being quite magnanimous in their efforts to reintegrate the residents of the former Biafran *de facto* state back into Nigeria. What Crawford Young refers to as 'the haunting fear of genocide' was ultimately laid to rest: 'for the most part, Federal troops remained under control, and did not exact vengeance upon the Ibo populace' (1983, p. 211). Thus, the Biafran example can be used to illustrate two important points regarding the evolution or transformation of *de facto* states: 1) complete military defeat need not lead to massive population movements; and 2) even after a long and bitter struggle, successful non-violent reintegration is still quite possible.

Our final scenario in this regard is a partial military defeat that transforms the *de facto* state into something more akin to isolated enclaves of rebellion or a mere terrorist threat. In other words, an entity which once would have qualified as a *de facto* state suffers such a decline in capabilities that it now falls afoul of our second theoretical criterion in chapter two which distinguishes these entities from other groups or situations such as terrorists, riots, sporadic violence, and random banditry. Though it is far too early to make any definitive judgments in this regard, perhaps the best potential example here might be the position of the LTTE following the Sri Lankan army's capture of Jaffna city in December 1995. Along these lines, *The Straits Times* reported that the fall of Jaffna and other subsequent losses sustained in 1996 signified that 'In less than a year, the Tigers had been reduced from a rebel movement in effective control of the northern third of Sri Lanka, to a guerilla force operating from the jungles...'.[2] The LTTE can, however, be seen as trying to maintain or recreate its *de facto* state within the context of new and altered boundaries through its attempts at forcibly resettling displaced civilians into areas still under its control. Whether this attempt ultimately succeeds or not remains to be seen.

Unlike the situations in Krajina and Biafra, should the LTTE ultimately fail in its attempt to maintain or recreate its *de facto* state, its challenge to the Sri Lankan government will not disappear. In this regard, A. Jeyaratnam Wilson and Chelvadurai Manogaran (1994) argue that while the Sri Lankan army can conceivably regain control of the northeast, 'it can never win the hearts and minds of the Tamil people or bring to a complete halt what will be a continuing guerrilla struggle...'. They go on to maintain that the army's hopes of dealing the LTTE a 'death blow' like they did to the JVP are misplaced for the latter 'was not broad-based whereas the Tigers have the support of the civilian population' (1994, p. 240). Rather than disappear, the LTTE *de facto* state would likely mutate into an exclusively terrorist threat or some sort of a low-level guerrilla war. In some ways, this is an artificial distinction—even when functioning as a *de facto* state, the LTTE has never been adverse to the use of terrorist tactics. What would be different now is that whereas those tactics had previously been carried out within the context of also providing some form of civil administration to the local population, they would now be the organization's sole *raison d' être*.

This type of evolution would return the LTTE to a situation somewhat analogous to the state of affairs prevailing at the height of the IPKF intervention. During this time, the LTTE 'survived for more than two years in the jungles of the North and retained the potential to wage a hit and run war in the urban centres' (Hoole, Somasundaram, Sritharan, and Thiranagama, 1990, p. 411). This scenario potentially poses a number of problems for the Sri Lankan government. In particular, it could find itself facing the same type of dilemma that the IPKF did in being 'unable to scale down the level of conflict, or to reduce the tempo of human rights violations carried out by its troops in frustrated reprisal raids' (Hoole, Somasundaram, Sritharan, and Thiranagama, 1990, p. 411). The result would be further alienation of the Tamil population. Should such a scenario unfold, the LTTE might even be able to reconstruct its *de facto* state at a later date—as it did after the withdrawal of the IPKF.

Obviously, from the perspective of the existing sovereign government, either of the first two scenarios presented above is preferable to the third. This is because the first two scenarios each imply a degree of finality, whereas the third implies a continued challenge to sovereign authority, albeit at a somewhat lower level than before. Conversely, from the perspective of the *de facto* state's political leadership, the third scenario is the 'least bad' alternative in that it at least allows for the possibility of some continuation of the struggle and perhaps even a return to *de facto* statehood at a later date. From the standpoint of the civilian population, however, the second scenario (successful reintegration into the existing state) may be preferable to continued struggle in that they will no longer be subjected to reprisal attacks or other abuses as the government struggles to eradicate the remaining guerrilla forces.

International society generally directs its efforts towards the successful reintegration or accommodation of dissident groups within the fixed borders of existing states. In some cases, however, either the first or the third scenarios presented above may be preferred by individual states. In the case of Krajina, the first scenario was more or less palatable in that it paved the way for a final settlement to the various conflicts in the former Yugoslavia. The elimination of the Krajina *de facto* state removed a major impediment to Croatia's acceptance of a settlement and it also relieved the pressure on the isolated Bosnian Muslim enclave of Bihac. The mass exodus from Krajina also poignantly reinforced to the Bosnian Serbs their own vulnerability and hence their interest in reaching some sort of accord. Obviously no international leader is going to go on record in favor of the mass creation of refugees as a means of conflict resolution, but this is in effect what happened in Krajina. The third scenario of having the *de facto* state transformed into some sort of terrorist threat or low-level guerrilla war may be appealing to states which do not want to condone the break-up of their neighbors but which wish to limit domestic irredentist pressure to intervene on behalf of their ethnic brethren in another state. Such a guerrilla force may also be useful for harassing and thereby preoccupying one's neighbors.[3]

3 Continued Existence as a *De Facto* State

Although this chapter is concerned with potential transformations of the *de facto* state, one distinct possibility for these entities is a continuation of the *status quo*. Indeed, there are a number of reasons to suspect that non-transformation or stasis may be the most likely outcome for these entities. The single leading reason to expect this is likely to be the continued persistence of the various international norms and regimes identified in chapter five on such things as fixed territorial borders, juridical statehood, collective non-recognition, and an extremely narrow interpretation of self-determination. All of these factors are designed to ensure that *de facto* states remain just that: graduation to sovereign statehood, though not impossible, is extremely unlikely. As advancing beyond *de facto* statehood is so difficult, if these entities are able to avoid military defeat, peaceful implosion, or a gradual loss of capabilities and support, one might expect to see a continuation of the *status quo* in a number of cases.

A second reason to expect a continuation of the present state of affairs is the past track record of many of these entities. Although Biafra and Krajina each failed to reach their fifth birthdays, all of the four cases examined in this study have crossed the five-year threshold of *de facto* statehood. The TRNC will likely celebrate its fifteenth anniversary in 1998 and there has been a Northern Cypriot *de facto* state for more than twenty years now. Contrary to the plethora of diplomatic expressions on the subject, the *status quo* in Northern Cyprus appears viable—at least in the short-to-medium term future. The vast majority of Turkish Cypriots continue to support trading the costs of economic embargo for the benefits of communal security.[4] Additionally, the costs of assisting the TRNC are not an insurmountable burden for Turkey. As Chaim Kaufmann points out, 'Although the weakness of the Turkish Republic of Northern Cyprus has required a permanent Turkish garrison, the almost equal weakness of the Greek Cypriots allows the garrison to be small, cheap, and inactive' (1996, p. 166). In the case of Somaliland, economic conditions have actually improved under the SNM's leadership and one would be hard-pressed to come up with any concrete reasons why the civilian population here would want to trade its present *de facto* statehood for future reintegration with Somalia.

Further, many sovereign states are unlikely to become efficient, effective, or attractive places to be anytime soon. As such, they are unlikely to be successful in their attempts to force their *de facto* state challengers into submission or to seduce their civilian supporters with offers of a better deal. The various components of the weak state security problematic are exceedingly difficult to overcome. The structural nature of this problematic leads Joel Migdal (1988) to conclude that the elapse of time will not necessarily lead to more success in the state-building enterprise. As he sees it, 'slim prospects now exist for qualitative leaps in the consolidation of social control on the part of states in societies that now have fragmented social control'.[5] As such, 'Without severe social dislocations and additional conducive conditions, it is unlikely that new strong states will emerge in the foreseeable future'.[6] Thus, although the *de facto* state may not be able to translate its empirical success into juridical recognition, the continued ineptitude of its quasi-state parent assists it in maintaining its present status.

The prospects for continued *de facto* statehood also depend to some degree on international society's reaction to these entities. Going back to our three models in chapter seven, the TRNC example clearly shows that even an extended isolate and embargo strategy need not preclude continued existence as a *de facto* state. Other things being equal, however, one suspects that the ability of these entities to maintain their present status would be greater under either the benign neglect or the limited acceptance scenarios than it would be in the face of concerted opposition.

Continued *de facto* statehood, at least in the short-to-medium term future, may be the safest prediction for Chechnya, Somaliland, and the TRNC. In the case of Chechnya, the Russians no longer appear to have the will to attempt to subdue it by force. As the Chechens do not appear at risk for any type of substantive military defeat, continued *de facto* statehood appears likely. The big question here is whether or not the Russians will go ahead with their reported plans to allow the Chechens to hold a referendum on independence after a five-year transition period. Should they do so, graduation to sovereign statehood would then become a distinct possibility for Chechnya. Short of extending diplomatic recognition, the international community has shown some signs of willingness to accommodate Somaliland. This, combined with the SNM's relative economic success, its consociational politics, and the chaotic state of affairs in Mogadishu should allow the Somaliland *de facto* state to survive. As for sovereign statehood,

Somaliland has yet to secure any international recognition. The US has told President Egal that it will not extend diplomatic recognition until after Somaliland's neighbors and the OAU have already done so.[7] Considering the OAU's almost sacrosanct commitment to fixed territorial borders, such action appears unlikely. As for the TRNC, the biggest question mark hanging over its continued *de facto* statehood is whether or not the combination of the recent violence along the green line, increased Greek Cypriot arms purchases, and the EU's soon-to-be commenced entry negotiations with the Republic of Cyprus generate sufficient impetus for an overall settlement. Should such a settlement fail to materialize, a continuation of the *status quo* would appear to be the safest bet.

4 Evolution into Some Alternate Status Short of Sovereign Statehood

A potentially infinite number of options exist for the transformation of the *de facto* state through peaceful negotiated agreement into something other than an independent sovereign state. Such arrangements may be distinguished broadly in terms of their international content. At one end of the spectrum would be such things as UN trust territories or internationally-imposed conditions such as the Kurdish safe havens in northern Iraq. At this end of the spectrum there would be active international involvement in the domestic affairs of a sovereign state—and, in some cases, legal guarantees which provided for such involvement. At the other end of the spectrum would be purely domestic agreements on such things as regional autonomy or federalism in which there were no provisions for any international involvement whatsoever. In between one might find something like the original Ethio-Eritrean federation—negotiated and drafted under UN auspices, but with no provisions for subsequent international involvement. Here we first consider international options and then use examples from our four case studies to examine more purely domestic scenarios for the peaceful evolution of the *de facto* state.

International law has traditionally encompassed a wide variety of entities including such things as condominia, internationalized territories, free cities, neutralized states, protectorates, mandates, associated states, and trust territories. Even though developments have generally moved decisively in the direction of a system based on the participation of legally equal sovereign states and no one else, there are still a number of post-1945 examples of groups or peoples who have been granted some sort of international status short of sovereign statehood. Here we consider five such examples: the UN Council for Namibia; the PLO; the Palestinian Authority; the Kurdish safe havens; and post-Dayton accords Bosnia. Conceivably, a number of *de facto* states could evolve in such directions or be the subject of their own *sui generis* agreements.

The UN Council for Namibia (originally the UN Council for South West Africa) was established by the General Assembly in 1967—one year after it had terminated South Africa's mandate over Namibia and two years before the Security Council approved that decision. According to Lynn Berat, 'The Council enjoyed a dual status as both an organ of the United Nations and as the legal administering authority for Namibia' (1991, p. 31). Although South Africa effectively prevented it from assuming its responsibilities inside Namibia, the Council was able to represent Namibia as an observer at a number of international organizations including the World Health Organization, the International Labor Organization, and the Food and Agricultural Organization. The Council functioned alongside the South West Africa People's Organization (SWAPO) which had been designated by various UN and OAU resolutions as the 'sole and authentic' representative of the Namibian people. In Heather Wilson's (1988) view, the distinction between the two groups is that the UN Council 'is supposedly the legitimate administrative and governmental authority for the territory until independence, while SWAPO expresses the views of the people but does not represent Namibia, as a territory, internationally'.[8] Considering the special circumstances of *apartheid* and Namibia's history as a Class C mandate under the League of Nations system and later a UN trust territory, it is unlikely that such a precedent will ever be followed in regards to any contemporary *de facto* states. Conceivably, however, aspects of such a model may be useful if there is ever again any extended transition period to a referendum on independence as happened in Eritrea.

The PLO has been perhaps the most active non-state participant in international politics. Amongst other things, it participated in the Third Law of the Sea Conference, the International Telecommunications Union Conference, the World Food Conference, and the ICRC Diplomatic Conference. In 1974, the PLO was granted observer status at the UN General Assembly and invited to participate in plenary deliberations there on the question of Palestine. Heather Wilson argues that the criterion for the PLO's participation in the General Assembly was that it had been recognized not as a State, but as a representative of a people entitled to certain rights.... In effect, the Palestinians were the first nation without a State to be granted status as a 'non-voting member' based on their as yet unrealized right to self-determination (1988, p. 74).

The PLO's status in international relations thus stemmed not from its possession of territory, but rather from the fact that the Palestinians were recognized as a distinct people with the PLO as their representatives. Theoretically, one could see a group such as the Tamils or the Turkish Cypriots being given some sort of similar status based on their existence as a people. One suspects, however, that this scenario is quite unlikely to develop. In the eyes of the UN, decolonization is over and few *de facto* state populations are likely to be seen to be suffering from military occupation at the hands of a pariah state.

Since the signing of the Oslo peace accords, the PLO's status has now been upgraded somewhat from being a recognized liberation movement to being the basis of the Palestinian Authority (PA). Though not (or not yet) a sovereign state, the PA does have recognized powers in certain areas that are guaranteed under international treaties. Obviously, the mere fact that treaties have been signed does not guarantee their implementation—witness the PA's recent frustrations over Israel's reluctance to engage in the 'further redeployments' called for in its agreements with the Palestinians. Still, the PA's status compares favorably to groups whose autonomy is only protected by domestic laws or constitutions. This model may potentially have a greater impact on future transformations of the *de facto* state than any of the others considered here. One could, for example, see the TRNC or Somaliland evolving in the direction of something like the Palestinian Authority. In effect, these entities would not be considered states or recognized as such, but they would have some international standing and perhaps even some form of international recourse should their status be unilaterally revoked or substantively altered by the sovereign state on whose territory they resided. Obviously, sovereign states like Cyprus or Somalia would be extremely reluctant to enter into such an arrangement unless they perceived it to be their only choice.

The establishment of the Kurdish safe haven in northern Iraq followed shortly after the passage of UN Security Council Resolution 688 on 5 April 1991. Ignoring the vocal opposition of the Iraqi government, paragraph three of Resolution 688 '*insists* that Iraq allow immediate access by international humanitarian organizations to all those in need of assistance in all parts of Iraq and to make available all necessary facilities for their operations'. Subsequent to the passage of this resolution, American, British, and French troops set up a number of camps and tent cities for the Kurds and imposed a no-fly zone on Iraqi aircraft north of the 36th parallel.

Whatever its other successes and failures, the Kurdish safe haven is unlikely to provide any sort of a model for future *de facto* state transformation for a number of reasons. First, Resolution 688 was the least-supported of all the Security Council resolutions on Iraq.[9] Given the extended duration of the Kurdish safe havens and the dismal experience with such entities in Bosnia, there is unlikely to be a mass ground swell demanding the establishment of new international safe havens. Second, the legal basis for the safe havens is highly questionable. As Simon Duke (1994) points out, Resolution 688 said nothing about military intervention or the establishment of air-exclusion zones. Duke argues that the provision of humanitarian assistance, regardless of whatever objections the host country may have, had already been established as permissible by the International Court of Justice in *Nicaragua v. U.S.* The legality of establishing the exclusion zones is, however, disputed. Apart from providing humanitarian aid, the allied troops also established tent cities for the refugees. Having done this, it followed that these areas should be protected—thus the practical justification for the exclusion zones (Duke, 1994, p. 41). Such a practical justification is, however, unlikely to convince skeptics of this action's legality. Third, the unique allied responsibility for this situation after actively inciting the Kurdish and Shiite populations of Iraq to rebel leads one to emphasize the special circumstances of this experience. As James Mayall puts it, 'the obligation towards the Kurds does not arise merely from a general principle of human solidarity.... It arises as a result of the attribution of responsibility for the consequence of specific acts' (1993, p. 175). Finally, the whole idea of a safe haven implies a degree of helplessness that is not characteristic of the *de facto* state. Perhaps the only way that such a model could ever come into play would be: 1) if a *de facto* state appeared to be headed toward a crushing military defeat with dire humanitarian consequences; and 2) the international community decided to intervene in such a fashion before this could happen. Such a combination of events does not appear likely.

The final non-sovereign entity with international standing to consider comes from post-Dayton accords Bosnia. Designed to end the war in Bosnia, the Dayton accords were originally initialed by the presidents of Bosnia, Croatia, and Serbia on 21 November 1995. The accords provide for the theoretical preservation of the Bosnian state within its existing territorial boundaries. That preservation, however, is achieved by federating two constituent units under a very loose central government arrangement. The two constituent units are a Muslim-Croat Federation comprising 51 percent of Bosnia's total land area and a Bosnian Serb Republic comprising the remaining 49 percent of the land area. Tensions within the Muslim-Croat Federation may conceivably lead to Bosnia ultimately being divided into three constituent units.

Theoretically, the Bosnian Serbs will participate in a central government that features such things as a parliament, a rotating presidency, a central bank, and a court. The central government is given authority over such areas as immigration, foreign policy, international trade, and monetary policy. Each of the constituent units will maintain its own defense forces. Further, the Muslim-Croat Federation will have the right to have 'special links' with Croatia, while the Bosnian Serbs will be granted similar rights in regard to Serbia. So far, the progress in implementing the accords has been mixed at best. Additionally, whether or not the Dayton accords survive the withdrawal of the foreign troops presently assisting in their implementation remains an open question.

One likely possibility is that the Bosnian Serbs in effect maintain their *de facto* state within the context of an internationally-recognized Bosnia. In essence, the Bosnian Serb *de facto* state would cooperate with the central institutions on matters of common interest and go its own way on others. Their *de facto* statehood may even be bolstered by the fact that they now have international agreements guaranteeing such things as their right to maintain their own defense force. In this scenario, unacknowledged yet viable *de facto* statehood coexists within the framework of preserving existing sovereign states and maintaining fixed territorial boundaries. As *The Economist* notes, 'In name Bosnia remains a single entity; in most other respects it looks like two'.[10] Once again, we see the *de facto* state having utility as a messy solution to a messy problem. This model has obvious attractions for international society in that norms are preserved and secession is not seen to be rewarded. As with the Palestinian Authority example, though, existing sovereign states are unlikely to be interested in such an arrangement unless they perceive themselves as having no other choice.

Outside of any international arrangements, the potential for alternate domestic options is nearly unlimited. Looking at this issue in regard to Sri Lanka, Marshall Singer (1990) argues that one can envision the devolution of powers between central and local authorities as points along a continuum. In the Sri Lankan case,

> At one end would be a unitary state with virtually no local autonomy, except perhaps for garbage collection and similar activities. At the other extreme would be a completely independent Tamil Eelam, with no ties between it and what was left of Sri Lanka. An almost endless variety of options range between the two, and the key factors are (1) how much power is actually devolved, and (2) the size of the unit being given power (1992, p. 718).

In the remainder of this section we will not attempt to delineate Singer's 'almost endless variety of options'. Rather, we will examine each of our four case studies to see what sort of possibilities exist in the domestic context for the peaceful transformation of the *de facto* state into some sort of non-sovereign entity with federal or confederal status.

As Eritrea has already achieved sovereign statehood, it might appear that its experience has little to offer us in this regard. This is not necessarily the case. Despite its ultimate failure, the original Federal Act of 1952 in which Eritrea had its own government which possessed 'legislative, executive and judicial powers in the field of domestic affairs' and was considered to be an 'autonomous unit federated with Ethiopia under the sovereignty of the Ethiopian crown' might serve as a future model for other *de facto* state situations (Scholler, 1994, pp. 10-18). The powers and standing of the Provisional Government of Eritrea between 1991 - 1993 might also serve as a template for negotiating end results which fall short of sovereign statehood. Andreas Escheté, for example, argues that the authority of the PGE exceeded that of federal Eritrea in only three areas: defense; interstate communication (notably the ports); and foreign affairs (1994, pp. 28-31). None of these need pose a problem for two entities living under the same sovereign roof. The PGE entered into a mutual defense pact with the Ethiopian government and it also reached agreements with it on the use of Assab and Massawa as free ports. As for its ability to enter into international relations, Escheté maintains that 'Independent external ties have been successfully maintained elsewhere by self-governing territories in the same political community' (1994, p. 31).

In essence, something akin to the PGE model is what Hussein Adam (1994b) identifies as the 'confederal solution' for Somaliland and Somalia. In his conception, the alternatives to this are either renewed fighting that produces a Yugoslav-type scenario, or ultimate independence for Somaliland along the lines of what happened in Eritrea. In Adam's vision, the confederal solution would be 'a two equal states arrangement' in which Somaliland would have greater autonomy than Québec now enjoys within Canada. Internally, Somaliland would have its own president who would constitutionally be either the first vice-president or even the co-president of the confederation. In addition, Somaliland would also have its own parliament, cabinet, and civil service. Following the precedents set by Ukraine and Belarus, Somaliland could even be admitted to full UN membership under this plan. The essence of this proposal is that 'Somaliland would gain virtually all the substance of an independent state retaining slim, practical links: currency, passports, jointly shared foreign embassies' (1994b, pp. 36-37).

The problem, of course, is that political leaders in Mogadishu would probably not agree to such a loose confederal arrangement while political leaders in Hargeisa would likely not trade in their present *de facto* statehood for anything less. Somaliland's President Egal is, for one, dismissive of any federalist solution. As he sees it, 'The federal solution never had any future.... These people lock themselves in rooms and think up fictitious scenarios that they think might be acceptable to the Security Council in New York. But it has no basis in reality, nothing' (Bryden, 1994a, pp. 41-42). Ken Menkhaus and John Prendergast (1995) are also somewhat dismissive of any attempts to reconstruct centralized state institutions in Somalia. As they see it, Somalia today is chaotic, but it is not chaos. Nor is it anarchy. Rather, it 'is a mosaic of fluid, highly localized polities... that are stepping in to fill the vacuum created by the prolonged collapse of the state...'. Instead of seeking to reconstruct a new Somali state, 'The challenge to the international community... is to learn to work constructively with these local polities rather than against them. This will not be easy' (1995, p. 22).

As both sides in Cyprus are nominally committed to a bi-communal and bi-zonal federal republic, one might think that the federal solution would be an obvious choice here. Yet, reconciling the Greek Cypriot preference for a strong federal government with sharply-delineated areas of limited regional competence and the Turkish Cypriot preference for a weak federal government in what is more or less a confederation of two equal republics has so far proved impossible. In broader terms, the Greek Cypriot view of the island in the unitary terms of majority and minority does not lend itself easily to political harmonization with the Turkish Cypriot view of the island in the confederal terms of two equal founding peoples. In terms of the above discussion, from the Turkish Cypriot perspective, the Greek Cypriots offer little better than Singer's scenario of 'virtually no local autonomy, except perhaps for garbage collection and similar activities'. Correspondingly, from the Greek Cypriot perspective, the Turkish Cypriot view of federalism is akin to Adam's 'confederal solution' for Somalia and would only succeed in producing the unacceptable outcome of two partitioned states. Conceivably, the island's original 1960 constitution with its detailed provisions on such things as the composition of the legislature, the council of ministers, and the civil service might serve as the basis of a future federal union between the two communities. The Greek Cypriot view of this constitution as inherently unworkable and imposed upon them by outside parties, however, militates against this.

Of all our four cases, Sri Lanka has perhaps the least experience with any kind of federal or confederal arrangements. Marshall Singer (1990) maintains that part of the problem here has been an inability on the part of Sinhalese civilians and politicians to understand the meaning of the word 'federalism'. He argues that for the Sinhalese federalism 'meant splitting the island into two separate states—which they could not distinguish from two separate countries. Thus, they were, and are still, totally opposed to it'.[11] The fact that Sinhalese Buddhists comprise such a large proportion of the population has meant that they have generally been able to secure whatever they wanted from the island's unitary system of government. Therefore, the incentives for them to move toward a federal system are far from compelling.

There have been, however, two attempts to move in the federal direction. The first was the establishment of District Development Councils in 1981. These councils were hampered by having a miniscule budget that did not even amount to one percent of the national budget. According to four Tamil scholars, the political will to devolve real power was completely lacking: 'On nearly all matters where a devolution of responsibility had to evolve, the centre used every hidden mechanism to maintain its hold' (Hoole, Somasundaram, Sritharan, and Thiranagama, 1990, p. 28). Following the collapse of the District Development Councils, the next major attempt came with the establishment of Provincial Councils in 1987. Though ostensibly drawn up to emulate the devolution of powers found in India, Amita Shastri argues that the responsibilities devolved to the Provincial Councils 'have been critically cut down and hedged in by restrictions, while the Concurrent List and the Reserved List have been expanded to allow the center control over all significant subjects and functions' (1992, p. 729). Some creative interpretation on the part of the central government could have resulted in the granting of considerably more power to the Provincial Councils than they now possess. Such an interpretation would have resulted in 'a *de facto* federalism, which Sinhalese extremists wouldn't like but which would not need another constitutional amendment and could therefore conceivably be implemented fairly easily' (Singer, 1992, pp. 719-720). Unfortunately, no such creative interpretation was forthcoming.

Essentially, the Tamils have three main objections to the Provincial Council system. First, even the most moderate Tamils want a more substantial devolution of powers. Second, Tamils want a more entrenched devolution of powers. The present system can be changed by a two-thirds vote of parliament along with passage in a popular referendum. As Tamils constitute less than one-third of the population, this system can therefore be unilaterally changed by the Sinhalese without their consent. Third, and most importantly, the Tamils insist on a permanent merger of the Northern and Eastern Provinces—something which the present system does not provide for.[12] Barring a permanent merger of the Northern and Eastern provinces and a much more substantial devolution of powers in a genuinely federal system, one can expect that Tamil separatist claims will continue to be pressed.

Overall, a near-endless variety of federal, confederal, or autonomous arrangements exist which may facilitate the peaceful transformation of the *de facto* state into some alternate status short of sovereign statehood. Of the international arrangements considered here, only the Palestinian Authority and Dayton accords examples are likely to serve as any kind of template for a future *de facto* state evolution. Even here, though, the existing sovereign state will strongly resist such international arrangements unless it perceives itself as having no other choice. Entire separate books have been written on the relative advantages and disadvantages of particular federal or confederal arrangements carried out in a purely domestic context. Unfortunately, the historical experience of our four case studies with such arrangements has been uniformly negative. The work of Thomas Franck (1968) on 'why federations fail' is of some relevance here. According to Franck, the presence of certain secondary factors such as a common language, common religion, or the potential for mutually beneficial economic interactions may be useful, indeed may even be necessary, but is not sufficient to ensure the success of a federal arrangement. However, in each of the four cases Franck studied, 'the absence of a positive political or ideological commitment to the *primary* goal of federation *as an end in itself* among the leaders and people of each of the federating units did... make success improbable, if not impossible'. Thus, Franck concludes that 'It is not enough that the units of a potential federation have the same idea of "the Good" but that "the Good" for any *one* must be consciously subordinate to or compatible with "the Good" for *all*' (1968, p. 173, italics in original). Such a paramount political commitment is seldom found in states whose own failures have helped create *de facto* state challengers to their own legitimacy. With its natural preference for discouraging secession and maintaining existing boundaries, there will always be a strong constituency in international society for trying to resolve the *de facto* state 'problem' through some sort of federal or confederal arrangements. Theoretically, the prospects for such a resolution are wide open. Practically, the chances of success may not be that great.

5 Successful Graduation to Sovereign Statehood

The *de facto* state is not supposed to achieve sovereign statehood. All of the assorted norms and regimes discussed in chapter five are specifically designed to prevent just such a possibility from ever happening. With a very few exceptions, these norms have been extremely successful at preserving the existing territorial map. If, as I have argued, the ending of the Cold War has not substantially affected the strong international consensus surrounding these norms, then one should expect them to continue to be quite successful—at least into the medium-term future. Therefore, the overall prospects for *de facto* states becoming sovereign states remain bleak.

Eritrea is obviously the classic example of a *de facto* state successfully graduating to widely-recognized sovereign statehood. It may not, however, be the last example. Here we will examine three possible routes that might conceivably lead from *de facto* statehood to sovereign statehood. None of these routes has a great probability of success, but they do merit consideration.

The first route, of which Eritrea is representative, is through the imposition of a military *fait accompli*. In effect, this means that either the *de facto* state's military forces have achieved a position of absolute military superiority or they have made the cost of defeating themselves so prohibitive that the existing sovereign state decides not to pursue any further military action against them. Achieving such a status may or may not be accompanied by the existing sovereign state granting its consent to juridical independence. In the Eritrean case, the new Ethiopian government could have refused to give its consent to the Eritrean referendum on sovereignty. In this, they might conceivably have succeeded in keeping Eritrea juridically yoked to Ethiopia. It is extremely unlikely, however, that they could have forcibly recaptured Eritrea after 1991—at least not at a cost which Ethiopian society was able or willing to bear. At least in part, the decision to allow Eritrea to proceed to independence was taken because Eritrean cooperation was needed to ensure the continued use of Assab and Massawa as free ports for the now landlocked remainder of Ethiopia. Obviously, such cooperation might not have been forthcoming if sovereignty was denied. Thus, while many commentators emphasize the fact that Eritrean independence was secured only after Ethiopia granted its consent, it should be remembered that this same Ethiopian consent was forthcoming in no small part due to Eritrea's military prowess.

Chechnya is perhaps the *de facto* state most likely to follow Eritrea in this regard. Barring the ascension to power of an extreme nationalist in Russia, it appears that the Chechens have now succeeded in raising the costs of defeating them militarily to such a level that Russia is either unwilling or unable to bear those costs any longer. The big question, however, is whether or not Russia will allow the Chechens to translate their 'ungovernability' into sovereign independence. The most recent peace treaty signed between the presidents of Chechnya and Russia skirts this question but does provide that relations between the two entities 'will be governed by the norms of international law'.[13] It is extremely doubtful, though, that Chechnya will receive any substantive recognition of its independence without Russian consent. In this regard, the Chechens' military success could still lead to two divergent outcomes: 1) Russian consent to Chechen sovereignty along the lines of the Eritrean experience with an extended transition period leading to a referendum vote; or 2) a continued Russian refusal to allow Chechen sovereignty, thus leading to a Chechen *de facto* state within the juridical confines of Russia itself. Whereas the Eritreans may have been able to force Addis Ababa's hand through their control of the ports, the Chechens have no such trump card to play against Moscow. As such, in contemporary international society, their military success still leaves the decision as to whether or not they graduate to sovereign statehood in Russian hands.

A second potential route to sovereign statehood, somewhat similar to the first, is through the imposition of what might be termed a broadly-based *fait accompli*. One potential example here might be the TRNC. In this regard, Kwaw Nyameke Blay's (1985) arguments on Indonesia and East Timor are of some relevance. Noting the decline in support for resolutions in the UN General Assembly condemning Indonesia's invasion of East Timor and affirming the East Timorese people's right to self-determination, Blay argues that this does not represent a weakening of support for the principle of self-determination, but 'rather indicates an increasing recognition in the Assembly of the fact that the Indonesian takeover is now a *fait accompli*' (1985, pp. 396-397). In spite of this, a majority in the General Assembly still refuses to sanction Indonesia's annexation of East Timor. The problem that both Indonesia and the TRNC run up against here is the legal concept of *ex injuria jus non oritur*—a right cannot originate in an illegal act or, in these cases, a legal title cannot be acquired through an illegal act. Blay notes that notwithstanding this principle, 'international law may also make a concession to a situation of fact and occasionally allow this general maxim to be overruled by the rule of *ex facto oritur jus*' (1985, footnote # 43, p. 397). In other words, states might, in exceptional circumstances, connive to recognize a situation of fact arising from an illegal act if such recognition was necessary to preserve a larger value such as international order. Theoretically, Blay might be right. Realistically, it seems that *ex injuria jus non oritur* continues to trump *ex facto oritur jus*. As such, one should only expect to see continued *de facto* statehood for the TRNC. Growing recognition of its *fait accompli* may someday lead a few sympathetic states to extend it *de jure* recognition. Without Greek Cypriot consent, however, it is highly unlikely that such recognitions will ever be so widespread as to make the TRNC's sovereignty uncontested.

The other main possible candidate for graduation to sovereign statehood in this regard is Taiwan. There can be no question of the Taiwanese government's capabilities. Unlike every other case considered here, the Taiwanese may have succeeded in making themselves an economic *fait accompli* whose foreign currency reserves, high-tech manufacturing expertise, rapid growth rates, and prodigious exporting ability make them a major player in the global political economy. Beyond this, Taiwan's recent successful moves toward democratization have also earned it widespread praise and sympathy. Yet, Taiwan's ultimate graduation to uncontested sovereign statehood is still far from assured or even likely. Since the PRC's admission to the UN in 1971 and US derecognition in 1979, Taiwan has been able to maintain official diplomatic relations with somewhere between twenty and thirty states at any given time. The number of states may go up or down a bit, but it has held more or less constant for the better part of two decades now. However, Taiwan has suffered a continual loss of recognition from some of its most important allies. Saudi Arabia switched its recognition to the PRC in 1990, South Korea switched in 1992, and South Africa switched in 1998. As such, Taiwan is left with the recognition of a few dozen smaller states, nearly all of them in Africa, Central America, and the Caribbean. John Copper argues that rather than successful graduation to unquestioned sovereign statehood, 'Taiwan's destiny may be to become a true international actor whose nation-state status is permanently unclear or weak or unique. It is possible its status will become the subject of an international agreement or one involving Washington and Beijing' (1990, p. 127). As with the other *fait accompli* considered here, widespread sovereign recognition of Taiwan appears unlikely without Beijing's consent.

The final potential route to sovereign statehood is what might be termed the flawed or improper union approach. As opposed to a territorial argument based on prior conquest or annexation, this type of argument 'concentrates on a wrongdoing committed by a third party. At some previous point in history, a state with no current stake in the dispute improperly joined the territories of the currently dominant state and the separatist group' (Brilmayer, 1991, p. 190). One could argue that a strong reason Eritrea's independence was so widely accepted was at least partly due to its former colonial status and some international misgivings both on how it was federated to Ethiopia and how Ethiopia wantonly violated the provisions of that federal arrangement. The only other *de facto* state that might benefit in such a way is Somaliland. Following its strong rejection of the country's new constitution in a June 1961 referendum, it is highly questionable whether or not Somaliland's union ever met the test prescribed in General Assembly Resolution 1541 of 15 December 1960 that

> Integration should be the result of the freely expressed wishes of the territory's peoples acting with full knowledge of the change in their status, their wishes having been expressed through informed and democratic processes impartially conducted and based on universal adult suffrage.[14]

The fact that Somaliland has yet to secure any recognition highlights the considerable weaknesses of this potential route to sovereign statehood. Additionally, while this argument may have aided the Eritreans in their quest for sovereignty, it is extremely unlikely that it would have won them that sovereignty in the absence of either their military *fait accompli* or the consent of Addis Ababa.

The overwhelming probability is that most *de facto* states will never attain widespread recognition as sovereign states. The *de facto* state does not fail here because it lacks popular support or cannot provide effective governance. Rather, it fails because there is a strong global consensus against secessionist self-determination and in favor of preserving the existing territorial map. Barring an unforeseen fundamental shift in this normative environment, the odds-on bet is that the Eritrean experience will remain exceptional: few, if any, *de facto* states are likely to follow in its footsteps to widely-recognized sovereign statehood. Of the various cases considered here, the two most likely candidates to succeed in this regard are probably Chechnya (due to its military *fait accompli*) and Somaliland (due to the legitimacy derived from its former colonial status). Even here, though, without consent from the existing sovereign state, the prospects for widespread juridical recognition of their substantive empirical capabilities remain remote.

6 What Determines Success or Failure in Securing Recognition

Whether it likes it or not, the factors determining the *de facto* state's ultimate prospects for successful graduation to sovereign statehood are beyond its control. Regardless of whatever internal successes it has, the *de facto* state cannot admit itself to full membership in international society. Within the context of international society's overwhelming hostility to secession and its clear preference for preserving existing territorial boundaries, there are in essence three main factors which determine the *de facto* state's prospects for success or failure in attaining recognition. These three factors are an assortment of secondary attributes and characteristics which are of peripheral importance; force; and the consent of the existing sovereign.

Most attempts to devise criteria for 'legitimate' or 'just' secessions focus on an assortment of factors that serve either to strengthen or weaken the secessionist's overall case.[15] While these factors are certainly worth considering, they are not ultimately determinative of whether a given secession succeeds or not. Rather, they are of secondary or peripheral importance. Obviously, the merits of a secessionist's argument will be strengthened if the group can show prolonged oppression, massive human rights violations directed against its members, and systemic economic exploitation. Any sort of unjust or questionable incorporation also adds to the secessionist's case. Certainly groups that can demonstrate strong cohesiveness; racial, religious, historic and/or linguistic differentiation; widespread popular support; and a high degree of internal legitimacy are better off than those which cannot demonstrate any of these things. Territorially concentrated populations are likely to present fewer problems when seceding than widely-dispersed and intermingled populations are. The emerging importance of fixed internal borders also favors groups which can tailor their secessionist demands to correspond to recognized internal boundaries. Conversely, secessionists whose departure will dramatically impoverish the remainder of the existing sovereign state pose greater problems than those whose departures will not. Secessionist regions like Sri Lanka's Eastern Province which will result in the creation of large numbers of new 'trapped' minorities are more problematic than those like the more homogenous Northern Province which will produce fewer such minorities in the future.

All of these assorted internal merits or mitigating factors must also be considered in conjunction with a secession's affect on the larger international system. Lee Buchheit's criteria is, in effect, an attempt to balance the internal merits of the secessionist claim against the disruption it is likely to cause—both to the existing sovereign state and to the international community as a whole (Buchheit, 1978, pp. 228-245). As Buchheit sees it, 'Where the disruption factor is high, the claimant must make out an extraordinarily good case for its entitlement to self-determination'. On the other hand, 'Where little disruption is liable to ensue from the secession, or where the amount of current disruption outweighs the future risk, the community can afford to be less strict in its requirements...' (1978, p. 241). While Buchheit's criteria have been criticized for overemphasizing international political considerations at the expense of legal criteria and the internal merits of the claim (White, 1981-82, p. 161), they do highlight some of the complex calculations which political leaders may have to entertain in order to assess the relative merit of any given secessionist claim. All of these factors, however, are only of peripheral importance. Without success in either of the next two categories, no secessionist can ever hope to overcome international society's desire to freeze the existing territorial map.

In spite of all the scholarly attention devoted in recent years to such things as international cooperation and growing levels of economic interdependence, the importance of our second factor, force, in securing international recognition cannot be understated. As Rupert Emerson points out, 'The realistic issue is still not whether a people is qualified for and deserves the right to determine its own destiny but whether it has the political strength, which may well mean the military force, to validate its claim' (1971, p. 475). Obviously, force is not everything—witness the international community's continuing refusal to grant juridical legitimacy to the TRNC or to Indonesia's occupation of East Timor. Yet, one cannot get around the fact that there is an independent Eritrea while there is not an independent Tamil Eelam in large measure due to the fact that the EPLF was able to secure its independence on the battlefield while the LTTE has not been able to do so. One can also compare Biafra and Bangladesh in this regard. As Conor Cruise O'Brien puts it, 'Bangladesh is now recognized by all, Biafra by none. The reason is not that Bangladesh had necessarily a better moral case than Biafra, though perhaps it had. The reason is that the Indian army beat the army of Pakistan. Biafra, having no such ally, died' (1973, p. 48). Should the Chechens ultimately succeed in upgrading their *de facto* state to a sovereign state, it will not be due to their distinct ethnic, linguistic, or religious heritage or to the justness or morality of their cause. Rather, it will be due to their successful application of force.

The main reason that force does not count for everything is our third factor—the importance of prior sovereign consent. As James Crawford argues, 'modern practice demonstrates with some consistency the proposition that, prima facie, a new State granted full formal independence by the former sovereign has the international right to govern its territory as a State' (1976-77, p. 135). The swift and widespread recognitions following the peaceful dissolutions of Czechoslovakia and the Soviet Union attest to the continuing validity of this position. Indeed, in the contemporary international system one can probably state with some certainty that the consent of the existing sovereign will automatically lead to widespread juridical acceptance with or without any prior success on the battlefield while military force will usually, but not always, fail to produce such acceptance in the absence of sovereign consent. Robert Jackson notes in this regard that many secessionists 'believe they can use force to coerce such consent, but this has rarely happened and usually requires the total defeat of a sovereign government—as in Ethiopia in 1991' (1993a, p. 357). Force matters, but as such total defeats seldom occur, the prospects for widespread recognition of a contemporary secessionist movement without the consent of the existing sovereign are almost non-existent. As such, one should not expect to find many *de facto* states capable of translating their empirical success into juridical recognition.

7 Conclusion

This chapter has concluded our birth, life, and death or evolution examination of the *de facto* state with a discussion of some of the various possible transformations one might expect to see these entities undergo. While their lack of juridical standing obviously increases their volatility, death, evolution, or transformation is not preordained: one distinct possibility is continued *de facto* statehood. Indeed, this is far from the worst option available to these entities. As graduation to sovereign statehood remains unlikely, the *status quo* is probably preferable to some form of military defeat or to a reluctantly entered into federal arrangement that lacks the requisite political commitment necessary for success. In any case, past historical experience is likely to make most *de facto* states extremely skeptical of any such proposed arrangements—particularly if they lack provisions for international involvement.

From the standpoint of the existing sovereign state, the usual preferred option is to attempt to defeat these entities militarily. If that does not appear to be working, the next best option may be to try and negotiate some sort of federal or autonomous arrangements that keep the *de facto* state firmly tethered within the juridical confines of its existing territorial boundaries. The existing sovereign state will prefer to keep such arrangements purely domestic and avoid any international involvement whatsoever unless it perceives itself as having no other choice. If the existing state is unable to function or to function effectively, as is the case in Somalia today, it may have no other choice than to reach some sort of uneasy accommodation with its secessionist challenger. Only in the rarest of instances, usually brought about by a military *fait accompli*, will an existing state consent to dismembering itself and grant sovereignty to its *de facto* state challenger.

The interests of international society as a whole are obviously with finding a solution or functional non-solution to the *de facto* state within the confines of the existing territorial map. International society has some interests in avoiding a crushing military defeat of one of these entities that leads to a massive population displacement, but on the whole it is generally not adverse to the existing sovereign state's decision to respond militarily. In the long-run, some sort of federal or autonomous arrangement within the confines of existing borders is probably the preferred choice of international society. Such arrangements can address the concerns which may have originally given rise to the *de facto* state in the first place, but do so without offering undue encouragement to any other secessionists. If the existing sovereign state is unable or unwilling to negotiate such arrangements on its own, international society may, in rare cases, step in and seek to find some sort of internationally-guaranteed solution to the problem. Such involvement will generally come only if the costs of the existing situation in terms of refugees, fatalities, or regional instability are high. As the *de facto* state may serve a number of useful purposes for international society, the *status quo* is often acceptable to most outside parties.

The next chapter examines the impact of the *de facto* state on academic International Relations. In particular, it addresses the question of what, if any, changes do the existence of these entities suggest might be required in international theory? This chapter essentially proceeds along two main tracks: first, an evaluation of the *de facto* state's significance to international theory as a whole and, second, an evaluation of what challenges or opportunities these entities pose for specific theoretical traditions such as realism, rationalism, and the various post-modernist approaches.

Notes

[1] Kaufmann, 1996, p. 163; 'Former Yugoslavia: Turn of the Tide?' *The Economist*, 5 August 1995; 'Croatia's Blitzkrieg', *The Economist*, 12 August 1995; 'The Flight of the Krajina Serbs', *The Economist*, 12 August 1995; and '9 Elderly Serbs Found Slain in Croat Town', *The New York Times*, 5 October 1995.

[2] 'Sri Lanka's Civil War: What Chance for Peace?', *The Straits Times*, 16 April 1997.

[3] These possibilities are discussed in section four of chapter six.

[4] Dr. Sazil Korküt, the TRNC representative in New York, points out that the economic embargo provides the Turkish Cypriots with strong incentives to reach an overall settlement but that a settlement without a Turkish security guarantee is worse, from their perspective, than a continuation of the present situation. Telephone interview, 15 April 1997.

[5] Migdal, 1988, pp. 268-269. A somewhat similar conclusion was reached twenty years earlier in Nettl, 1968, p. 589.

[6] Migdal, 1988, p. 277. See more generally chapters six and eight.

[7] Telephone interview with Mr. Ken Shivers, US State Department desk officer for Djibouti and Somalia, 10 April 1997.

[8] H. A. Wilson, 1988, p. 122. See also Berat, 1991, p. 32.

[9] China abstained from using its permanent veto against this resolution. India also abstained while Cuba, Yemen, and Zimbabwe all voted against the resolution. A number of other states not on the Security Council were also vociferous in their opposition.

[10] 'Bosnia's Bitter Peace', *The Economist*, 25 November 1995. The above paragraphs have also drawn from a variety of other media sources.

[11] Singer, 1990, p. 412. A somewhat similar argument is also advanced in Oberst, 1992, p. 131.

[12] For more on these Tamil objections, see Shastri, 1992, pp. 727, 733, and 741-742.

[13] 'A Budding Chechen Peace', *The Economist*, 17 May 1997.

[14] Cited on pp. 149-150 of White, 1981-82.

[15] The listing of such factors below is partially drawn from McMullen, 1992, pp. 118-123.

9 The *De Facto* State and International Theory

1 Introduction

Whereas previous chapters have mainly focused on the reasons for and the practical implications of *de facto* states in international society, this chapter considers the significance of these entities for academic international theory. This examination is divided into two main parts. I address the general relationship of the *de facto* state to international theory as a whole first. The second main part of this discussion considers the potential significance of these entities to specific theoretical traditions such as realism, rationalism, and post-modernism.

Some theoretical traditions are ill-equipped to deal with *de facto* states, while others may find them of distinctly peripheral interest. The theoretical attractions of this phenomenon are therefore likely to be varied: realists, for example, may find much more to interest them in this subject than feminists do. While the *de facto* state will never be all things to all theorists, its theoretical relevance is worth probing.

2 International Theory and the *De Facto* State

The *de facto* state has not featured prominently in international theory for a number of reasons. Foremost among them are the limited number of cases and their small size. Even when compared to other non-sovereign actors, the *de facto* state does not appear to have the same magnitude of impact as, for example, multinational corporations, the bond market, epistemic communities, or non-governmental organizations. Further, the logic of the *de facto* state is similar to that of the sovereign state. As it only wants to be allowed to play the same game and does not try to change the rules of the game itself, it might be seen as less interesting than an entity like the multinational corporation whose logic and motives diverge from those of existing sovereign states.

Another main reason for this lack of attention is international theory's general inability to deal with ambiguity. Richard Ashley (1988) sarcastically refers to this as a 'heroic practice'. In Ashley's conception, this heroic practice is the need to invoke sovereignty as a principle of interpretation so that a dichotomous distinction can be imposed between 'what can be represented as rational and meaningful (because it can be assimilated to a sovereign principle of interpretation) and what must count as external, dangerous, and anarchic (because it has yet to be brought under the control of the sovereign principle invoked)'. As Ashley sees it, 'only those contributions that replicate this interpretative attitude and invoke a sovereign voice as an absolute ground can be taken seriously...'. Other more ambiguous phenomena, of which the *de facto* state could be one example, 'are either to be assimilated to a sovereign voice or, failing that, regarded under the sign of a dangerous anarchy, as a problem to be solved' (1988, p. 230). One need not support Ashley's entire argument to see how an inherently nebulous entity like the *de facto* state might suffer from theoretical neglect in a discipline that places such a high value on parsimonious explanation.

One interesting method of assessing the potential impact of these entities on international theory is by considering their effect on the states system itself. More specifically, what does their existence say about the assorted challenges to that system? As the question of whether or not the states system is itself fundamentally being transformed is far too vast a subject to address adequately here, our comments will be limited to a few brief observations.

According to Ferguson and Mansbach (1991), the state is being challenged on a variety of fronts by such things as dramatically increased international economic transactions, more assertive and better informed citizens, and rapidly evolving technologies. As they see it,

> *What we are witnessing appears to be nothing less than a widespread revolt against the prerogatives and pretensions of "the state."* In other words, we may be approaching one of those historical sea changes... in which one form of organization yields pride of place to others (1991, p. 371, italics in original).

There are three main responses to this and other such claims of impending transformation. First, the state has never been exclusively predominant in international politics. It has always co-existed with other units and it continues to do so today. This point has been made both by theorists who see great possibilities for transformation in the present era and by those who are often ridiculed for their narrowly 'state-centric' viewpoints.[1]   Second, challenges to the state are nothing new.   By some measures there was a higher level of economic interdependence just before World War I than there is today. As Stephen Krasner (1995-96) observes, 'It is historically myopic to take the Westphalian model as a benchmark that accurately describes some golden age when all states exercised exclusive authority within their own borders'.[2] Finally, there is scant evidence that the state is being overwhelmed by interdependence or any other challenges to its rule. In other words, one can reasonably expect continued state predominance in the foreseeable future. As Robert Jackson (1993a) puts it, 'the majority of existing States and regions and the global States system as a whole seem destined to persist indefinitely more or less in their existing shape'.[3]

Regardless of whether or not one accepts the proposition that the states system is far from being overwhelmed or superseded, it is still worth considering the impact of *de facto* states in this regard. On the whole, their effect on the states system is likely to be minimal. There are two main reasons for this. First, the *de facto* state tries to follow the same basic logic as the sovereign state. Entities like Somaliland and the TRNC do not seek to challenge or overthrow the states system. Rather, they want to join that system and become members of the club. In John Ruggie's view, 'the distinctive feature of the modern system of rule is that it has differentiated its subject collectivity into territorially defined, fixed, and mutually exclusive enclaves of legitimate dominion' (1993, p. 151). *De facto* state challengers seek to alter the boundaries within such a system; they do not seek to alter the system itself. Thus, the TRNC may pose a serious threat to the territorial integrity of the Republic of Cyprus but it does not pose much of a threat to the states system as a whole. Even here, though, it must be pointed out that a sovereign and internationally recognized TRNC would not lead to the extinction of the Republic of Cyprus. Similarly, Eritrean independence may have led to Ethiopia becoming landlocked; it did not, however, lead to the juridical death of the Ethiopian state itself.[4] The second reason to doubt the impact of *de facto* states on challenges to the states system as a whole is their limited numbers, relatively small size, and general lack of substantive economic power.

Rather than viewing the *de facto* state as part of a 'challenge' to the states system, it might be more productive to view these entities as part of a cyclical return to a more diverse international system. While the sovereign state presently appears to have crowded out all other options, the world has historically contained a variety of political units other than sovereign states. There have been colonies, protectorates, guaranteed or neutralized states, trusteeship arrangements, associated states, condominia, and internationalized territories (Hannum, 1990, pp. 16-18). This idea of *de facto* states being a part of some sort of cyclical return to a more diverse states system should only be advanced cautiously for the evidence of such a return is tentative and the role that *de facto* states could play in such a return is open to question. Still, Hurst Hannum and Richard Lillich (1980) maintain that we may be seeing 'the beginning of a trend away from independence and full statehood as the only answer to the problems perceived either by ethnic communities within existing states or by non-self-governing territories that have yet to emerge fully on the international stage' (1980, p. 889). Stephen Krasner (1995-96) goes even further in arguing that what he terms 'compromising Westphalia' is not only inevitable, but can also be beneficial. According to Krasner,

> Explicitly recognizing that different principles ought to vary with the capacity and behavior of states would not only make normative discourse more consistent with empirical reality, it would also contribute to the more imaginative construction of institutional forms—forms that compromise Westphalia—that could create a more stable and peaceful international system (1995-96, p. 151).

For the *de facto* state to play a significant role in such a more diverse international system, one would have to see evidence that these entities were: 1) remaining in their present ambiguous status (i.e., neither attaining sovereignty as constitutional independence nor being successfully reincorporated into the existing sovereign state) and 2) that international society was coming to grips (albeit non-sovereign grips) with their continued existence. From the standpoint of international theory, it is the first of these two conditions—the *de facto* state remaining stuck in some sort of permanent intermediate status—that is potentially the most significant. For if, as Hedley Bull (1977) pointed out, the end result of these secession attempts is just that Chechnya and Somaliland take their seat in the exclusive club of sovereign states, then the number of those states in the world would have increased, but the institution of the sovereign state itself would have been largely unaffected. Even less interesting theoretically are militarily defeated *de facto* states like Biafra and Krajina. In these cases, not only is the institution of the sovereign state unaffected, but the actual number of such entities remains unchanged. As Bull argues, 'the disintegration of states would be theoretically important *only* if it were to remain transfixed in an intermediate state' (1977, p. 267, my italics). He goes on to elaborate that we cannot ignore the possibility that should these new units

> advance far enough towards sovereign statehood both in terms of accepted doctrine and in terms of their command of force and human loyalties, to cast doubt upon the sovereignty of existing states, and yet at the same time were to stop short of claiming that same sovereignty for themselves, the situation might arise in which the institution of sovereignty itself might go into decline (1977, p. 267).

The *de facto* state does not fully correspond to Bull's adumbrated scenario for two main reasons. First, in regard to the first part of his statement, it is far from clear that these entities have 'advanced far enough' to cast doubt upon the sovereignty of existing states. They certainly have cast doubt on the effectiveness and the completeness of the sovereign's control. From the standpoint of international society, however, the evidence does not indicate that they have effectively cast doubt upon the sovereign's legitimate authority to rule. The assorted norms and regimes discussed in chapter five all support the premise that casting doubt upon a sovereign's actual *control* and casting doubt upon a sovereign's legitimate *authority* are two fundamentally different things. Second, and perhaps more importantly, the *de facto* state does not stop short of claiming that same sovereignty for itself. A more exact fit for Bull's scenario may be an entity like the Eastern Kasai region of Zaire which does not claim such sovereignty for itself.

While the *de facto* state might not be a perfect fit for the above scenario, it could easily be a part of what Bull terms 'a new mediaevalism'— a potential scenario for a change in the states system which results in a system whose central characteristic is 'a system of overlapping authority and multiple loyalty' (1977, p. 254). In such a system, the sovereign state's authority would be shared with regional and world entities on the one hand and sub-state or sub-national entities on the other. Though it is purely speculative, one might see the *de facto* state here playing the role of the effective and powerful regional baron while its quasi-state parent is akin to the monarch who is nominally in charge but whose power ultimately rests on delicately balancing the competing interests of the various barons below him or her. It is not claimed here that international relations has entered into a period of new mediaevalism or even that the arrival of such a system is likely. Though it is now more than twenty years old, Bull's own conclusion on this matter remains valid: 'it would be going beyond the evidence to conclude that "groups other than the state" have made such inroads on the sovereignty of states that the states system is now giving way to this alternative' (1977, p. 275).

There are two main points to be made on the *de facto* state in this regard. First, the most significant impact these entities could have on international theory is if they remain in an indeterminate condition. If every *de facto* state either graduated to sovereign statehood or was defeated militarily, the subject would not be of much theoretical relevance. If, on the other hand, the number of *de facto* states were to grow and they were to remain effective yet unrecognized entities which commanded support from the local populations concerned, then the subject might prove a fruitful vehicle from which to launch new theoretical departures. Second, while the evidence for a return to a more diverse states system is tentative, it is worth keeping an eye on the *de facto* state in this regard. The ability or inability of these entities to carve out a long-term secure position for themselves in the international system may be one indication of just how strong (or weak) the trends are in that direction of states system transformation. This phenomenon would only be one indicator among many, but its future role here may still be of some importance.

3 The *De Facto* State and Specific Theoretical Traditions

It is a common practice to delineate the various strands of international theory according to a tripartite division. For Martin Wight, this division was between realists, rationalists, and revolutionists. Similarly, Hedley Bull divided the field into the Hobbesian, Grotian, and Kantian traditions of thought. Robert Jackson substitutes Machiavelli for Hobbes and argues that 'At the risk of oversimplification, these terms denote the contrasting ideas of national self-interest and prudent statecraft (Machiavellism), international law and civility (Grotianism), and global political community (Kantianism)' (1990, p. 164). In this section, we analyze the implications of *de facto* statehood for each of these traditions, as well as for three other distinct avenues of theoretical inquiry: feminism, post-modernism, and international law. The focus here is not on exploring the nuances and subtleties of these various theoretical traditions or on highlighting the distinctions within or between them. Thus, we are not elaborating the differences between critical theorists, post-modernists, constructivists, and post-structuralists or examining the debates between pluralists and solidarists within the Grotian tradition. Our focus is merely on the challenges or opportunities the existence of *de facto* states poses for each of these traditions conceived in broad, general terms.

Realism

Although it is much maligned by its critics, realism is highly relevant to the study of *de facto* statehood. Its emphasis on prudent diplomacy, power defined in terms of the national interest, and the importance of military force as an ultimate arbiter does not appear outdated when examining the *de facto* state. Indeed, one suspects that a number of the issues surrounding these entities offer quite bountiful avenues for future realist inquiries. The answers to such questions as why did Bangladesh survive when Biafra could not?; why has Ethiopia consented to Eritrea's independence while Somalia refuses to grant Somaliland the same acknowledgment?; how has the TRNC been able to survive in spite of all the concerted international hostility directed against it?; and why is Chechnya presently in a better position than Tamil Eelam? are all likely to be found within the general realist framework of analysis. The hypocrisy and manifest inconsistency which has characterized the application of the principle of self-determination and the granting of recognition to aspiring states is another major area where realism, with its focus on the national interest, is likely to provide interesting avenues of inquiry.

The contrast between quasi-states and *de facto* states provides another useful window from which to view the applicability of a realist approach in this regard. As Robert Jackson (1990) argues, realism is deficient in providing an explanation for the survival of quasi-states because it is premised on a competitive international environment where state survival is open to question and far from assured. The quasi-state, though, exists today by virtue of the fact that the members of international society have in effect guaranteed its survival with an external insurance policy premised on the sanctity of existing territorial borders. The *de facto* state, on the other hand, benefits from no such external insurance policy. It does function in the more traditional realist setting of a competitive international environment where its survival is open to question and contingent upon its own abilities to provide for itself alone or in alliance with others.

Realism, though, is only partially successful in describing the international environment in which the *de facto* state must operate. It accurately portrays the omnipresent uncertainty, constant potential for hostility, and never-ending need for self-reliance that is the daily cut-and-thrust of life as a *de facto* state. What it fails to describe adequately, however, is the true nature of the challenge facing these entities. Just as realism underestimates the importance of international law, organization, and normative consensus in explaining the survival of quasi-states, so it underestimates the importance of these same factors in explaining the failure (at least in terms of securing sovereignty) of most *de facto* states. Put in the terms of the discussion on securing recognition in chapter eight, realism captures the essential importance of force but it fails to understand fully the importance of prior sovereign consent and societal norms in explaining the existence of *de facto* states. While these entities offer a number of potentially fruitful avenues for realist inquiry, they also highlight realism's neglect of international law and the power of ideas.

Rationalism

The Grotian or rationalist tradition is frequently portrayed as occupying a 'middle ground' somewhere between the two extremes of realism and cosmopolitanism. Like realists, the rationalists view independent sovereign states as the dominant actors in world politics. Unlike realists, however, they do not view the existing international order as the product merely of a fortuitous balance of power that is lacking any legal or moral content. Where realists deny the possibility of an international society, rationalists see states as bound by the normatively-based rules and institutions of the society they form. Unlike cosmopolitan idealists, however, the rationalists do not advocate overthrowing the society of states so that it can be replaced by a universal community of global humanity. As Hedley Bull (1977) explains,

> As against the view of the Hobbesians, states in the Grotian view are bound not only by rules of prudence or expediency but also by imperatives of morality and law. But, as against the universalists, what these imperatives enjoin is not the overthrow of the system of states and its replacement by a universal community of mankind, but rather acceptance of the requirements of coexistence and co-operation in a society of states (1977, p. 27).

The strength of the rationalist approach in studying *de facto* statehood is its focus on the laws, norms, institutions, and organizations which bind sovereign states together in a contractual sense. An approach with such an emphasis is certainly well-suited to launching inquiries into many of the factors such as collective non-recognition, fixed territorial borders, changing conceptions of sovereignty, and narrow interpretations of self-determination that help produce the *de facto* state phenomenon. The relevance of the rationalist approach here is also highlighted by the societal importance placed on securing prior sovereign consent in order to attain widespread international recognition. Quite simply, there probably would not be any such thing as *de facto* statehood to study if international norms could not indeed trump force on most occasions.

That said, there are a number of areas highlighted in this study where further research is required by scholars operating from within the rationalist tradition. First, as the international consensus surrounding such things as sovereignty and self-determination has evolved over the years, more work is required on explaining how such international agreements are reached in the first place and how and why they are subsequently changed. Second, further research is required to explain the violations and exceptions to such rules and norms: why, for instance, does *ex injuria jus non oritur* apply to the TRNC but not to Bangladesh and Tibet? Third, and perhaps most importantly, as the *de facto* state can survive, yet has very limited prospects for overcoming the array of factors which keep it unrecognized, rationalists must devote more attention to learning how to cope with the existence of these entities in the international system. The evidence indicates that *de facto* states can endure for quite long periods of time. As such, it is time to move beyond ritual condemnation to focus on how best to accommodate (juridically or non-juridically) the existence of these entities within the context of larger goals such as international order, human rights, and stability. Such an accommodation does not necessarily imply recognizing all *de facto* states. Minimal non-juridical accommodation of these entities may simply be one aspect of a necessary shift toward coping with a more diverse international system.

There may be a role in all of this for what Timothy Dunne (1995) terms 'critical international society theorists'. In his vision, 'If the strength of the classical wing of international society thinking hinges on its *correspondence* to state practice, then the task for critical international society theory is to *shape* state practice' (1995, p. 146, italics in original). Such scholars may also be well positioned to address Hedley Bull's concern with the fragility of international society and the need not only to preserve, but to extend the area of consensus underlying it.[5] Obviously, the explicitly activist and subjective value bias inherent in any such project will raise objections from some scholars. The point to be made here is merely that 'critical international society theorists' may find much to interest them in the world of *de facto* statehood and that international theory as a whole might benefit from their engagement in this regard.

Revolutionism

Revolutionism is often subdivided into a cosmopolitan variant which draws its original inspiration from Kant and a structural economic variant which derives from Marx. These two broad traditions are considered in turn here. In general, the *de facto* state is an awkward fit for theories based on Kantian cosmopolitanism. The logic of the *de facto* state mimics that of the sovereign state. It is therefore more concerned with the advancement and preservation of *sovereign* rights than it is with the universal advancement of *human* rights. In other words, *de facto* states are much more interested in securing their place within the existing system than they are in transforming that system.

There is only a very remote and extremely tenuous possibility that the *de facto* state could have any sort of positive impact on the cosmopolitan or universalist project to advance global human dignity. One might try to advance the thesis that if *de facto* states are more effective and have a higher degree of internal legitimacy than their quasi-state parents, then they might be better candidates to fulfill the requirements for Kant's proposed confederation of republican states—which is, in his scheme, preferable to world government and perhaps an inevitable step on the road to a universal community of global individuals.[6] This would seem, however, to be stretching an argument beyond its breaking point. The TRNC clearly advances the specific humanitarian interests of the Turkish Cypriot community. Whether or not it does anything to advance the interests of global humanity at large, however, remains far from certain. In general, the human rights scorecard of *de facto* states is mixed. While some of these entities (Eritrea and Somaliland for example) compare favorably in this regard to their juridical parents, others (Tamil Eelam) do not. In yet other cases (Chechnya), the *de facto* state may ultimately lead to an improvement in the human condition of its local inhabitants but whether or not this improvement will justify the cost in human lives at which it was purchased is debatable. Regardless of which scenario applies in any given case, the overwhelming importance these entities place on securing sovereignty makes them unlikely vehicles from which to build the ultimate global community of humankind. As such, the *de facto* state is likely to be of very limited interest to any scholars operating from a Kantian or cosmopolitan framework of analysis.

The Marxist or structural variant of revolutionism will be interpreted broadly here to include any of the various theoretical approaches (dependency, world systems, neo-Marxism, and the like) which elevate the systemic role of global capitalism to a primary place of explanatory analysis and which have as their general problematic 'the causes of inequality/exploitation and the conditions for equality...'.[7] While such approaches may perhaps have some insights to offer into the study of *de facto* statehood, they are not particularly well-suited to this research project. The main reason is that such approaches emphasize the primacy of economic factors while the logic of the *de facto* state (Taiwan perhaps being one exception) generally advances political considerations over economic ones. The *de facto* state is interested in securing sovereignty for itself, not in advancing the condition of the global proletariat. Similarly, one is unlikely to find a global capitalist interest in the creation of these entities.[8] Whereas states and sovereignty are only derivative factors in the various structural approaches, they are the primary *raison d' être* for these entities. Robert Jackson's (1990) view on the relevance of these approaches to the study of quasi-states is equally applicable in regards to the study of this phenomenon. As he puts it, structuralist approaches have grave difficulty in this area 'because of blindness to the significance of sovereignty and legal institutions generally' (1990, p. 179).

Beyond this, any theory which is predominantly economically-based will have difficulty explaining the tremendous diversity of economic situations found in most secessionist attempts. Secessionist movements have arisen in regions that are relatively disadvantaged economically (Bangladesh, Tamil Eelam) and in regions that are relatively well-off economically (Biafra, the Basque country, northern Italy)—sometimes even within the same country (Kashmir and Punjab in India; Kosovo and Slovenia in the former Yugoslavia).[9] While some authors theorize that disadvantaged regions are less likely to pursue secession (Bookman, 1992, pp. 44-46), others highlight the potential economic advantages to these same regions of seceding (Jacobs, 1984, pp. 205-206 and 214-216). Assessing the global data produced by the Minorities at Risk study, Ted Robert Gurr concludes that 'material inequalities and economic discrimination had negligible correlations with ethnonationalist grievances and rebellions' (1994, p. 358).

None of this is to deny that economic analysis—whether or not it is structurally-based—has a role to play in the study of secession in general or *de facto* states in specific. While the relative importance of economic factors in explaining secession is a hotly-debated subject,[10] there is no question that economic issues are involved, one way or another, in *all* secessionist bids—including those that result in the establishment of *de facto* states. As Eisuke Suzuki observes, 'Separation claims inevitably involve claims for wealth resources whether or not a claimant group's primary demand is for wealth' (1976, p. 825).

Indeed, a number of areas related to the focus of this study where further economic research is necessary can be specified. First, specific political-economic analyses of each of our four case studies and of other cases referenced in this study would be helpful. Perhaps most important would be a general study on the political economy of *de facto* statehood—i.e., what kinds of challenges does a lack of widely-recognized sovereignty pose for these entities and what various coping strategies have they devised to address these problems? The relationships between *de facto* state political and business leaders also need to be elaborated. Another relevant area for further research is the whole question of what effects continued regional and global economic integration are likely to have both on currently-existing *de facto* states and on the prospects for the creation of more such entities in the future.[11] Whether such work could most fruitfully be carried out from within neo-Marxist or neo-classical economic traditions probably depends upon one's own ideological biases in this regard. The main point, though, is that the study of *de facto* statehood is likely to be of limited interest to scholars operating from within any of the structural variants of revolutionism. While some insights may be generated on this subject, the structuralist blind spot to the importance of such things as sovereignty and international law is likely to ensure that their contributions are of a marginal or peripheral nature at best.

Feminism

As with many of the other theoretical traditions canvassed here, to speak of feminism as if it was one distinct and coherent body of thought probably obscures as much as it reveals. As J. Ann Tickner asserts, 'there is no *one* feminist approach but many, which come out of various disciplines and intellectual traditions' (1991, p. 35, italics in original). For our purposes, we will somewhat simplistically dichotomize feminism into liberal and radical variants to examine what, if anything, either of these approaches may have to offer the study of *de facto* statehood.

On the whole, feminists are unlikely to find much that appeals to them in this area of study. This is especially true for radical feminists and is due in large part to their open hostility to the state in general. Anne Sisson

Runyan and V. Spike Peterson, for example, maintain that 'State formation is the process of reordering social relations such that the exploitation of gender and class is consolidated, institutionalized, legitimated, and reproduced' (1991, p. 90). While acknowledging that patriarchal customs precede state formation, these authors emphasize that it is only with the state that these relations are institutionalized. Beyond the state's role in constituting profoundly gendered identities and divisions of labor which have 'systemic implications for the production and reproduction of women's insecurities' (Peterson, 1992, p. 44), there is also its problematic role in impeding the radical feminist's desired transformation away from national security and toward world security. As Peterson argues, 'moving toward world security requires moving beyond state sovereignty and the limiting construction of political community and identity it has historically imposed' (1992, p. 32). As the *de facto* state emulates the same general logic as the sovereign state and seeks merely to join rather than transform the existing international society, there is little about it that will likely pique the interest of radical feminists. In other words, while radical feminists will probably continue to devote much time to gendered analyses of the state, there is little of distinction to draw them to the more specific study of *de facto* statehood.

While the study of *de facto* states as a whole is probably of no greater appeal to liberal feminists, these scholars may show moderate interest in evaluating specific examples of this phenomenon. According to Runyan and Peterson, for liberal feminists, 'the "problem" of the state is primarily its patriarchal definition of citizenship, which excludes women from legal equality'. As such, their ultimate goal in this regard is 'the elimination of barriers to women's equal participation with men' (1991, pp. 87-88). Such an orientation may lead these scholars to consider an examination of the status of women in various *de facto* states—perhaps in comparison to their prior status in the juridical parent state. Of the cases evaluated in this study, the Eritreans would likely win the most praise for their persistent and considerable efforts at improving the general status of women and ensuring their active participation in all facets of social, economic, political, and military life. On the other hand, Somaliland, with its reliance on more traditional clan-based structures of authority, would likely come in for some sharp criticism from liberal feminists—as would the LTTE for its wanton disregard of women's security and their human rights. The gendered analysis of individual *de facto* state case studies would certainly bring a new perspective to much of the literature on these entities. From the perspective of this study, though, the important point to note is that while liberal feminists might find particular policies or actions of various individual *de facto* states commendable or reprehensible, they are unlikely to find much of interest to them in the general study of this phenomenon.

One area where the experiences of these entities may be of some interest to feminist scholars is the whole question of women's participation in war. Again, Eritrea may be the individual case study that is most interesting to feminists in this regard but the struggle to establish and maintain *de facto* states impacts women's security in every instance. The issue of women's participation in war is one that is likely to divide liberal and radical feminists. The implications of this are well-captured by Rebecca Grant (1992):

> Death, so rarely mentioned in connection with security, snaps us out of the theoretical reverie on women's experience. How much of a victory is women's participation if it ultimately funnels into the same tragic waste? Here we are face to face with the dilemma of being pleased with equality and dismayed at the lack of transformation (1992, p. 90).

The whole question of whether or not women's participation in *de facto* state situations differs substantially from their participation in other such things as terrorist groups, isolated rebellions, or the regular armies of sovereign states remained unanswered at present. The claim here is not that women's participation in conflicts surrounding the creation or maintenance of *de facto* states is necessarily unique or precedent-setting. Rather, it is merely that their participation in these cases may be of some interest to feminist scholars concerned with the larger issue of women and war.

Critical or Post-modern Approaches

As with feminism and most of the other traditions considered here, post-modernism is a broad tent that contains much diversity within its ranks. Our purpose again is not to highlight the distinctions between post-modernists, constructivists, post-structuralists, critical theorists, or post-positivists. Rather, it is to examine what these various approaches taken broadly might have to offer to the study of *de facto* statehood.

According to Alexander Wendt (1995), the main factor that unites these approaches to international relations is their concern with how world politics is 'socially constructed'. As he sees it, these approaches seek 'to analyze how processes of interaction produce and reproduce the social structures—cooperative or conflictual—that shape actors' identities and interests and the significance of their material contexts' (1995, p. 81). While some post-modernists are derided for their ideological commitment to 'emancipation', their denial of the possibility of objective knowledge, and their rejection of positivist methodology, their primary focus on social construction is highly relevant to the subject matter of this study. In this regard, Keith Krause (1996) identifies six foundational claims at the core of critical approaches to international relations. At least three of them may open up some interesting avenues for further research on the *de facto* state. In essence, these three claims are that: 1) the principal actors or subjects in world politics are social constructs; 2) that these subjects are constituted and reconstituted through political practices that create shared social understandings—in the process endowing these subjects with interests and identities that are not 'given' or carved in stone; and 3) that world politics is not static because its 'structures' are also ultimately social constructs (1996, p. 5). As Krause points out, the focus on social construction does not mean that scholars operating from within such a tradition ignore the importance of institutions such as sovereignty and the state. Nor does it mean that identities are infinitely malleable or here today and gone tomorrow. Rather, it signifies that the interests of political subjects are not determined by structures, but are produced through social interactions between those subjects. Similarly, despite the rhetoric on emancipation in some of this literature, adopting a critical approach does not commit a scholar to any particular political position, 'except insofar as the acceptance that world politics is not static, and that its structures and identities are constructed, implies the *possibility* of change' (1996, p. 10, italics in original).

Certainly any theoretical approach that implies even the possibility of change is likely to be received favorably by those who are sympathetic to the plight of *de facto* states. One might speculate therefore that these approaches will become increasingly popular among Northern Cypriot political scientists. Beyond this, however, the focus on how shared social understandings are constructed through interactive political processes also appears well-suited to explain the ways in which international society's consensus on such things as sovereignty, territorial borders, and self-determination has shifted and permutated over the years. The locus of where sovereignty resides, the degree to which borders are fixed or permeable, and the extent of the 'selves' eligible to determine have all evolved dramatically over the years. World politics has not been static in any of these areas. As the constellation of how such factors are interpreted in the post-1945 period has helped produce the entire phenomenon of *de facto* statehood, any theoretical approach which emphasizes the ways in which such shared understandings are constructed—and hence may be deconstructed or reconstructed—will likely be of vital importance in gauging the future prospects for these entities.

In regard to the subject matter of this study, the critical approach to international relations has probably advanced furthest in the area of sovereignty. Following the pioneering work of Rob Walker and Richard Ashley, the literature emphasizing the socially constructed nature of sovereignty has expanded considerably.[12] Moving beyond sovereignty, virtually all of the factors analyzed in chapter five could probably benefit from a critical analysis. The concepts of self-determination, collective non-recognition, and fixed territorial borders seem especially likely candidates for such scrutiny in the future. While all of these factors constitute the environment which helps produce *de facto* states, those entities themselves can also be seen as social constructions. Critical research on why political leaderships attempt to construct these entities rather than non-secessionist federal components would be helpful. Perhaps even more important is the whole question of why some leaderships (the EPLF, for example) choose to construct diverse, pluralistic, multi-ethnic, civic, and broad-based identities while other leaderships (the LTTE) choose to construct extremely narrow, intolerant, and exclusively ethnic-based identities from which to support their sovereign aspirations. The argument here is not that critical or post-modern approaches have any exclusive claim to the ability to provide answers to such questions. Many of the other traditions prevalent in international theory may also be capable of generating such insights. The point is merely that *de facto* states and many of the issues surrounding them and constitutive of their environment can be seen as socially constructed concepts. As such, approaches that place such concepts at the heart of their research program should offer productive starting points from which to launch inquiries in this regard.

International Law

As noted in chapter seven, the *de facto* state does not present any insurmountable theoretical problems for international legal scholars. International law has proven itself to be adaptable to new developments in the past and there is no reason to assume that it cannot conceptually accommodate the *de facto* state and other such related entities. That said, however, while topics such as self-determination, criteria for 'just' secessions, and non-intervention are the subjects of seemingly endless debates, the literature available on specific case studies of interest to this study is extremely sparse. The fact that many *de facto* states can survive for a long time while their juridical status is questionable or contentious indicates the need for such academic work. Taiwan has received some attention from international lawyers, particularly since the US decision to switch recognition to Beijing in 1979,[13] but there has really only been one substantial study of the international legal position of the Turkish Cypriot *de facto* state—despite its more than twenty years of existence.[14] Perhaps most surprising is the near complete lack of attention devoted to the Provisional Government of Eritrea and its extended transition period to independence. The dearth of literature on this subject is particularly telling since, after the traumas associated with the rush to independence in the former Yugoslavia, the Eritrean extended transition to independence may serve as a template for future cases such as Chechnya and Somaliland.

Beyond the specific cases described as *de facto* states in this study, there exists a much wider range of territorially-based political entities which also function and exist at what might be termed the margins of international society. Examples here would include such things as the Palestinian Authority; non-secessionist rebel groups in Angola and Sierra Leone; the Kurdish safe havens; and the constituent units of the post-Dayton accords Bosnia. More work in all of these individual areas is needed. Even more desirable, however, would be a comparative international legal study of *de facto* states and other such entities on the margins of international society. Such work would be of tremendous assistance to future scholars interested in comparing apples to apples or at least in knowing that they are comparing apples to oranges and bananas. It would also be of assistance to policy-makers and non-governmental aid organizations as well.

Obviously, this whole agenda ties into the larger question of whether or not international society is evolving in the direction of a more diverse system characterized by a wider-range of participants than hitherto has been the case. How best to deal with the implications of such an evolution (if it is indeed taking place) may be one of the leading questions facing international lawyers in the near future. The *de facto* state is obviously only one small part of such a possible scenario but the significance of its presence should be of interest to international legal scholars. One interesting avenue of inquiry suggested here by Hurst Hannum and Richard Lillich (1980) focuses on the concept of autonomy. After arguing that the increasing complexity of world politics no longer corresponds 'to the sovereign nation-state simplicity of the nineteenth century', these authors suggest that autonomy 'remains a useful, if imprecise, concept within which flexible and unique political structures may be developed to respond to that complexity' (1980, p. 889). Such a focus may appeal to those international lawyers whose work is normatively committed to bringing additional areas of world politics under the domain of international law. While the proactive, and explicitly ideological nature of their work may put off some hardened international relations scholars, there is a case to be made for not just chronicling moves toward a more diverse international system but also seeking to pave the way to ensure that such moves occur smoothly and cause the minimum amount of disruption and suffering possible.

4 Conclusion

The combination of their small size, their limited numbers, their ambiguous status, and their conventional goals (sovereignty as constitutional independence) have all kept *de facto* states out of the international theoretical limelight. As such, the theoretical study of these entities remains in its infancy. While the existence of *de facto* states does not force us to rethink our existing theories, the presence of these entities in the international system does open up some potentially interesting avenues of theoretical inquiry. Without question, the largest theoretical impact that these entities could have would be if their numbers were to increase and they were to remain locked in some sort of indeterminate or intermediate status. In other words, neither their potential graduation to sovereign statehood nor their potential eradication poses novel theoretical challenges. Continued indeterminate status, on the other hand, might conceivably be seen as an indication of fundamental challenges to the existing consensus on sovereignty and a shift in the direction of a more diverse international system. While such claims may not be likely or self-evident at present, it is at least worth noting the possible role continued *de facto* statehood may play in this regard. Obviously, these entities do not exist in isolation and they would merely be one part of other, larger transformations taking place throughout the international system. While their potential role may be somewhat minor, the possibilities it suggests are interesting enough to warrant placing the *de facto* state on our theoretical radar screens.

As so little theoretical work to date has been carried out on this phenomenon, there are few areas where further research would not be helpful. Certainly it is not claimed that the work done here will serve as a definitive statement on this subject. Rather, it is to be hoped that it will serve as a starting point and that future scholars following on from it will seek to add to, modify, or challenge its various premises. That said, of the different traditions evaluated in this chapter, it is unlikely that either feminists or revolutionists will find much to pique their curiosity in the study of *de facto* statehood. Realists, rationalists, post-modernists, and international lawyers on the other hand should all be interested in this phenomenon to varying degrees. No hierarchy of relevant traditions is offered here. Rather, it is postulated that the study of *de facto* statehood is most likely to be advanced if it is carried out by a wide variety of scholars operating from a diverse plurality of perspectives.

This chapter concludes the main body of analysis in this study. As it has focused on the theoretical implications of *de facto* statehood, our conclusion in chapter ten shifts the focus back toward the practical and policy implications of these entities. In addition to summing up some of the main findings of this work, chapter ten also seeks to assess the likely prospects for the *de facto* state's growth or demise in the future. It concludes by asking what, if anything, international society can or should do about this phenomenon.

Notes

[1] Compare in this regard Elkins, 1995, pp. 75-76; Ruggie, 1993, p. 167; Waltz, 1979, pp. 93-95; and Thomson and Krasner, 1989, p. 198.
[2] Krasner, 1995-96, p. 150. See also Holsti, 1985, p. 688.
[3] Jackson, 1993a, p. 361. See also Holsti, 1985, p. 689; and Thomson and Krasner, 1989, pp. 196-198.
[4] The argument that territorial losses are not necessarily fatal to a state's existence is put forward in Buzan, 1991, p. 92.
[5] See Bull, 1977, p. 295 for more on this.
[6] One excellent introduction to the Kantian tradition of thought in international relations is Donaldson, 1992, pp. 136-157.
[7] Holsti, 1985a, p. 66. This is in italics in the original.
[8] Donis Christofinis, though, does find just such an interest in his Marxist analysis of the creation of the TRNC. See Christofinis, 1984, pp. 86-88.
[9] See Bookman, 1992, pp. 94-95; and Hannum, 1990, pp. 7-8 for more on this.
[10] Contrast in this regard Connor, 1972, pp. 342-343 with Nafzinger and Richter, 1976, p. 92.
[11] An initial attempt to apply economic theory to secession by Alberto Alesina and Enrico Spolaore suggests that greater economic integration may lead to more

secessionist bids in the future. Their work is summarized in 'A Wealth of Nations', *The Economist*, 29 April 1995.

[12] See Walker, 1993; Ashley, 1988; Barkin and Cronin, 1994; Weber, 1992; and the various contributions in Biersteker and Weber (eds.), 1996.

[13] See, for example, Li, 1979, pp. 134-162; Ling, 1983, pp. 163-184; Mangelson, 1992, pp. 231-251; Randolph, 1981, pp. 249-262; and Sheikh, 1980, pp. 323-341.

[14] Necatigil, 1989. There have, of course, been other studies of the broader Cyprus dispute, but few that place much emphasis on the Turkish Cypriot *de facto* state itself. Some of the other literature includes Jacovides, 1995; Palmer, 1986; and Rossides, 1991.

10 Conclusion

1 Main Objectives

This concluding chapter solely aims to achieve three main objectives. First, it will briefly summarize some of the broadest key findings to come out of this study. Second, it will attempt to assess the future prospects for these entities. Third, from a policy perspective, it will evaluate what, if anything, international society can or should do about the existence of *de facto* states.

2 Key Findings of This Study

While hundreds of points or arguments have been put forth in this study, here we will limit our attention to five fundamental observations. The first key point to reiterate is simply that *de facto* states do exist. Though they are inherently more nebulous and harder to come to grips with than their sovereign counterparts, these entities can be discerned and they can be shown to exist. In this study we have primarily considered four examples of this phenomenon: Eritrea before independence, the LTTE-controlled parts of Sri Lanka, the Republic of Somaliland, and the Turkish Republic of Northern Cyprus. Other potential examples include Biafra, Chechnya, Krajina, the Bosnian Serb Republic, UDI Rhodesia, and Taiwan. Two potential future *de facto* states to watch for might be Kosovo and the southern Sudan. While this phenomenon may not be global (at present, none of these entities is found in the western hemisphere), it is multi-regional.

As with other terms like 'sovereign state', 'weak state', and 'capitalist state', the term '*de facto* state' incorporates a wide diversity of entities under its umbrella. The four case studies examined here, for example, differ in terms of such things as their degree of popular support, the extent of governance provided, their dependence (or lack thereof) on external support, their territorial justifications, their level of democratic accountability, and their organizational principle (the liberal and civic ideals of the state principle or the ethnic-based ideals of the national principle). In spite of these various differences, it does still make sense to refer to these

249

four entities as *de facto* states. In the terms of our working definition, all of these cases feature organized political leaderships which have risen to power through some degree of indigenous capability. These leaderships all receive some form of popular support and they have achieved sufficient capacity to provide governmental services to a specific population in a given territorial area, over which effective control is maintained for an extended period of time. All of them see themselves as capable of entering into relations with other states and they all seek widespread recognition as constitutionally independent sovereign states. None of them, however, has been able to garner such recognition. As such, they all remain illegitimate in the eyes of international society.

The second main point to be emphasized is that theoretical criteria can be elaborated to distinguish the *de facto* state from other participants in international relations. In other words, in addition to merely being out there, this phenomenon can also be distinguished as a separate category worthy of analysis in its own right. In chapter two, ten such theoretical criteria were advanced that speak to such things as the *de facto* state's capabilities and its goals. Some of these criteria more specifically serve to differentiate these entities from other phenomena such as puppet states and peaceful secession movements. One can argue over the finer points of such criteria, as well as over their relative importance. The main point to be made, though, is that one can meaningfully distinguish the *de facto* state as a distinct type of actor in international politics.

Third, despite the extensive academic literature surrounding such topics as sovereignty, secession, and self-determination, almost no attention has been devoted to the study of *de facto* statehood itself. At best, entities like the TRNC are given what might be termed footnote treatment—briefly mentioned in a paragraph or two as exceptions to the dominant sovereign paradigm and then quickly glossed over. At worst, they are treated merely as deviant problems that require solutions. While the term '*de facto* state' may have tentatively entered into our political lexicon, there have been few, if any, attempts to study this phenomenon comparatively or to assess systematically its implications for contemporary international society.[1] Similarly, while some of the individual conflicts surrounding *de facto* states (such as those in Cyprus and Sri Lanka) have been the subject of intensive scrutiny, almost no attention has been devoted to considering these entities together as a coherent phenomenon worthy of distinct analysis. It is this gap in the existing literature that this study has attempted to redress.

Fourth, this widespread academic neglect of the *de facto* state is unjustified. *De facto* states are not the most significant actors in international politics. That said, however, the near-total academic neglect of these entities is a serious problem. The case for devoting more attention to the phenomenon of *de facto* statehood is multi-faceted. First, the evidence indicates that many of these entities can survive for extended periods of time. They are not here today and gone tomorrow. Indeed, depending on how one calculates it, the average time of existence for our four case studies is 15.25 years.[2] Second, *de facto* states do have measurable impacts on global political economy and, especially, on the number of fatalities and refugees produced. Beyond this, the question of how to deal with specific cases may have spillover effects on much larger issues. Current disputes over whether or not the Turkish Cypriots should be consulted in upcoming negotiations on the question of that island's accession to EU membership, for example, threaten to disrupt the planned expansions of both NATO and the EU.[3] Third, *de facto* states may be of some significance to international theory. Their greatest potential theoretical impact would be if they remained in some sort of continued indeterminate status. The ability of these entities to survive or flourish in coming years may also serve as one indicator of just how strong (or weak) the trends are in the direction of a more diverse international system. While their overall impact on both international politics and international theory may be relatively modest, it is not negligible. *De facto* states deserve more academic interest than they have received to date.

Finally, these entities should not be viewed solely in negative terms. It is not argued here that they all deserve sovereign recognition or that they have all demonstrated enlightened, moral, or just leadership. The widespread diversity among *de facto* states means that one cannot state that these entities are categorically 'good' or 'legitimate'. They are unlikely to make for ideal solutions to most international or intra-state problems. The argument is thus not put forward here that *de facto* states should be seen solely in positive terms. A case can be made, though, that these entities are deserving of more balanced and less judgmental treatment than they have often received in the past.

The *de facto* state may indeed provide some form of international utility. To use the Somaliland example, it is hard to argue in favor of forcibly yoking these people against their wishes to Mogadishu. Yet, international society has a legitimate interest in not wishing to grant them recognition and thereby set a precedent for others to follow. Reaching some sort of non-juridical accommodation with the Somaliland *de facto* state may be the best option available here. The *de facto* state's inherent lack of juridical acceptance is well-suited to serve two important purposes here: 1) international norms are maintained as secession is not seen to be rewarded; and 2) the existence of a *de facto* state in no way precludes any future settlement arrangements. This study has deliberately used such terms as 'functional non-solutions' and 'messy solutions to messy problems' to indicate that these entities probably do not offer the best of all possible worlds. Viewing them solely in the negative terms of problems that require solutions, however, obscures as much as it reveals.

One can also argue along these lines that *de facto* states are sometimes held up to unrealistic standards or condemned in a vacuum. The Turkish Cypriots, for example, can legitimately be criticized for the fact that some of their demands may indeed be unreasonable given their small share of the total Cypriot population. Such criticisms are, however, often made with the unstated presumption that the Greek Cypriots have always behaved reasonably and treated the Turkish Cypriot minority with enlightened sensitivity. The events of the early 1960s clearly show, however, that this has not been the case. Similarly, Somaliland's decision to print its own currency may be superfluous or economically irrational. The sins of the Somaliland *de facto* state, however, are seen in a different light when compared to those of Siad Barre, Mohamed Farah Aideed, and the warlords of Mogadishu. One need not shirk from criticizing specific *de facto* states or abandon the hope that problems can be resolved within the context of existing territorial borders. *De facto* states should not, however, be seen solely in disparaging terms.

3 Future Prospects for These Entities

In the short-to-medium term future, the safest prediction is probably for an approximate continuation of the status quo in terms of the numbers of *de facto* states present in the international system. In other words, one is likelier to see something similar to the present state of affairs—more or less a handful of these entities in existence—than one is to see either their total abolition or an explosive increase in their numbers. This prediction is based on a number of factors. First, the assorted systemic-level factors identified in chapter five as helping to produce this phenomenon have not been fundamentally altered by the end of the Cold War. The international consensus on such things as fixed territorial borders, state-based sovereignty, and an extremely narrow interpretation of self-determination still holds. As the figurative ceiling that prevents *de facto* states from graduating to sovereign statehood still remains in place, one should not expect to see many of these entities being welcomed into international society anytime soon.

On the other side of the equation, however, there are still a number of reasons to expect that the search for sovereignty will continue. The state-nation disjunction is a structural feature of international relations. In and of itself, this will not necessarily produce future secession attempts, let alone new *de facto* states. Yet, the number of ineffective, corruption-plagued, and human rights-violating governments does not seem to be abating rapidly. If the chances of most weak states overcoming their insecurity dilemmas are not great, then one should not be surprised to see future secession attempts. As Ralph Premdas puts it,

> we live in a divided world where cleavages abound and where secessionist claims for a separate autonomous existence are more 'normal' than are often perceived. It is the homogenous state that is the deviant case.... we are not dealing with a peripheral phenomenon, but with one that is indeed predominant in the world... (1990, p. 17).

A major question mark here will be the importance of ethnicity in the future. Not all *de facto* states are ethnically-based. Indeed, the growing importance placed by international society on fixed internal borders suggests that future sovereign aspirants may have a better chance of acceptance by inclusively crafting their claims toward all those who live within set internal boundaries rather than exclusively crafting them toward specific ethnic groups. A relative increase or decrease in the importance attached to ethnicity may, however, impact upon the number of secessionist state-creation bids in the future. In this regard, Walker Connor (1967) argued more than thirty years ago that for the vast majority of the world's population, ethnic consciousness still lies in the future. This is because such a consciousness presupposes an awareness of other distinct groups but, for most people, their relevant world still ends at the village. As such, Connor expects that the end-result of the spread of communications will be that 'the ethnic hodgepodges that are Asia and Africa will produce a host of new demands for the redrawing of political borders' (1967, p. 46). While most secessionist movements do not result in the creation of *de facto* states, if Connor's hypothesis is correct, then the explosion in new demands for the revision of existing frontiers would likely lead to at least some notable increase in the number of these entities.

The available evidence, however, does not necessarily support Connor's position. Ted Robert Gurr (1994), for example, finds no evidence of any dramatic increase in ethnic conflicts in recent years. After noting that new secessionist conflicts have been almost exclusively confined to the Soviet and Yugoslav successor states, Gurr argues that 'The most likely scenario is an increase in communal contention about access to power in new, weak, heterogeneous states like those of Africa: Sudan and Angola are archetypes, Zaire is on the brink' (1994, p. 364). Such a scenario might produce a modest increase in the number of *de facto* states. Even this, however, is questionable. A number of potential *de facto* states, such as the Eastern Kasai region of Zaire and the UNITA-controlled parts of Angola have not (as yet) chosen to pursue secessionist aims. Even if they were to do so in the future, Gurr's scenario is still unlikely to lead to any explosion in the numbers of these entities.

The work of Michael Desch (1996) on the effects of a decline in the external threat environment on state cohesion is also of some relevance here. Examining the use of external threats to maintain internal cohesion, Desch focuses on the end of the Cold War and its possible implications for state disintegration. He does not forecast any radical change in the existing states system but does argue that

> Since war and preparation for war have played such important roles in expanding the scope and maintaining the cohesion of the modern state, the changed international security environment ought to make the continued growth or maintenance of broad scope, and in certain cases even the viability of some states doubtful (1996, p. 259).

According to Desch, the implications of all of this are quite mixed for Third World states. While many of these states suffer from deep cleavages, many of them also still face challenging external threat environments. Thus, two separate sets of outcomes are predicted. On the one hand, 'States with deep ethnic, social, or linguistic cleavages facing a more benign threat environment should find it harder to maintain cohesion'. On the other hand, 'deeply divided Third World states that are facing a challenging external threat environment will probably find it easier to maintain cohesion' (1996, p. 260). Again, on such a scenario one might perhaps expect a modest increase in the number of *de facto* states. One would not, however, expect a dramatic increase in their numbers.

Another influential factor here is the success or failure of existing sovereign governments in responding to a *de facto* state challenge. The record of existing sovereign states here is at best mixed. While there are a few examples of *de facto* states which have been eradicated (Krajina) or successfully reincorporated (Biafra), there are many other cases where governments have been unable to solve their *de facto* state problem with either the carrot or the stick (Chechnya, Somaliland, Tamil Eelam, the TRNC, arguably the Bosnian Serbs). Once established then, most *de facto* states probably have better than a 50-50 chance of surviving for extended periods of time. Barring any unforeseen change in the ability of weak states to consolidate the legitimacy of their rule, there is unlikely to be much downward pressure on the number of these entities in the states system.

Arguably the biggest factor holding back any potential future growth in the numbers of *de facto* states is simply the sheer difficulties inherent in any attempt to establish one. The substantive requirements for *de facto* statehood in terms of such things as popular support, effective control of a given territorial area, the provision of governance services, and the like are simply beyond the reach of most secessionist groups. As such, even if the number of active secessionist movements in the world expanded by a dozen or more this still might not result in the creation of any new *de facto* states. Would-be *de facto* state leaders must overcome many of the same difficulties that prevent the consolidation of effective and legitimate sovereign rule by their quasi-state parents. Unlike those same quasi-states, however, they must do so without any substantive outside diplomatic or financial support, and often in the face of concerted external hostility. Even with other favorable conditions in place, one would still not be wise to predict any massive increase in the number of these entities.

The final factor influencing the number of *de facto* states is the reaction to these entities from other members of international society. Other things being equal, one would expect these entities to have a better chance of survival if international society chose to ignore them or to come to some sort of working accommodation with them than if it chose to try actively to undermine them. Perhaps the two most interesting cases to watch for future clues in this regard are Chechnya and Somaliland—Chechnya because the attempt at a military solution so obviously failed; Somaliland because of the bankruptcy of its sovereign parent, its former colonial status, and its high comparative levels of legitimacy, efficiency, and democratic accountability.

Putting all of these various factors together, it seems that the most likely bet is for the continued presence of about a handful of *de facto* states in the international system. One cannot absolutely rule out the possibility that the strong consensus on fixed territorial borders or the extremely narrow interpretation of self-determination will someday give way to looser arrangements that facilitate the creation of new *de facto* states or even their graduation to sovereign statehood. The odds at present, though, must be seen as set strongly against those possibilities.[4] Barring such fundamental changes, one can expect a continued small (but not negligible) number of *de facto* states in the contemporary states system.

4 What, if Anything, Should Be Done About This Phenomenon?

Although this study has been concerned with an entity that lives on or outside the margins of international society, its policy prescriptions are relatively modest. In spite of the total inconsistency and manifest hypocrisy which has characterized such things as self-determination, secession, and recognition, this study still gives international society's presumption in favor of maintaining existing states a qualified endorsement. Beyond the more hysterical versions of the domino theory and the self-interested whining of threatened states, there are a whole host of reasons to operate under a general presumption in favor of existing states and against secession. These reasons include such things as the clarity and simplicity afforded by such a system; the desire not to subvert majority rule; the inability ever to solve the structural state-nation disjunction; the fear of creating new trapped minorities; the fact that a shift away from such a system would probably lead to at least short-term increases in instability; and the extremely difficult questions thrown up by any divorce. Therefore, operating from a general presumption in favor of maintaining existing states within their fixed territorial borders is prudent.

Yet, this study's endorsement of the present state of affairs regarding secession is a distinctly qualified one. There are a number of reasons for this. First, international society's position on secession is based on some practical and philosophical inconsistencies. Philosophically, the distinction between legitimate decolonization and illegitimate secession makes little sense. The argument that salt-water colonial oppressors cannot stand in the way of self-determination while domestic internal colonialists can is one that is lost on most dissatisfied minorities. Practically, tremendous inconsistencies have characterized the application of these various policies. International society's divergent responses to the invasions of Kuwait, Goa, East Timor, Cyprus, and East Pakistan are seemingly devoid of principled explanation. Such double standards undermine the legitimacy of supposedly absolute rules on such things as fixed territorial borders and *ex injuria jus non oritur*. Second, nothing about the present system is natural, permanent, or inevitable. There are no territorial givens and state sovereignty is not divinely ordained. The states system has shown itself able to cope with substantial amounts of change and there is no reason to assume that any of the various options canvassed in chapter eight for Somaliland, Chechnya, or the TRNC will bring about that system's collapse. Third, while the present system does promote a particular kind of stability, it is not necessarily the only or the best kind of stability available. The more than twenty million (overwhelmingly civilian) conflict fatalities since 1945 attests to this fact.

One must always question the value of an existing state that does not provide for what Robert Jackson (1992) has termed 'the domestic good life'. As he points out, the state is not an end. Rather, it is only a means to the end of individuals and their well-being. Fixed territorial borders facilitate the maintenance of external security. Yet, 'External security enabling privileged ruling classes to keep populations in servitude, want, and even fear is not exactly consistent with the value assumptions of national security theory' (1992, p. 82). Charles Beitz's argument (1979, pp. 121-122) that the principle of state autonomy needs to be evaluated against appropriate principles of justice can be seen in a similar light. Metin Tamkoç (1988) pursues this logic even further in arguing for a dynamic conception of state legitimacy. This contrasts with our present static conception of state legitimacy where, by virtue of its supposed legitimacy at birth (the sovereign equivalent of the immaculate conception), the state is deemed eternal. Tamkoç, on the other hand, sees the state merely as another means devised by people to serve a specific purpose. He compares the state in this regard to a building which can be constructed in different sizes, shapes, or configurations depending upon the needs it is designed to serve. Further, the owners of the original building can decide at some point in the future to expand, remodel, abandon, or destroy it. In Tamkoç's conception,

> No State, no legal order is so sacred that it cannot be altered and abolished by the people, by force, if necessary. If and when the State systematically undermines and violates the human and political rights of its citizens, it loses its reason for being, and therefore, its legitimacy although it may continue to 'govern effectively' (1988, pp. 22-23).

Most international relations scholars will recoil from the potential instability that an unrestrained pursuit of Tamkoç's approach might lead to. Surely, it will be argued, there is no reason why the Catalans and the

Quebecois cannot resolve their differences within the context of current borders. The general presumption in favor of existing states indicates that in most cases, most of the time, such an argument is justifiable. A qualified (as opposed to an absolute) presumption in favor of existing states leads one to wonder, however, if such a position has any validity when dealing with an Ethiopia under Mengistu or a Somalia under Siad Barre. As K. J. Holsti asks,

> Do the Christian and animist southern Sudanese really have any realistic alternatives except to rebel against a fundamentalist Muslim regime expropriating their lands, excluding them from any form of national political participation, and attempting to convert them forcibly to Islam? (1996, p. 195)

If international society wishes to ensure that secession is rarely resorted to, then progress must be made in terms of promoting individual human rights, protecting group minority rights, and identifying viable federal solutions within the context of existing territorial borders. Aside from the logic of state sovereignty itself, the fundamental problem here remains the lack of political will and commitment needed to ensure the success of whatever arrangements are agreed to. After scores of broken promises and, in some cases, decades of bitter fighting, convincing Tamils, Kurds, or Chechens of the merits and viability of a non-secessionist solution remains a formidable task.

To reduce the demand for secession, international society can pursue one or both of two main approaches. The first is the protection and promotion of individual human rights. Despite the plethora of human rights documents signed by governments around the world, success on this front remains elusive. Even a casual glance through any of the Amnesty International or Human Rights Watch annual reports shows how minimal the progress to date has been at securing individual civil and political liberties. A fundamental problem here is that the agenda of individual rights runs smack up against the agenda of sovereign rights and non-intervention. The United Nations is an organization of states and its Charter is based on territorial inviolability and exclusive areas of domestic sovereign jurisdiction. Existing states defend their sovereign privileges tenaciously and are unlikely vehicles for the furtherance of an individual rights agenda. While recent years have seen perhaps the beginnings of a move away from sovereign rights and toward human rights, such moves have been selective, tentative, and reluctant.

The other main option is the promotion and protection of group minority rights. This approach is sometimes advocated because it is felt that simply granting individuals equal treatment under the law may be inadequate to deal with minorities' concerns over such things as language and culture. In particular, it is seen as especially important in the case of what are so-called 'permanent minorities'. Whereas democracy and the principle of majority rule are often justified on the basis of shifting majorities on different issues,[5] groups such as the Tamils and the Turkish Cypriots are permanent minorities who can always be outvoted in a straight majority rule system. Thus, they may need to be given special group rights to ensure that their concerns are addressed properly.

The international protection of minority rights is an idea that goes back at least as far as the Final Act of the Congress of Vienna in 1815 and perhaps even further.[6] This idea arguably reached its peak with the 1919-1920 series of peace treaties which primarily applied to the defeated powers of World War I and some newly-created or reconfigured states in Central and Eastern Europe. The minority provisions here essentially comprised two main elements: the first ensured racial, religious, or linguistic minorities of equal treatment under the law, while the second sought to ensure suitable means for the preservation of distinct minority traditions and characteristics.[7]

The international position of minority rights declined substantially from the post-World War I era to the United Nations. The UN Charter contains no specific provisions for minority rights. Rather, the UN approach was to emphasize individual human rights in the Universal Declaration of Human Rights and to grant all peoples the right of self-determination. This second component was, of course, limited mainly to cases of decolonization. The one exception to this UN neglect of minority rights came with Article 27 of the International Covenant on Civil and Political Rights. Even here, though, the beneficiaries of this article's limited protections are 'persons belonging to' ethnic minorities, not ethnic minorities themselves.[8]

One can now see a shift back toward the direction of internationally recognizing minority rights. This is most apparent regionally in the work of the CSCE (now OSCE). At its June 1990 Copenhagen meeting, the CSCE included an entire section on the rights of national minorities in its final communiqué. The CSCE reiterated its support for minority rights on 21 November 1990 in its Charter of Paris for a New Europe. Perhaps its strongest wording on the subject came in the July 1991 Geneva Report which states that,

Issues concerning national minorities, as well as compliance with international obligations and commitments concerning the rights of persons belonging to them, are matters of legitimate international concern and consequently do not constitute exclusively an internal affair of the respective state.[9]

Based on such statements, Jennifer Jackson Preece (1997) concludes that there has been a 'substantial normative shift' on the issue of minority rights since the end of the Cold War. Ironically, as she observes, 'The most important change of all is perhaps the most easily overlooked: after 1989, *minority questions were once again legitimate subjects of international society*' (1997, p. 91, italics in original). While Preece is undoubtedly correct in her assessment, from the perspective of most minorities, it is K. J. Holsti's conclusion that remains compelling: 'the logic of an official "minority" status is permanent insecurity because what can be granted can also be taken away' (1996, p. 55).

In theory, a general respect for individual human rights combined with specific minority rights protections in a federal or confederal system should ensure that secession need not be resorted to in international relations. Unfortunately, though, human rights and minority rights often count for little in a world of sovereign states jealously protective of their domestic autonomy. As Michael Shapiro (1994) points out, rights 'are predicated on juridical *standing*. The metaphor is crucial: a fixed address based on a historically legitimated title is a prerequisite for exercising rights in the world of bordered entities' (1994, p. 496, italics in original). Lacking such an address, some minorities will likely continue to seek solutions to their problems through secession. As such, we must expect a future in which secession will continue to be pursued and in which some secession attempts may result in the creation of *de facto* states. The question therefore becomes how qualified should the presumption in favor of existing states be?

In a few cases, international society may have to come to grips with the fact that widespread recognition of a secession attempt is its best option. A strong argument can be made that this was the case with Eritrea, and that it may well be the case with Chechnya and Somaliland today. Even the mere possibility that such an acceptance of successful secessions *may* be on the cards can encourage existing states to adopt a more accommodative position toward the dissatisfied groups within their boundaries. Jeffrey Herbst (1996-97) makes a retrospective argument along these lines in regard to Africa. As he puts it,

If secession had been a viable threat,... African politicians would have had a profound incentive to reach accommodation with disaffected populations, especially those that were spatially defined, lest they threaten to leave the nation-state. However, the international community's view that the boundaries were inviolable and that, therefore, the use of force was justified against potential secessionists, removed incentives for ethnic accommodation (1996-97, p. 131).

It is important to note here that successful secessions need not preclude future amicable agreements. Indeed, they may even be a prerequisite for such agreements. The best example here is the post-1991 state of relations between Eritrea and Ethiopia. Although the Eritreans voted overwhelmingly for independence in 1993, their government has entered into dozens of cooperative agreements with Ethiopia before and after the referendum. Perhaps the most important of these have been the arrangements making Assab and Massawa available to Ethiopia as free ports. It is also interesting to note that, even after receiving its independence, Eritrea continued to use the Ethiopian *birr* as its currency for more than four years while Somaliland, with its less secure status, has insisted on creating its own separate currency. While the recent border skirmishes between Ethiopia and Eritrea are a cause for concern, they do not change the fact that successful secessions need not preclude amicable relations in the future.

Perhaps the most interesting question here concerns the Turkish Cypriots. A number of provisions in the actual declaration proclaiming the establishment of the TRNC specifically prohibit it from uniting with any state or anyone other than the Greek Cypriots to form a federal Republic of Cyprus. In the Turkish Cypriot view, the establishment of the TRNC was not a final exercise of their right to self-determination. Rather, they have reserved the right to self-determine once again in order to form a federal union with the Greek Cypriots. In their view, the establishment of the TRNC does not hinder, but rather can facilitate a final Cypriot settlement.[10] While the Turkish Cypriots have thus been careful not to close the door on a future federation, they have yet to convince either the Greek Cypriots or the rest of the world of their credibility on this issue. As A. J. R. Groom notes, the question remains: 'was the establishment of the TRNC a move of separation as a prelude for integration - a case of *reculer pour mieux sauter* - or was it a case of separation *tout court*? It is a question that is still with us...' (1993, p. 25).

While this study does not specifically call for the recognition of the TRNC, it does argue that either: a) widespread recognition of secession as in the Eritrean case or b) international society coming to some sort of working non-juridical accommodation with a *de facto* state (option three in chapter seven) may facilitate future cooperative arrangements. Indeed, the *de facto* state may be an excellent choice here as its inherently nebulous status can act as an impetus for reaching future agreements. On the other hand, Michael Mangelson argues that the recognition of both governments in divided nation situations like Germany and Korea might actually be more conducive to reunification (1992, p. 249). Barbara Thomas-Woolley and Edmond Keller (1994) also hypothesize that federation may become more viable as autonomy becomes more secure. As they observe,

> It may be that, in order to form a sustainable federal union, some countries need to split apart completely and then later decide to federate after having experienced the problems/dangers inherent in complete autonomy, or after having developed a sense of equality and mutual respect (1994, p. 418).

The policy recommendation of this study is therefore that while international society should continue to operate from a presumption in favor of existing states, in some cases it should either recognize a successful secession or at least reach some form of non-juridical coexistence with a successful *de facto* state. Recognizing the TRNC or adopting a more accommodative approach to its *de facto* existence *may* not lead to an ultimate settlement of the Cyprus problem. It is, however, certain that twenty-some years of the isolate and embargo strategy *has* failed to produce such a settlement. Further, showering the Somaliland *de facto* state with hostility and contempt is unlikely to do much for the cause of peace and security in the Horn of Africa. Therefore, in most cases, international society should seek to work with and not against viable *de facto* states. This does not mean that all *de facto* states should be recognized. It does mean that they should be engaged and offered opportunities to participate in the technical work of organizations such as the UNDP. Their concerns and interests should be listened to and their residents should not be deprived of humanitarian assistance merely because they seek separation from a failed parent state. Even a wholly non-juridical acknowledgment of the *de facto* state's effective control may provide a means for establishing a framework within which these entities may be engaged on issues of importance before a final settlement can be reached. The one possible exception to this non-juridical accommodation strategy might be a *de facto* state like Tamil Eelam which has such an atrocious human rights record that international society recoils from even limited cooperative engagements with it.

What of the response to existing states faced with a *de facto* state challenge? In general, international society has chosen to offer such states both strong diplomatic support and, in many cases, substantial amounts of economic and military assistance as well. The argument advanced here in favor of a more qualified presumption in favor of existing states suggests that both of these types of support should be more conditional and less automatic than they have been in the past. Consider first the provision of economic and military assistance. Surely there is something wrong with the provision of massive amounts of such aid to criminal regimes such as those of Mengistu in Ethiopia, Mobutu in Zaire, and Siad Barre in Somalia. It is hard to get around the fact that the provision of such assistance has served to promote sustained military campaigns which have routinely led to massive human rights abuses, gross violations of the laws of war, and regionally-destabilizing refugee flows.

The western economic support for Russia during its brutal and inept war against Chechnya is one recent case in point. Of the cases considered here, Sri Lanka is arguably the leading candidate for a massive reduction in such outside support. Foreign aid has at times comprised over 40 percent of the government's total budget (O'Ballance, 1989, p. 92). With so many other calls on limited aid resources, one must ask why western governments continue to support a succession of regimes in Sri Lanka that choose to spend enormous sums of money fighting a dirty war against their own population. While the Sri Lankan government forces are far from alone in contributing to the awful human rights situation on that island, their own record in this regard is abysmal. It is one thing to support diplomatically the preservation of the Sri Lankan state within its present borders. It is quite another thing to fund a multi-million dollar a year dirty war machine that is repeatedly turned loose on innocent civilians.

This study therefore supports the efforts of countries such as Norway which have substantially reduced assistance to Sri Lanka in protest at its dismal human rights record and its inability to find a political solution to this long-running conflict. Correspondingly, it criticizes countries such as the United States which have continued to support the Sri Lankan government. In making this criticism, it is important to note that this study is requesting nothing more than that the US government obey its own domestic laws in this regard. Section 701 of the International Financial Institutions Act of 1977, for example, mandates US opposition to World Bank and regional development bank loans to governments that consistently engage in gross violations of human rights, except when such loans expressly meet basic

264 International Society and the De Facto State

human needs. Section 116 of the US Foreign Assistance Act places a number of human rights conditions on development assistance and US law also prohibits military aid 'to consistent violators of human rights' (Human Rights Watch, 1992, p. 468; Chege, 1991-92, pp. 160-161). In most cases, the qualified presumption in favor of existing states argues against granting sovereign recognition to *de facto* states. Such a policy need not, however, be coupled with the provision of hundreds of millions of dollars a year in foreign assistance to governments that have consistently demonstrated that they are unable to meet even the most minimal human rights standards.

One can also question the unflagging diplomatic support granted to some governments. In this, it is argued that international society often fails to make the distinction between supporting the preservation of an existing state within its current borders and supporting the preservation of a particular government. Perhaps the best example here comes from Cyprus. At the end of 1963, the system of government established in Cyprus under the 1960 constitution and associated treaties had collapsed. The international community could have responded to this situation in a number of different ways.[11] First, it could have argued that the Republic of Cyprus continued to exist under international law but that, as the legal 'shell' of the state was no longer occupied by representatives of both communities as provided for under the 1960 constitution, neither of the two communities could claim to represent Cyprus. In other words, while the Republic of Cyprus would continue to exist internationally as a state, it would not have a recognized government. Second, it could have argued that the Republic of Cyprus no longer existed even as a juridical shell covering two separate governments but that it had been superseded by two new states—one for the Greek Cypriots and one for the Turkish Cypriots. Instead, following the precedent set in Security Council Resolution 186 of 4 March 1964, the international community chose to recognize the now exclusively Greek Cypriot government as the 'Government of Cyprus'.

The international recognition of the Greek Cypriot administration as the government of *all* of Cyprus is galling to the Turkish Cypriots. Zaim Necatigil (1993), for example, finds objectionable

> the assumption of the Greek-Cypriot side, in complete disregard of the present realities, that a unitary 'Government of Cyprus' still exists and that the Greek-Cypriot administration is *that* 'Government.' In fact there is no 'common' or 'national' parliament in Cyprus. Northern Cyprus and Southern Cyprus elect their representatives separately and neither of these parliaments can represent Cyprus by itself (1993, p. 60).

This recognition also flies in the face of section 5 of the Geneva Declaration of 30 July 1974 (issued jointly on behalf of the governments of Greece, Turkey, and the UK) which 'noted the existence in practice in the Republic of Cyprus of two autonomous administrations, that of the Greek Cypriot Community and that of the Turkish Cypriot Community'. While the Greek Cypriots justify outside recognition as their only defense against Turkish military superiority, most Turkish Cypriots and many outside observers see this recognition as the main impediment to a future Cyprus settlement. In the words of Nancy Crawshaw, 'It is not surprising that the Greek Cypriots should be reluctant to exchange the monopoly of sovereignty, with its huge advantages, for a constitution which involves sharing power with the Turkish Cypriots'.[12]

The argument put forth here does not require recognizing the TRNC or condoning the partition of Cyprus. It does, however, maintain that it is foolish to pretend that the Greek Cypriot government represents or controls all of Cyprus or that whichever warlord prevails in Mogadishu governs all of Somalia. Perhaps the best manner of dealing with such situations in the future would be to couple recognition of the existing state's fixed territorial borders with a frank acknowledgment that its present government does not control or represent the entire population of that state. The present American position on Somalia—where the US does not recognize the existence of any government in Mogadishu—is perhaps one example of such a policy.[13] Jeffrey Herbst advocates an even more radical variant on this scheme which he refers to as 'decertification' (1996-97, pp. 142-144).

For those who do not want to go this far, there may be a case for a return to such traditional international law categories as a recognition of belligerency or insurgency, or for the creation of entirely new such categories. Along these lines, Michael Shapiro argues that 'The struggles of indigenous peoples for recognition on a map where they do not exist.... have to be recognized and given political legitimacy' (1994, p. 498). Similarly, Gidon Gottlieb (1993) advocates what he terms a 'states-plus-nations' approach to international politics. Gottlieb's system, which is explicitly designed to prevent the creation of new territorial states, entails a number of related concepts including the delimitation of a variety of functional borders for different purposes; the formal recognition of nations within the international system; the recognition of the concept of a national home that is distinct from the state; and the adoption of different layers of citizenry that can express an individual's link to the nation, as well as to the state. As Gottlieb sees it,

> It is possible to create a 'new space' for nations that have not achieved
> independence without encouraging the forces of disintegration.... Nations
> and peoples that have no state of their own can be recognized as such and
> endowed with an international legal status.[14]

It is not claimed here that the *de facto* state necessarily accords well with
either Shapiro or Gottlieb's ideas. Rather, it is claimed that international
society must creatively move beyond the mere reassertion of the sanctity of
existing borders if it is to come to grips with the assorted problems and
opportunities posed by *de facto* states and other such dissatisfied groups.

Related to the above, both individual states and the society of states
as a whole have an interest in bringing *de facto* states further into the
international legal system. *De facto* states control natural resources, they
engage in various types of commerce, and they play host to foreign nationals
who enter their territories as aid workers, businesspersons, journalists, and
tourists. Further, their actions contribute greatly to regional stability or
instability. It is therefore in international society's interest to see that these
entities are brought further into the current international legal framework. No
matter how explicitly it is reiterated that this incorporation does not
necessarily imply recognition of sovereignty, the existing parent state will
object vociferously. Finding a way around this conundrum will require
innovative legal and political thinking.

Finally, it needs to be emphasized that nothing advocated here
requires fundamentally changing the existing international legal or political
order. The present system is generally capable of coping with the long-term
existence of *de facto* states within its midst. The call here is mainly for
individual states such as the US to obey their own domestic laws on not
providing assistance to human rights violators and for international society to
insist on proper adherence to its relevant rules on internal conflicts—
principally those found in Common Article 3 of the Geneva Conventions of
1949 and in the Second Additional Protocol of 1977 to those same
conventions—as the *quid pro quo* for its support of existing state boundaries.
The call here is also for the creation of some political space that
acknowledges the reality of *de facto* states and other such entities on the
margins of international society. In other words, there is a need to recognize,
as Christopher Clapham puts it, that the post-Cold War world is not 'crisply
divided into entities which do and do not count as "states". It consists instead
of a mass of power structures which, regardless of formal designation, enjoy
greater or lesser degrees of statehood' (1998, p. 157). We do not need to
throw out the general presumption in favor of existing states and grant

widespread recognition to any and all would-be challengers. We do, however, need to find some creative options between the two extremes of sovereign recognition and full-scale military assaults on groups of people that often have quite legitimate concerns and grievances. It is time to move beyond purely ritualistic condemnations of *de facto* states and toward innovative forms of accommodating their existence short of and, in some cases, perhaps including sovereignty.

Notes

[1] Perhaps the closest thing to a comparative study of *de facto* statehood is the work of Hussein Adam and Ronald McMullen on Somaliland and Eritrea. See Adam, 1994b; and McMullen, 1993.

[2] This figure is arrived at by considering the Turkish Cypriot *de facto* state to have been in existence from 1975-1998; the Somaliland one from 1991-1998; the LTTE one from 1983-1998; and the Eritrean one from 1977-1993. One might wish to revise the LTTE figure downward. The Turkish Cypriot figure could perhaps be revised upward. Depending on which part of Eritrea one is referring to, the 1977 figure could also be modified in either direction. The average of 23, 7, 15, and 16 years is 15.25 years.

[3] The threat here comes from Greece and Turkey vetoing EU and NATO expansion plans respectively if the Turkish Cypriots are (or are not) consulted on admitting the Republic of Cyprus to the EU. For more on this, see 'Turkey's Troubles', *The Economist*, 8 March 1997.

[4] An argument that we should expect to see a rapid growth in the number of sovereign states in the future is made in Boniface, 1998.

[5] The classic statement here perhaps being James Madison in The Federalist Papers, Number 10.

[6] For more on the general history of minority rights, see Preece, 1997, pp. 75-92; and Thornberry, 1980, pp. 421-458.

[7] For more on the post-World War I minorities regime, see Buchheit, 1978, pp. 67-70; and Thornberry, 1980, pp. 429-430.

[8] For more on the UN approach to minority rights, see Addis, 1991, pp. 1241-1242; and Thornberry, 1980, pp. 438-439.

[9] Cited in Halperin and Scheffer with Small, 1992, pp. 58-59.

[10] See, for example, Necatigil, 1989, pp. 174-175, 197-198, and 279; and Denktash, 1988, p. 149.

[11] This account draws from Necatigil, 1993, pp. 52-53.

[12] Crawshaw, 1984, p. 78. For the Turkish Cypriot view, see Denktash, 1988, p. 158.

[13] The US does not recognize any government in Somalia at present. It encourages peaceful reconciliation and has told any would-be governments that they must first secure recognition from their neighbors and the OAU before the US will consider

extending recognition. Telephone interview with Mr. Ken Shivers, US State Department desk officer for Djibouti and Somalia, 10 April 1997.
[14] Gottlieb, 1993, pp. 36 and 39. The various components of the 'states-plus-nations' approach are outlined on pp. 1-5.

Bibliography

General

Adam, H.M. (1994a), 'Eritrea, Somalia, Somaliland and the Horn of Africa',
in Amare Tekle (ed.), *Eritrea and Ethiopia: From Conflict to
Cooperation*, Lawrenceville, NJ: The Red Sea Press, pp. 139-168.

Adam, H.M. (1994b), 'Formation and Recognition of New States:
Somaliland in Contrast to Eritrea', *Review of African Political Economy*,
Vol. 21, pp. 21-38.

Adam, H.M. (1995), 'Somalia: A Terrible Beauty Being Born?', in I.
William Zartman (ed.), *Collapsed States: The Disintegration and
Restoration of Legitimate Authority*, Boulder: Lynne Rienner Publishers,
pp. 69-89.

Adam, H.M. (1994c), 'Somalia: Federalism and Self-Determination', in Peter
Woodward and Murray Forsyth (eds.), *Conflict and Peace in the Horn of
Africa: Federalism and Its Alternatives*, Aldershot: Dartmouth Publishing
Company, pp. 114-123.

Addis, A. (1991), 'Individualism, Communitarianism, and the Rights of
Ethnic Minorities', *Notre Dame Law Review*, Vol. 66, pp. 1219-1280.

Alemdar, S. (1993), 'International Aspects of the Cyprus Problem', in C.H.
Dodd (ed.), *The Political Social and Economic Development of Northern
Cyprus*, Huntingdon: The Eothen Press, pp. 75-101.

Alexandrowicz, C.H. (1969), 'New and Original States: The Issue of
Reversion to Sovereignty', *International Affairs*, Vol. 45, pp. 465-480.

Amare Tekle (1994) (ed.), *Eritrea and Ethiopia: From Conflict to
Cooperation*, Lawrenceville, NJ: The Red Sea Press.

Amnesty International (1995), *Amnesty International Report 1995*, New
York: Amnesty International USA.

Amnesty International (1997), *Amnesty International Report 1997*, New
York: Amnesty International USA.

Anderson, B. (1983), *Imagined Communities: Reflections on the Origin and
Spread of Nationalism*, London: Verso.

Araia Tseggai (1994), 'A New Perspective on Ethio-Eritrean Partnership', in
Amare Tekle (ed.), *Eritrea and Ethiopia: From Conflict to Cooperation*,

Lawrenceville, NJ: The Red Sea Press, pp. 55-66.

Ashley, R.K. (1988), 'Untying the Sovereign State: A Double Reading of the Anarchy Problematique', *Millennium: Journal of International Studies*, Vol. 17, pp. 227-262.

Ayoob, M. (1992), 'The Security Predicament of the Third World State: Reflections on State Making in a Comparative Perspective', in Brian L. Job (ed.), *The Insecurity Dilemma: National Security of Third World States*, Boulder: Lynne Rienner Publishers, pp. 63-80.

Ayoob, M. (1991),'The Security Problematic of the Third World', *World Politics*, Vol. 43, pp. 257-283.

Barkin, J.S. and Cronin, B. (1994), 'The State and the Nation: Changing Norms and the Rules of Sovereignty in International Relations', *International Organization*, Vol. 48, pp. 107-130.

Barnett, M. and Wendt, A. (1992), 'The Systemic Sources of Dependent Militarization' in Brian L. Job (ed.), *The Insecurity Dilemma: National Security of Third World States*, Boulder: Lynne Rienner Publishers, pp. 97-119.

Bastiampillai, B.E.S.J. (1990), 'Ethnic Conflicts in South Asia and Inter-State Relations Especially in Relation to Sri Lanka', in Shelton U. Kodikara (ed.), *South Asian Strategic Issues: Sri Lankan Perspectives*, New Delhi: Sage Publications, pp. 82-114.

Beitz, C.R. (1979), *Political Theory and International Relations*, Princeton: Princeton University Press.

Beitz, C.R. (1991), 'Sovereignty and Morality in International Affairs', in David Held (ed.), *Political Theory Today*, Cambridge: Polity Press, pp. 236-254.

Beran, H. (1984), 'A Liberal Theory of Secession', *Political Studies*, Vol. XXXII, pp. 21-31.

Berat, L. (1991), 'Namibia: The Road to Independence and the Problem of Succession of States', in Yossi Shain (ed.), *Governments-in-Exile in Contemporary World Politics*, London: Routledge, pp. 18-41.

Beres, L.R. (1994), 'Self-Determination, International Law and Survival on Planet Earth', *Arizona Journal of International and Comparative Law*, Vol. 11, pp. 1-26.

Biersteker, T.J. and Weber, C. (1996) (eds.), *State Sovereignty as Social Construct*, Cambridge: Cambridge University Press.

Biles, P. (1993), 'Eritrea: Birth of a Nation', *Africa Report*, Vol. 38, pp. 13-19.

Biles, P. (1992), 'Somalia: Going It Alone', *Africa Report*, Vol. 37, pp. 58-

61.

Binder, G. (1993), 'The Case for Self-Determination', *Stanford Journal of International Law*, Vol. 29, pp. 223-270.

Birch, A.H. (1984), 'Another Liberal Theory of Secession', *Political Studies*, Vol. XXXII, pp. 596-602.

Blaney, D.L. (1992), 'Equal Sovereignty and an African Statehood: Tragic Elements in the African Agenda in World Affairs', in Martha L. Cottam and Chih-yu Shih (eds.), *Contending Dramas: A Cognitive Approach to International Organizations*, New York: Praeger, pp. 211-226.

Blay, K.N. (1985), 'Self-Determination Versus Territorial Integrity in Decolonization Revisited', *Indian Journal of International Law*, Vol. 25, pp. 386-410.

Blum, Y.Z. (1975), 'Reflections on the Changing Concept of Self-Determination', *Israel Law Review*, Vol. 10, pp. 509-514.

Bookman, M.Z. (1992), *The Economics of Secession*, New York: St. Martin's Press.

Booth, K. (1995), 'Human Wrongs and International Relations', *International Affairs*, Vol. 71, pp. 103-126.

Branthwaite, A. (1993), 'The Psychological Basis of Independent Statehood', in Robert H. Jackson and Alan James (eds.), *States in a Changing World: A Contemporary Analysis*, Oxford: Clarendon Press, pp. 46-65.

Brewin, C. (1982), 'Sovereignty', in James Mayall (ed.), *The Community of States: A Study in International Political Theory*, London: George Allen & Unwin, pp. 34-48.

Briggs, H.W. (1949), 'Recognition of States: Some Reflections on Doctrine and Practice', *American Journal of International Law*, Vol. 43, pp. 113-121.

Brilmayer, L. (1991), 'Secession and Self-Determination: A Territorial Interpretation', *Yale Journal of International Law*, Vol. 16, pp. 177-202.

Brown, C. (1995), 'International Theory and International Society: The Viability of the Middle Way?', *Review of International Studies*, Vol. 21, pp. 183-196.

Brownlie, I. (1984), 'The Expansion of International Society: The Consequences for the Law of Nations', in Hedley Bull and Adam Watson (eds.), *The Expansion of International Society*, Oxford: Clarendon Press, pp. 357-369.

Bryden, M. (1994a), 'Interview: President Mohamed Haji Ibrahim Egal', *Africa Report*, Vol. 39, pp. 41-42.

Bryden, M. (1994b), 'Somaliland: Fiercely Independent', *Africa Report*, Vol.

39, pp. 35-40.

Buchanan, A. (1991), *Secession: The Morality of Political Divorce from Fort Sumter to Lithuania and Quebec*, Boulder: Westview Press.

Buchanan, A. (1992), 'Self-Determination and the Right to Secede', *Journal of International Affairs*, Vol. 45, pp. 347-365.

Buchheit, L.C. (1978), *Secession: The Legitimacy of Self-Determination*, New Haven: Yale University Press.

Bull, H. (1977), *The Anarchical Society: A Study of Order in World Politics*, London: Macmillan.

Bull, H. (1966), 'The Grotian Conception of International Society', in Herbert Butterfield and Martin Wight (eds.), *Diplomatic Investigations*, London: Allen & Unwin, pp. 51-73.

Bull, H. and Watson, A. (1984) (eds.), *The Expansion of International Society*, Oxford: Clarendon Press.

Bullion, A. (1994), 'The Indian Peace-Keeping Force in Sri Lanka', *International Peacekeeping*, Vol. 1, pp. 148-159.

Buzan, B. (1993), 'From International System to International Society: Structural Realism and Regime Theory Meet the English School', *International Organization*, Vol. 47, pp. 327-352.

Buzan, B. (1991a), 'New Patterns of Global Security in the Twenty-First Century', *International Affairs*, Vol. 67, pp. 431-451.

Buzan, B. (1991b), *People, States and Fear: An Agenda for International Security Studies in the Post-Cold War Era*, 2nd ed., Boulder: Lynne Rienner Publishers.

Carroll, A.J. and Rajagopal, B. (1992-93), 'The Case For the Independent Statehood of Somaliland', *American University Journal of International Law and Policy*, Vol. 8, pp. 653-681.

Cassese, S. (1986), 'The Rise and Decline of the Notion of State', *International Political Science Review*, Vol. 7, pp. 120-130.

Chazan, N. (1991), 'Irredentism, Separatism, and Nationalism' in Naomi Chazan (ed.), *Irredentism and International Politics*, Boulder: Lynne Rienner Publishers, pp. 139-151.

Chege, M. (1991-92), 'Remembering Africa', *Foreign Affairs*, Vol. 71, pp. 146-163.

Chen, L.-C. (1991), 'Self-Determination and World Public Order', *Notre Dame Law Review*, Vol. 66, pp. 1287-1297.

Christofinis, D. (1984), 'The Partition of Cyprus: A Threat to International Security', *World Marxist Review*, Vol. 27, pp. 84-90.

Clark, R.S. (1980), 'The "Decolonization" of East Timor and the United

Nations Norms on Self-Determination and Aggression', *Yale Journal of World Public Order*, Vol. 7, pp. 2-44.

Claude, I.L., Jr. (1966), 'Collective Legitimization as a Political Function of the United Nations', *International Organization*, Vol. XX, pp. 367-379.

Claude, I.L., Jr. (1986), 'Myths About the State', *Review of International Studies*, Vol. 12, pp. 1-11.

Cliffe, L. (1994), 'Eritrea: Prospects for Self-Determination', in Peter Woodward and Murray Forsyth (eds.), *Conflict and Peace in the Horn of Africa: Federalism and Its Alternatives*, Aldershot: Dartmouth Publishing Company, pp. 52-69.

Cliffe, L. (1989), 'Forging a Nation: The Eritrean Experience', *Third World Quarterly*, Vol. 11, pp. 131-147.

Cohen, Y.; Brown, B.R. and Organski, A. F. K. (1981), 'The Paradoxical Nature of State Making: The Violent Creation of Order', *American Political Science Review*, Vol. 75, pp. 901-910.

Commerce Commission, EPLF (1993), 'Trade Policy Proposals for the Transitional Period', in Gebre Hiwet Tesfagiorgis (ed.), *Emergent Eritrea: Challenges of Economic Development*, Trenton: The Red Sea Press, pp. 169-175.

Connor, W. (1978), 'A Nation is a Nation is a State, is an Ethnic Group is a....', *Ethnic and Racial Studies*, Vol. 1, pp. 377-400.

Connor, W. (1972), 'Nation-Building or Nation-Destroying?', *World Politics*, Vol. XXIV, pp. 319-355.

Connor, W. (1967), 'Self-Determination: The New Phase', *World Politics*, Vol. XX, pp. 30-53.

Construction Commission, EPLF (1993), 'Construction: Plan of Action and Policies', in Gebre Hiwet Tesfagiorgis (ed.), *Emergent Eritrea: Challenges of Economic Development*, Trenton: The Red Sea Press, pp. 253-259.

Cooper, R. and Berdal, M. (1993), 'Outside Intervention in Ethnic Conflicts' *Survival*, Vol. 35, pp. 118-142.

Coplin, W.D. (1965), 'International Law and Assumptions About the State System', *World Politics*, Vol. XVII, pp. 615-634.

Copper, J.F. (1990), *Taiwan: Nation-State or Province?*, Boulder: Westview Press.

Coughlan, R. (1991), 'Negotiating the Cyprus Problem: Leadership Perspectives from Both Sides of the Green Line', *The Cyprus Review*, Vol. 3, pp. 80-100.

Crawford, J. (1976-77), 'The Criteria for Statehood in International Law',

British Year Book of International Law, Vol. 48, pp. 93-182.

Crawshaw, N. (1984), 'Cyprus: A Failure in Western Diplomacy', *The World Today*, Vol. 40, pp. 73-78.

Cutler, A.C. (1991), 'The "Grotian Tradition" in International Relations', *Review of International Studies*, Vol. 17, pp. 41-65.

David, S.R. (1991), 'Explaining Third World Alignment', *World Politics*, Vol. 43, pp. 233-256.

de Silva, K. M. (1990), 'Separatism in Sri Lanka: The "Traditional Homelands" of the Tamils', in Ralph R. Premdas, S.W.R. de A. Samarasinghe and Alan B. Anderson (eds.), *Secessionist Movements in Comparative Perspective*, London: Pinter Publishers, pp. 32-47.

Deibel, T.L. (1993), 'Internal Affairs and International Relations in the Post-Cold War World', *The Washington Quarterly*, Vol. 16, pp. 13-33.

Denktash, R. R. (1988), *The Cyprus Triangle*, 2nd ed., London: K. Rustem & Brother.

Desch, M.C. (1996), 'War and Strong States, Peace and Weak States?', *International Organization*, Vol. 50, pp. 237-268.

Deutsch, K.W. (1986), 'State Functions and the Future of the State', *International Political Science Review*, Vol. 7, pp. 209-222.

Dodd, C. H. (1993a) (ed.), *The Political Social and Economic Development of Northern Cyprus*, Huntingdon: The Eothen Press.

Dodd, C.H. (1993b), 'The Ascendancy of the Right: 1985-1993', in C.H. Dodd (ed.), *The Political Social and Economic Development of Northern Cyprus*, Huntingdon: The Eothen Press, pp. 136-166.

Dodd, C.H. (1993c), 'Conclusion', in C.H. Dodd (ed.), *The Political Social and Economic Development of Northern Cyprus*, Huntingdon: The Eothen Press, pp. 373-379.

Dodd, C.H. (1993d), 'From Federated State to Republic: 1975-1984', in C.H. Dodd (ed.), *The Political Social and Economic Development of Northern Cyprus*, Huntingdon: The Eothen Press, pp. 103-135.

Dodd, C.H. (1993e), 'Historical Introduction', in C.H. Dodd (ed.), *The Political Social and Economic Development of Northern Cyprus*, Huntingdon: The Eothen Press, pp. 1-13.

Dodd, C.H. (1993f), 'Political and Administrative Structures', in C.H. Dodd (ed.), *The Political Social and Economic Development of Northern Cyprus*, Huntingdon: The Eothen Press, pp. 167-192.

Donaldson, T. (1992), 'Kant's Global Rationalism', in Terry Nardin and David R. Mapel (eds.), *Traditions of International Ethics*, Cambridge: Cambridge University Press, pp. 136-157.

Donnelly, J. (1984), 'Human Rights, Humanitarian Intervention and American Foreign Policy', *Journal of International Affairs*, Vol. 37, pp. 311-328.

Doob, L.W. (1986), 'Cypriot Patriotism and Nationalism', *Journal of Conflict Resolution*, Vol. 30, pp. 383-396.

Drysdale, J. (1992), *Somaliland: The Anatomy of Secession*, revised ed., Hove: Global-Stats Ltd.

Duke, S. (1994), 'The State and Human Rights: Sovereignty Versus Humanitarian Intervention', *International Relations*, Vol. XII, pp. 25-48.

Dunne, T. (1995), 'International Society — Theoretical Promises Fulfilled?', *Cooperation and Conflict*, Vol. 30, pp. 125-154.

Eastwood, L.S., Jr. (1993), 'Secession: State Practice and International Law After the Dissolution of the Soviet Union and Yugoslavia', *Duke Journal of Comparative and International Law*, Vol. 3, pp. 299-349.

Elkins, D.J. (1995), *Beyond Sovereignty: Territory and Political Economy in the Twenty-First Century*, Toronto: University of Toronto Press.

Emerson, R. (1971), 'Self-Determination', *American Journal of International Law*, Vol. 65, pp. 459-475.

Escheté, A. (1994), 'Why Ethio-Eritrean Relations Matter: A Plea for Future Political Affiliation', in Amare Tekle (ed.), *Eritrea and Ethiopia: From Conflict to Cooperation*, Lawrenceville, NJ: The Red Sea Press, pp. 21-40.

Etzioni, A. (1992-93), 'The Evils of Self-Determination', *Foreign Policy*, no. 89, pp. 21-35.

Ferguson, Y.H. and Mansbach, R.W. (1991), 'Between Celebration and Despair: Constructive Suggestions for Future International Theory', *International Studies Quarterly*, Vol. 35, pp. 363-386.

Fleiner-Gerster, T. and Meyer, M.A. (1985), 'New Developments in Humanitarian Law: A Challenge to the Concept of Sovereignty', *International and Comparative Law Quarterly*, Vol. 34, pp. 267-283.

Flint, J. (1994), 'Somaliland: Struggling to Survive', *Africa Report*, Vol. 39, pp. 36-38.

Forbes, I. (1993), 'Beyond the State', in Ian Forbes and Mark Hoffman (eds.), *Political Theory, International Relations and the Ethics of Intervention*, New York: St. Martin's Press, pp. 212-229.

Fowler, M.R. and Bunck, J.M. (1995), *Law, Power, and the Sovereign State: The Evolution and Application of the Concept of Sovereignty*, University Park, PA: Pennsylvania State University Press.

Fowler, M.R. and Bunck, J.M. (1996), 'What Constitutes the Sovereign

State?', *Review of International Studies*, Vol. 22, pp. 381-404.

Franck, T.M. (1992), 'The Emerging Right To Democratic Governance', *American Journal of International Law*, Vol. 86, pp. 46-91.

Franck, T.M. (1988), 'Legitimacy in the International System', *American Journal of International Law*, Vol. 82, pp. 705-759.

Franck, T.M. (1968), 'Why Federations Fail', in Thomas M. Franck (ed.), *Why Federations Fail: An Inquiry into the Requisites for Successful Federalism*, New York: New York University Press, pp. 167-199.

Franck, T.M. and Rodley, N.S. (1973), 'After Bangladesh: The Law of Humanitarian Intervention by Military Force', *American Journal of International Law*, Vol. 67, pp. 275-305.

French, S. and Gutman, A. (1974), 'The Principle of National Self-Determination', in Virginia Held, Sidney Morgenbesser and Thomas Nagel (eds.), *Philosophy, Morality and International Affairs*, New York: Oxford University Press, pp. 138-153.

Friedlander, R.A. (1980), 'Self-Determination: A Legal-Political Inquiry', in Yonah Alexander and Robert A. Friedlander (eds.), *Self-Determination: National, Regional, and Global Dimensions*, Boulder: Westview Press, pp. 307-331.

Gallie, W. B. (1962), 'Essentially Contested Concepts', in Max Black (ed.), *The Importance of Language*, Englewood Cliffs: Prentice Hall, pp. 121-146.

Gebre Hiwet Tesfagiorgis (1993) (ed.), *Emergent Eritrea: Challenges of Economic Development*, Trenton: The Red Sea Press.

Gellner, E. (1983), *Nations and Nationalism*, Ithaca: Cornell University Press.

Goldgeier, J.M. and McFaul, M. (1992), 'A Tale of Two Worlds: Core and Periphery in the Post-Cold War Era', *International Organization*, Vol. 46, pp. 467-491.

Gong, G.W. (1984), *The Standard of 'Civilization' in International Society*, Oxford: Clarendon Press.

Gottlieb, G. (1993), *Nation Against State: A New Approach to Ethnic Conflicts and the Decline of Sovereignty*, New York: Council on Foreign Relations Press.

Gow, J. and Freedman, L. (1992), 'Intervention in a Fragmenting State: The Case of Yugoslavia', in Nigel Rodley (ed.), *To Loose the Bands of Wickedness: International Intervention in Defense of Human Rights*, London: Brassey's, pp. 93-132.

Grader, S. (1988), 'The English School of International Relations: Evidence and Evaluation', *Review of International Studies*, Vol. 14, pp. 29-44.

Grant, R. (1992), 'The Quagmire of Gender and International Security', in V. Spike Peterson (ed.), *Gendered States: Feminist (Re) Visions of International Relations Theory*, Boulder: Lynne Rienner Publishers, pp. 83-97.

Groom, A.J.R. (1993), 'The Process of Negotiation, 1974-1993', in C.H. Dodd (ed.), *The Political Social and Economic Development of Northern Cyprus*, Huntingdon: The Eothen Press, pp. 15-45.

Gross, L. (1975), 'The Right of Self-Determination in International Law', in Martin Kilson (ed.), *New States in the Modern World*, Cambridge: Harvard University Press, pp. 136-157.

Gurr, T.R. (1994), 'Peoples Against States: Ethnopolitical Conflict and the Changing World System', *International Studies Quarterly*, Vol. 38, pp. 347-377.

Gurr, T.R. (1993), 'Why Minorities Rebel: A Global Analysis of Communal Mobilization and Conflict Since 1945', *International Political Science Review*, Vol. 14, pp. 161-201.

Halliday, F. (1994), *Rethinking International Relations*, Vancouver: UBC Press.

Halperin, M.H. and Scheffer, D.J. with Small, P.L. (1992), *Self-Determination in the New World Order*, Washington, D.C.: Carnegie Endowment for International Peace.

Hannum, H. (1990), *Autonomy, Sovereignty, and Self-Determination: The Accommodation of Conflicting Rights*, Philadelphia: University of Pennsylvania Press.

Hannum, H. and Lillich, R.B. (1980), 'The Concept of Autonomy in International Law', *American Journal of International Law*, Vol. 74, pp. 858-889.

Hassen, M. (1994), 'Eritrean Independence and Democracy in the Horn of Africa', in Amare Tekle (ed.), *Eritrea and Ethiopia: From Conflict to Cooperation*, Lawrenceville, NJ: The Red Sea Press, pp. 85-113.

Helman, G.B. and Ratner, S.R. (1992-93), 'Saving Failed States', *Foreign Policy*, no. 89, pp. 3-20.

Hendrie, B. (1989), 'Cross-Border Relief Operations in Eritrea and Tigray', *Disasters*, Vol. 13, pp. 351-360.

Henze, P.B. (1994), 'Eritrea: The Economic Challenge', in Peter Woodward and Murray Forsyth (eds.), *Confict and Peace in the Horn of Africa: Federalism and Its Alternatives*, Aldershot: Dartmouth Publishing Company, pp. 70-77.

Henze, P.B. (1986), 'Eritrea: The Endless War', *The Washington Quarterly*, Vol. 9, pp. 23-36.

Heraclides, A. (1992), 'Secession, Self-Determination and Nonintervention: In Quest of a Normative Symbiosis', *Journal of International Affairs*, Vol. 45, pp. 399-420.

Heraclides, A. (1990), 'Secessionist Minorities and External Involvement', *International Organization*, Vol. 44, pp. 341-378.

Herbst, J. (1989), 'The Creation and Maintenance of National Boundaries in Africa', *International Organization*, Vol. 43, pp. 673-692.

Herbst, J. (1996), 'Is Nigeria a Viable State?', *The Washington Quarterly*, Vol. 19, pp. 151-172.

Herbst, J. (1996-97), 'Responding to State Failure in Africa', *International Security*, Vol. 21, pp. 120-144.

Herbst, J. (1990), 'War and the State in Africa', *International Security*, Vol. 14, pp. 117-139.

Higgins, R. (1971), 'Internal War and International Law', in Cyril E. Black and Richard A. Falk (eds.), *The Future of the International Legal Order, Volume III*, Princeton: Princeton University Press, pp. 81-121.

Higgins, R. (1972), 'International Law and Civil Conflict', in Evan Luard (ed.), *The International Regulation of Civil Wars*, New York: New York University Press, pp. 169-186.

Hinsley, F. H. (1967), 'The Concept of Sovereignty and the Relations Between States', *Journal of International Affairs*, Vol. 21, pp. 242-252.

Hinsley, F.H. (1986), *Sovereignty*, 2nd ed., Cambridge: Cambridge University Press.

Holsti, K. J. (1985a), *The Dividing Discipline: Hegemony and Diversity in International Theory*, Boston: Allen & Unwin.

Holsti, K.J. (1992), 'International Theory and War in the Third World', in Brian L. Job (ed.), *The Insecurity Dilemma: National Security of Third World States*, Boulder: Lynne Rienner Publishers, pp. 37-60.

Holsti, K.J. (1985b), 'The Necrologists of International Relations', *Canadian Journal of Political Science*, Vol. XVIII, pp. 675-695.

Holsti, K.J. (1991), *Peace and War: Armed Conflicts and International Order 1648 – 1989*, Cambridge: Cambridge University Press.

Holsti, K.J. (1996), *The State, War, and the State of War*, Cambridge: Cambridge University Press.

Holsti, K.J. (1995), 'War, Peace, and the State of the State', *International Political Science Review*, Vol. 16, pp. 319-339.

Hoole, R.; Somasundaram, D.; Sritharan, K.; and Thiranagama, R. (1990),

The Broken Palmyra: The Tamil Crisis in Sri Lanka - An Inside Account, 2nd ed., Claremont: The Sri Lanka Studies Institute.

Horowitz, D.L. (1991), 'Irredentas and Secessions: Adjacent Phenomena, Neglected Conclusions', in Naomi Chazan (ed.), *Irredentism and International Politics*, Boulder: Lynne Rienner Publishers, pp. 9-22.

Human Rights Watch (1992), *Human Rights Watch World Report 1992*, New York: Human Rights Watch.

Human Rights Watch/Asia (1995), 'Sri Lanka: Stop Killings of Civilians', Human Rights Watch/Asia Newsletter 7, pp. 1-10.

Ijalaye, D.A. (1971), 'Was "Biafra" at Any Time a State in International Law?', *American Journal of International Law*, Vol. 65, pp. 551-559.

Inayatullah, N. and Blaney, D.L. (1995), 'Realizing Sovereignty', *Review of International Studies*, Vol. 21, pp. 3-20.

Jackson, R.H. (1993a), 'Continuity and Change in the States System', in Robert H. Jackson and Alan James (eds.), *States in a Changing World: A Contemporary Analysis*, Oxford: Clarendon Press, pp. 346-367.

Jackson, R.H. (1986), 'Negative Sovereignty in sub-Saharan Africa', *Review of International Studies*, Vol. 12, pp. 247-264.

Jackson, R.H. (1987), 'Quasi-States, Dual Regimes, and Neoclassical Theory: International Jurisprudence and the Third World', *International Organization*, Vol. 41, pp. 519-549.

Jackson, R.H. (1990), *Quasi-States: Sovereignty, International Relations and the Third World*, Cambridge: Cambridge University Press.

Jackson, R.H. (1992), 'The Security Dilemma in Africa', in Brian L. Job (ed.), *The Insecurity Dilemma: National Security of Third World States*, Boulder: Lynne Rienner Publishers, pp. 81-94.

Jackson, R.H. (1993b), 'The Weight of Ideas in Decolonization: Normative Change in International Relations', in Judith Goldstein and Robert O. Keohane (eds.), *Ideas and Foreign Policy: Beliefs,Institutions, and Political Change*, Ithaca: Cornell University Press, pp. 111-138.

Jackson, R.H. and James, A. (1993), 'The Character of Independent Statehood', in Robert H. Jackson and Alan James (eds.), *States in a Changing World: A Contemporary Analysis*, Oxford: Clarendon Press, pp. 3-25.

Jackson, R.H. and Rosberg, C.G. (1986), 'Sovereignty and Underdevelopment: Juridical Statehood in the African Crisis', *Journal of Modern African Studies*, Vol. 24, pp. 1-31.

Jackson, R.H. and Rosberg, C.G. (1982), 'Why Africa's Weak States Persist: The Empirical and the Juridical in Statehood', *World Politics*,

280 *International Society and the De Facto State*

Vol. XXXV, p. 1-24.

Jacobs, J. (1984), *Cities and the Wealth of Nations: Principles of Economic Life*, New York: Random House.

Jacovides, A.J. (1995), 'Cyprus—The International Law Dimension', *American University Journal of International Law and Policy*, Vol. 10, pp. 1221-1231.

James, A. (1986a), 'Comment on J. D. B. Miller', *Review of International Studies*, Vol. 12, pp. 91-93.

James, A. (1992), 'The Equality of States: Contemporary Manifestations of an Ancient Doctrine', *Review of International Studies*, Vol. 18, pp. 377-391.

James, A. (1986b), *Sovereign Statehood: The Basis of International Society*, London: Allen & Unwin.

Job, B.L. (1992) (ed.), *The Insecurity Dilemma: National Security of Third World States*, Boulder: Lynne Rienner Publishers.

Jones, D.V. (1992), 'The Declaratory Tradition in Modern International Law', in Terry Nardin and David R. Mapel (eds.), *Traditions of International Ethics*, Cambridge: Cambridge University Press, pp. 42-61.

Kamanu, O.S. (1974), 'Secession and the Right of Self-Determination: an O.A.U. Dilemma', *Journal of Modern African Studies*, Vol. 12, pp. 355-376.

Kapil, R.L. (1966), 'On the Conflict Potential of Inherited Boundaries in Africa', *World Politics*, Vol. XVIII, pp. 656-673.

Kaufmann, C. (1996), 'Possible and Impossible Solutions to Ethnic Civil Wars', *International Security*, Vol. 20, pp. 136-175.

Kearney, R.N. (1987-88), 'Territorial Elements of Tamil Separatism in Sri Lanka', *Pacific Affairs*, Vol. 60, pp. 561-577.

Keller, E.J. (1994), 'The United States, Ethiopia and Eritrean Independence', in Amare Tekle (ed.), *Eritrea and Ethiopia: From Conflict to Cooperation*, Lawrenceville, NJ: The Red Sea Press, pp. 169-185.

Kidane Mengisteab (1994), 'Ethio-Eritrean Cooperation in National Reconstruction and Development', in Amare Tekle (ed.), *Eritrea and Ethiopia: From Conflict to Cooperation*, Lawrenceville, NJ: The Red Sea Press, pp. 67-84.

Kiss, A. (1986), 'The Peoples' Right to Self-Determination', *Human Rights Law Journal*, Vol. 7, pp. 165-175.

Klieman, A.S. (1980), 'The Resolution of Conflicts Through Territorial Partition: The Palestine Experience', *Comparative Studies in Society and History*, Vol. 22, pp. 281-300.

Knight, D.B. (1983), 'The Dilemma of Nations in a Rigid State Structured World', in Nurat Kliot and Stanley Waterman (eds.), *Pluralism and Political Geography*, New York: St. Martin's Press, pp. 114-132.

Knight, D.B. (1993), 'Geographical Considerations in a World of States', in Robert H. Jackson and Alan James (eds.), *States in a Changing World: A Contemporary Analysis*, Oxford: Clarendon Press, pp. 26-45.

Knight, D.B. (1984), 'Geographical Perspectives on Self-Determination', in Peter Taylor and John House(eds.), *Political Geography: Recent Advances and Future Directions*, Totowa: Barnes & Noble Books, pp. 168-190.

Knight, D.B. (1985), 'Territory and People or People and Territory? Thoughts on Postcolonial Self-Determination', *International Political Science Review*, Vol. 6, pp. 248-272.

Kodikara, S.U. (1990a) (ed.), *South Asian Strategic Issues: Sri Lankan Perspectives*, New Delhi: Sage Publications.

Kodikara, S.U. (1990b), 'The Indo-Sri Lankan Agreement of July 1987: Retrospect', in Shelton U. Kodikara (ed.), *South Asian Strategic Issues: Sri Lankan Perspectives*, New Delhi: Sage Publications, pp. 160-174.

Krasner, S.D. (1984), 'Approaches to the State: Alternative Conceptions and Historical Dynamics', *Comparative Politics*, Vol. 16, pp. 223-246.

Krasner, S.D. (1995-96), 'Compromising Westphalia', *International Security*, Vol. 20, pp. 115-151.

Krasner, S.D. (1988), 'Sovereignty: An Institutional Perspective', *Comparative Political Studies*, Vol. 21, pp. 66-94.

Kratochwil, F. (1986), 'Of Systems, Boundaries, and Territoriality: An Inquiry into the Formation of the State System', *World Politics*, Vol. XXXIX, pp. 27-52.

Kratochwil, F.; Rohrlich, P.; and Mahajan, H. (1985), *Peace and Disputed Sovereignty: Reflections on Conflict over Territory*, Lanham: University Press of America, Inc.

Krause, K. (1996), 'Critical Theory and Security Studies', YCISS Occasional Paper # 33, February 1996.

Lafrenière, F. and Mitchell, R. (1990), 'Cyprus -- Visions for the Future', Working Paper # 21, Ottawa: Canadian Institute for International Peace and Security.

Lapidoth, R. (1992), 'Sovereignty in Transition', *Journal of International Affairs*, Vol. 45, pp. 325-346.

Lauterpacht, H. (1985), 'The Grotian Tradition in International Law', in Richard Falk, Friedrich Kratochwil and Saul H. Mendlovitz (eds.),

International Law: A Contemporary Perspective, Boulder: Westview Press, pp. 10-31.

Li, V.H. (1979), 'The Law of Non-Recognition: The Case of Taiwan', *Northwestern Journal of International Law and Business*, Vol. 1, pp. 134-162.

Ling, A.M. (1983), 'The Effects of Derecognition of Taiwan on United States Corporate Interests', *Loyola of Los Angeles International and Comparative Law Journal*, Vol. 6, pp. 163-184.

Little, R. (1991), 'Liberal Hegemony and the Realist Assault: Competing Ideological Theories of the State', in Michael Banks and Martin Shaw (eds.), *State and Society in International Relations*, New York: Harvester Wheatsheaf, pp. 19-38.

Lockhart, D. (1994), 'Tourism in Northern Cyprus: Patterns, Policies and Prospects', *Tourism Management*, Vol. 15, pp. 370-379.

Lowenkopf, M. (1995), 'Liberia: Putting the State Back Together', in I. William Zartman (ed.), *Collapsed States: The Disintegration and Restoration of Legitimate Authority*, Boulder: Lynne Rienner Publishers, pp. 91-108.

Lyon, P. (1973), 'New States and International Order', in Alan James (ed.), *The Bases of International Order: Essays in Honour of C. A. W. Manning*, London: Oxford University Press, pp. 24-59.

MacKenzie, Major-General L. (1993), *Peacekeeper: The Road to Sarajevo*, Vancouver: Douglas & McIntyre.

Mangelson, M.E. (1992), 'Taiwan Re-recognized: A Model for Taiwan's Future Global Status', *Brigham Young University Law Review*, #1, pp. 231-251.

Mann, M. (1988), *States, War and Capitalism: Studies in Political Sociology*, Oxford: Basil Blackwell.

Manogaran, C. (1994), 'Colonization as Politics: Political Use of Space in Sri Lanka's Ethnic Conflict', in Chelvadurai Manogaran and Bryan Pffafenberger (eds.), *The Sri Lankan Tamils: Ethnicity and Identity*, Boulder: Westview Press, pp. 84-125.

Manogaran, C. and Pfaffenberger, B. (1994) (eds.), *The Sri Lankan Tamils: Ethnicity and Identity*, Boulder: Westview Press.

Manufacturing Commission, EPLF (1993), 'Features of the Eritrean Industry: Its Prospects for Development and Policy', in Gebre Hiwet Tesfagiorgis (ed.), *Emergent Eritrea: Challenges of Economic Development*, Trenton: The Red Sea Press, pp. 189-197.

Maoz, Z. (1989), 'Joining the Club of Nations: Political Development and

International Conflict, 1816 – 1976', *International Studies Quarterly*, Vol. 33, pp. 199-231.

Mapel, D.R. and Nardin, T. (1992), 'Convergence and Divergence in International Ethics', in Terry Nardin and David R. Mapel (eds.), *Traditions of International Ethics*, Cambridge: Cambridge University Press, pp. 297-322.

Markakis, J. (1995), 'Eritrea's National Charter', *Review of African Political Economy*, Vol. 22, pp. 126-129.

Markakis, J. (1988), 'The Nationalist Revolution in Eritrea', *Journal of Modern African Studies*, Vol. 26, pp. 51-70.

Martin, J. (1993), 'The History and Development of Tourism', in C.H. Dodd (ed.), *The Political Social and Economic Development of Northern Cyprus*, Huntingdon: The Eothen Press, pp. 335-372.

Mayall, J. (1990), *Nationalism and International Society*, Cambridge: Cambridge University Press.

Mayall, J. (1993), 'Non-Intervention, Self-Determination and the New World Order', in Ian Forbes and Mark Hoffman (eds.), *Political Theory, International Relations and the Ethics of Intervention*, New York: St. Martin's Press, pp. 167-176.

Mayall, J. (1983), 'Self-Determination and the OAU', in I.M. Lewis (ed.), *Nationalism and Self-Determination in the Horn of Africa*, London: Ithaca Press, pp. 77-92.

Mayall, J. (1991), 'The Variety of States', in Cornelia Navari (ed.), *The Condition of States: A Study in International Political Theory*, Milton Keynes: Open University Press, pp. 44-60.

McDonald, R. (1984), 'Cyprus: The UN Tries Again', *The World Today*, Vol. 40, pp. 420-427.

McDonald, R. (1988-89), *The Problem of Cyprus*, Adelphi Papers, no. 234, London: International Institute for Strategic Studies.

McMullen, R.K. (1992), 'Secession in Asia: The Emerging Criteria for International Acceptance', *Asian Thought and Society*, Vol. XVII, pp. 113-125.

McMullen, R.K. (1993), 'Somaliland: The Next Eritrea?', *Low Intensity Conflict & Law Enforcement*, Vol. 2, pp. 421-433.

Menkhaus, K. and Prendergast, J. (1995), 'Somalia: The Stateless State', *Africa Report*, Vol. 40, pp. 22-25.

Mesfin Araya. (1990), 'The Eritrean Question: An Alternative Explanation', *Journal of Modern African Studies*, Vol. 28, pp. 79-100.

Migdal, J.S. (1988), *Strong Societies and Weak States: State-Society*

Relations and State Capabilities in the Third World, Princeton: Princeton University Press.

Miller, J.D.B. (1986), 'Sovereignty as a Source of Vitality for the State', *Review of International Studies*, Vol. 12, pp. 79-89.

Miller, J.D.B. (1984), 'The Sovereign State and Its Future', *International Journal*, Vol. XXXIX, pp. 284-301.

Minasse Haile. (1994), 'Legality of Secessions: The Case of Eritrea', *Emory International Law Review*, Vol. 8, pp. 479-537.

Modelski, G. (1964), 'The International Relations of Internal War', in James N. Rosenau (ed.), *International Aspects of Civil Strife*, Princeton: Princeton University Press, pp. 14-44.

Mojekwu, C.C. (1980), 'Self-Determination: The African Perspective', in Yonah Alexander and Robert A. Friedlander (eds.), *Self-Determination: National, Regional, and Global Dimensions*, Boulder: Westview Press, pp. 221-239.

Morvaridi, B. (1993a), 'Agriculture and the Environment', in C.H. Dodd (ed.), *The Political Social and Economic Development of Northern Cyprus*, Huntingdon: The Eothen Press, pp. 235-251.

Morvaridi, B. (1993b), 'Demographic Change, Resettlement and Resource Use', in C.H. Dodd (ed.), *The Political Social and Economic Development of Northern Cyprus*, Huntingdon: The Eothen Press, pp. 219-234.

Nafzinger, E.W. and Richter, W.L. (1976), 'Biafra and Bangladesh: The Political Economy of Secessionist Conflict', *Journal of Peace Research*, Vol. XIII, pp. 91-109.

Naldi, G.J. (1987), 'The Case Concerning the Frontier Dispute (Burkina Faso/Republic of Mali): *Uti Possidetis* in an African Perspective', *International and Comparative Law Quarterly*, Vol. 36, pp. 893-903.

Nanda, V.P. (1972), 'Self-Determination in International Law: The Tragic Tale of Two Cities -- Islamabad (West Pakistan) and Dacca (East Pakistan)', *American Journal of International Law*, Vol. 66, pp. 321-336.

Nardin, T. (1983), *Law, Morality, and the Relations of States*, Princeton: Princeton University Press.

Navari, C. (1993), 'Intervention, Non-Intervention and the Construction of the State', in Ian Forbes and Mark Hoffman (eds.), *Political Theory, International Relations and the Ethics of Intervention*, New York: St. Martin's Press, pp. 43-60.

Navari, C. (1991), 'Introduction: The State as a Contested Concept in

International Relations', in Cornelia Navari (ed.), *The Condition of States: A Study in International Political Theory*, Milton Keynes: Open University Press, pp. 1-18.

Necatigil, Z.M. (1993), 'The Cyprus Conflict in International Law', in C.H. Dodd (ed.), *The Political Economic and Social Development of Northern Cyprus*, Huntingdon: The Eothen Press, pp. 46-74.

Necatigil, Z.M. (1989), *The Cyprus Question and the Turkish Position in International Law*, Oxford: Oxford University Press.

Nettl, J.P. (1968), 'The State as a Conceptual Variable', *World Politics*, Vol. XX, pp. 559-592.

Oakeshott, M. (1975), 'The Vocabulary of a Modern European State', *Political Studies*, Vol. XXIII, pp. 319-341.

O'Ballance, E. (1989), *The Cyanide War: Tamil Insurrection in Sri Lanka 1973-88*, London: Brassey's.

Oberling, P. (1982), *The Road to Bellapais: The Turkish Cypriot Exodus to Northern Cyprus*, New York: Columbia University Press.

Oberst, R.C. (1992), 'A War Without Winners in Sri Lanka', *Current History*, Vol. 91, pp. 128-131.

O'Brien, C.C. (1973), 'On the Rights of Minorities', *Commentary*, Vol. 55, pp. 46-50.

Okbazghi Yohannes (1993), 'Eritrea: A Country in Transition', *Review of African Political Economy*, Vol. 20, pp. 7-28.

Olgun, M.E. (1993), 'Economic Overview', in C.H. Dodd (ed.), *The Political Social and Economic Development of Northern Cyprus*, Huntingdon: The Eothen Press, pp. 270-298.

Omaar, R. (1993), 'Somalia: The Best Chance for Peace', *Africa Report*, Vol. 38, pp. 44-48.

Omaar, R. (1994) 'Somaliland: One Thorn Bush at a Time', *Current History*, Vol. 93, pp. 232-236.

Ottaway, M. (1991), 'Mediation in a Transitional Conflict: Eritrea', in I.William Zartman (ed.), *Resolving Regional Conflicts: International Perspectives*, Newbury Park: Sage Publications, pp. 69-81.

Palmer, S. (1986), 'The Turkish Republic of Northern Cyprus: Should the United States Recognize It as an Independent State?', *Boston University International Law Journal*, Vol. 4, pp. 423-450.

Parkinson, F. (1993), 'Ethnicity and Independent Statehood', in Robert H. Jackson and Alan James (eds.), *States in a Changing World: A Contemporary Analysis*, Oxford: Clarendon Press, pp. 322-345.

Pateman, R. (1994), 'Eritrea Takes the World Stage', *Current History*, Vol.

93, pp. 228-231.

Pateman, R. (1990a), 'The Eritrean War', *Armed Forces and Society*, Vol. 17, pp. 81-98.

Pateman, R. (1990b), 'Liberté, Egalité, Fraternité: Aspects of the Eritrean Revolution', *Journal of Modern African Studies*, Vol. 28, pp. 457-472.

Paust, J.J. (1980), 'Self-Determination: A Definitional Focus', in Yonah Alexander and Robert A. Friedlander (eds.), *Self-Determination: National, Regional, and Global Dimensions*, Boulder: Westview Press, p. 3-18.

Pegg, S. (1994), 'Interposition and the Territorial Separation of Warring Forces: Time for a Rethink?', *Peacekeeping & International Relations*, Vol. 23, pp. 4-5.

Peterson, M.J. (1982), 'Political Use of Recognition: The Influence of the International System', *World Politics*, Vol. XXXIV, pp. 324-352.

Peterson, V.S. (1992), 'Security and Sovereign States: What Is at Stake in Taking Feminism Seriously?', in V. Spike Peterson (ed.), *Gendered States: Feminist (Re) Visions of International Relations Theory*, Boulder: Lynne Rienner Publishers, pp. 31-65.

Pfaffenberger, B. (1994), 'Introduction: The Sri Lankan Tamils', in Chelvadurai Manogaran and Bryan Pfaffenberger (eds.), *The Sri Lankan Tamils: Ethnicity and Identity*, Boulder: Westview Press, pp. 1-27.

Poggi, G. (1978), *The Development of the Modern State: A Sociological Introduction*, Stanford: Stanford University Press.

Pomerance, M. (1984), 'Self-Determination Today: The Metamorphosis of an Ideal', *Israel Law Review*, Vol. 19, pp. 310-339.

Pomerance, M. (1976), 'The United States and Self-Determination: Perspectives on the Wilsonian Conception', *American Journal of International Law*, Vol. 70, pp. 1-27.

Pool, D. (1993), 'Eritrean Independence: The Legacy of the Derg and the Politics of Reconstruction', *African Affairs*, Vol. 92, pp. 389-402.

Posen, B.R. (1993), 'The Security Dilemma and Ethnic Conflict', *Survival*, Vol. 35, pp. 27-47.

Preece, J.J. (1997), 'Minority Rights in Europe: From Westphalia to Helsinki', *Review of International Studies*, Vol. 23, pp. 75-92.

Premdas, R.R. (1990), 'Secessionist Movements in Comparative Perspective', in Ralph R. Premdas, S.W.R.deA. Samarasinghe and Alan B. Anderson (eds.), *Secessionist Movements in Comparative Perspective*, London: Pinter Publishers, pp. 12-29.

Rajanayagam, D.-H. (1994), 'The "Groups" and the Rise of Militant

Secessionism', in Chelvadurai Manogaran and Bryan Pfaffenberger (eds.), *The Sri Lankan Tamils: Ethnicity and Identity*, Boulder: Westview Press, pp. 169-207.

Randolph, R.S. (1981), 'The Status of Agreements Between the American Institute in Taiwan and the Coordination Council for North American Affairs', *The International Lawyer*, Vol. 15, pp. 249-262.

Reisman, W.M. and Suzuki, E. (1976), 'Recognition and Social Change in International Law: A Prologue for Decisionmaking', in W. Michael Reisman and Burns H. Weston (eds.), *Toward World Order and Human Dignity: Essays in Honor of Myres S. McDougal*, New York: The Free Press, pp. 403-470.

Reno, W. (1995), 'Reinvention of an African Patrimonial State: Charles Taylor's Liberia', *Third World Quarterly*, Vol. 16, pp. 109-120.

Rentmeesters, V. (1993), 'Women and Development Planning', in Gebre Hiwet Tesfagiorgis (ed.), *Emergent Eritrea: Challenges of Economic Development*, Trenton: The Red Sea Press, pp. 72-85.

Republic of China. (1993), *The Republic of China Yearbook, 1994*, Taipei: Government Information Office.

Roberts, D. (1991), 'War and the Historical Formation of States: Evidence of Things Unseen', in Michael Banks and Martin Shaw (eds.), *State and Society in International Relations*, New York: Harvester Wheatsheaf, pp. 137-168.

Røling, B.V.A. (1976), 'The Legal Status of Rebels and Rebellion', *Journal of Peace Research*, Vol. XIII, pp. 149-163.

Ronen, D. (1979), *The Quest for Self-Determination*, New Haven: Yale University Press.

Rosecrance, R. (1996), 'The Rise of the Virtual State', *Foreign Affairs*, Vol. 75, pp. 45-61.

Rosenau, J.N. (1988), 'The State in an Era of Cascading Politics: Wavering Concept, Widening Competence, Withering Colossus, or Weathering Change?', *Comparative Political Studies*, Vol. 21, pp. 13-44.

Rosenau, J.N. (1990), *Turbulence in World Politics: A Theory of Change and Continuity*, Princeton: Princeton University Press.

Rossides, E.T. (1991), 'Cyprus and the Rule of Law', *Syracuse Journal of International Law and Commerce*, Vol. 17, pp. 21-90.

Rothman, J. (1991), 'Conflict Research and Resolution: Cyprus', in I. William Zartman (ed.), *Resolving Regional Conflicts: International Perspectives*, Newbury Park: Sage Publications, pp. 95-108.

Ruggie, J.G. (1993), 'Territoriality and Beyond: Problematizing Modernity in

International Relations', *International Organization*, Vol. 47, pp. 139-174.

Runyan, A.S. and Peterson, V.S. (1991), 'The Radical Future of Realism: Feminist Subversions of IR Theory', *Alternatives*, Vol. 16, pp. 67-106.

Rupesinghe, K. (1988), 'Ethnic Conflicts in South Asia: The Case of Sri Lanka and the Indian Peace-keeping Force (IPKF)', *Journal of Peace Research*, Vol. 25, pp. 337-350.

Ryan, S. (1988), 'Explaining Ethnic Conflict: The Neglected International Dimension', *Review of International Studies*, Vol. 14, pp. 161-177.

Sabaratnam, L. (1987), 'The Boundaries of the State and the State of Ethnic Boundaries: Sinhala-Tamil Relations in Sri Lankan History', *Ethnic and Racial Studies*, Vol. 10, pp. 291-316.

Samarasinghe, S.W.R.de A. (1990), 'The Dynamics of Separatism: The Case of Sri Lanka', in Ralph R. Premdas, S. W. R. de A. Samarasinghe and Alan B. Anderson (eds.), *Secessionist Movements in Comparative Perspective*, London: Pinter Publishers, pp. 48-70.

Saravanamuttu, P. (1989), 'Ethnic Conflict and Nation-Building in Sri Lanka', *Third World Quarterly*, Vol. 11, pp. 313-320.

Sardeshpande, Lt. Gen. S.C. (1992), *Assignment Jaffna*, New Delhi: Lancer Publishers.

Sayigh, Y. (1990), *Confronting the 1990s: Security in the Developing Countries*, Adelphi Papers, no. 251, London: International Institute of Strategic Studies.

Scholler, H. (1994), 'The Ethiopian Federation of 1952: An Obsolete Model or a Guide for the Future?', in Peter Woodward and Murray Forsyth (eds.), *Conflict and Peace in the Horn of Africa: Federalism and Its Alternatives*, Aldershot: Dartmouth Publishing Company, pp. 10-18.

Schroeder, G.E. (1992), 'On the Economic Viability of New Nation-States', *Journal of International Affairs*, Vol. 45, pp. 549-574.

Shain, Y. (1991), 'Governments-in-Exile and International Legitimation', in Yossi Shain (ed.), *Governments-in-Exile in Contemporary World Politics*, London: Routledge, pp. 219-237.

Shapiro, M.J. (1994), 'Moral Geographies and the Ethics of Post-Sovereignty', *Public Culture*, Vol. 6, pp. 479-502.

Shastri, A. (1994), 'The Material Basis for Separatism: The Tamil Eelam Movement in Sri Lanka', in Chelvadurai Manogaran and Bryan Pfaffenberger (eds.), *The Sri Lankan Tamils: Ethnicity and Identity*, Boulder: Westview Press, pp. 208-235.

Shastri, A. (1992), 'Sri Lanka's Provincial Council System: A Solution to the

Ethnic Problem?', *Asian Survey*, Vol. XXXII, pp. 723-743.

Shaw, M. (1992), 'Global Society and Global Responsibility: The Theoretical, Historical and Political Limits of "International Society"', *Millennium: Journal of International Studies*, Vol. 21, pp. 421-434.

Shaw, M. (1991), 'State Theory and the Post-Cold War World', in Michael Banks and Martin Shaw (eds.), *State and Society in International Relations*, New York: Harvester Wheatsheaf, pp. 1-17.

Sheikh, A. (1980), 'The United States and Taiwan After Derecognition: Consequences and Legal Remedies', *Washington and Lee Law Review*, Vol. XXXVII, pp. 323-341.

Singer, M.R. (1990), 'New Realities in Sri Lankan Politics', *Asian Survey*, Vol. XXX, pp. 409-425.

Singer, M.R. (1992), 'Sri Lanka's Tamil-Sinhalese Ethnic Conflict: Alternative Solutions', *Asian Survey*, Vol. XXXII, pp. 712-722.

Sivarajah, A. (1990), 'Indo-Sri Lankan Relations and Sri Lanka's Ethnic Crisis: The Tamil Nadu Factor', in Shelton U. Kodikara (ed.), *South Asian Strategic Issues: Sri Lankan Perspectives*, New Delhi: Sage Publications, pp. 135-159.

Smith, A.D. (1983), 'Ethnic Identity and World Order', *Millennium: Journal of International Studies*, Vol. 12, pp. 149-161.

Smith, A.D. (1981), 'States and Homelands: the Social and Geopolitical Implications of National Territory', *Millennium: Journal of International Studies*, Vol. 10, pp. 187-202.

Stone, J. (1983), 'Ethnicity Versus the State: The Dual Claims of State Coherence and Ethnic Self-Determination', in Donald Rothchild and Victor A. Olorunsola (eds.), *State Versus Ethnic Claims: African Policy Dilemmas*, Boulder: Westview Press, pp. 85-99.

Suganami, H. (1983), 'The Structure of Institutionalism: An Anatomy of British Mainstream International Relations', *International Relations*, Vol. II, pp. 2363-2381.

Suzuki, E. (1976), 'Self-Determination and World Public Order: Community Response to Territorial Separation', *Virginia Journal of International Law*, Vol. 16, pp. 779-862.

Tamkoç, M. (1988), *The Turkish Cypriot State: The Embodiment of the Right of Self-Determination*, London: K. Rustem & Brother.

Tekie Fessehatzion (1994), 'Prospects for Regional Economic Cooperation Between Eritrea and Its Neighbors', in Amare Tekle (ed.), *Eritrea and Ethiopia: From Conflict to Cooperation*, Lawrenceville, NJ: The Red Sea Press, pp. 41-53.

Tesfatsion Medhanie (1994), 'Remarks on Eritrea and a Possible Framework for Peace', in Peter Woodward and Murray Forsyth (eds.), *Conflict and Peace in the Horn of Africa: Federalism and Its Alternatives*, Aldershot: Dartmouth Publishing Company, pp. 19-26.

Thomas, R.G.C. (1994), 'Secessionist Movements in South Asia', *Survival*, Vol. 36, pp. 92-114.

Thomas-Woolley, B. and Keller, E.J. (1994), 'Majority Rule and Minority Rights: American Federalism and African Experience', *Journal of Modern African Studies*, Vol. 32, pp. 411-427.

Thomson, J.E. (1995), 'State Sovereignty in International Relations: Bridging the Gap Between Theory and Empirical Research', *International Studies Quarterly*, Vol. 39, pp. 213-233.

Thomson, J.E. and Krasner, S.D. (1989), 'Global Transactions and the Consolidation of Sovereignty', in Ernst-Otto Czempiel and James N. Rosenau (eds.), *Global Changes and Theoretical Challenges: Approaches to World Politics for the 1990s*, Lexington: Lexington Books, pp. 195-219.

Thornberry, P. (1980), 'Is There a Phoenix in the Ashes?—International Law and Minority Rights', *Texas International Law Journal*, Vol. 15, pp. 421-458.

Thornberry, P. (1989), 'Self-Determination, Minorities, Human Rights: A Review of International Instruments', *International and Comparative Law Quarterly*, Vol. 38, pp. 867-889.

Tickner, J.A. (1991), 'Hans Morgenthau's Principles of Political Realism: A Feminist Reformulation', in Rebecca Grant and Kathleen Newland (eds.), *Gender and International Relations*, Milton Keynes: Open University Press, pp. 27-40.

Tilly, C. (1975a), 'Reflections on the History of European State-Making', in Charles Tilly (ed.), *The Formation of National States in Western Europe*, Princeton: Princeton University Press, pp. 3-83.

Tilly, C. (1985), 'War Making and State Making as Organized Crime', in Peter B. Evans, Dietrich Rueschemeyer, and Theda Skocpol (eds.), *Bringing the State Back In*, Cambridge: Cambridge University Press, pp. 69-191.

Tilly, C. (1975b), 'Western State-Making and Theories of Political Transformation', in Charles Tilly (ed.), *The Formation of National States in Western Europe*, Princeton: Princeton University Press, pp. 601-638.

Valentine, D.A. (1980), 'The Logic of Secession', *Yale Law Journal*, Vol. 89, pp. 802-824.

Vanniasingham, S. (1989), *Sri Lanka: The Conflict Within*, New Delhi: Lancer International.

Vincent, R.J. (1990), 'Grotius, Human Rights, and Intervention', in Hedley Bull, Benedict Kingsbury and Adam Roberts (eds.), *Hugo Grotius and International Relations*, Oxford: Clarendon Press, pp. 241-256.

Vincent, R.J. (1986), *Human Rights and International Relations*, Cambridge: Cambridge University Press.

Vincent, R.J. (1974), *Nonintervention and International Order*, Princeton: Princeton University Press.

Vincent, R.J. (1984), 'Racial Equality', in Hedley Bull and Adam Watson (eds.), *The Expansion of International Society*, Oxford: Clarendon Press, pp. 239-254.

Vincent, R.J. and Wilson, P. (1993), 'Beyond Non-Intervention', in Ian Forbes and Mark Hoffman (eds.), *Political Theory, International Relations and the Ethics of Intervention*, New York: St. Martin's Press, pp. 122-130.

Wæver, O. (1992), 'International Society — Theoretical Promises Unfulfilled?', *Cooperation and Conflict*, Vol. 27, pp. 97-128.

Walker, R.B.J. (1993), *Inside/Outside: International Relations as Political Theory*, Cambridge: Cambridge University Press.

Wallace-Bruce, N.L. (1985), 'Africa and International Law - the Emergence to Statehood', *Journal of Modern African Studies*, Vol. 23, pp. 575-602.

Wallensteen, P. and Axell, K. (1993), 'Armed Conflict at the End of the Cold War, 1989-92', *Journal of Peace Research*, Vol. 30, pp. 331-346.

Waltz, K.N. (1979), *Theory of International Politics*, New York: McGraw-Hill Publishing Company.

Walzer, M. (1992), *Just and Unjust Wars: A Moral Argument with Historical Illustrations*, 2nd ed., New York: Basic Books.

Walzer, M. (1970), *Obligations: Essays on Disobedience, War and Citizenship*, Cambridge: Harvard University Press.

Warner, J. (1993), 'Political Choice: Parliamentary and Presidential Elections', in C.H. Dodd (ed.), *The Political Social and Economic Development of Northern Cyprus*, Huntingdon: The Eothen Press, pp. 193-217.

Watson, A. (1992), *The Evolution of International Society: A Comparative Historical Analysis*, London: Routledge.

Weber, C. (1992), 'Reconsidering Statehood: Examining the Sovereignty/Intervention Boundary', *Review of International Studies*, Vol. 18, pp. 199-216.

Weber, M. (1947), *The Theory of Social and Economic Organization*, edited with an introduction by Talcott Parsons, New York: Oxford University Press.

Weiss, H. (1995), 'Zaire: Collapsed Society, Surviving State, Future Polity', in I. William Zartman (ed.), *Collapsed States: The Disintegration and Restoration of Legitimate Authority*, Boulder: Lynne Rienner Publishers, pp. 157-170.

Weiss, T.G. (1994), 'Intervention: Whither the United Nations?', *The Washington Quarterly*, Vol. 17, pp. 109-128.

Weller, M. (1992), 'The International Response to the Dissolution of the Socialist Federal Republic of Yugoslavia', *American Journal of International Law*, Vol. 86, pp. 569-607.

Wendt, A. (1995), 'Constructing International Politics', *International Security*, Vol. 20, pp. 71-81.

Wheeler, N.J. (1992), 'Pluralist or Solidarist Conceptions of International Society: Bull and Vincent on Humanitarian Intervention', *Millennium: Journal of International Studies*, Vol. 21, pp. 463-487.

White, R.C.A. (1981-82), 'Self-Determination: Time for a Re-Assessment?', *Netherlands International Law Review*, Vol. XXVIII, pp. 147-170.

Wiberg, H. (1983), 'Self-Determination as an International Issue', in I.M. Lewis (ed.), *Nationalism and Self-Determination in the Horn of Africa*, London: Ithaca Press, pp. 43-65.

Wight, M. (1977), *Systems of States*, edited with an introduction by Hedley Bull, Leicester: Leicester University Press.

Willets, P. (1981), 'The United Nations and the Transformation of the Inter-State System', in Barry Buzan and R.J. Barry Jones (eds.), *Change and the Study of International Relations: The Evaded Dimension*, London: Frances Pinter Publishers, Ltd., pp. 100-119.

Wilson, A.J. (1988), *The Break-up of Sri Lanka: The Sinhalese-Tamil Conflict*, London: C. Hurst & Company.

Wilson, A.J. and Manogaran, C. (1994), 'Afterword: The Future of Sinhala-Tamil Relations', in Chelvadurai Manogaran and Bryan Pfaffenberger (eds.), *The Sri Lankan Tamils: Ethnicity and Identity*, Boulder: Westview Press, pp. 236-241.

Wilson, H.A. (1988), *International Law and the Use of Force by National Liberation Movements*, Oxford: Clarendon Press.

Wilson, P. (1989), 'The English School of International Relations: A Reply to Sheila Grader', *Review of International Studies*, Vol. 15, pp. 49-58.

Woodward, P. and Forsyth, M. (1994) (eds.), *Conflict and Peace in the*

Horn of Africa: Federalism and Its Alternatives, Aldershot: Dartmouth Publishing Company.

Ya Qin (1992), 'GATT Membership for Taiwan: An Analysis in International Law', *New York University Journal of International Law and Politics*, Vol. 24, pp. 1059-1105.

Yesilada, B.A. (1989), 'Social Progress and Political Development in the Turkish Republic of Northern Cyprus', *The Cyprus Review*, Vol. 1, pp. 91-112.

Young, C. (1983), 'Comparative Claims to Political Sovereignty: Biafra, Katanga, Eritrea', in Donald Rothchild and Victor A. Olorunsola (eds.), *State Versus Ethnic Claims: African Policy Dilemmas*, Boulder: Westview Press, pp. 199-232.

Young, C. (1984), 'Zaire: Is There a State?', *Canadian Journal of African Studies*, Vol. 18, pp. 80-82.

Young, R.A. (1994), 'How Do Peaceful Secessions Happen?', *Canadian Journal of Political Science*, Vol. XXVII, pp. 773-792.

Zarembo, A. (1995), 'Controlled Democracy', *Africa Report*, Vol. 40, pp. 52-55.

Zartman, I.W. (1995a) (ed.), *Collapsed States: The Disintegration and Restoration of Legitimate Authority*, Boulder: Lynne Rienner Publishers.

Zartman, I.W. (1995b), 'Introduction: Posing the Problem of State Collapse', in I. William Zartman (ed.), *Collapsed States: The Disintegration and Restoration of Legitimate Authority*, Boulder: Lynne Rienner Publishers, pp. 1-11.

Zartman, I.W. (1995c), 'Putting Things Back Together', in I. William Zartman (ed.), *Collapsed States: The Disintegration and Restoration of Legitimate Authority*, Boulder: Lynne Rienner Publishers, pp. 267-273.

Media

Africa News
African Business
Agence France Presse
BBC Summary of World Broadcasts
Christian Science Monitor
Daily Telegraph
Economist

Far Eastern Economic Review
Financial Times
Guardian
Independent
Indian Ocean Newsletter
Inter Press Service
Maclean's
New York Times
Reuter Library Report
Reuter's World Service
Russian Press Digest
Straits Times
Times
Washington Times

Index